STRENGTH TRAINING

FOR

FOOTBALL

Library of Congress Cataloging-in-Publication Data

Library of Congress Cataloging in Publication Data is available. LCCN 2019021066 (print)

ISBN: 978-1-4925-7142-1 (print)

This publication is written and published to provide accurate and authoritative information relevant to the subject matter presented. It is published and sold with the understanding that the author and publisher are not engaged in rendering legal, medical, or other professional services by reason of their authorship or publication of this work. If medical or other expert assistance is required, the services of a competent professional person should be sought.

The web addresses cited in this text were current as of April 2019, unless otherwise noted.

Senior Acquisitions Editor: Roger W. Earle; **Senior Developmental Editor:** Cynthia McEntire; **Managing Editor:** Miranda K. Baur; **Copyeditor:** Kevin Campbell; **Indexer:** Nan Badgett; **Permissions Manager:** Dalene Reeder; **Senior Graphic Designer:** Sean Roosevelt; **Graphic Designer:** Dawn Sills; **Cover Designer:** Keri Evans; **Cover Design Associate:** Susan Rothermel Allen; **Photograph (cover):** Joe Robbins/ Getty Images; **Photographs (interior):** © Human Kinetics, unless otherwise noted; **Photo Asset Manager:** Laura Fitch; **Photo Production Coordinator:** Amy M. Rose; **Photo Production Manager:** Jason Allen; **Senior Art Manager:** Kelly Hendren; **Illustrations:** © Human Kinetics; **Printer:** Sheridan Books

We thank Matthew Sandstead, NSCA-CPT,*D and Scott Caulfield, MA, CSCS,*D, RSCC*D at the National Strength and Conditioning Association in Colorado Springs, Colorado, for overseeing the photo shoot for this book.

Human Kinetics books are available at special discounts for bulk purchase. Special editions or book excerpts can also be created to specification. For details, contact the Special Sales Manager at Human Kinetics.

Printed in the United States of America   10 9 8 7 6 5 4 3 2 1

The paper in this book is certified under a sustainable forestry program.

Human Kinetics
P.O. Box 5076
Champaign, IL 61825-5076
Website: www.HumanKinetics.com

In the United States, email info@hkusa.com or call 800-747-4457.
In Canada, email info@hkcanada.com.
In the United Kingdom/Europe, email hk@hkeurope.com.

For information about Human Kinetics' coverage in other areas of the world, please visit our website: **www.HumanKinetics.com**

E7410

Tell us what you think!
Human Kinetics would love to hear what we can do to improve the customer experience. Use this QR code to take our brief survey.

STRENGTH TRAINING
FOR
FOOTBALL

NSCA®
NATIONAL STRENGTH AND
CONDITIONING ASSOCIATION

Jerry Palmieri, MA, CSCS, RSCC*E

Darren Krein, MA, CSCS, PES, CES

EDITORS

HUMAN KINETICS

PART I: PRINCIPLES OF SPORT-SPECIFIC RESISTANCE TRAINING

PART II: EXERCISE TECHNIQUE

PART III: PROGRAM DESIGN GUIDELINES AND SAMPLE PROGRAMS

TOM COUGHLIN

Football is a physical game played by big, powerful athletes who need to be strong and fast to excel in this sport. Therefore, I have always been a proponent of an outstanding strength program for my teams. It was imperative to win the line of scrimmage with strong offensive and defensive lines. The best way to accomplish this goal was to have my players training in the weight room. Having the more physical team on the field was such a priority for me that I required my strength coach to watch the game film and determine which team won the physical battle on offense, defense, special teams, and overall.

When it came to personnel, I was determined to build my teams with strong, physical people who demonstrated a great work ethic. In my first NFL draft in 1995, as the head coach for the expansion Jacksonville Jaguars, I selected Tony Boselli as the second overall pick and the first pick of the organization. Tony was a big, strong, talented left tackle. Our second pick in that draft was a physical running back from the University of Tennessee named James Stewart. The third pick was another big, strong offensive lineman named Brian DeMarco, followed by a physical linebacker named Bryan Schwartz. I wanted to set an expectation of the kind of team that we would be. Years later, when I was the head coach for the New York Giants, one of their great linebackers, Jesse Armstead, spoke to our players. He told them that whenever he played the Jaguars he didn't know if his team was going to win or lose, but he knew they were going to be in for a very physical game.

Our two Super Bowl champion teams with the Giants were very physical. Defensive players like Michael Strahan, Osi Umenyiora, Justin Tuck, Jason Pierre Paul, Linval Joseph, and Antonio Pierce punished the opposition. Our offensive line included physical men named Chris Snee, Shaun Ohara, Kareem McKenzie, David Diehl, Rich Seubert, and Kevin Boothe. We also had powerful running backs in Brandon Jacobs and Ahmad Bradshaw. Our team leader, Eli Manning, was very devoted to weight room training year-round. For the entire 12 years I was his head coach, Eli would come to the facility every Tuesday during the season to get in an extra training session.

Strength training is a vital component in the development of high school and collegiate football players because many of them are still physically maturing. Athletes who are not exposed to a quality strength program will not only come up short in their performance on the field but will also be more vulnerable to injury. There is such a vast difference in the rate at which these younger athletes develop that failing to train properly can put one athlete at a physical disadvantage compared to another. Because of the physical nature of the game, such a disadvantage can lead to injuries.

If you are a football coach, I encourage you to educate yourself in strength training your athletes for football. This book is a great place to start because some very talented and experienced strength coaches have shared their wealth of knowledge here. Additionally, I suggest you hire a good strength coach. In 1993 when I was the head football coach at Boston College, I hired Jerry Palmieri as our strength coach. Jerry was committed to making better football players rather than powerlifters, Olympic lifters, or bodybuilders. It is imperative to understand that training for football is more than going into the gym and doing biceps and triceps exercises. While the upper body is important, your athletes must have strong, powerful hips and legs. They need to be able to run fast, jump high, push people off the ball, and tackle the ball carrier.

If you are an athlete, commit yourself to getting bigger, stronger, and faster. Train hard with the weights, but train wisely. Do the exercises that will help you get better on the field so that you can excel in football. This book will be an excellent guide for you to follow. Understand that there are no shortcuts to greatness.

In closing, I strongly believe in the value of the weight room and the physical development of athletes. Our success as a team would never have been achieved without physical players. Do not underestimate the value of strength training in the preparation for football. Train hard, train well, and be a dominant force on the field.

MIKE GENTRY

The strength and conditioning profession has evolved since its inception. According to the National Strength and Conditioning Association's website, the history of the profession dates back to the late 1960s and early 1970s. Nebraska athletics director and head football coach Bob Devaney, and then-assistant football coach Tom Osborne, noticed a young track and field athlete named Boyd Epley training in the Cornhusker weight room. Legend has it that Osborne was so impressed with the results of Epley's voluntary workouts with injured Husker football athletes, who returned stronger than before their injuries, that in 1969 he convinced Coach Devaney to hire Boyd as the first-ever strength and conditioning coach at the University of Nebraska. In a recent personal conversation with Coach Epley, he confided in me that Coach Devaney told him that if even one of his athletes got slower because of lifting weights, he would fire Epley. For the sake of the strength and conditioning profession, thankfully, this must not have happened. The emergence of Epley as the first high-profile strength and conditioning professional started a trend that has led to the profession that we have today.

As the University of Nebraska and other successful collegiate and professional football teams became known for resistance training, their competition soon sought knowledgeable instructors or coaches to help develop their athletes. Most of these early coaches had backgrounds in one of three areas of competition related to resistance training: Bodybuilding, powerlifting, or Olympic lifting. The most consistent tests for maximal strength and power evaluation were one repetition maximum (1RM) effort in the bench press, back squat, and power clean exercises. The bench press and back squat exercises represented upper and lower body strength proficiency, and the power clean was chosen to evaluate total body power.

Through the 1980s, the predominant strategy for offensive football became power football, where running the football with the use of at least two running backs on the field was the norm. The bigger, faster, and stronger team had the advantage. The role of strength and conditioning gained acceptance, and most schools had some level of involvement.

The profession grew in both size and mission as most coaches saw the opportunity to improve individual and team performance with the help of organized resistance training. With the growth of collegiate sports revenue (due to money generated by television contracts and athletic donors), athletic departments entered a recruiting arms race, which often featured strength and conditioning facilities and staffs. This arms race further solidified the strength and conditioning profession within collegiate athletics.

The cycle of collegiate offensive football gradually evolved into a more passing-oriented spread offense, using more receivers spread out on the field. This offensive strategy required the defense to use more speed-oriented defensive backs to defend against the pass. These strategic changes led to a shift in recruiting emphasis, and strength and conditioning professionals adapted the training to better fit the needs. Often these adaptations were away from the emphasis on traditional, slower absolute strength exercises to a more diverse exercise menu, such as Olympic lifting variations of the clean, jerk, and snatch exercises, more plyometric exercises, emphasis on posterior chain strength exercises, and unilateral strength exercises.

Further evolution of sport-specific and position-specific exercises has resulted in the use of bands and chains to achieve accommodated resistance and various methods of measuring the athlete's bar speed. These advanced training methods allowed football athletes to train for explosive power more effectively. Most recently, the use of flexible bars has been shown to enhance power output and engage stabilizer muscles, and it is gaining in popularity among college and professional football teams.

All of these exercise tools and training strategies have certainly required strength and conditioning professionals to be open to change and learning. It is an exciting time because the coach must not only learn the use of new methods but also understand the art of application. To make the best use of modalities and strategies, coaches must appreciate the training level of the athlete and the relevance of the time in the training year.

For the football athlete, there is still a place for absolute strength development and hypertrophy training, as well as more specific power exercises, speed and acceleration training, and reactive and predetermined skill agility training. Most of these activities are trained concurrently. The priority placed in each of these areas is most often based on the experience and training age of the athlete, the position requirements, and the proximity of the competitive season. Today, maximizing performance in football athletes requires this prioritized approach to address all aspects of physical training.

One of the major roles of the strength and conditioning professional is to condition athletes to minimize the risk of injury. Most football coaches would agree that keeping the athletes injury-free throughout the competitive season is critical to success. Far too many times, a highly ranked team drops in the rankings due to a loss as a direct result of injuries to key athletes. It's a cruel reality of the sport.

Modern football strength and conditioning professionals must be well educated in many aspects of performance improvement training—from increasing strength and power to linear speed development, functional movement and agility training, and metabolic conditioning. They must also work closely with the team's athletic trainers and develop effective pre-habilitation training protocols to address and reduce the incidence of common and significant injury risks associated with football.

Modern strength and conditioning professionals must be proficient in the science of training and the proper application of training methods to the sport. They must be able to gain the trust of the athlete and earn the confidence of the coach.

In my opinion, football teams from the high school to the professional level that understand the importance of a comprehensive, scientifically sound, yearly strength and conditioning program and are further blessed with a strength and conditioning professional who can effectively communicate with the athletes, sports medicine staff, and football coaches will have a distinct competitive advantage over the programs that lack these important components.

PART I

PRINCIPLES OF SPORT-SPECIFIC RESISTANCE TRAINING

IMPORTANCE OF RESISTANCE TRAINING

ANTHONY CATERISANO

Just as the strength and conditioning profession has evolved, the science and application of strength and conditioning training have also evolved through scientific research and improvements in technology related to training athletes. Most coaches recognize that football athletes today are bigger, faster, and stronger than they were a few decades ago. This is due in part to the growth of the body of knowledge about strength and conditioning and to technological advances in training equipment. Today's strength and conditioning professionals are more knowledgeable, especially since the National Collegiate Athletic Association (NCAA) has mandated that all college strength and conditioning professionals must be certified to establish a minimum standard of scientific knowledge required of all coaches at this level. In addition to better programming, new and innovative training equipment provides new tools with which coaches can target specific adaptations in their athletes. This not only serves to improve performance, but it also helps prevent injuries and gives athletes the best chance for success on the field. These innovations, blended with the tried and true methods of the past, provide the best foundation for training athletes.

MAXIMIZING PERFORMANCE: THE ROLE OF RESISTANCE TRAINING

Exercise physiology textbooks often have several general definitions of **maximum strength**. Some see it as simply the ability to exert force (16). A more detailed definition would be the maximal amount of force a muscle or muscle group can generate in a specified movement pattern at a specified velocity (23). Later in this chapter, the relationship between strength and velocity is discussed, especially with regard to the acquisition of power via resistance training. But to the strength and conditioning professional, training for strength is much more than these simple definitions describe. Strength is the foundation of sport performance, the major factor in injury prevention, a critical factor in developing a healthy body composition, and a great motivator for athletes because it is measurable and an achievement that is universally recognized among one's peers. Many athletes use their **one repetition maximum** (1RM) as a source of pride and distinction to help develop their athletic identity. So, let's look at the role strength plays in each of these.

THE ATHLETIC PYRAMID: MAXIMUM STRENGTH IS THE FOUNDATION

Maximum strength is the foundation upon which power is developed, and studies show a strong correlation between strength and power (2, 34, 36, 39, 40). Maximum strength is the force generated in an unlimited amount of time. Maximum power is performing work in the shortest period of time (1, 45). Thus, maximum strength is defined as the capacity to generate maximal force through a muscle action with no time limits (12). The time factor becomes very important in distinguishing between maximum strength and maximum power. From a pure physics application, strength is force production (mass times acceleration), and work is calculated as force times distance or displacement. **Power**, using a pure physics application, is calculated as force times distance divided by time. It makes logical sense that improving an athlete's capacity to generate force will have a positive effect on the ability to generate power, as long as the time it takes to generate that force does not change. Figure 1.1 shows the **athleticism pyramid** and the relationship between maximum strength, power, speed, and agility, with maximum strength being the foundation upon which power is built (12).

Power (or what some describe as **explosive strength**) is defined as the ability to generate the greatest amount of force in the shortest amount of time (12). In untrained persons, an increase in strength alone can result in an increase in power, which demonstrates the direct role that force production plays in the acquisition of power (39, 40). For trained athletes, power probably transfers more directly to athletic performance, so reducing the time it takes to generate maximum force becomes a high priority.

When untrained athletes increase their measurable maximum strength, there is a measurable increase in power, as measured by the standing vertical and horizontal jumps (2). There is also an increase in speed for short-distance sprints, such as 10-yard (9 m) sprints (26). Being able to apply more force into the ground will improve jumping power and short-distance sprint speed for the untrained or undertrained athlete. Because of this relationship, it is believed that increasing maximum strength is the component of training that most affects the other com-

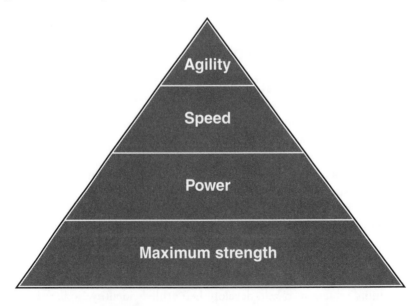

Figure 1.1   Athleticism pyramid.

Reprinted by permission from M. Gentry and A. Caterisano, *The Ultimate Guide to Physical Training for Football* (New York: Sports Publishing, 2013), 6-18.

ponents of the pyramid of athleticism. This is why it is so important to effectively and safely train less experienced athletes to increase their maximum strength. It is also important to train more experienced football athletes to increase absolute strength during the off-season and to maintain this strength safely and efficiently during the preseason and in-season.

The concept of **explosive strength deficit** (ESD) describes the difference between the amount of force an athlete can generate in an unlimited time and the amount of force he or she can generate in the limited time of sport performance. This concept is critical to power development (45). Due to the time–force relationship, many sport movements will not give athletes the time they need to generate maximum force. For example, think about sprinting, which involves explosive hip extension. The time the athlete's foot is in contact with the ground is not the same as when that athlete performs a maximal back squat exercise. In the maximal back squat, the hip extension takes place over a longer period of time. The window of opportunity to generate force is very short in sprinting, probably hundredths of a second, but unlimited in the back squat. Reducing ESD may require a combination of speed-specific training and heavy resistance training to enable athletes to generate the highest percentage of their 1RM within the time limitations of real sport performance.

Speed is the application of power and is defined as distance moved per unit time (16). Speed requires the ability to accelerate and to achieve maximum velocity. The application most people think of is sprinting. Sprinters try to generate the highest possible ground reaction force and explosive hip extension to increase their stride length, along with rapid leg turnover to increase their stride frequency. Power is applied with every foot strike into the floor to maximize ground reaction force, but it is also applied in the muscles that flex and extend the hips and knees to increase stride frequency.

Agility is much more complex than the first three components of the athleticism pyramid because it requires good reaction time, balance, coordination, and other motor skills. The two main components of agility are speed and cognitive factors (16). Agility is defined as the ability to quickly accelerate, decelerate, and change direction in response to a sport-specific stimulus (16). Research suggests that this cognitive component involves perception and decision-making skills that are trainable through reactive agility drills (35).

INCREASE STRENGTH

Developing strength through resistance training requires heavy resistance. Coaches usually achieve this by applying the principle of progressive resistance over time through some variation of the concept of periodization. At its core, the concept of periodization represents a training schedule that over time, often six to nine weeks, shifts from a higher volume of lesser intensity or resistance in the important multijoint exercises toward lesser volume and higher intensity or resistance. Neural and muscular adaptations that occur over the course of the training cycle allow the athlete to increase maximal strength.

Understanding why this is so requires a bit of review on how muscle cells are activated. Muscle cells are unique among cells in the human body because they can contract or shorten through the action of contractile proteins, **actin** and **myosin**, coupling and uncoupling in a ratchetlike motion. Two factors influence how fast a muscle contraction occurs: The **twitch rate** (differentiated by muscle fiber type: Fast-twitch or slow-twitch) and the **rate coding** of the muscle, which describes the firing frequency, which eventually builds up a maximal level of force (45). A **motor unit** is a group of muscle cells stimulated by a single alpha motoneuron that innervates all the muscle cells associated with that motoneuron. Each motor unit is activated as needed, depending on the amount of force required to perform a task. If low forces are required, only a few motor units are activated. As greater force is required, like in the case of lifting a heavy resistance, either the rate coding of the motor unit increases or more motor units are activated, or both. Increased rate coding typically occurs in smaller muscle groups that rely on increased firing rate to increase contraction force (9). Large muscle groups typically will increase force by recruiting more motor units as well as by increasing their firing rate (12, 45). Even in a large muscle, increases in force (even from 0-70% of maximum) are still achieved in part by firing rate modulation (9).

The pattern of motor unit recruitment is not random but instead follows a very orderly hierarchy known as the **Henneman's size principle**. The size principle states that the smallest motoneurons (low-threshold motor units), which are associated with the slow-twitch muscle fibers, are recruited first, but as greater force is needed, larger and larger motoneurons are activated (higher-threshold motor units). The addition of more and more force eventually results in the 1RM that recruits most of the available motor units, including those made up of type IIx fibers. Once known as type IIb fibers (some textbooks refer to fast-twitch muscle fibers as type IIb), type IIx fibers are the largest and fastest-twitch muscle cells.

INCREASE POWER

Power training is a bit more complex than strength development, but it is closely related. Power is a multifaceted construct that combines force production, displacement, velocity, and time (25). It does not appear to be as cut-and-dried as simply recruiting more motor units. Instead, it has more to do with neural factors involved in the process of generating force, and subsequently work, in less time. Velocity-specific training such as plyometric training, speed repetitions, and other high-velocity resistance training is often used to reduce ESD, allowing the athlete to generate more force in less time. Research suggests that muscle fiber conduction velocity plays a major role in how quickly force can be developed in a muscle (11). This ability to recruit motor units more quickly, along with achieving faster firing rates, are critical factors in power training.

Strength and conditioning professionals understand that to optimize performance for a power sport like football, it is critical to focus on training methods that develop power. One such method may be resistance training. Coaches have learned that if the traditional barbell, dumbbell, or kettlebells are used, the speed of the bar or implement is very important and must be emphasized. A device that can measure bar speed and provide feedback to coaches and athletes is very useful. This feedback is also highly motivating for athletes.

Plyometric exercises that consist of hops, skips, or jumps are proven power developers for the lower body (7). Plyometric exercises take advantage of the stretch-shortening characteristics of muscle, which couple eccentric and concentric muscle actions (15). Most plyometric exercises take advantage of the inherent elastic characteristics of the muscle and the stretch reflex to perform speed-specific muscle actions. Muscle spindles are sensory structures in the muscle that detect when a muscle is stretched quickly or extensively. This triggers a reflex contraction of that muscle to protect it from injury. Medicine balls are often used in a plyometric fashion (such as the medicine ball lying plyo press) to increase upper body power (7). The Tsunami Bar and other such flexible barbells may increase ground reaction forces and activate stabilizer muscles by requiring maximal forces to reverse the direction of the bar while maintaining the speed of movement needed for explosive strength and power (19). A study compared a Tsunami Bar training program to a more traditional training regimen that included Olympic lifts and plyometric exercises. The Tsunami-trained athletes demonstrated greater improvements in lower body power than the traditionally trained group (6). Thus, there is a variety of methods to incorporate speed-specific exercises into a training program to increase power.

Traditionally, the power clean or push jerk (and their many variations) are thought to be most helpful to football offensive and defensive linemen who, by the nature of the sport, must collide with and move other athletes of similar size and body weight. As mentioned previously, the effort to move a heavier object with velocity will also increase power (29).

Football athletes who play away from the line of scrimmage may best increase their explosive power by using a lower percentage of a theoretical 1RM for Olympic lifting exercises than football linemen due to their greater movement velocity compared to the linemen. These speed oriented athletes of lesser body weight than their linemen teammates may more safely perform higher level jumping and plyometric drills for power development than linemen.

Resistance training is also effective in developing power through **postactivation potentiation** (PAP), which is a method of activating the neuromuscular system with resistance just before performing a power-related activity. PAP is based on the idea that skeletal muscle has a "contractile history" when it is activated. Activation is akin to priming the distribution of calcium ions throughout the muscle cells, preparing the cells for use in subsequent muscle contractions (33). Calcium ion supply is the major regulator of muscle contraction, and increasing it is critical for improving motor unit twitch forces. This results in the ability to produce more force at lower stimulation frequencies. This phenomenon is commonly referred to as **twitch potentiation** (18). Through preactivation of those pathways, it becomes easier to reactivate them and to positively affect rate coding. This PAP phenomenon has been shown to be most prevalent in the fast-twitch muscle fibers. A common method of incorporating the PAP training concept with football athletes is termed **complex training**. Many strength and conditioning professionals use the complex of immediately following a set of heavy squats with a set of explosive box jumps.

IMPROVE SPEED AND AGILITY

Speed is the application of power to a very sport-specific movement, such as straight-line sprinting, but it can also include hand speed and foot speed in many different football positions (12). Some resistance training programs use training methods such as plyometric exercises and speed lifting to try to mirror the same velocity of movement used in competition. This approach uses speed-specific resistance training, such as plyometric and speed exercises, to improve speed (32). Past research suggests that resistance training, regardless of the speed at which it is performed, can be effective in increasing speed (3). It appears that a combination of both types of training, high-intensity and speed-specific with lower intensities, may work best for speed development.

For strength and conditioning professionals, speed training for football athletes begins with developing maximum strength as an effective way to put more force into the ground. As the athletes also train for lower body power with velocity-specific resistance training, this ability to apply force into the ground is enhanced by decreasing the time needed to apply the force. The ESD is reduced through power training.

Football-position-specific speed training usually refers to the heavier training loads placed on weighted sleds that are pushed or pulled by linemen and other athletes who line up close to the line of scrimmage. The heavier loads are pushed or pulled for shorter distances than the lighter loads usually pulled by the sprinting athletes in speed-oriented positions such as offensive backs, receivers, and defensive backs.

Agility is probably the most complex parameter of the athleticism hierarchy because it involves skills such as balance, reaction time, coordination, and mobility, in addition to sheer physical prowess. Not only does agility require force to be developed quickly for acceleration, but it also requires **impulse** to decelerate quickly and potentially to change direction (17). The role

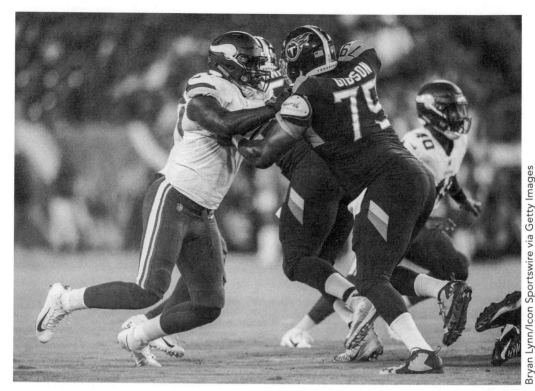

The strength and conditioning professional can reduce risk of injury through resistance training and metabolic conditioning.

of resistance training in developing agility is not as clear-cut as it is for other parameters, but there is some evidence that it plays a part in making athletes more athletic (37, 42). Two studies looked at plyometric training and motor training as effective ways to train change-of-direction skills in young athletes (35, 37).

Agility drill training must be practiced so that balance, acceleration, and deceleration can all be improved. However, the building blocks of maximum strength, power, and speed all contribute to the ability to move with agility. Power training, which improves the efficiency of quickly applying force into the ground, is a key component of acceleration, which is an agility cornerstone. Movement patterns learned and practiced during resistance training, such as the eccentric catch of a clean, jerk, or snatch, may help improve the efficiency and safety of decelerations on the field of play.

PREVENT INJURIES

As mentioned in the introduction, it is important to keep athletes healthy and able to perform. Failure to have the best athletes competing on game day will significantly affect the team's success. One of the major roles of the strength and conditioning professional is to condition athletes to minimize their risk of injury. This must include metabolic conditioning achieved through sprint intervals, resisted running, and up-tempo practice methods, in addition to resistance training. Proper metabolic conditioning will reduce the risk of potentially catastrophic events such as heat stroke, sickle cell trait incidence, and exertional rhabdomyolysis.

Much research, including both individual case studies and the meta-analysis of multiple case studies, supports the hypothesis that resistance training prevents injuries (4, 10, 14, 36, 41,

44). A stronger muscle is less likely to tear, and when opposing muscle groups are in balance, the risk of a strong muscle working against a weak muscle is reduced.

Probably the most common injury associated with poor muscle balance is a hamstring strain (biceps femoris, semitendinosus, gracilis, and semimembranosus) that occurs when an athlete is sprinting (13, 41, 44). This can happen when an athlete overdevelops the quadriceps muscles and neglects to train the hamstring group equally. One of the training shifts that has accompanied the more speed-oriented football philosophy is a focus on training the **posterior chain muscles**. The exercises used are designed to increase speed through a more powerful leg drive as the glute, hamstring, and lower back muscles are strengthened. This strength increase also better addresses the quad-to-hamstring muscular imbalance. Common posterior chain exercises include the glute ham extension, reverse back extension, and Romanian deadlift.

Researchers in Scandinavia provide some evidence that heavy resistance training may affect selected collagen XIV and macrophage density in the **myotendinous junction** (MTJ), which is where the muscle and the tendon meet, and which is a common hamstring injury site (20, 21). The MTJ is the weak link in the connection between the tendon, which is relatively dense connective tissue, and the muscle fibers, which are more sparsely distributed near the tendon when compared to the belly of the muscle. Collagen is a basic building block of connective tissue that makes up muscles and tendons, and the research found that after only four weeks of heavy resistance training, levels of collagen XIV were higher when compared to a control group who did no training (20, 21).

Strength development is also important in preventing injury, especially to the lower back. The muscles associated with the appendicular skeleton that attach to the pelvis, almost like the spokes of a wheel that connect to a central axis, are commonly referred to as the **anatomical core** (see chapter 8 for more details). The muscles that originate from the pelvis and insert above it include the abdominal muscles (rectus abdominis, internal and external obliques, and transversus abdominis), which are counteracted by the low back muscles (erector spinae) to help humans maintain an upright position. A quality resistance training program should target these core muscles, and since many of these core muscles are postural muscles, a targeted flexibility program is also strongly recommended. The muscles that originate from the lower aspects of the pelvis include the gluteal, hamstring, and quadriceps muscle groups. Dynamic stretching can be included in warm-up activities before a workout. In addition, encouraging athletes to move through a full range of motion during resistance training is also a good strategy for gaining flexibility. Static stretching can be included once the muscles are well warmed up, especially at the end of the workout.

In addition to reducing mechanical injuries to the musculature, there is indirect evidence that resistance training may help prevent muscle damage or other injuries. One study found that there was less muscle damage, as indicated by lower serum creatine kinase levels, in stronger athletes compared to those with lower muscular strength (28). This could have ramifications in preventing exertional rhabdomyolysis and other overuse types of injuries. Another published paper suggested that joint injury risks such as ACL tears may be reduced with a preventive resistance training program (24). Two common applications of preventive ACL tear training include reducing excessive knee valgus during flexion and teaching the athlete to properly land after a jump.

There is also strong evidence that neck strengthening protocols may be effective in reducing the number of concussions in contact sports such as football (8, 17). A stronger neck helps stabilize the head during high-impact collisions. A more stable head position can minimize brain movement within the skull, thus reducing the injuries that are caused by excessive brain movement in the cranium. Due to the potential severity of head and neck injuries associated with football, strength and conditioning professionals must place great emphasis on effectively training the muscles of the upper back and neck to lower the risks. Exercises that achieve this

略

include those that feature the motion of shrugging the shoulder girdle, such as Olympic lifting pulling exercises such as clean-and-snatch variations, and direct-shrug exercises using the barbell, dumbbell, and machines. Directly targeting the muscles of the neck with four-way neck machines and manual resistance exercises of the neck with a partner through four directions are also recommended.

Resistance training has also been shown to increase bone density over time with proper nutrition (13, 30, 31, 38). The implication of these findings is that resistance training may reduce the risk of bone breaks and other associated mechanical injuries, which are common in a sport like football.

IMPROVE BODY COMPOSITION

Body composition describes the relative ratio of fat mass to fat-free mass in the human body. **Fat mass** includes the fat between the skin and the muscle (subcutaneous fat), fat surrounding the organs (visceral adipose tissue), intramuscular fat (engrained in the muscle), and other fats that make up blood lipids, cell membranes, and myelin, which is a component of nerve tissue. **Fat-free mass** includes muscle, tendons, ligaments, cartilage, organs, and bone tissue. The fact that the fat-free mass varies greatly in density makes it a challenge to measure body composition with most of the total body assessments that are typically available to strength and conditioning professionals (e.g., skinfold, bioelectrical impedance, hydrostatic densitometry or underwater weighing, the BOD POD or air-displacement plethysmography, etc.) (27). That being said, many body fat assessment techniques have good test–retest reliability, so the change in body fat content from one test to the next test is measurable (22, 43). These tests can be valuable in monitoring athletes' changes in body fat percentage as they gain or lose body weight.

Longitudinal studies have demonstrated that football players do benefit from strength and conditioning programs by gaining lean body mass, which improves their body composition (5, 38). This includes increased bone mass and muscle mass, even if body fat levels stay relatively the same in some cases.

CONCLUSION

Veteran strength and conditioning professionals will probably say that their original mission was simply to develop strength and size in the football player. Early programs led to bigger and stronger athletes. This was especially evident among high-profile teams such as the University of Nebraska, and the profession took hold. Over the years, every major college athletics department started some sort of strength and conditioning program. The mission also evolved as priorities shifted from training for strength and size to recognizing that other performance parameters, such as power, speed, and agility, played an important role in the physical development of football players. Maximum strength is still the foundation of athleticism, and it holds a high priority at certain times of the year. Power is the application of strength in a short time frame since it is velocity specific. Speed is the application of power to a specific skill, such as running or jumping. Agility is a more complex parameter that involves accelerating, decelerating, and changing direction in response to a sport-specific stimulus. Speed plays a key role in optimizing agility. It is difficult to maximize each of these four parameters of athleticism at the same time without overtraining athletes. The key to success is to understand how to prioritize training to fit each stage of the season. Other benefits beyond performance improvement include injury prevention and improved body composition. A stronger and more balanced musculoskeletal system reduces the risk of preventable injury. Improved body composition not only makes an athlete more efficient and well-conditioned, but it also positively affects confidence and self-esteem.

2

ANALYSIS OF THE SPORT AND SPORT POSITIONS

BRETT BARTHOLOMEW

When most strength and conditioning professionals started out, they were taught that before they did anything else in terms of planning, they must conduct a thorough needs analysis of both the sport itself and the athletes they would be working with. Moleskin notebooks, Excel spreadsheets, and whiteboards became filled with notes, timelines, logistical information, and physiological data such as the length of a play, the length of a game, yards covered, and the like. Sadly, as professionals progress in their careers, they sometimes neglect or even omit this step, relying on experience instead of gathering and analyzing data. Football is a rapidly evolving sport, and to take this approach with today's football athletes would be foolish. Simply getting athletes bigger, stronger, or even faster is no longer enough to develop the modern football athlete.

GENERAL PHYSIOLOGICAL ANALYSIS

To keep up with the modernization of the sport and the increased pace of the game, strength and conditioning professionals must be able to help their athletes to become more efficient in their movements and better conditioned in order to handle the greater physical demands. The following sections examine the physiological demands of football and provide an overview of each quality in terms of the requirements of high-level competition.

The Role of Muscular Strength and Power

Regardless of the level of play, the ability to exert both submaximal and near-maximal levels of physical strength rapidly and explosively is critical not only to performance but also to reducing the risk of injury (2). Football is both a collision sport and an invasion/evasion sport (33), so athletes will not only produce large amounts of force, they will also absorb them every time they collide with other athletes or with the ground.

Muscular strength is the ability to exert force on an external object or resistance (22, 24). The development of muscular strength is a necessary prerequisite to increasing and efficiently directing power. Muscular strength can greatly influence not only acceleration and top speed, but also agility and the ability to change direction and jump (5, 31, 34). These qualities are important to all positions in football. Efficiency of movement is a critical trait for a quarterback trying to fit a pass through a tight window, a defensive end trying to beat an offensive lineman to the edge, or a free safety moving into the best position to make a play.

There are many ways football athletes can enhance their muscular strength and power. Whether it is the use of ballistic exercises with loads ranging from 0 to 50 percent of 1RM, or weightlifting variations performed with loads between 50 and 90 percent of 1RM (7), the key responsibility of the strength and conditioning professional is to determine the methods most appropriate for the athletes, their experience level, training age, the resources they have access to, and their medical history, just to name a few.

It is important to note that strength and the rate of force development are important not only to football training, but also to optimal athletic development (26). Elite football athletes are first and foremost elite athletes. Increases in overall athleticism are what truly transfer to the field, not just increases in strength alone. By increasing the athletic reservoir from which the athlete can draw, the strength and conditioning professional can also increase the athlete's durability and maneuverability. This idea has been lost in recent years to some degree, partly because there is a growing trend of early specialization among young football athletes as well as organizations that now enable them to compete almost year-round.

Coaches must remember that increasing strength alone is not going to make one a better football athlete but increases in muscular strength serve as a gateway through which athletes can produce, resist, and counteract the many forces that will act upon them during competition. Muscular strength is the foundation on which other physical qualities for performance and injury prevention are based.

Rate of Force Development

Given the highly explosive nature of the sport, football athletes must not only produce a tremendous amount of force, but they also must produce it rapidly, in multiple planes of motion, and with clinical precision. A great deal of research supports the idea of a significant and synergistic relationship between muscular strength and rate of force development (1, 10, 18, 25, 26). **Rate of force development** is the rate of rise in force over the change in time. Also called **explosive strength**, the rate of force development can be seen during some of the most dynamic plays in the sport, many of which can abruptly influence the outcome of a game. Furthermore, the highly reactive nature of football dictates that regardless of their position on the field, athletes must all be able to track, block, pursue, or evade an opponent as quickly as possible. This is why many training programs call for a variety of exercises to be performed at different loads (intensities) and speeds (velocities).

Lean Body Mass

Despite the importance of the physiological traits just described, football training programs must address far more than just strength and power. Athletes who can significantly improve body composition and strength levels will at the same time increase their strength-to-body-weight ratio, thus making them more explosive, elusive, resistant to fatigue, and perhaps most importantly, more durable and able to withstand collisions.

This point is especially important in light of public discussions about the dangers of football. If athletes are trained appropriately, play by the rules, and work to improve their motor-skill proficiency, the risk of injuries will be significantly reduced. It is also important to note that all sports pose an inherent risk of injury, which is why a properly implemented resistance training program and an analysis of an athlete's LBM are crucial to injury prevention. Lean body mass is especially important for athletes returning from injury. If extensive muscle atrophy due to immobilization is allowed to occur and is not addressed, it can lengthen the rehabilitation process and impede the return-to-play timeline (4, 12, 13).

Previous research has suggested optimal percent body fat ranges for certain football positions (32). However, the information in this study and others like it is from an era when offensive strategies and the pace of the game differed tremendously from the game today. With the relatively recent emergence of hybrid-spread and up-tempo offenses in collegiate football, not only are different types of athletes now being recruited to play common positions, but some previously important positions, such as the fullback, have been eliminated.

Regardless, the take-home point here is that improvements in lean body mass play a critical role in the successful performance of football athletes of all ages and at all levels, and there is no substitute for a practical, periodized resistance training regimen for improving lean body mass.

Speed

An athlete who can move quickly from a given point on the gridiron to another within a short amount of time (that is, who can exhibit **speed**) is a coveted commodity for any head football coach. Whether it is depicted by a running back sprinting down the sidelines after eluding defenders and finding space in the backfield, or a member of special teams chasing down a would-be returner, football is not only a game of inches but also one of moments. The ability to achieve and maintain high levels of speed gives athletes in all positions an edge over their counterparts. To maximize speed, it must be trained often and with great care during both the off-season and in-season.

Mobility

People often consider mobility to be synonymous with flexibility or absolute range of motion in a joint or system of joints. In fact, **mobility** within a joint is more accurately defined by how much the **articulation** (space where two bones meet) can move before being restricted by surrounding tissue such as tendons, muscles, or ligaments. The practical takeaway is that great flexibility does not equate with great mobility or even with the ability to move efficiently. The highly flexible person may not have the strength, coordination, or stability needed to execute a given movement. Mobility is also a reflection of neural characteristics and motor programming just as much if not more than genetic factors or anthropometry. Though many mobility fixes have popped up in recent years, performing both dynamic warm-up movements and resistance training exercises through a full range of motion and with great focus are easy and effective ways for athletes to continue to improve their mobility. This is especially true given the sheer number of repetitions one will perform during a playing career since warm-up and resistance training activities are performed with ritualistic frequency.

Coordination

The Greek philosopher Aristotle stated, "to be ignorant of motion is to be ignorant of nature." The truth of this cannot be overstated given what is known today about motor learning and sport performance. In football, it is critical for athletes to have not only precise control over their own movements, but also a keen awareness of the various types of motion occurring around them. Both are forms of biofeedback; athletes must use them continually to get into the best position to make a play. **Coordination** is defined as the process of constraining a system's available degrees of freedom in order to organize an efficient movement pattern that will effectively achieve the goal of the desired task (23, 27). It may be helpful to consider coordination to refer to one's awareness of the relationship of the head, body, and limbs at a specific point in time during a movement skill.

The way in which skilled movements such as sprinting, cutting, jumping, and catching are performed is known as the **degrees of freedom problem** (6). To perform movements that are often taken for granted or considered automatic, the nervous system must work nonstop to manage independent elements such as nerves, muscles, and many possible joint movements. For this reason, strength and conditioning professionals must always be mindful of the contributions of various neural mechanisms to performance. This is yet one more nod to the importance of participating in a well-rounded strength and conditioning program, which includes not only traditional resistance training exercises such as the squat, bench press, and deadlift but also more explosive movements such as cleans, snatches, jerks, medicine ball throws, and various plyometrics. Taken together, these exercises conduct an orchestra that elicits a symphony of changes throughout the human body.

Agility and Change of Direction

Much like mobility and flexibility, at first glance, agility and change of direction seem synonymous. For years these terms have been used interchangeably by the strength and conditioning community. The difference between the two is that **change of direction** (COD) refers to a specific moment in which an athlete uses the skills and abilities needed to change a movement's direction, velocity, or modes (8), whereas **agility** is a rapid total body movement with change of velocity or direction in response to a sport-specific stimulus (21). The reaction to a stimulus is the key element that separates the two. It separates the cone-drill superstars from those who truly know how to read the environment, their opponent, and the context of the moment.

Technically, both agility and COD would be classified as more coordinative abilities than physiological capacities, especially since athletes can get stronger and more fit without becoming more agile. This is where it is critical to remember that the importance of resistance training extends far beyond performance enhancement into injury reduction. Improving one's agility and ability to change direction can enable one to avoid some of the impact forces that account for cumulative wear and tear on the body.

Energy System Demands

Football is characterized by short, intense bursts of activity ranging anywhere from three to six seconds (the variance depends on scheme, personnel, result of the play, field position, and clock-management situations) followed by periods of rest that can range from 20 to 40 seconds (depending on the aforementioned variables). Although there are guidelines consisting of more specific time frames (20), the chaotic and unpredictable nature of football does not lend itself to an exact work-to-rest ratio. These numbers and ranges, while important to note, provide only a general rule of thumb.

Moreover, the evolution of the sport, particularly in its offensive strategies, requires coaches to continuously adapt their methods and programs to best fit the current scheme of the head coach, the needs of the athletes, and the feedback obtained by monitoring athletic performance. It is also worth mentioning that one should not apply the principle of specificity to the point where one tries to mimic game demands in every training activity. To do so would defeat the purpose of eliciting an enhanced physiological adaptation. Constantly exposing athletes to the same stressors would fail to apply principles of overload that lead to true adaptation.

In a closer examination of the specific energy systems that football calls upon, the first critical point to reinforce is that no one energy system ever works alone. Despite the fact that the **phosphagen system** (also called the **ATP-PC system**) and the **aerobic (oxidative) systems** are the primary systems to be stressed during play (the latter playing a more significant role in recovery between plays or offensive/defensive series), they all have a role in the larger scheme of things. A helpful analogy to illustrate this interdependence and integration between energy systems is that of various form of currency—specifically one's salary, the amount of cash on hand, and a credit card (table 2.1).

A person's salary, in this example, would serve as an analogy to the aerobic (oxidative) energy system in that it "funds" or replenishes all other forms of spending. This speaks specifically to the recovery benefits of having a well-developed aerobic system as well as overall capacity in terms of bioenergetic "currency." The anaerobic energy system functions much like cash; it is quick to access and thus can be called upon in a pinch, yet it is not quickly or easily replenishable without going to a bank or ATM. Finally there is the phosphagen pathway, which can be thought of as the body's credit card. Credit cards allow for near instant access to available resources, but if used too often they also make it easier for one to accumulate "debt," which, in a sport context, would lead to decrements in performance.

This example illustrates the point that all energy systems should be considered parts of an integrated system in which each pathway is dependent on the robustness of the others. No matter the activity, athlete, or intensity of the activity, all of the body's energy systems are contributing in some way to fuel the metabolic demands of explosive movement during a play or to aid in the replenishment of ATP between plays.

The second critical point to consider about energy systems is that special circumstances occur where athletes are pushed into more of a metabolic by-product-rich environment (e.g., H^+ ions, ammonia, K^+, P_i). These situations can include 2-minute drills, the rigors of training camp, and even when football coaches decide to punish the team with extreme or excessive forms of conditioning exercise. From a clinical or research standpoint, it is best to steer clear of these metabolic by-product-rich environments if the goal is to optimize training-induced adaptations. In reality, though, athletes will experience them at some point, and thus they must occasionally be exposed to this type of stressor in order to be fully prepared for the competitive sport environment. While the accumulation of lactate is commonly associated with fatigue and decrements in performance (11), lactate is not the "bad guy." In fact, lactate can be converted into a pyruvate and can subsequently be oxidized or even used as a substrate to synthesize glucose and glycogen, both of which can be readily used for energy by the body (8). This process is yet another testament to the importance of addressing all of the body's energy systems during training because it requires all of the metabolic pathways to work together.

As a final note, it is important to remember that while each team, position, and scheme will have its own unique demands, discerning coaches should focus on building a strong general foundation on which to develop their athletes' motor skills and physiological attributes. Coaches who aggressively rush their athletes into overly advanced or specific methods early in the training process can be setting the stage for future injuries or overtraining.

Table 2.1 Analogy Comparing Energy Systems to Payment Systems

Energy system	Analogy example
Phosphagen (ATP-PC)	Credit card
Anaerobic (lactic)	Cash
Aerobic (oxidative)	Salary

Despite current trends in nomenclature, the terms *phosphagen* and *ATP-PC* are used instead of *alactic* due to literature showing that lactate is present even in extremely short bursts of high-intensity activity.

GENERAL BIOMECHANICAL ANALYSIS

Football provides one of the premier examples in sport of both the resilience and the complexity of the human body during movement. This is due in part to the unique range and diversity of size, positional assignments, scheme or style of play, and cultural background of each athlete and team. Taken together, the movements performed on a football field are a symphony of coordination, rhythm, explosiveness, precision, and timing that even the most casual of onlookers would be hard-pressed not to notice or appreciate. Football is not just a game of strength, power, and speed; it is also a game of position, timing, and movement quality. Despite the importance of speed, it is not uncommon for faster athletes to be run down, contained, or otherwise bested by slower or less talented athletes due to their superior use of pursuit angles or body position. Whether this occurs because of superior knowledge, experience, or instinct—or a combination of all of these—the point is that being strong or fast by itself does not guarantee success in football. Success is a relative concept, too, since an athlete may have a productive year personally while the team struggles to win. Football is the ultimate team sport in that dominant individual performances do not always produce victories.

For all of the reasons mentioned, it is critical that football athletes be exposed to a wide variety of movement skills during their training. This not only helps improve overall motor skills, but it also helps reduce the risk of soft-tissue injuries that can occur as a result of inappropriate or insufficient exposure to stressors associated with sprinting, jumping, cutting, or landing during games, practice, or training. The assorted yet integrated movements that occur during the course of a game (backpedaling, shuffling, sprinting, etc.) are the reason for football's classification as an **acyclic sport**. In contrast, an activity such as distance running, which calls upon a more singular and highly repetitive action in one primary plane of movement, would be classified as a **cyclic sport** (19). Common modes of locomotion or transitioning to another movement plane may include one or more of the following:

- Shuffle
- Sprint
- Jump cut or side step
- Crossover run
- Backpedal
- Crossover
- Open step
- Drop step
- Dive
- Jump
- Angle cut

None of these movements are better than the others. The decision about which is most appropriate will depend on the athletes' positions on the field; their athletic profile, body structure, and physical capacity; game situations; and the movement strategies of their opponents. When training these movements, it is critical that there be consistency between what is being taught in the weight room and the movements that occur on the field of play. For example, helping linebackers understand how lateral lunges and squats performed in the weight room can also help them move more efficiently and safely on the field is a critical way to not only gain more

Peter G. Aiken/Getty Images

Football involves an assortment of integrated movements during the course of a game.

buy-in from athletes, but also to help them better understand the big picture of a program and how it helps to extend the longevity and productivity of their playing careers.

POSITION-SPECIFIC ANALYSIS

In football, athletes are divided into six positional groups: Offensive and defensive lineman; tight end, fullback, and linebacker; wide receiver and running back; defensive back; quarterback; and kicker and punter. Each faces different tactical and physical demands (19). The sample programs in the season-specific chapters in Part III are divided into these positional groups.

Understanding the positional demands and differences between groups is imperative given their implications in creating appropriate periodization strategies and programming options for athletes. An analysis of collegiate football athletes has shown that generally, non-linemen (e.g., wide receiver, defensive back, running back, quarterback) run more and wide receivers and defensive backs specifically cover greater total distances than any of the other positions on the field (29). While elements of individualization are often over-hyped in popular media, factors such as athlete load, distance covered, and readiness must be taken into account when designing resistance training programs, especially those that target the muscles of the lower body.

From a contact adaptation standpoint, an evaluation of impacts in collegiate football revealed that running backs and defensive tackles engaged in a larger number of severe and heavy collisions (defined as >10 g-forces) than other position groups (30). This lends further support to the fact that positional differences must be taken into consideration by strength and conditioning professionals. This research has its limitations because the position groups listed in the literature are often broad and will vary by offensive or defensive scheme, the athletes' level of gross and discrete motor skill competency, practice design, the instruments used to capture the data, roster size, time of year (e.g., training camp, preseason, in-season), and the age of the athletes and level of play (e.g., youth, collegiate, pro) Due to the recent emergence of more organized and refined GPS data collection within the sport, there is also limited quantification of all of the physical demands specific to each group. That being said, some brief points have been included here for quick reference that better clarify the key physiological characteristics for each position or group.

Offensive and Defense Linemen

Football games are often won or lost in the trenches; hence the need for strong, powerful, and quick offensive linemen. Offensive linemen will usually start plays in a crouched or squatting position. Due to the impact loads they must absorb and deliver, their need for maximal strength is often much greater than that of nearly any other position on the field. Unlike athletes at other positions, offensive linemen are constantly trying to move or to fend off opponents for the entire length of nearly every play. Offensive linemen must be highly conditioned to adapt to this type of contact. The biomechanics and postures required by the position, plus the fact that offensive linemen often fall or are fallen on by others, mean that offensive linemen and their strength and conditioning professionals must take special precautions to protect against knee, shoulder, hand, and ankle injuries, among others.

Defensive linemen are typically some of the largest athletes on the field. For the purposes of this book, it is not practical to give a range of ideal weights or heights—they will vary significantly from the Pop Warner level to the NFL, and they will differ according to the defensive scheme preferred by the head football coach. Typically, defensive linemen exhibit a more aggressive style of play than their offensive counterparts do, but both defensive linemen and offensive linemen collectively perform a larger number of movements that are highly specific to their positions (swim, rip, spin, rush, shuffle, kick-step, etc.) compared to positions such as running back or wide receiver. Defensive linemen may line up in varied positions (stand-up, three-point) based on the defensive package and their individual abilities. Due to their large body mass and the frequency and nature of their collisions with others, interior linemen especially are at risk for knee and ankle injuries, so they must pay careful attention to lower body resistance training and mobility strategies.

Tight Ends, Fullbacks, and Linebackers

In what is one of the most unique of the positions, tight ends may serve as additional linemen or run blockers on some plays, while they may serve as additional receivers on others. They do more sprinting than both offensive linemen and defensive linemen but typically less than running backs, defensive backs, and wide receivers. Tight ends must be strong and durable in order to take on opposing linebackers, linemen, and even defensive backs blitzing at maximal speed. They must also possess the grace, timing, hand-eye coordination, and precision of a wide receiver.

Once a trademark role for hard-hitting, power-based offenses at every level, the fullback position is now less common in modern football, or the role has become more diverse. While fullbacks are primarily expected to block or clear the way during both running and passing plays, it is not uncommon for them to serve as auxiliary receiving targets. Fullbacks usually have a short, wide stature (i.e., a low center of gravity), which is a tremendous benefit for blocking or running through would-be defenders. Fullbacks will not make contact with an opposing athlete as often as an offensive lineman or defensive lineman will, but they do so far more than running backs and wide receivers. The collision and locomotive loads imparted on them are more similar to those of a linebacker or a tight end. Fullbacks are often some of the strongest athletes on the team in their lower bodies, and although they do not stand out in terms of absolute speed (30-yard [27-m] sprints and beyond), their high levels of lower body strength and force production are evident when they accelerate or explode through a pack of defenders.

Often referred to as the quarterbacks of the defense, linebackers can be some of the most exciting athletes to both watch and train. The position is highly physical, with impact forces often surpassing even those of offensive and defensive linemen, but it also requires the speed and finesse needed to drop back into pass coverage or pick up a wide receiver coming across the middle. Like their defensive back counterparts, linebackers will call upon a wide movement cache, including linear and lateral sprinting, shuffling, crossover running, backpedaling, and jumping. Linebackers will also typically do more high-speed sprinting than defensive linemen, but not as much as defensive backs.

Wide Receivers and Running Backs

Wide receivers and defensive backs often face the highest amount of athlete load of any position in football (28). The combination of high-speed linear sprinting, variable cutting maneuvers during route running, and blocking responsibilities over the course of not only weekly practice but also competitive games can quickly take a toll on the calves, ankles, Achilles tendons, and hamstrings of the wide receiver. Special care must be taken by the strength and conditioning professional to ensure that high-volume resistance training for the lower body is reduced during times in which athlete load is highest. This is, of course, true across all positions, but aside from defensive back, few positions are exposed to the same volume of specialized workloads as wide receiver. The best way to foster an adaptive and resilient stimulus is to repeatedly expose it to stress. In the case of the wide receiver, this means athletes must not only develop adequate strength qualities (especially those of an eccentric nature, which are inherently protective), but they must also be exposed to higher-velocity movements in the weight room that target the posterior chain, such as the two-arm kettlebell swing, various weightlifting exercise derivatives, and even ballistic exercises such as medicine ball tosses and throws.

Running backs are some of the most elusive and explosive athletes on the football field. Although their involvement and total high-speed running distance and athlete load will vary tremendously based upon scheme, running backs must have significant levels of lower body strength in order to run through tackles and maintain a solid athletic base and a lower center of gravity when blocking opposing defenders. They also must have great vision and catching ability because they are often called upon to catch screen passes out of the backfield and other short passes in order to misdirect the defense. Compared to their offensive teammates, running backs will traditionally cover more cumulative sprint distances than offensive linemen, fullbacks, tight ends, and quarterbacks but fewer than wide receivers (depending on offensive system). Like defensive backs and fullbacks, running backs are subject to higher-velocity impact forces, which may increase the risk of injury from concussion, ACL tear, shoulder separation, and the like. Thus, durability and strength and power qualities must be emphasized throughout the physical preparation process.

Defensive Backs

Due to not only the demands of the sport, but also the unique roles assigned to their position, defensive backs are often required to use multivariate modes of locomotion, including back-pedaling, shuffling, drop-step and open-step techniques, linear (straight-line) running, and crossover running. When pursuing a wide receiver in coverage, or when trying to knock down or intercept a ball that has been thrown, a defensive back may open or drop back at 45-, 90-, or even 180-degree angles. Even when performed at submaximal speeds, this requires tremendous proprioception, mobility, visual acuity, and timing. Additionally, although no current research has directly compared backpedaling and crossover running, there is research that has examined general forms of lateral, backward, and forward locomotion. This has shown that during linear running, propulsive forces are generated by the hip extensor muscles (gluteus maximus and hamstring group), the knee extensors, and to a lesser degree the plantar flexors, whereas during backward running, most of the propulsive forces are driven by knee extensors and hip flexors (3, 9, 15, 16, 17). Along with wide receivers and running backs, defensive backs typically cover some of the greatest total distances on the field (if not the greatest total running volume), and although they do not have to withstand the same frequency of collisions that offensive linemen, defensive linemen, tight ends, and linebackers do, the impact forces they do experience are often much higher due to their velocity at the time of impact.

Quarterbacks

Over the years, few positions have evolved as much as the quarterback position. Body types of quarterbacks can vary broadly, and one should not expect the same physical attributes for a quarterback in a pro-style offense that would be found in one who leads a triple-option attack. This holds true regardless of whether one is analyzing the NFL or the collegiate level. In one week a defense may have to prepare for the likes of a true dual threat such as Cam Newton, and in the next week they may need to adjust to a more traditional pocket passer such as Matt Ryan. Even when these athletes retire, the archetypes (dual threat and pocket passer) will still exist, as they have for well over 40 years. Quarterbacks of all types must have upper body strength, shoulder mobility and stability, trunk stability, and lower body strength and mobility. All of these collectively help to both produce and transfer force through the kinetic chain. These physical qualities are crucial for all positions in football because the sport calls upon the entire system to function well in order to maximize both performance and resilience.

Kickers and Punters

While often overlooked and underappreciated, quality special teams play is a critical contributor to team success. Kickers and punters alike are expected to jump into action during some of the most stressful situations, and they must be able to focus under tremendous pressure and deliver with preternatural accuracy, timing, and precision. Due to the unilaterally dominant nature of the position, strength and conditioning professionals must place a premium on addressing and improving the mobility and stability of not only the kicking leg but also the stance leg. Some strength, power, and mobility asymmetries will exist between the stance leg and the kicking leg due to the frequency with which the activity is performed (which affects such things as motor learning, rate coding, and force production), but coaches should aim to manage those asymmetries as much as possible through the regular inclusion of both single-leg hip- and quad-dominant exercises (e.g., split-squat and lunge variations, single-leg Romanian deadlift variations, bridging and leg curl variations, and mini-band walks) as well as single-leg power movements (hops to a box, over hurdles, etc.). Furthermore, stability and proprioception can be improved through the inclusion of exercises and drills where the athlete drops off a box and lands softly on one foot, or even performs a level change by dropping from two feet to one foot. All of these exercises should be performed under varying conditions (e.g., strength and plyometric exercises performed in frontal, sagittal, and transverse planes), to ensure the well-rounded development of multiple qualities.

CONCLUSION

Due to the popularity of football, the media coverage it draws, and the training protocols of many of the athletes who compete at the highest level (many of whom become celebrities), countless myths have arisen about the best way to train. Most of these practices are not based on scientific evidence. More often they serve as eye candy or as ways to sell expensive training equipment, not as ways to do the simple things savagely well. The information presented here should serve as a solid starting point for both further reflection and investigation into the physiological and positional demands on football athletes, and it will complement the training regimens prescribed in other chapters of this text.

Neither performance enhancement nor the art of coaching in general are topics that can fit into a vacuum. Just as football athletes must call upon a wide variety of movement skills in order to succeed, strength and conditioning professionals must use a wide array of strategic plans, evidenced-based approaches, assessments, and even, at times, improvisations to ensure that none of the physical capacities and complex motor skills that produce explosive multiplanar movement are neglected. To date, no long-term, peer-reviewed scientific data exist to show a definitive relationship between a team's resistance training program and its win–loss record (14). Nevertheless, strength and conditioning professionals have a responsibility to their athletes not only to develop the technical aspects of their movement, but also to educate their athletes about why achieving certain biomechanical positions can both enhance performance and prevent injuries. The collective aim should be to help athletes to have long and productive careers, and this can be done by developing a strategic framework to help guide programming decisions.

3

TESTING PROTOCOLS AND ATHLETE ASSESSMENT

ZAC WOODFIN

This chapter provides information on testing protocols and athlete assessment and the appropriate time to use each one. It will also provide the testing protocols to use with athletes of any sport or age and information on assessing where an athlete falls in a normative range for that specific test based on age or level of competition. Testing protocols should take place at various times during an athlete's development.

GENERAL TESTING GUIDELINES

Opinions differ on whether an athlete should be tested right away when starting a training program. There are pros and cons, and it will be up to the strength and conditioning professional to make that judgment. Testing protocols are best used when an athlete has proven technical proficiency in the movement pattern that will be tested. If a coach does choose to test at the beginning of a training program, the strength, power, and speed tests should be administered in a way that minimizes the risk of injury. An example of this would be a 3- to 5-repetition maximum (RM) test instead of a 1RM test, or a 10-yard (9 m) sprint instead of a 40-yard (37 m) sprint. Maximal loading or maximal sprinting by an athlete who has poor movement quality will often result in injury either in the short term or in the long term.

A benefit of testing an athlete before starting a training program is that it provides the coach with appropriate loading strategies to write into the training plan. All testing should be administered by highly educated, trained, and certified professionals. This will ensure the consistency, reliability, and validity of the testing protocols.

Testing also provides objective information for athletes and coaches to use in setting and achieving goals. The test must be administered the same way every time to ensure validity. The **validity** of a test is how well the test actually measures what it is supposed to measure (2). Reliability is also critical when testing athletes. The **reliability** of a test is its ability to consistently repeat the test in exactly the same manner (5). Testing also provides motivation and competition among athletes who are trying to achieve goals that were set.

TESTING PROTOCOLS

The testing protocols provided will be descriptive and exact, and they will include instructions to ensure validity and reliability. When testing an athlete or athletes, follow the testing protocols closely to make sure it is done properly.

Test Finder

STRENGTH TESTS

The strength tests provided will allow the coach or strength and conditioning professional to measure an athlete's strength in the upper body and lower body. The tests provided are reliable and valid.

1RM BENCH PRESS

Purpose

Measure maximal upper body strength in a horizontal pressing movement

Equipment

Weight plates or bumper plates

Bar

Safety collars

Weight rack or bench press stand

Bench

Setup

The coach loads the appropriate weight onto the bar. The athlete performs a proper warm-up (see testing protocol).

Testing Protocol

1. Refer to the exercise technique description for the bench press (chapter 7, page 125).

2. The athlete performs 5 to 10 repetitions with a light resistance.

3. After a one-minute rest, add 5 to 10 percent more weight on the bar and have the athlete performs three to five repetitions.

4. After a two-minute rest, add 5 to 10 percent more weight on the bar and have the athlete performs two to three repetitions.

5. After another two- to four-minute rest, add 5 to 10 percent more weight on the bar and have the athlete attempt a 1RM.

6. If the athlete is successful, go back to step 4. If the athlete fails, give a two- to four-minute rest, decrease the load by 2.5 to 5 percent and re-attempt a 1RM.

7. Keep adjusting the load until the 1RM is determined; ideally within three to five attempts (1).

Coaching Tips

- The athlete must be mentally prepared for the test. This test takes the athlete to failure. The athlete must have the mental focus to give it his absolute best.

- This test should never be performed without a spotter. When a single spotter is used, the spotter stands at the head of the bench behind the athlete's head and grasps the bar in a closed, alternated grip inside the athlete's hands. In some cases, three spotters are used: One directly behind the head of the athlete and one on each side of the barbell.

Descriptive Data

Tables 3.1, 3.2, and 3.3 on pages 27 and 28 provide descriptive data that can be used to evaluate a high school and college football athlete's 1RM bench press.

1RM BACK SQUAT

Purpose

Measure lower body strength

Equipment

Squat rack or squat stand with adjustable spotter arms

Bar

Bumper or weight plates

Safety collars

Setup

The coach loads the appropriate weight onto the bar. The athlete performs a proper warm-up (see testing protocol).

Testing Protocol

1. Refer to the exercise technique description for the back squat (chapter 6, page 91).

2. The athlete performs 5 to 10 repetitions with a light resistance.

3. After a one-minute rest, add 10 to 20 percent more weight on the bar and have the athlete performs three to five repetitions.

4. After a two-minute rest, add 10 to 20 percent more weight on the bar and have the athlete performs two to three repetitions.

5. After another two- to four-minute rest, add 10 to 20 percent more weight on the bar and have the athlete attempt a 1RM.

6. If the athlete is successful, go back to step 4. If the athlete fails, give a two- to four-minute rest, decrease the load by 5 to 10 percent, and re-attempt a 1RM.

7. Keep adjusting the load until the 1RM is determined; ideally within three to five attempts (1).

Coaching Tips

- The athlete should undergo a medical screening before he performs the back squat test. Any previous injuries to the spine are indicators for possibly choosing another lower body strength test.

- The athlete may wear a weight belt during the back squat test to provide added stability to the spine.

- Firm footwear is best for the back squat test. Some athletes prefer to perform the back squat in a shoe that has an elevated heel. This increases ankle mobility and allows the hips to sit lower while the athlete maintains an upright trunk posture.

- There should be two spotters for the 1RM back squat test, one spotter on each side of the barbell. The spotters grasp the bar and take it out of the rack for the athlete. On the downward movement phase, the spotters keep their thumbs crossed and hands close to the bar but do not touch it. The spotters use the same technique during the upward movement phase and when the athlete completes the squat. After the athlete finishes, the spotters grasp the bar and guide it back into the rack.

Descriptive Data

Tables 3.1, 3.2, and 3.3 on pages 27 and 28 provide descriptive data that can be used to evaluate a high school and college football athlete's 1RM back squat.

1RM POWER CLEAN

Purpose

Measure total body power

Equipment

Olympic bar

Bumper plates

Safety clips

Setup

The coach loads the appropriate weight onto the bar. The athlete performs a proper warm-up (see testing protocol).

Testing Protocol

1. Refer to the exercise technique description for the power clean (chapter 5, page 64).

2. The athlete performs 5 to 10 repetitions with a light resistance.

3. After a one-minute rest, add 10 to 20 percent more weight on the bar and have the athlete performs three to five repetitions.

4. After a two-minute rest, add 10 to 20 percent more weight on the bar and have the athlete performs two to three repetitions.
5. After another two- to four-minute rest, add 10 to 20 percent more weight on the bar and have the athlete attempt a 1RM.
6. If the athlete is successful, go back to step 4. If the athlete fails, give a two- to four-minute rest, decrease the load by 5 to 10 percent and re-attempt a 1RM.
7. Keep adjusting the load until the 1RM is determined; ideally within three to five attempts (1).

Coaching Tips

• Other variations of the power clean include the *full clean* (the athlete catches the bar in the bottom position of a squat), *hang clean* (barbell starts below the knees), *high hang clean* (barbell starts mid-thigh), and *low hang clean* (barbell starts mid-shin).
• The power clean should not be spotted (see chapter 5 for more details).

Descriptive Data

Tables 3.1, 3.2, and 3.3 provide descriptive data that can be used to evaluate a high school and college football athlete's 1RM power clean.

Table 3.1   Percentile Values of the 1RM Bench Press, Squat, and Power Clean in High School and College Football Athletes

% rank	1RM bench press Lb	Kg	1RM squat Lb	Kg	1RM power clean Lb	Kg	1RM bench press Lb	Kg	1RM squat Lb	Kg	1RM power clean Lb	Kg
	High school 14-15 years						**High school 16-18 years**					
90	243	110	385	175	213	97	275	125	465	211	250	114
80	210	95	344	156	195	89	250	114	425	193	235	107
70	195	89	325	148	190	86	235	107	405	184	225	102
60	185	84	305	139	183	83	225	102	365	166	223	101
50	170	77	295	134	173	79	215	98	335	152	208	95
40	165	75	275	125	165	75	205	93	315	143	200	91
30	155	70	255	116	161	73	195	89	295	134	183	83
20	145	66	236	107	153	70	175	80	275	125	165	75
10	125	57	205	93	141	64	160	73	250	114	145	66
Average	179	81	294	134	176	80	214	97	348	158	204	93
SD	45	20	73	33	32	15	44	20	88	40	43	20
n	214		170		180		339		249		284	
	NCAA DI						**NCAA DIII**					
90	370	168	500	227	300	136	365	166	470	214		
80	345	157	455	207	280	127	325	148	425	193		
70	325	148	430	195	270	123	307	140	405	184		
60	315	143	405	184	261	119	295	134	385	175		
50	300	136	395	180	252	115	280	127	365	166		
40	285	130	375	170	242	110	273	124	350*	159*		
30	270	123	355	161	232	105	255	116	335	152		
20	255	116	330	150	220	100	245	111	315	143		

(continued)

Table 3.1 *(continued)*

% rank	1RM bench press Lb	Kg	1RM squat Lb	Kg	1RM power clean Lb	Kg	1RM bench press Lb	Kg	1RM squat Lb	Kg	1RM power clean Lb	Kg
	NCAA DI						NCAA DIII					
10	240	109	300	136	205	93	225	102	283	129		
Average	301	137	395	180	252	115	287	130	375	170		
SD	53	24	77	35	38	17	57	26	75	34		
n	1,189		1,074		1,017		591		588			

*Hoffman 2006 reported 365 lb, 166 kg, for the 40% rank of the NCAA DIII 1RM squat. Lb = pounds, SD = standard deviation, *n* = sample size.

Reprinted by permission from J. Hoffman, *Norms for Fitness, Performance, and Health* (Champaign, IL: Human Kinetics, 2006), 36-37.

Table 3.2   Average Values of the 1RM Bench Press, Squat, and Power Clean in College NCAA Division I Football Athletes

Position	1RM bench press Lb	Kg	1RM squat Lb	Kg	1RM power clean Lb	Kg
Average	363 ± 59*	165 ± 27	510 ± 90	232 ± 41	306 ± 42	139 ± 19
DL	396 ± 53	180 ± 24	543 ± 77	247 ± 35	323 ± 37	147 ± 17
LB	352 ± 53	160 ± 24	530 ± 81	241 ± 37	317 ± 35	144 ± 16
DB	312 ± 37	142 ± 17	458 ± 88	208 ± 40	279 ± 44	127 ± 20
QB	359 ± 48	163 ± 22	440 ± 99	200 ± 45	275 ± 42	125 ± 19
RB	385 ± 53	175 ± 24	513 ± 73	233 ± 33	304 ± 33	138 ± 15
WR	332 ± 59	151 ± 27	453 ± 88	206 ± 40	282 ± 33	128 ± 15
OL	383 ± 62	174 ± 28	552 ± 75	251 ± 34	315 ± 35	143 ± 16
TE	378 ± 37	172 ± 17	510 ± 81	232 ± 37	310 ± 31	141 ± 14

*±1 standard deviation. DL = defensive lineman, LB = linebacker, DB = defensive back, QB = quarterback, RB = running back, WR = wide receiver, OL = offensive lineman, TE = tight end.

Reprinted by permission from J. Hoffman, *Norms for Fitness, Performance, and Health* (Champaign, IL: Human Kinetics, 2004), 38; Data from M.A.Garstecki, R.W. Latin, and M.M. Cuppett. "Comparison of Selected Physical Fitness and Performance Variables Between NCAA Division I and II Football Players," *Journal of Strength and Conditioning Research* 18 (2004): 292-297.

Table 3.3   Average Values of the 1RM Bench Press, Squat, and Power Clean in College NCAA Division II Football Athletes

Position	1RM bench press Lb	Kg	1RM squat Lb	Kg	1RM power clean Lb	Kg
Average	321 ± 57*	146 ± 26	449 ± 90	204 ± 41	277 ± 46	126 ± 21
DL	356 ± 46	162 ± 21	482 ± 79	219 ± 36	293 ± 48	133 ± 22
LB	321 ± 48	146 ± 22	460 ± 84	209 ± 38	290 ± 51	132 ± 23
DB	277 ± 40	126 ± 18	389 ± 84	177 ± 38	255 ± 42	116 ± 19
QB	284 ± 51	129 ± 23	394 ± 88	179 ± 40	264 ± 42	120 ± 19
RB	323 ± 44	147 ± 20	473 ± 88	215 ± 40	279 ± 48	127 ± 22
WR	271 ± 44	123 ± 20	383 ± 77	174 ± 35	273 ± 37	124 ± 17
OL	352 ± 55	160 ± 25	488 ± 79	222 ± 36	290 ± 37	132 ± 17
TE	317 ± 35	144 ± 16	447 ± 64	203 ± 29	271 ± 42	123 ± 19

*±1 standard deviation. DL = defensive lineman, LB = linebacker, DB = defensive back, QB = quarterback, RB = running back, WR = wide receiver, OL = offensive lineman, TE = tight end.

Reprinted by permission from J. Hoffman, *Norms for Fitness, Performance, and Health* (Champaign, IL: Human Kinetics, 2004), 38; Data from M.A. Garstecki, R.W. Latin, and M.M. Cuppett. "Comparison of Selected Physical Fitness and Performance Variables Between NCAA Division I and II Football Players," *Journal of Strength and Conditioning Research* 18 (2004): 292-297.

POWER TESTS

The power tests provided will allow the coach or strength and conditioning professional to safely and properly evaluate and test an athlete's ability to express explosive strength.

VERTICAL JUMP

Purpose
Measure the athlete's lower body power

Equipment
Jump mat

Vertec stand

Force plate

Chalk

Wall

Testing Protocols
There are four ways to measure a noncountermovement and a countermovement vertical jump: With a jump mat, a Vertec stand, a force plate, or chalk on a wall.

Jump Mat
A jump mat is an indirect assessment of vertical jump height. It uses flight time to predict jump height. Therefore, it is very important that the athlete does not land with significant flex in his knees or hips because this will influence flight time and jump height. The setup for using a jump mat is shown in figure 3.1.

1. The coach instructs the athlete to stand on the mat.

2. The coach instructs the athlete to stand tall then quickly dip down and jump as high as possible.

3. Once the athlete lands on the mat, a height number appears on the screen of the remote box. This number is the measure of the countermovement vertical jump height.

4. To measure the noncountermovement vertical jump height, all directions are the same except the athlete starts in a quarter-squat position instead of a tall position and jumps from the quarter-squat position.

Figure 3.1   Jump mat setup.

Figure 3.2 Vertec stand.

Vertec Stand

Using a Vertec stand (figure 3.2) is a bit more complex, but it directly assesses vertical jump performance. The athlete's reach must be measured first, before the jump is measured.

1. To properly measure the athlete's reach, the Vertec should be set high enough for the athlete's outstretched arm to touch and move the highest bar when the athlete walks up and touches the Vertec.
2. Once the reach is recorded, the coach raises the Vertec even higher for the jump.
3. After the Vertec is raised, the athlete stands tall under and slightly behind the bars of the Vertec.
4. When instructed by the coach, the athlete dips quickly and jumps as high as possible, touching the highest vane he can with the dominant arm.
5. To measure the noncountermovement vertical jump on a Vertec stand, all instructions are the same except the athlete begins in a quarter-squat position instead of a tall standing position.
6. The best of three trials is recorded.

Force Plate

Using a force plate (figure 3.3) is much easier because the force plate does the measurement for the coach. However, force plates are expensive and are not yet common in most strength and conditioning settings.

1. The coach instructs the athlete to stand on the force plate and then tells the athlete when to jump.
2. The computer connected to the force plate automatically gives the coach the height of the jump.

Figure 3.3 Force plate.
Courtesy of Andrius Ramonas

Chalk and Wall

The most inexpensive way to measure vertical jump is by putting chalk on the athlete's fingers and measuring his reach and jump height on a blank wall (figure 3.4).

1. The athlete puts chalk on the tips of his fingers.
2. The athlete extends his arm until completely locked out. He touches the wall for a measurement of standing reach height.
3. After the standing reach height is measured, the athlete performs a maximum vertical jump and touches the wall at the highest point possible.
4. To measure the noncountermovement vertical jump height, all directions are the same except the athlete starts in a quarter-squat position instead of a tall position and jumps from the quarter-squat position.
5. The coach measures the distance between the two marks on the wall to get the vertical jump height.

Coaching Tip

Lower body power is not solely about quickly applying force into the floor. It also is about absorbing force upon landing (6).

Descriptive Data

Tables 3.4 and 3.5 provide descriptive data for a vertical jump test for high school and NCAA Division I and III

Figure 3.4 Chalk and wall.

college football athletes. Table 3.6 provides descriptive data for NCAA Division I and II college football athletes. Figure 3.5 provides classifications from the NFL Scouting Combine.

Table 3.4 Percentile Values of the Vertical Jump in High School Football Athletes (in Inches)

Percentile rank	DB	DL	LB, DE, TE	OL	QB	RB	WR
90	31.0	28.0	29.2	25.5	30.0	31.0	31.0
80	29.0	26.0	27.5	24.0	28.0	29.0	29.0
70	28.0	24.8	26.5	22.5	27.0	28.0	27.5
60	27.0	23.5	25.0	21.0	26.0	27.0	26.5
50	26.0	22.5	24.5	20.0	25.0	26.0	26.0
40	25.0	21.5	23.5	19.5	24.5	25.0	25.0
30	24.0	20.5	22.5	18.5	23.0	24.0	24.0
20	23.0	19.5	21.5	18.0	22.5	23.0	23.0
10	22.0	17.5	20.0	16.5	21.0	21.5	22.0
Mean (±SD)							
Freshman	23.7 (3.1)*	20.9 (3.7)*	22.7 (3.3)*	19.7 (3.5)*	23.9 (3.3)*	24.5 (3.1)*	24.4 (3.1)*
Sophomore	26.1 (3.2)*	22.2 (3.9)*	24.4 (3.3)*	20.4 (3.5)*	24.9 (3.4)*	26.2 (3.7)*	26.0 (3.4)*
Junior	27.1 (3.8)*	23.4 (4.3)*	25.4 (3.7)*	21.2 (4.0)*	26.5 (4.0)*	26.7 (3.9)*	26.8 (3.6)*
n	1,308	847	1,196	670	625	1,161	1,455

*Significant differences among classes (p ≤ 0.05). DB = defensive back, DL = defensive lineman, LB = linebacker, DE = defensive end, TE = tight end, OL = offensive lineman, QB = quarterback, RB = running back, WR = wide receiver. SD = standard deviation, *n* = sample size.

Reprinted by permission from B.D. McKay, A.A. Miramonti, Z.M. Gillen, T.J. Leutzinger, A.I. Mendez, N.D.M. Jenkins, and J.T. Cramer, "Normative Reference Values for High School-Aged American Football Players," *Journal of Strength and Conditioning Research* (2019).

Table 3.5 Percentile Values of the Vertical Jump in College NCAA Division III and Division I Football Athletes

| Percentile rank | NCAA DIII | | NCAA DI | |
	In.	Cm	In.	Cm
90	30.0	76.2	33.5	85.1
80	28.5	72.4	31.5	80.0
70	27.5	69.9	30.0	76.2
60	26.5	67.3	29.0	73.7
50	25.5	64.8	28.0	71.1
40	24.5	62.2	27.0	68.6
30	23.5	59.7	25.5	64.8
20	22.0	55.9	24.0	61.0
10	20.0	50.8	21.5	54.6
Average	25.3	64.3	27.6	70.1
SD	4	10.2	4.4	11.2
n	567		1,495	

SD = standard deviation, *n* = sample size.

Reprinted by permission from J. Hoffman, *Norms for Fitness, Performance, and Health* (Champaign, IL: Human Kinetics, 2006), 60.

Table 3.6 Average Values of the Vertical Jump in College NCAA Division I and Division II Football Athletes

| Position | NCAA DI | | NCAA DII | |
	In.	Cm	In.	Cm
Average	31.5 ± 4.0*	80.1 ± 10.2	27.6 ± 4.8	70.1 ± 12.1
DL	30.7 ± 3.2	77.9 ± 8.2	26.3 ± 4.4	66.9 ± 11.3
LB	34.0 ± 3.1	83.2 ± 7.8	28.5 ± 4.3	72.4 ± 10.8
DB	34.6 ± 3.1	87.8 ± 7.8	30.7 ± 4.1	78.0 ± 10.3
QB	31.8 ± 2.5	80.7 ± 6.4	27.7 ± 3.7	70.3 ± 9.3
RB	33.8 ± 3.0	85.9 ± 7.7	29.2 ± 4.3	74.2 ± 11.0
WR	34.4 ± 2.8	87.4 ± 7.0	30.6 ± 4.8	77.8 ± 12.1
OL	27.1 ± 2.4	68.8 ± 6.2	23.8 ± 3.4	60.4 ± 8.6
TE	31.3 ± 2.8	79.6 ± 7.2	27.6 ± 3.4	70.1 ± 8.7

*±1 standard deviation, DL = defensive lineman; LB = linebacker, DB = defensive back, QB = quarterback, RB = running back, WR = wide receiver, OL = offensive lineman, TE = tight end.

Reprinted by permission from J. Hoffman, *Norms for Fitness, Performance, and Health* (Champaign, IL: Human Kinetics, 2006), 63; Data from M.A. Garstecki, R.W. Latin, and M.M. Cuppett. "Comparison of Selected Physical Fitness and Performance Variables Between NCAA Division I and II Football Players," *Journal of Strength and Conditioning Research* 18 (2004): 292-297.

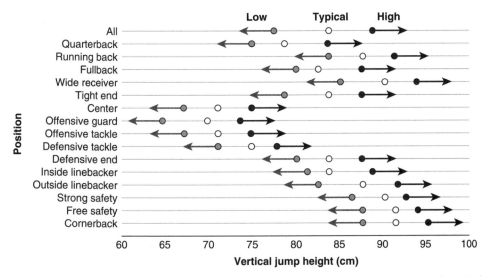

Figure 3.5 Vertical jump classifications from the NFL Scouting Combine: high—70th percentile; typical—50th percentile; low—30th percentile.

Reprinted by permission from D.H. Fukuda, *Assessments for Sport and Athletic Performance* (Champaign, IL: Human Kinetics, 2019), 140; Data from J.L. Nuzzo, "The National Football league scouting combine from 1999 to 2014: Normative reference values and an examination of body mass normalization techniques," *Journal of Strength and Conditioning Research* 29 (2015):279-289.

STANDING LONG (BROAD) JUMP

Purpose
Measure horizontal jumping power and the athlete's ability to decelerate and land

Equipment
    Tape measure
    Grass or turf surface (ideal)
    Weight room floor or court (secondary option)

Setup
The coach marks a starting line and sets up a measuring tape perpendicular to the starting line and extending 10 feet (3 m) away from the starting line (Note: The athlete is not quite behind the line in the photo.).

Testing Protocol
1. The coach instructs the athlete to stand behind the starting line.
2. From a tall standing position, the athlete performs a countermovement and jumps forward as far as possible, landing under control (figure 3.6). If the feet move or the athlete falls forward or backward on landing, the test is invalid.
3. The jump is measured from the starting line to the back of the foot closest to the starting line.
4. The best of three trials is recorded.

Coaching Tips
- Although a grass or turf surface is best, a weight room floor or court surface can be used.

- Both countermovement and noncountermovement jumps can be tested using the standing long (broad) jump.

Figure 3.6 Setup for the standing long (broad) jump.

Descriptive Data

Table 3.7 provides descriptive data for a standing long (broad) jump test for high school football athletes. Table 3.8 provides descriptive data for college football athletes. Figure 3.7 provides classifications from the NFL Scouting Combine.

Table 3.7 Percentile Values of the Standing Long (Broad) Jump in High School Football Athletes (in Inches)

Percentile rank	DB	DL	LB, DE, TE	OL	QB	RB	WR
90	112.0	104.0	108.0	94.0	109.0	111.0	112.0
80	109.0	99.0	104.0	90.0	105.0	107.0	109.0
70	107.0	95.0	101.0	88.0	102.0	105.0	106.0
60	104.0	92.0	98.0	85.0	100.0	103.0	104.0
50	102.0	90.0	96.0	83.0	98.0	100.0	102.0
40	100.0	87.0	94.0	81.0	96.0	98.0	100.0
30	98.0	85.0	91.0	78.0	93.0	96.0	97.0
20	95.0	81.0	88.8	75.0	91.0	93.0	95.0
10	91.0	75.0	85.0	70.0	87.0	89.0	90.0
Mean (±SD)							
Freshman	95.5 (8.4)	83.7 (11.2)	90.5 (8.2)	77.6 (10.8)	93.4 (7.9)	95.8 (8.4)	95.9 (8.2)
Sophomore	100.0 (7.7)	88.9 (10.2)	95.0 (8.5)	81.4 (9.2)	97.5 (8.0)	100.3 (8.4)	100.6 (7.6)
Junior	104.2 (7.6)	91.7 (10.7)	98.5 (8.8)	84.0 (8.9)	100.3 (8.7)	101.2 (9.9)	103.6 (8.0)
n	1,311	836	1,198	676	626	1,169	1,475

DB = defensive back, DL = defensive lineman, LB = linebacker, DE = defensive end, TE = tight end, OL = offensive lineman, QB = quarterback, RB = running back, WR = wide receiver. SD = standard deviation, *n* = sample size.

Reprinted by permission from B.D. McKay, A.A. Miramonti, Z.M. Gillen, T.J. Leutzinger, A.I. Mendez, N.D.M. Jenkins, and J.T. Cramer, "Normative Reference Values for High School-Aged American Football Players," *Journal of Strength and Conditioning Research* (2019).

Table 3.8 Average Values of the Standing Long (Broad) Jump in College Football Athletes

Position	Feet	Meters
Average	8.8 ± 0.68*	2.7 ± 0.21*
Backs	9.3 ± 0.52	2.8 ± 0.16
LB	8.9 ± 0.30	2.7 ± 0.09
OL/DL	8.2 ± 0.62	2.50 ± 0.19

*±1 standard deviation. LB = linebacker, OL = offensive lineman, DL = defensive lineman.

Adapted by permission from S. Seiler et al., "Assessing Anaerobic Power in Collegiate Football Players," *Journal of Applied Sport Science Research* 4, no. 1 (1990): 9-15.

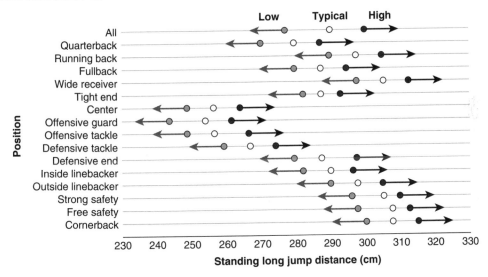

Figure 3.7 Standing long (broad) jump classifications from the NFL Scouting Combine: high—70th percentile; typical—50th percentile; low—30th percentile.

Reprinted by permission from D.H. Fukuda, *Assessments for Sport and Athletic Performance* (Champaign, IL: Human Kinetics, 2019), 143; Data from J.L. Nuzzo, "The National Football League Scouting Combine from 1999 to 2014: Normative Reference Values and an Examination of Body Mass Normalization Techniques," *Journal of Strength and Conditioning Research* 29 (2015): 279-289.

SPEED AND AGILITY TESTS

Speed and agility tests are important to assess and track an athlete's athleticism and progress. The tests covered will provide the coach with detailed instruction on how to implement and administer speed and agility testing.

40-YARD (37 M) SPRINT

Purpose
Measure linear speed

Equipment
Cones or markers

Timing devices (two)

Measured running space, such as a football field

Setup

The coach marks a starting line and sets up a timer on the 20-yard (18 m) mark and the 40-yard (37 m) mark (figure 3.8).

Testing Protocol

1. The athlete begins at the starting line.
2. On the coach's command, the athlete sprints down the course.
3. The athlete's time at the 20-yard (18 m) mark is noted. The coach looks for proper posture, leg action, and arm action.
4. The athlete's time at the 40-yard (37 m) mark is noted.
5. After 40 yards (37 m), the athlete decelerates safely.
6. The best of three trials is recorded (with 3-5 min of rest in between).

Coaching Tips

- Getting times at the two points of the sprint—the 20-yard (18 m) mark and the 40-yard (37 m) mark—gives the coach a great understanding of what part of the test the athlete exceeds in and what part can be improved through speed training.
- There are three phases of the sprint: The start phase, acceleration phase, and top speed phase; the efficiency with which athletes can link these skills together and transition from one to the next will determine their success (7).
- The acceleration phase consists of the first 20 yards (18 m) (7). The athlete's performance during this phase provides great feedback on the athlete's power and ability to create force quickly. During the acceleration phase, the coach should look for proper posture: Leaning forward with a neutral spine and a stiff trunk. This posture allows

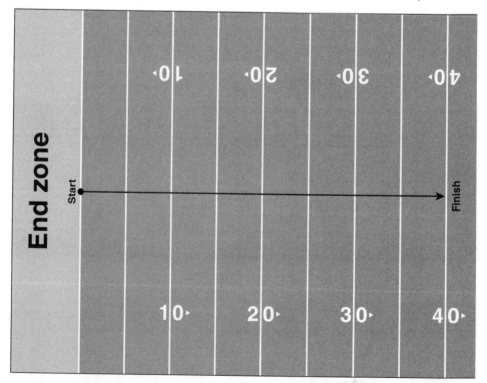

Figure 3.8 Setup for the 40-yard (37 m) sprint.

proper leg action, and the stiff trunk allows the force applied into the running surface to be transferred efficiently. Leg action should be piston-like, and all force should be applied behind the athlete's center of mass.

- During the top speed phase of the sprint, the coach also looks for proper posture, leg action, and arm action. In the top speed phase, the posture rises from a stiff leaning trunk to a stiff vertical upright trunk. The leg action moves from piston-like to cyclical, and the foot contact point should be right under the body's center of mass instead of behind the center of mass as in the acceleration phase.

- Improving mechanics and stride frequency are important and specific to increased performance (3).

Descriptive Data

Table 3.9 provides descriptive data for a 40-yard (37 m) sprint test for high school football athletes. Tables 3.10 and 3.11 provide descriptive data for college football athletes. Figure 3.9 provides classifications from the NFL Scouting Combine.

Table 3.9 Percentile Values of the 40-Yard (37 m) Sprint in High School Football Athletes

Percentile rank	DB	DL	LB, DE, TE	OL	QB	RB	WR
90	4.83 s	5.10 s	4.97 s	5.43 s	4.91 s	4.80 s	4.80 s
80	4.91 s	5.23 s	5.06 s	5.55 s	4.89 s	4.89 s	4.88 s
70	4.96 s	5.34 s	5.13 s	5.65 s	4.96 s	4.96 s	4.95 s
60	5.01 s	5.44 s	5.20 s	5.75 s	5.00 s	5.00 s	5.01 s
50	5.06 s	5.52 s	5.27 s	5.85 s	5.05 s	5.05 s	5.06 s
40	5.11 s	5.61 s	5.33 s	5.95 s	5.11 s	5.11 s	5.12 s
30	5.17 s	5.71 s	5.40 s	6.06 s	5.18 s	5.18 s	5.19 s
20	5.26 s	5.87 s	5.49 s	6.20 s	5.25 s	5.25 s	5.28 s
10	5.38 s	6.09 s	5.63 s	6.41 s	5.41 s	5.41 s	5.42 s
Mean (±SD)							
Freshman	5.26 (0.29)*	5.81 (0.55)*	5.44 (0.27)*	6.04 (0.49)*	5.35 (0.30)*	5.21 (0.25)*	5.23 (0.25)*
Sophomore	5.10 (0.20)*	5.59 (0.39)*	5.32 (0.26)*	5.93 (0.44)*	5.24 (0.25)*	5.07 (0.25)*	5.11 (0.25)*
Junior	5.02 (0.19)*	5.51 (0.39)*	5.22 (0.25)*	5.85 (0.40)*	5.15 (0.23)*	5.04 (0.23)*	5.03 (0.23)*
n	1,308	855	1,200	681	627	1,174	1,464

*Significant differences among classes (p ≤ 0.05). DB = defensive back, DL = defensive lineman, LB = linebacker, DE = defensive end, TE = tight end, OL = offensive lineman, QB = quarterback, RB = running back, WR = wide receiver. SD = standard deviation, n = sample size.

Reprinted by permission from B.D. McKay, A.A. Miramonti, Z.M. Gillen, T.J. Leutzinger, A.I. Mendez, N.D.M. Jenkins, and J.T. Cramer, "Normative Reference Values for High School-Aged American Football Players," *Journal of Strength and Conditioning Research* (2019).

Table 3.10 Percentile Values of the 40-Yard (37 m) Sprint in College NCAA Division III and Division I Football Athletes (in Seconds)

Percentile rank	NCAA DIII	NCAA DI
90	4.59	4.58
80	4.70	4.67
70	4.77	4.73
60	4.85	4.80
50	4.95	4.87

(continued)

Table 3.10 *(continued)*

Percentile rank	NCAA DIII	NCAA DI
40	5.02	4.93
30	5.12	5.02
20	5.26	5.18
10	5.47	5.33
Average	4.99	4.92
SD	0.35	0.32
n	538	757

SD = standard deviation, *n* = sample size.

Reprinted by permission from J. Hoffman, *Norms for Fitness, Performance, and Health* (Champaign, IL: Human Kinetics, 2006), 109.

Table 3.11   Average Values of the 40-Yard (37 m) Sprint in College NCAA Division I and Division II Football Athletes (in Seconds)

Position	NCAA DI	NCAA DII
Average	4.74 ± 0.3*	4.88 ± 0.3
DL	4.85 ± 0.2	5.03 ± 0.3
LB	4.64 ± 0.2	4.76 ± 0.2
DB	4.52 ± 0.2	4.61 ± 0.1
QB	4.70 ± 0.1	4.81 ± 0.1
RB	4.53 ± 0.2	4.69 ± 0.2
WR	4.48 ± 0.1	4.59 ± 0.2
OL	5.12 ± 0.2	5.25 ± 0.2
TE	4.78 ± 0.2	4.84 ± 0.1

*±1 standard deviation. DL = defensive lineman; LB = linebacker, DB = defensive back, QB = quarterback, RB = running back, WR = wide receiver, OL = offensive lineman, TE = tight end.

Reprinted by permission from J. Hoffman, *Norms for Fitness, Performance, and Health* (Champaign, IL: Human Kinetics, 2006), 111; Data from M.A. Garstecki, R.W. Latin, and M.M. Cuppett, "Comparison of Selected Physical Fitness and Performance Variables Between NCAA Division I and II Football Players," *Journal of Strength and Conditioning Research* 18 (2004): 292-297.

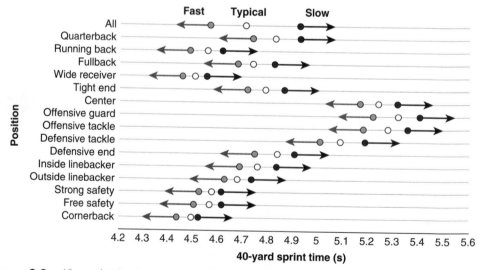

Figure 3.9   40-yard (37 m) sprint classifications from the NFL Scouting Combine: fast—70th percentile; typical—50th percentile; slow—30th percentile.

Reprinted by permission from D.H. Fukuda, *Assessments for Sport and Athletic Performance* (Champaign, IL: Human Kinetics, 2019), 124: Data from J.L. Nuzzo, "The National Football League Scouting Combine From 1999 to 2014: Normative Reference Values and an Examination of Body Mass Normalization Techniques," *Journal of Strength and Conditioning Research* 29 (2015): 279-289.

5-10-5 AGILITY TEST (ALSO CALLED THE *PRO AGILITY DRILL* OR *20-YARD SHUTTLE RUN*)

Purpose
Measure lateral speed and ability to change direction

Equipment
Cones

Stopwatch or timing system

Grass turf or good running surface

Setup
The coach places three cones in a straight line on a field marked with three parallel lines 5 yards (4.6 m) apart (figure 3.10). If there are not lines on the field, use a tape measure to ensure reliability and validity. Once the cones are set up and the coach has the stopwatch or timing system ready, the test is administered.

Testing Protocol
1. The athlete lines up right behind the middle cone and gets in a three-point stance. If starting to the right first, the right hand should be down. If starting to the left first, the left hand should be down.

2. The stopwatch or timing system starts at the athlete's first movement; if he is going to the right first, he will start by turning and sprinting to his right until he touches the line with his right hand.

3. After touching the far right line with his right hand, the athlete will turn to his left and sprint past the middle line until he touch the far left line with his left hand.

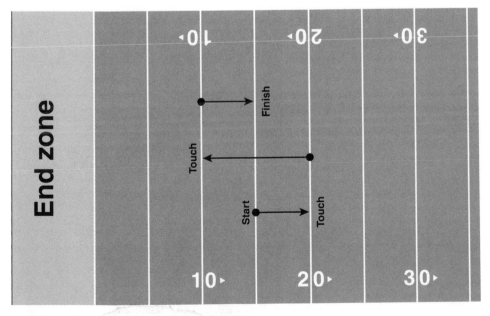

Figure 3.10   Setup for the 5-10-5 agility test.

4. After touching the far left line with his left hand, he will turn back to his right and sprint past the middle line to complete the test.

5. The coach will stop the time as soon as the athlete crosses the finish line at the middle cone. The time of the test determines the score.

6. The best of two trials is recorded (with 3-5 min of rest in between).

Coaching Tip

The test can begin with the athlete starting to the right or left. The coach has the discretion to begin in either direction. Both directions should be tested (with 3-5 min of rest in between).

Descriptive Data

Table 3.12 provides descriptive data for the 5-10-5 agility test for high school football athletes. Tables 3.13 and 3.14 provide descriptive data for college football athletes. Figure 3.11 provides classifications from the NFL Scouting Combine.

Table 3.12   Percentile Values of the 5-10-5 Agility Test in High School Football Athletes (in Seconds)

Percentile rank	DB	DL	LB, DE, TE	OL	QB	RB	WR
90	4.26	4.47	4.35	4.67	4.33	4.27	4.25
80	4.33	4.57	4.43	4.77	4.40	4.35	4.32
70	4.38	4.65	4.50	4.87	4.45	4.41	4.37
60	4.43	4.71	4.56	4.94	4.51	4.46	4.43
50	4.48	4.79	4.61	5.01	4.56	4.51	4.48
40	4.53	4.87	4.68	5.10	4.61	4.57	4.53
30	4.59	4.97	4.76	5.16	4.67	4.63	4.60
20	4.66	5.11	4.83	5.28	4.74	4.71	4.68
10	4.77	5.29	4.95	5.44	4.86	4.83	4.81
Mean (±SD)							
Freshman	4.61 (0.24)*	5.00 (0.43)*	4.76 (0.24)*	5.18 (0.37)*	4.66 (0.24)*	4.63 (0.23)*	4.62 (0.24)*
Sophomore	4.52 (0.22)*	4.85 (0.31)*	4.66 (0.23)*	5.05 (0.31)*	4.59 (0.21)*	4.53 (0.23)*	4.52 (0.22)*
Junior	4.46 (0.20)*	4.81 (0.34)*	4.59 (0.24)*	5.02 (0.33)*	4.53 (0.20)*	4.50 (0.24)*	4.46 (0.22)*
n	1,307	839	1,189	677	627	1,172	1,462

*Significant differences among classes (p ≤ 0.05). DB = defensive back, DL = defensive lineman, LB = linebacker, DE = defensive end, TE = tight end, OL = offensive lineman, QB = quarterback, RB = running back, WR = wide receiver. SD = standard deviation, n = sample size.

Reprinted by permission from B.D. McKay, A.A. Miramonti, Z.M. Gillen, T.J. Leutzinger, A.I. Mendez, N.D.M. Jenkins, and J.T. Cramer, "Normative Reference Values for High School-Aged American Football Players," *Journal of Strength and Conditioning Research* (2019).

Table 3.13   Percentile Values of the 5-10-5 Agility Test in College NCAA Division I Football Athletes (in Seconds)

Percentile rank	NCAA DI
90	4.21
80	4.31
70	4.38
60	4.44
50	4.52
40	4.59

Percentile rank	NCAA DI
30	4.66
20	4.76
10	4.89
Average	4.54
SD	0.27
n	869

Data collected using an electronic timer. SD = standard deviation, *n* = sample size.

Reprinted by permission from J. Hoffman, *Norms for Fitness, Performance, and Health* (Champaign, IL: Human Kinetics, 2006), 113.

Table 3.14 Average Values of the 5-10-5 Agility Test in College NCAA Division I and Division III Football Athletes (in Seconds)

Position	NCAA DI[a]	NCAA DIII[b]
Average	4.53 ± 0.22*	4.6 ± 0.2*
DL	4.35 ± 0.11	4.8 ± 0.2
LB	4.6 ± 0.2	—
DB	4.35 ± 0.12	4.6 ± 0.2
OB	—	4.5 ± 0.2
RB	4.6 ± 0.2	—
WR	4.35 ± 0.12	—
OL	4.35 ± 0.11	4.8 ± 0.2
TE	4.6 ± 0.2	—

*±1 standard deviation, DL = defensive lineman; LB = linebacker, DB = defensive back, OB = offensive back, RB = running back, WR = wide receiver, OL = offensive lineman, TE = tight end.

Reprinted by permission from J. Hoffman, *Norms for Fitness, Performance, and Health* (Champaign, IL: Human Kinetics, 2006), 114; [a]Data from D.T. Sawyer et al., "Relationship Between Football Playing Ability and Selected Performance Measures," *Journal of Strength and Conditioning Research* 16 (2002): 611-616; [b]Data from K.J. Stuempfle, et al., "Body Composition Relates Poorly to Performance Tests in NCAA Division III Football Players" *Journal of Strength and Conditioning Research* 17 (2003): 238-244.

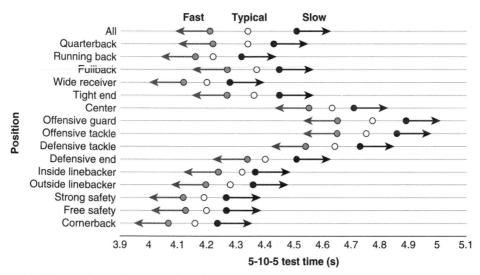

Figure 3.11 5-10-5 agility test classifications from the NFL Scouting Combine: fast—70th percentile; typical—50th percentile; slow—30th percentile.

Reprinted by permission from D.H. Fukuda, *Assessments for Sport and Athletic Performance* (Champaign, IL: Human Kinetics, 2019), 124; Data from J.L. Nuzzo, "The National Football League Scouting Combine from 1999 to 2014: Normative Reference Values and an Examination of Body Mass Normalization Techniques," *Journal of Strength and Conditioning Research* 29 (2015): 279-289.

L-DRILL AGILITY TEST (ALSO CALLED THE *3-CONE AGILITY TEST*)

Purpose
Measure ability to change direction

Equipment
Cones

Tape measure

Stopwatch or timing system

Grass, turf, or other good running surface

Setup
The coach needs three cones to set up the test (figure 3.12). The coach places the first cone anywhere on the running surface. The coach places the second cone exactly 5 yards (4.6 m) in front of the first cone. If lines are not present on the field, a tape measure should be used to ensure reliability and validity. The third and final cone is placed exactly 5 yards (4.6 m) to the right of the second cone. A tape measure will be needed to measure out to the third cone. Once the three cones are set up properly and the coach has the stopwatch or timing system ready, the test is ready to be administered.

Testing Protocol
1. The athlete begins in a three-point stance with his hand behind the first cone.
2. The coach starts the stopwatch at the athlete's first movement.

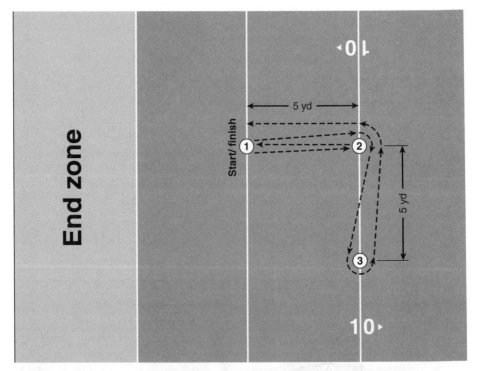

Figure 3.12   Setup for the L-drill agility test.

3. The athlete sprints forward 5 yards (4.6 m), touching the line next to the second cone with his right hand.

4. After touching the line, the athlete changes direction and returns to the starting line, touching it with his right hand.

5. The athlete changes direction again and runs back toward the second cone. Once the athlete gets to the second cone, he makes a sharp right turn and runs toward the third cone, which is 5 yards (4.6 m) to the right of the second cone.

6. The athlete approaches the right side of the third cone and circles it, heading back toward the second cone.

7. The athlete stays to the right of the second cone and curves around it toward the finish line (the first cone).

8. After the athlete crosses the finish line, the coach stops the stopwatch and records the athlete's time.

9. The best of three trials is recorded (with 3-5 min of rest in between).

Coaching Tips

- It is important that the athlete touch both the first and second lines with his right hand.
- The test can also be performed with a left-hand turn or as a reaction test with a left or right signal given to the athlete when he is between the first and second cone.

Descriptive Data

Table 3.15 provides descriptive data for the L-drill agility test for high school football athletes. Table 3.16 provides standards for college football athletes. Figure 3.13 provides classifications from the NFL Scouting Combine.

Table 3.15 Percentile Values of the L-Drill Agility Test in High School Football Athletes (in Seconds)

Percentile rank	DB	DL	LB, DE, TE	OL	QB	RB	WR
90	7.18	7.60	7.39	7.92	7.26	7.18	7.21
80	7.37	7.79	7.57	8.16	7.41	7.38	7.35
70	7.47	7.98	7.69	8.31	7.55	7.50	7.46
60	7.56	8.10	7.80	8.45	7.66	7.62	7.56
50	7.66	8.21	7.91	8.58	7.75	7.73	7.65
40	7.76	8.37	8.02	8.74	7.85	7.81	7.74
30	7.86	8.51	8.15	8.89	7.95	7.94	7.86
20	7.98	8.73	8.28	9.10	8.08	8.09	8.00
10	8.17	9.08	8.54	9.38	8.28	8.31	8.21
Mean (±SD)							
Freshman	7.87 (0.56)*	8.61 (0.74)*	8.13 (0.44)*	8.80 (0.72)*	7.87 (0.43)*	7.94 (0.47)*	7.88 (0.49)*
Sophomore	7.73 (0.39)*	8.33 (0.56)*	7.97 (0.46)*	8.73 (0.58)*	7.78 (0.40)*	7.75 (0.48)*	7.70 (0.41)*
Junior	7.60 (0.42)*	8.20 (0.60)*	7.86 (0.47)*	8.56 (0.59)*	7.72 (0.44)*	7.67 (0.47)*	7.62 (0.39)*
n	1,163	769	1,046	585	547	1,047	1,278

*Significant differences among classes ($p \leq 0.05$). DB = defensive back, DL = defensive lineman, LB = linebacker, DE = defensive end, TE = tight end, OL = offensive lineman, QB = quarterback, RB = running back, WR = wide receiver. SD = standard deviation, n = sample size.

Reprinted by permission from B.D. McKay, A.A. Miramonti, Z.M. Gillen, T.J. Leutzinger, A.I. Mendez, N.D.M. Jenkins, and J.T. Cramer, "Normative Reference Values for High School-Aged American Football Players," *Journal of Strength and Conditioning Research* (2019).

Table 3.16 Standards for the L-Drill Agility Test in College Football Athletes (in Seconds)

Position	Time
OL	7.7
TE	7.2
RB	7.1
WR	7.0
QB	7.2
DT	7.7
DE	7.4
LB	7.2
S	7.0
CB	6.9
K, P	7.2

OL = offensive lineman, TE = tight end, RB = running back, WR = wide receiver, QB = quarterback, DT = defensive tackle, DE = defensive end, LB = linebacker, S = safety, CB = cornerback, K = picker, P = punter.

Reprinted data by permission from P. Ivey and J. Stoner, *Complete Conditioning for Football* (Champaign, IL: Human Kinetics, 2012), 20.

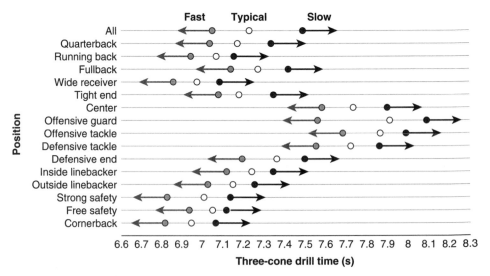

Figure 3.13 L-drill agility test classifications from the NFL Scouting Combine: fast—70th percentile; typical—50th percentile; slow—30th percentile.

Reprinted by permission from D.H. Fukuda, *Assessments for Sport and Athletic Performance* (Champaign, IL: Human Kinetics, 2019), 115; Data from J.L. Nuzzo, "The National Football League Scouting Combine From 1999 to 2014: Normative Reference Values and an Examination of Body Mass Normalization Techniques," *Journal of Strength and Conditioning Research* 29 (2015): 279-289.

ANAEROBIC CAPACITY TESTS

Testing for anaerobic capacity gives the coach or strength and conditioning professional an indication of an athlete's ability to perform maximal-effort tests but over a moderate duration rather than a few seconds (i.e., maximal anaerobic power). The following tests will give the coach exact instruction on implementation and execution.

300-YARD (274 M) SHUTTLE RUN

Purpose
Measure anaerobic capacity

Equipment
Cones

Stopwatch or timing system

Grass, turf, or other good running surface

Setup
The coach places cones at the starting line and 25 yards (23 m) away from the starting line (figure 3.14). If the field does not have lines, a tape measure should be used for validity. Once the cones are set up at the appropriate distances and the coach is ready with the stopwatch or timing system, the test can begin.

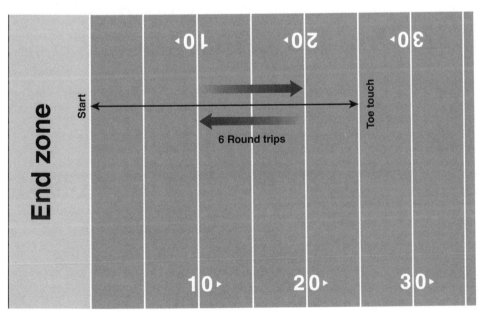

Figure 3.14 Setup for the 300-yard (274 m) shuttle run.

Testing Protocol

1. The athlete starts behind the starting line in a three-point stance. The coach starts the time at the athlete's first movement.
2. The athlete sprints forward 25 yards (23 m) then turns and runs back to the starting line.
3. The athlete runs back and forth six times, for a total of 300 yards (274 m).
4. The athlete always touches the 25-yard (23 m) line with his right foot and touches the starting line with his left foot. This will ensure that the athlete is being efficient during the test.
5. Once the athlete crosses the line after finishing 300 yards (274 m), the coach stops the time and records the number for the test result.
6. The athlete gets a five-minute rest and then performs the test again.
7. The times of the two tests are averaged for the final test score.

Coaching Tip

Athletes may walk and stretch during the five-minute rest interval, but they need to begin the second trial on time.

Descriptive Data

Table 3.17 provides guidelines for college football athletes for the 300-yard (274 m) shuttle run.

Table 3.17   25-Yard (23 m) Times by Position for the 300-Yard (274 m) Shuttle Run in College Football Athletes (in Seconds)

Position	Time ranges for the 25-yard (23 m) increments
OL	65-75
DL, K, P	60-70
LB, TE	55-65
RB, WR, DB, QB	50-60

OL = offensive lineman, DL = defensive lineman; K = kicker, P = punter, LB = linebacker, TE = tight end, RB = running back, WR = wide receiver, DB = defensive back, QB = quarterback.

Reprinted data by permission from P. Ivey and J. Stoner, *Complete Conditioning for Football* (Champaign, IL: Human Kinetics, 2012), 181.

60-50-40-YARD (55-46-37 M) TEST

Purpose

Measure anaerobic capacity

Equipment

Cones

Stopwatch or timing system

Grass, turf, or other good running surface at least 60 yards (55 m) long

Setup

The coach places cones at the starting point and ending point of the test (figure 3.15).

Testing Protocol

1. The athlete lines up behind the starting line in a three-point stance.
2. The coach starts the time at the athlete's first movement.
3. The athlete runs in a linear direction for the yardage within the time prescribed based on playing position:
   - Offensive and defensive linemen run 40 yards (37 m) in 6 seconds.
   - Linebackers, running back, quarterback, tight ends, and specialist positions run 50 yards (46 m) in 7 seconds.
   - Wide receivers and defensive backs run 60 yards (55 m) in 8 seconds.
4. When the athlete crosses the finish line, the coach stops the time.
5. All positions get the same rest time (30 sec) between repetitions.
6. All positions must complete 10 repetitions.
7. The athletes get a three-minute recovery break after the first 10 repetitions, then complete a second set of 10 repetitions with the same finish times and rest times as the first set.
8. This is a pass/fail test; athletes who do not make all of the goal times during both sets fail the test.

Coaching Tip

The running surface should be at least 80 yards (73 m) long to make sure there is enough space for the athlete to decelerate.

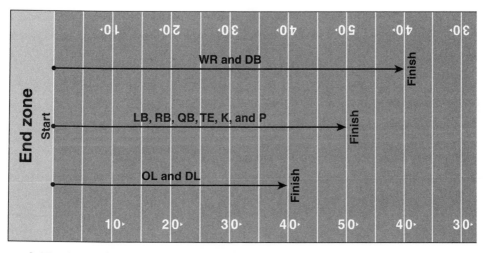

Figure 3.15   Setup for the 60-50-40-yard (55-46-37 m) test.

225-POUND BENCH PRESS MAXIMUM REPETITION TEST

Purpose
Evaluate upper body muscular endurance and strength

Equipment
Barbell

Bumper plates or weight plates

Collars

Bench press rack with bench

Setup
The coach loads the appropriate weight onto the barbell. The athlete performs a proper warm-up (see testing protocol).

Testing Protocol
1. Refer to the exercise technique description for the bench press (chapter 7, page 125).
2. The athlete completes 5 to 10 repetitions with a light weight (e.g., 95 lb [43 kg]) for the first warm-up set.
3. After a two-minute rest, another warm-up set is completed using with a heavier weight (e.g., 135 lb [61 kg]) for about six repetitions.
4. After a two-minute rest, another warm-up set is completed using with a heavier weight (e.g., 185 lb [84 kg]) for about three repetitions.
5. After a two-minute rest, another warm-up set is completed using with a heavier weight (e.g., 205 lb [93 kg]) for about two repetitions.
6. Once the athlete is warmed up, the coach instructs the athlete to complete as many repetitions as possible with 225 pounds (102 kg).
7. Once the athlete cannot complete a full repetition, the coach or spotter grasps the bar with an alternated grip and guides the bar back to the rack and then records the number of repetitions completed.

Coaching Tips
- Strict technique is required; the bar must touch the chest, the elbows must fully extend at the top, and the hips and gluteals must remain in contact with the bench and the feet must remain in contact with the floor throughout the test.
- The warm-up sequence described in the testing protocol is an example; there is no standardized regimen that is required before doing the test.
- The athlete must be mentally prepared. This test takes the athlete to failure. The athlete must have the mental focus to give it his absolute best.
- A consideration for the 225-pound (102 kg) bench press maximum repetition test is to lower the weight to 185 pounds (84 kg) for high school athletes. This can be a more appropriate weight for that age group in terms of maximum repetition testing.

- This test should never be performed without a spotter. When a single spotter is used, the spotter stands at the head of the bench behind the athlete's head and grasps the bar in a closed, alternated grip inside the athlete's hands. In some cases, three spotters are used: One directly behind the head of the athlete and one on each side of the barbell.

Descriptive Data

Table 3.18 provides descriptive data for the 225-pound (102 kg) bench press maximum repetition test from the NFL Scouting Combine.

Table 3.18 Repetitions for the 225-Pound (102 kg) Bench Press Maximum Repetition Test for Professional Football Athletes

Percentile	All	QB	RB	FB	WR	TE	C	OG
100	51	26	32	37	27	35	41	45
90	30	25	26	30	20	26	34	32
80	27	24	23	26	19	24	31	30
70	24	21	22	24	17	23	29	28
60	23	20	20	23	16	22	27	26
50	21	19	19	22	15	20	26	25
40	20	18	18	21	14	19	25	24
30	18	18	17	20	13	18	23	23
20	16	15	16	18	11	17	22	21
10	14	14	15	17	10	16	19	19
0.001	2	14	8	7	4	7	17	14
Mean	21.4	19.7	19.7	22.6	15.1	20.7	26.3	25.5
SD	6.4	3.9	4.4	5.2	4.3	4.5	5.4	5.2
n	3,424	13	332	98	225	233	130	271
Percentile	**OT**	**DT**	**DE**	**ILB**	**OLB**	**SS**	**FS**	**CB**
100	40	51	45	36	41	31	28	27
90	31	35	31	28	29	24	22	20
80	29	32	27	26	26	22	19	18
70	27	30	26	25	25	20	18	17
60	26	28	25	24	24	19	17	15
50	24	27	24	23	22	17	16	15
40	23	26	22	21	21	16	15	14
30	22	25	21	20	20	15	14	12
20	21	23	20	19	18	14	14	11
10	19	21	17	17	16	12	11	10
0.001	9	8	12	8	10	7	5	2
Mean	24.8	27.6	23.7	22.6	22.5	17.9	16.3	14.5
SD	4.9	5.7	5.0	4.6	4.9	4.6	4.0	4.2
n	309	307	320	180	297	147	178	380

QB = quarterback, RB = running back, FB = fullback, WR = wide receiver, TE = tight end, C = center, OG = offensive guard, OT = offensive tackle, DT = defensive tackle, DE = defensive end, ILB = inside linebacker, OLB = outside linebacker, SS = strong safety, FS = free safety, CB = cornerback. SD = standard deviation, *n* = sample size.

Reprinted by permission from J.L. Nuzzo, "The National Football League Scouting Combine From 1999 to 2014: Normative Reference Values and an Examination of Body Mass Normalization Techniques," *Journal of Strength and Conditioning Research* 29 (2015): 279-289.

Testing protocols should be appropriate for, and applicable to, an athlete's sport, position, and level of play.

CONCLUSION

Testing protocols and athlete assessment are key components in all strength and conditioning programs. Furthermore, testing and evaluation are key components in a football program (3). It is important to note that there are many tests, some of which are not listed in this chapter, that can be beneficial for certain positions and certain sizes of athletes. This chapter lists most of the commonly known tests and explains how to administer them. It is also important to note that individual coaches have their own preferences for certain tests over others. Their reasons may have to do with specific athlete populations, the football system being run (e.g., a tempo offense), or their own experiences with test administration. It is important to know why coaches use certain tests before deciding whether the tests they use should be the ones you use. The most important features in any testing program are safety, validity, reliability, and proper administration.

4

SPORT-SPECIFIC PROGRAM DESIGN GUIDELINES

JEFF HURD AND NATHANIEL D.M. JENKINS

There are many aspects to consider when designing a resistance training program for football. Not only are there training objectives that differ depending on the phase of the yearly cycle (typically simply referred to as **seasons**), but there are unique position-specific aspects that must be addressed to create the best overall team. In general, however, exercise selection, order, volume, intensity (load), and frequency are the critical factors of program design. The objective of this chapter is to describe the principles and guidelines that enable a coach to design a resistance training program that will help the athlete to excel at football.

SPECIFICITY, OVERLOAD, AND ADAPTATION

The first step to design a training program for football is to identify the physical attributes of the sport, such as the need for strength, speed, maximum power, repetitive power, lateral speed and quickness, acceleration, the ability to stop and redirect, muscular endurance, and anaerobic conditioning. Each of these must be addressed in the yearly training cycle to help the athlete excel on the field.

The term **specificity** was used by DeLorme in 1945 to explain that training results in adaptations or outcomes that are dependent on and specific to the training methods used (2). Consequently, for resistance training, Sale and MacDougall (3) suggested that exercises should simulate the movement pattern, velocities, contraction types, and contraction forces used in sport. However, while the movement patterns and skills needed to play football are complex and often difficult to match in the weight room, resistance training can be used to improve strength, speed, and power. Furthermore, training the body in the weight room in the same planes, using similar power outputs, and using movements that mimic positions during competition will maximize the muscular and neurological transfer when the athlete performs football-specific skills. Specific movement patterns and skills needed in football can then be further improved on the practice field.

When designing a resistance training program, it is also important to use the **overload principle**. To cause strength or power adaptation, the athlete must be subjected to a greater stress in training than he is accustomed to, while avoiding excessive overload and inadequate recovery (4). As the athlete achieves higher levels of performance, the training program must continue to increase in intensity to ensure continued adaptation. This principle, known as **progression**, promotes long-term training benefits when applied appropriately. Overload and progression are accomplished by modulating several program design variables, which are described in the paragraphs that follow.

EXERCISE SELECTION

After determining the needs of the athlete, the strength and conditioning professional should consider the **selection of exercises** to include in the resistance training program. In general, the more similar the exercise is to the movement patterns used in the sport, the more likely the exercise gains will produce performance gains on the field. The coach must also consider the athlete's ability to properly execute the exercises, the availability of exercise equipment, and the time available to devote to training in the weight room. Many movements in football require **triple extension**, which refers to the extension of the ankle, knee, and hip joints. For example, jumping, running, blocking, tackling, and cutting all require forceful and rapid triple extension. In the weight room, exercises such as the power clean and power snatch require high-velocity triple extension under load. While these exercises do not perfectly emulate the movements used on the field, the Olympic lifts and their derivatives will have a positive carryover effect to the football field, and in many cases they form the foundation for resistance training programs for football. Further, football is a pushing sport, often requiring athletes to push other athletes. Thus, pressing exercises, such as the flat and incline bench press and the front and back squat, are also specific to the demands of the sport and should be included in football resistance training programs. Later in this chapter we provide more details about choosing exercises that are specific to each of the position groups in football.

EXERCISE ORDER

The **order of exercises** included in the program is also an important factor to consider. When including exercises that are meant to develop maximal power, it is important that they are placed first in a training session. Power exercises require the most skill and technique, necessitate a strong stretch reflex, and are highly susceptible to fatigue. Thus, performing these exercises immediately after the warm-up will maximize exercise quality and athlete safety. Performing power exercises early in a workout may also help stimulate and prepare the athlete to handle the loads required for the rest of the resistance training exercises, too.

After the power exercises, the strength and conditioning professional should program other multi-joint, non-power primary exercises (commonly called **core exercises**, not to be confused with exercises for the anatomical core; see chapter 8), such as squats and shoulder-pressing variations. These exercises also have high energy requirements, and they should not be preceded by any assistance exercises.

Finally, the **assistance exercises** should be performed after all power and non-power-core exercises have been completed. These may include, but are not limited to, exercises that isolate specific muscle groups, such lateral raises, hamstring curls, leg extensions, biceps curls, and triceps extensions. Typically, these exercises will be prescribed using higher repetitions, lighter loads, and less rest between sets. This approach will help with muscle endurance development or maintenance.

TRAINING FREQUENCY

Training frequency refers to the number of training sessions scheduled in a one-week period. The prescribed frequency will depend on the athletes' training status, their current season, the anticipated exercise load, the types of exercises prescribed, and the anticipated training and conditioning load of the athletes. For example, resistance training frequency may be greater during the off-season than during the season, when the physical stresses of practices and games are high.

Training frequencies can be assigned in various ways. Two very popular and successful routines are the three-day-per-week (total body) and the four-day-per-week (upper/lower split) routines. It is important to structure both routines so that each core exercise is trained heavily once per week. In addition, the strength and conditioning professional should provide at least 48 hours between the training of muscle groups. The three-day-per-week training routine should be divided into heavy-, light-, and medium-load training days. During the first training session of the week, the exercises selected should be those that allow athletes to handle the heaviest loads, with the lightest loads prescribed on day 2 and medium loads on day 3. The same philosophy applies to the four-day, upper/lower split. For example, a heavy lower body training session may be prescribed for the first day of the week, followed by a lighter upper body session, a lighter lower body session, and finally, a heavy upper body session.

Training frequency during the season or during a competition phase drops to two to three days a week, often with the third session optional for assistance exercises. The intensity should remain moderate to high, but volume should remain low. High volumes can create high levels of neuromuscular fatigue, which should be largely avoided during in-season training. Furthermore, the use of heavy loads, in conjunction with low volumes, may help maintain the athlete's strength.

VOLUME

Volume refers to the total amount of weight that is lifted in a training session, or it can be calculated as the total number of repetitions performed in a workout (sometimes called **repetition-volume**). Most often, however, volume is calculated as the **volume-load**, or the product of the repetitions performed and the load used for a given exercise (4). Volume-load is highly related to the mechanical work performed during exercise and, therefore, the physiological stress imposed by training. Consequently, volume-load is thought to be a primary determinant of physiological adaptations to resistance training. It is one of the primary variables that can be manipulated to ensure overload (1). Volume-load can also be tracked within and across workouts to quantify the nature of the training session(s). For example, volume-load can be calculated for all sets that were completed with hypertrophy, maximal strength, or maximal power as the primary goal in a given training session to identify the primary training stimulus. It is common to intentionally decrease volume through a training cycle as intensity builds, or to decrease volume when outside training or conditioning loads are high to ensure that the athlete can recover. The resistance training volume an athlete can recover from is likely to differ for each athlete and to depend on factors such as training status, nutritional status, stress, training frequency, and practice or conditioning loads.

INTENSITY (OR LOAD)

Intensity is an indicator of mechanical and metabolic power output. Therefore, it is a good indicator of the quality of work performed in a training session. The intensity of resistance exercise is influenced by the repetition and set schemes used and can be calculated by dividing the volume-load by the total number of repetitions performed during a training session. Thus, intensity can also be thought of as the average weight lifted (or load) per repetition in a training session. It is important that intensity be increased over time to ensure continued progression in strength programs. The number of times a load can be lifted is inversely related to the load used. In other words, when using greater relative loads, the athlete will be able to perform fewer repetitions in a set than if he were to use lower relative loads (table 4.1). Consequently, the load, and therefore the number of repetitions performed in a set, will be directly related to the training goal. Programs that are designed to maximize strength and power in the football athlete generally use high relative loads and low numbers of repetitions per set.

The off-season portion of the resistance training program will be broken down into three phases. Each phase will prescribe training loads in the core exercises as a percentage of a tested, projected, or estimated 1RM. In general, as athletes move from phase I to phase III, they will lift greater relative loads. For example, in the hypertrophy and strength endurance phase (e.g., phase I), athletes will probably not perform an exercise using a load greater than 85% of the 1RM (4). However, in the strength and power phase, they may routinely perform exercises using loads greater than 90% of the 1RM (4).

Increasing the loads required in each phase for the core exercises will help create overload, and the variation will allow for progression, or adaptation. This gives athletes a great way to advance toward their strength and power goals. It is best for them to complete each core exercise using heavy loads once per week, whether executing a three-day-per-week or four-day-per-week split routine. Specific examples of complete training programs and exercise intensities for the preseason, in-season, off-season, and postseason are detailed in later chapters.

Table 4.1 Percent of the 1RM and Repetitions Allowed

%1RM	Number of repetitions allowed
100	1
95	2
93	3
90	4
87	5
85	6
83	7
80	8
77	9
75	10
70	11
67	12
65	15

Reprinted by permission from J. Sheppard and T. Triplett, Program Design for Resistance Training, in *Essentials of Strength Training and Conditioning,* 4th ed., edited by G. Haff and T. Triplett (Champaign, IL: Human Kinetics, 2016), 452.

REST PERIODS

The final variable that can be manipulated to cause overload is the time provided for recovery between sets and exercises, commonly referred to as the **rest period**. The rest period is dependent on the training goal and the relative load lifted. In general, longer rest periods should be prescribed when heavier loads are lifted to maximize the quality and to ensure the completion of subsequently prescribed sets. This principle is also true for exercises prescribed to improve maximal power. In general, the common guideline for maximal strength and power exercises is to provide three to five minutes of rest between sets (4). For those exercises in which maximal strength and power development are not the primary goal, such as assistance exercises (e.g., biceps curl, lateral raise, leg extension), rest periods of 30 seconds to 1.5 minutes may be prescribed (4). If the training goal is muscular endurance, it is common to prescribe rest periods of 30 seconds or less (4). Finally, the coach may also consider prescribing exercises in pairs with no rest between sets to help enhance muscle endurance. For example, exercises that target the upper and a lower body can be paired, exercises that target opposing muscle groups can be paired, or a compound assistance exercise can be paired with an isolation exercise.

SPORT-SPECIFIC GOALS OF A RESISTANCE TRAINING PROGRAM

Football has many physiological requirements, but the primary goal of a resistance training program is to develop strength and power. Creating consistent overload will increase strength in the untrained athlete, but when training a more conditioned athlete, there is more to consider to create stimulus and variation that promote growth while preventing overtraining. It is advantageous to divide the time in the training period into phases. Each phase has its own goals for making progress toward the overall program goal of strength and power. The strategic manipulation of an athlete's preparedness using sequenced training phases (defined by cycles and stages of workload) is known as **periodization**.

A training period is often divided into three phases:

Phase I: Hypertrophy/strength endurance (fourth-quarter conditioning)

Phase II: Basic strength

Phase III: Strength/power

The first phase of the training cycle is known as the **hypertrophy/strength endurance phase**. There are two goals for this phase of training. The first goal is to increase the size of skeletal muscle; this is known as muscle hypertrophy. Increasing muscle size prepares the muscles to handle the heavier loads that follow in the next two phases. The second goal is to enhance muscular endurance. Muscular endurance is important not only for sustaining an athlete's strength and power into the fourth quarter of a game, but also for helping the athlete to complete the prescribed repetitions during the next two phases of training. To accomplish these goals, training volume must be high. When training volumes are high, it is necessary to use low to moderate intensities to avoid overtraining, especially during the initial phases of a strength program. Thus, during the hypertrophy/strength endurance phase, athletes should perform exercises with loads ranging from 50% to 85% of the 1RM, or 6 to 20RM (4). The hypertrophic and muscular endurance adaptations realized during this phase may be maintained through the basic strength and strength/power phases by providing adequate volume and using appropriate rest periods when performing supplemental or assistance exercises.

The second phase of the training cycle is known as the **basic strength phase**. During this phase, the primary goal is to improve the strength of the muscles that are essential to sport performance. Volume for the core exercises is decreased, while the intensity is increased. Progressing from lighter weights to heavier ones provides the necessary stimulus to promote strength adaptation. In addition, the exercises used during this cycle may become more specific to the sport. The loads used during this phase should range from 80% to 95% of the 1RM, or 2-6RM (4). In addition, athletes should complete between 2 and 6 sets per exercise (4).

The third phase of the training cycle is known as the **strength/power phase**. During this phase, the training volume will be lower and the intensity higher than the previous phases. The athlete should perform no more than five repetitions per set, while using loads of 87% to 95% of the 1RM to develop maximal strength and 30% to 85% of the 1RM to develop maximal power (4). During this phase, it is also common to reduce the total number of exercises performed within the training week. Heavy loads, which can be moved for lower repetitions, are necessary to promote the neuromuscular adaptations that will maximize muscle strength. Furthermore, moderate loads are used in this phase for power exercises, because moderate loads allow for maximal power development. For example, loads of 50% to 70% of the 1RM may be necessary to achieve maximal power production in the bench press (4). Thus, the training goal and specific exercises that are chosen in this phase will ultimately dictate the appropriate loading scheme. Finally, an unloading or variation week should be implemented between phases or every three to four training weeks, in addition to the week prior to training camp.

All position groups need the same basic attributes on the playing field. Football is demanding and violent, and athletes at all positions must be strong, fast, and powerful at some time during practice and game performances. Therefore, every football athlete must have strength, speed, and overall power. What differs is that athletes at different positions need more emphasis in certain areas than others. Receivers, defensive backs, and running backs require speed in longer distances, while offensive and defensive linemen require speed and quickness in shorter bursts. Offensive and defensive linemen require high levels of strength and power to push big bodies off the line of scrimmage, but wide receivers and defensive backs also need strength and power when trying to gain separation from a defender or playing press-man on defense. Furthermore, all athletes are required to block or tackle.

All positions must be strong, powerful, and explosive, even though each position may have a different emphasis. Linebackers, tight ends, and fullbacks need an equal balance of all of the attributes. They must be strong for blocking and tackling, fast for running or covering routes, and agile as they react in the open field. Furthermore, these athletes often are on cover or return special teams, which require them to be fast over longer distances. Even quarterbacks need to be strong and powerful in order to throw the ball with good velocity and distance. Without the necessary strength and power in their hips and legs, they will place more stress on the shoulder and increase their susceptibility to injury. Quarterbacks must also be able to take hits, run a quarterback sneak, avoid being tackled or sacked, keep the ball from being stripped away, and scramble when the pocket collapses.

These positional emphases can be addressed while maintaining a standard philosophy of training with some manipulation of exercise selection, intensity, and volume.

Because the physical attributes of strength and power are necessary for every football position, a base program should be established to develop these attributes. Once this program is designed, then the coach can alter the program to address the specific positional needs. Bench lockouts may be added to the offensive and defensive linemen's program to work on the finishing press of close line play. Burner-preventive exercises may be added to the programs for the tight ends, linebackers, fullbacks, and defensive backs, since these positions are susceptible to neck and shoulder burners. Wide receivers, running backs, and defensive backs may have more single-leg resistance training added to their programs because they often find themselves cutting or jumping off one leg. Quarterbacks may need more rotational exercises than the other positions.

Since offensive and defensive linemen need to place a greater emphasis on strength, they may handle heavier loads than their teammates, while the wide receivers and defensive backs may be programmed to use lighter loads and faster movement to emphasize speed development. Likewise, sets and repetitions can be altered to meet the specific goals of each position.

POSITION-SPECIFIC EXERCISE SELECTION

All positions need programs that build on a base of strength and power development. The types of exercises can differ according to the goals of the resistance training program, and they should include presses (of many types), squats, deadlifts, and Olympic lifts. The core exercises selected in a program should be dictated by the athlete's positional needs, training history, and exercise technique, and complemented with assistance exercises.

The exercise choices and sample workouts for the different seasons are presented in detail in later chapters. Following are specific examples of power and strength demands by position.

Offensive and Defensive Linemen

Offensive and defensive linemen are competing against athletes of equal size. These athletes are big and powerful. They must be able to deliver sudden, powerful bursts of strength. They must be able to withstand powerful forces generated against them and maintain their positions powerfully on the line of scrimmage. Their first objective is to overpower and defeat their opponent in order to make the play. They must also neutralize their opponent so a teammate can make the play. Controlling the line of scrimmage by physically dominating the opponent is crucial to the success of all other positions on both sides of the ball.

Tight Ends, Fullbacks, and Linebackers

The tight end position involves running pass routes and blocking. The fullback must block, run, and sometimes run pass routes. Linebackers must develop the ability to run, fill gaps, take on blocks, tackle, and cover pass routes.

Wide Receivers and Running Backs

Wide receivers must be able to run pass routes with speed and precision. They must also be able to physically gain separation from defensive backs, withstand hits and tackles, and block in the run or screen game. Running backs run the football with great speed and power. They must also block in pass protection and withstand hits and tackles.

Defensive Backs

Defensive backs must be able to cover pass routes with the speed of a wide receiver, tackle, and take on blocks on the edge while playing run support.

Don Juan Moore/Getty Images

Resistance training exercises should have a specific application to the demands of the position.

Quarterbacks

Quarterbacks must be able to throw the football with great velocity, avoid oncoming rushers, and occasionally run the football. The quarterback must also withstand violent tackles and hits.

Kickers and Punters

Kickers and punters are required to kick and punt a football with accuracy and with great distance or hang time.

THE BIG FOUR CORE EXERCISES AND THEIR MODIFICATIONS

The summary of the position-specific requirements is further verification of the need for strength- and power-based resistance training programs for all positions. Exercises that are selected must address those requirements.

All positions will do the Big Four exercises—presses, squats, deadlifts, and Olympic lifts—in some form or fashion. These exercises are preferred unless restricted by preexisting injury or current physical limitations. In that case, the listed alternatives can be considered.

1. Presses. Straight bar bench and incline press, push press and shoulder press, close grip bench press. Alternatives include the following:
   - Dumbbell press
   - Pin, rack, or floor press
   - Press machines
   - Landmine press

2. Squats with a straight bar. Back, front, and safety bar squats are preferred unless restricted by preexisting injury or current physical limitations. The following alternative exercises can be considered:
   - Trap bar squat (from blocks if needed)
   - Belt squat or deficit squat
   - Landmine squat
   - Dumbbell or kettlebell sumo squat
   - Smith machine squat

3. Deadlifts. The following alternative exercises can be considered:
   - Deadlifts with a trap bar
   - Different types of deadlift machines

4. Olympic lifts (i.e., exercises that involve triple extension). These include the power clean, clean pull, snatch, snatch pull, push jerk, split jerk, Olympic lift complexes, and the Olympic derivatives such as the power shrug and hang clean. Alternatives include the following:
   - Dumbbell Olympic lifts
   - Jumps or jump training machines
   - Medicine ball throw and toss
   - Ground-based triple extension machines
   - Landmine squat to press exercises

Each position will also have modifications to these exercises based on their position-specific variations.

Offensive and Defensive Linemen

It is particularly important for linemen to be strong and the deadlift is a great exercise to develop strength in their stances. Pulling heavy weight from the floor enables linemen to improve strength in their legs, glutes, and trunk so they can deliver force out of their beginning stance and hold the point of attack against their opponents. It also enables the linemen to drive opponents off the ball or take on a double-team block. It aids in helping an offensive lineman to move a defensive lineman off the line of scrimmage, sustain a run block, or make a pass protection block. Deadlifts in conjunction with squats help a lineman to develop very powerful lower body strength while also improving total body strength.

Tight Ends, Fullbacks, and Linebackers

These positions are unique in the fact that they need to be strong at the point of attack and still be able to run with speed. They need the same types of exercises as linemen, but the load will stay in accordance with their body structure. Variations for these positions that differ from exercises for linemen may include trap bar deadlifts instead of straight bar deadlifts, hang cleans in place of power cleans, and more single-leg exercises due to running requirements of the position. Two examples of single-leg exercises are the walking lunge and single-leg squat.

Running Backs and Wide Receivers

As with other positions, these positions require a high level of strength and power, but this is relative to their position and body size. The biggest difference with these positions is that they require highly developed sprinting speed and slightly less emphasis on pure strength. They still have a high need for explosive power. These positions require the physicality to take hits and tackles, perform perimeter blocking, deliver tackles, and gain separation from opponents. These needs must be addressed when designing their programs. Variations in exercises to consider for these positions include the following:

1. The use of the trap bar deadlift instead of the straight bar deadlift
2. An emphasis on single-leg exercises (e.g., walking lunge, step-up, single-leg squat, and single-leg hamstring exercises) due to the greater running requirements of the positions
3. The substitution of the hang clean and hang snatch for the power clean and power snatch
4. The use of dumbbells for pressing exercises

Defensive Backs

Similar to running backs and wide receivers, defensive backs must have high levels of strength and power relative to their body size. They must also have excellent speed, explosiveness, change-of-direction abilities, and agility. Defensive backs must mirror the movements of wide receivers, tight ends, and running backs, disrupt, anticipate and react to routes and throws, tackle athletes who are often bigger than they are, and challenge blockers in running and screen pass plays. Due to these positional requirements, the exercise variations to consider for defensive backs are similar to those for the wide receiver and running back position groups. These variations include the following:

1. The substitution of the trap bar deadlift for the straight bar deadlift
2. An emphasis on single-leg exercises due to the greater running requirements
3. The hang clean and hang snatch may be performed instead of the power clean and power snatch
4. Presses may be performed with dumbbells instead of the straight bar

Quarterbacks

This is truly a unique group with regard to position demands, especially with the throwing element. The strength and conditioning professional should pay close attention to avoid over-development of the chest compared to the upper back and rear deltoids. Variations in exercises for this position include the following:

1. Alternative squats, or the use of lighter loads for back squat
2. An emphasis on single-leg exercises
3. The use of dumbbells when performing pressing variations
4. The use of dumbbells when performing Olympic lifts
5. The use of lighter loads when performing deadlift variations
6. Deadlifts using a trap bar off blocks or with dumbbells off blocks
7. The inclusion of rotational exercises for the trunk and hips, due to the throwing requirements
8. The inclusion of external rotation and rotator cuff exercises for the shoulder
9. The use of lighter loads on all overhead presses

Kickers and Punters

Kickers and punters need a strong leg and trunk area to deliver power on contact with the ball. They also should include more rotational trunk and hip exercises for kicking and punting. Variations in exercises for these positions include the following:

1. A reduction in intensity for barbell squats
2. An increased emphasis on single-leg exercises
3. The inclusion of hip abduction and adduction exercises
4. The inclusion of more hip flexion and extension exercises
5. The inclusion of trunk rotational exercises
6. Deadlifts using lighter loads or deadlifts with the trap bar or dumbbells off blocks
7. The use of lighter loads or dumbbells for performance of the Olympic lifts

CONCLUSION

Programs designed with the tools and information provided in this chapter will have a sound structure and be based on a good philosophical approach. Once the physical requirements of football are understood, the principles discussed in this chapter will enable the professional to design programs that will challenge athletes to improve their strength and power.

PART II

EXERCISE
TECHNIQUE

TOTAL BODY EXERCISE TECHNIQUE

RICHARD LANSKY

The total body exercise classification includes exercises commonly associated with the Olympic sport of weightlifting (often simply referred to as **Olympic lifts**) as well as ballistic medicine ball throws. These exercises involve synergistic, coordinated movements that activate multiple joints and muscle groups to produce and absorb force. Total body exercises can help athletes to improve their ability to produce high levels of power in movement patterns such as jumping and sprinting (1, 2), which are needed and regularly performed on the football field.

Olympic lifts like the snatch, clean, jerk, and their variations have been associated with the athletic movement pattern known as **triple joint extension**: The rapid, forceful extension of the hip, knee, and ankle by recruiting the major muscle groups of the hips, thighs, and calves to apply force to the floor or platform (2, 6). This movement pattern is present not only in general athletic movements like jumping and sprinting but also in football-specific skills such as tackling.

The use of Olympic lifts has also been associated with increased levels of intra- and inter-muscular coordination, as well as an enhanced ability to produce high rates of force (4). These biomotor qualities could have a positive effect on a football athlete's on-field performance. It has also been suggested that the proper performance of Olympic lifts may improve an athlete's ability to absorb force eccentrically (4). This could prepare the body to absorb similar stresses on the football field and reduce the risk of injury during practice and competition.

Olympic lifts and ballistic medicine ball exercises also require the athlete to exhibit mobility, flexibility, balance, and coordination (5). Safe, efficient, and technically correct use of these exercises can have a beneficial effect on these physical attributes, all of which are important to football performance. When performing total body power exercises, it is important to use proper equipment and adhere to basic safety practices. Barbells should rotate smoothly and should not be warped or bent. If possible, use rubber bumper plates to allow missed attempts to be dropped without causing damage to the plates, barbell, or flooring.

Athletes should know how to safely bail out on a missed repetition, especially in the case of overhead exercises. If a barbell is going to be lost behind, the athlete should keep the arms locked before releasing the weight and step forward. If the barbell is going to be missed out front, the athlete should keep the arms locked and step backward.

Exercise Finder

POWER CLEAN

Primary Muscles Trained

Gluteus maximus, biceps femoris, semitendinosus, semimembranosus, vastus lateralis, vastus intermedius, vastus medialis, rectus femoris, soleus, gastrocnemius, trapezius

Beginning Position

- Face the barbell and assume a hip-width foot stance, similar to a vertical jump stance.
- Align the barbell over the area where the toes meet the foot, about an inch (2-3 cm) off the shins.
- Keep the chest up, shift the hips back, and squat down to grasp the bar.
- Fully extend the elbows straight down with a grip placement slightly wider than foot placement.

- A hook grip may be used by wrapping the thumb around the barbell and under the index and middle fingers (4).
- Set the back in a neutral or slightly lordotic arch, with shoulders ahead of the barbell (a).
- Set the hips higher than the knees and the shoulders higher than the hips.
- Balance and foot pressure should be on the mid-foot and slightly forward.
- Rotate the toes out slightly.
- Rotate the arms inward with the insides of the elbows facing toward the trunk (4).
- Cock the wrists in toward the body.
- Hold the head up, eyes looking straight ahead (unlike what is shown in [a] and [b]).

Movement Phases

1. Retract the scapula, pinching the shoulder blades to draw the slack out of the arms.
2. Maintain a rigid trunk and push hard into the floor with the legs to initiate lift-off of the barbell from the floor (b).
3. Shift the knees slightly back as the barbell rises up and slightly backward, keeping it close to the body at all times.
4. The trunk remains stable during this first pull, with a constant shoulder-to-hip relationship.
5. The shoulders remain ahead of the bar during the first pull, with balance shifting toward the heels.
6. As the barbell passes knee level, raise the chest to allow the hips and knees to re-flex. During this transition phase, the balance shifts back to mid-foot as the shoulders move slightly backward to a position even with the barbell.
7. Jump upward with maximum effort, extending the hips, knees, and ankles. This is often called the **second pull**, characterized by an increase in bar velocity and acceleration. The barbell will brush against the mid-thigh area during this phase.
8. Shrug the shoulders vigorously (c), driving the elbows straight up to help guide the trajectory of the barbell.
9. Rotate the elbows down and quickly drive them up and through to receive the barbell at clavicle level (d).
10. As the barbell is received, slide the feet out slightly in a lateral fashion with the toes rotated slightly out. The hips and knees flex to eccentrically absorb the force of the barbell and the landing.
11. The fully standing end position should resemble the beginning position of the front squat (e).
12. If using rubber bumper plates, release the grip on the bar and let it drop to the floor.
13. If using metal plates, lower the barbell to the waist under control, being careful to maintain a safe posture and a braced core while releasing the weight.

Breathing Guidelines

Take a deep breath, inflating the chest before initiating the first pull off the floor. Exhale while performing the aggressive, explosive jumping action of the second pull.

Figure 5.1 Power clean: (a) beginning position; (b) lift barbell off the floor; (c) shrug shoulders; (d) catch; (e) end position.

Exercise Modifications and Variations

Hang Clean

The hang position means that the exercise does not begin with the barbell on the floor. Instead, start in a standing position, holding the barbell at waist level. Set the back and hinge the hips, pushing them backward as the trunk leans forward and the barbell slides down to a position on the thigh or lower. This position could be mid-thigh, at the knee, or below the knee and is determined by the goal of the exercise. Starting below the knee will help refine the transition phase of the pulling motion, while starting at mid-thigh or higher can help improve the finishing phase of triple joint extension (4). From this beginning position, proceed to power clean the weight using the same methods described in the power clean description.

One-Arm Dumbbell Clean

Hold a dumbbell in one hand with a pronated grip and arm fully extended. Assume the same stance and posture as described with the power clean. Lower the dumbbell between the legs to a position 3 to 4 inches (8-10 cm) below knee level. Perform an explosive jumping action in the same manner as in the second pull of the power clean. At the top of the jump, pull down under the dumbbell to receive it at the shoulder. As with the barbell power clean, always keep the dumbbell close to the body. Carefully bring the dumbbell back down to the beginning position, controlling its descent. After completing the prescribed repetitions with one arm, perform the same number of repetitions with the other arm. A two-arm dumbbell clean can also be used. Hold a dumbbell in each hand with a neutral grip, arms extended at the sides of the body. Perform a dumbbell power clean with both arms simultaneously.

Coaching Tips

- Be careful to keep the barbell or dumbbell close at all times.
- Use the legs to push into the floor to initiate lift-off as the barbell moves up and back toward the shins.

POWER SNATCH

Primary Muscles Trained

Gluteus maximus, biceps femoris, semitendinosus, semimembranosus, vastus lateralis, vastus intermedius, vastus medialis, rectus femoris, soleus, gastrocnemius, deltoids, trapezius

Beginning Position

- Face the barbell and assume a hip-width foot stance, similar to a vertical jump stance.
- Align the barbell over the area where the toes meet the foot, about an inch (2-3 cm) off the shins.
- Keep the chest up, shift the hips back, and squat down to grasp the bar (a).
- Fully extend the elbows with a wide grip placement. (See the Coaching Tips for ways to determine the optimal grip spacing.)
- A hook grip may be used.
- Set the back in a neutral or slightly lordotic arch, with shoulders ahead of the barbell.
- Set the hips higher than the knees and the shoulders higher than the hips.
- Balance and foot pressure should be on the mid-foot and slightly forward.
- Rotate the toes out slightly.
- Rotate the shoulders and arms inward with the insides of the elbows facing the trunk.
- Cock the wrists in toward the body.
- Keep the head up with the eyes looking straight ahead (unlike what is shown in figure 5.2).

Movement Phases

1. Retract the scapula, pinching the shoulder blades to draw the slack out of the arms.
2. Maintain a rigid trunk and push hard into the floor with the legs to initiate lift-off of the barbell from the floor (b).
3. Shift the knees slightly back as the barbell rises up and slightly backward, keeping it close to the body at all times.
4. Keep the trunk stable during this first pull, with a constant shoulder-to-hip relationship.
5. Keep the shoulders well ahead of the bar during this first pull, with balance shifting toward the heels.

Figure 5.2   Power snatch: *(a)* beginning position; *(b)* lift barbell off the floor; *(c)* shift weight back; *(d)* shrug; *(e)* catch; *(f)* end position.

6. As the barbell passes knee level during the transition phase, raise the chest to allow the hips and knees to re-flex *(c)*. Balance shifts back to mid-foot as the shoulders move slightly backward to a position slightly ahead of or even with the barbell.

7. Jump upward with maximum effort, extending the hips, knees, and ankles *(d)*. The barbell will brush against the upper thigh or slightly below the abdomen during this phase, which is significantly higher than the clean brush point.

8. Shrug the shoulders vigorously, driving the elbows straight up to help guide the trajectory of the barbell while pulling the body underneath the rapidly rising bar.

9. As the barbell is propelled past the head, rotate the elbows down and quickly "punch" the arms upward to drive the body down and receive the weight overhead at arm's length (e).

10. Slide the feet out side-to-side as the barbell is received overhead. The feet make contact with the platform at the same time that the arms lock the bar out overhead.

11. Flex the hips and knees to eccentrically absorb the landing in a partial squatting posture.

12. The squat depth should be between a quarter squat and slightly higher than a half squat, depending on the load and the timing of the exercise performance.

13. The fully standing end position should resemble the beginning position of the overhead squat. The barbell is fixed overhead with a shrugging up of the trapezius muscles and fully extended arms (f). The barbell should be in line with or slightly behind the shoulders, over the body's center of gravity.

14. If using rubber bumper plates, allow the barbell to fall forward, keeping the arms locked to keep the bar well clear of the head, and guide the barbell down as it drops to the floor. Release the grip on the bar at waist level and let it drop to the floor.

15. If using metal plates, lower the barbell to the shoulders under control, being careful to maintain a safe posture and a braced core to absorb the weight. Flex at the hips and knees and bring the bar down to the waist before placing it back on the floor.

Breathing Guidelines

Take a deep breath, inflating the chest before initiating the first pull off the floor. Exhale while performing the aggressive, explosive jumping action of the second pull.

Exercise Modifications and Variations

Hang Snatch

Start in a standing position, holding the barbell at waist level. Foot stance width should be the same as in the power snatch. Set the back and hinge the hips, pushing them backward as the trunk leans forward and the barbell slides down to mid-thigh, at the knee or below the knee. The hang position is determined by the goal of the exercise. Starting below the knee will help refine the transition phase of the pulling motion, while starting at mid-thigh or higher can help improve the finishing phase of triple joint extension (4). From this beginning position, proceed to power snatch the weight.

One-Arm Dumbbell Snatch

Hold a dumbbell in one hand, assuming the same beginning position and posture as described for the power snatch. Instead of beginning on the floor, lower the dumbbell between the legs to a position 3 to 4 inches (8-10 cm) below knee level. Perform an explosive jumping action in the same manner as in the second pull of the power snatch. At the top of the jump, turn the wrist over to receive the dumbbell at arm's length overhead. The dumbbell should be in line with the body's center of gravity, even or slightly back over the shoulder.

Coaching Tips

- There are a number of ways to determine a proper grip width for snatch-related exercises. The scarecrow method involves holding the upper arms out to the sides, elbows flexed to 90 degrees. The upper arms should be parallel with the floor. Measure the distance between the elbows and mark off that same measurement on the barbell for the hand spacing. An alternative method is the shoulder-to-opposite-fist method. Hold one arm extended out to the side with the hand balled into a fist. Measure the distance from the fist to the end of the opposite shoulder and use that distance to approximate a hand spacing on the barbell (4). An alternative is to stand up holding the barbell in front of the body. Using the outer rings on the knurling as a general starting point, position the hand spacing so that the barbell is level with the lower abdomen. The exact hand spacing can be adjusted slightly from these starting points to suit individual preference.
- Keep the barbell or dumbbell close to the body at all times.
- Always use proper equipment for the reasons described in the power clean exercise.

HIGH PULL

Primary Muscles Trained

Gluteus maximus, biceps femoris, semitendinosus, semimembranosus, vastus lateralis, vastus intermedius, vastus medialis, rectus femoris, soleus, gastrocnemius, trapezius

Beginning Position

- Face the barbell and assume a hip-width foot stance, similar to a vertical jump stance.
- Align the barbell over the area where the toes meet the foot, about an inch (2-3 cm) or less from the shins.
- Keep the chest up, shift the hips back, and squat down to grasp the bar (a).
- Fully extend the elbows with either a clean or a snatch grip hand placement on the bar.
- A hook grip may be used.
- Set the back in a neutral or slightly lordotic arch, with shoulders ahead of the barbell.
- Position the hips higher than the knees and the shoulders higher than the hips.
- Balance and foot pressure should be on the mid-foot and slightly forward.
- Rotate the toes out slightly.
- Internally rotate the arms with the insides of the elbows facing the trunk.
- Cock the wrists in toward the body.
- Hold the head up with the eyes looking straight ahead.

Movement Phases

1. Retract the scapula, pinching the shoulder blades to draw the slack out of the arms.
2. Maintain a rigid trunk and push hard into the floor with the legs to initiate lift-off of the barbell from the floor (b).
3. Shift the knees slightly back as the barbell rises up and slightly backward, keeping it close to the body at all times.

Figure 5.3 High pull: *(a)* beginning position; *(b)* lift barbell off the floor; *(c)* second pull.

4. Keep the trunk stable during this first pull. The shoulder-to-hip relationship and the angle of the torso relative to the floor do not change during this phase.

5. The shoulders remain well ahead of the bar during this first pull, with balance shifting toward the heels.

6. As the barbell passes knee level during the transition phase, raise the chest to allow the hips and knees to re-flex. Balance shifts back to mid-foot as the shoulders move slightly backward to a position slightly ahead of or even with the barbell.

7. Jump upward with maximum effort, extending the hips, knees, and ankles for the second pull *(c)*. The bar will brush the upper thighs during this vertical jumping action. A snatch high pull will contact higher on the thigh than a clean high pull.

8. Shrug the shoulders vigorously, driving the elbows straight up to help guide the trajectory of the barbell.

9. The body should be fully extended up onto the toes as the barbell reaches the maximum height of the pull. The barbell remains close to the body during this phase.

10. If using rubber bumper plates, release the barbell and let it drop to the floor.

11. If using metal plates, flex at the hips and knees and bring the bar down to the waist before placing it back on the floor.

Breathing Guidelines
Take a deep breath to inflate the chest before initiating the first pull off the floor. Exhale while performing the aggressive, explosive jumping action of the second pull.

Exercise Modifications and Variations

Snatch High Pull and Clean High Pull From the Hang

Hold the barbell at waist level. Set the back and hinge the hips, pushing them backward as the trunk leans forward and the barbell slides down to mid-thigh, knee level, or below knee level. The beginning position of the barbell is determined by the goal of the exercise. Starting below the knee will help refine the transition phase of the pulling motion, while starting at mid-thigh or higher can help improve the finishing phase of triple joint extension (4). From this position, perform a snatch or clean grip high pull.

Dumbbell High Pull

Athletes may also choose to use the one-arm or two-arm dumbbell variation of the high pull. When performing the one-arm dumbbell high pull, take a dumbbell in one hand and assume the same beginning position and posture as described with the high pull. Lower the dumbbell between the legs to a position 3 to 4 inches (8-10 cm) below knee level. The knees should be flexed and the hips pushed back slightly. Balance should be on the mid-foot. The trunk should be inclined slightly with the back set in a neutral or slightly lordotic arch. Perform an explosive jumping action in the same manner as in the second pull of the high pull. At the top of the jumping action, drive the elbow straight up, pulling the dumbbell to the upper chest area. Keep the dumbbell close to the body throughout the pulling motion. Re-flex the knees and lower the dumbbell back to the beginning position. Depending on the identified needs, the athlete can perform all the repetitions with one arm before transitioning to the other arm or can hold a dumbbell in each hand and alternate arms for each repetition until all the repetitions for each arm are completed. (The two-arm dumbbell high pull is performed in the same fashion as the one-arm version, with a dumbbell in each hand held in front of the thighs at or slightly below knee level.)

Snatch Pull or Clean Pull

These variations are performed in the same manner as in the high pulls, except the arms remain locked the entire time. The first and second pull techniques are otherwise the same as described previously. Heavier loads may be used with the snatch pull and clean pull compared to the high pull versions.

Coaching Tips

- The beginning position of both the high pull and conventional pull described in the variations can be adjusted from the floor to a hang version, the exact positioning is dependent on the objective of the exercise.
- Keep the barbell or dumbbell close to the body at all times throughout the performance of the exercise.
- Finish tall, fully extending the hips, knees, and ankles while keeping the trunk upright.
- Always use proper equipment for each version of the exercise.
- Rubber-encased dumbbells are an option when performing the dumbbell variations.

PUSH PRESS

Primary Muscles Trained

Gluteus maximus, biceps femoris, semitendinosus, semimembranosus, vastus lateralis, vastus intermedius, vastus medialis, rectus femoris, deltoids, trapezius, triceps

Beginning Position

- Place the barbell on a squat rack or squat stand at mid-chest height.

- Face the barbell and assume a shoulder-width, pronated grip. Depending on individual comfort, the grip may also be slightly wider than shoulder-width.
- With the barbell balanced across the anterior deltoids, take a few steps back from the rack to allow enough room to safely execute the exercise.
- If a rack or stand is not available, power clean the barbell to set it up in the correct beginning position.
- Assume a hip-width stance, with the balance toward the heels.
- Elbows should be positioned underneath the barbell, pointed down toward the floor or slightly up (a).
- The head should be in a neutral position.

Movement Phases

1. Inflate the chest and perform a controlled dip, flexing the knees with a very slight hip hinge (b).
2. Keep the hips in line with the shoulders, with the balance and pressure on the heels.
3. Maintain a rigid trunk during the eccentric dipping motion.
4. Reverse the dipping motion, pushing into the floor with the feet to produce a forceful extension of the hips and knees.
5. The switch from an eccentric dip to a concentric upward drive should be quick and smooth. Keep the trunk stable and the barbell fixed on the upper chest throughout this phase.
6. Using momentum from the explosive extension of the hips and thighs, drive the barbell upward in a straight line (c). Keep the chin tucked in so there is a clear pathway for the barbell. Athletes may choose to pull the head back slightly to allow a more direct path for the barbell.
7. While the initial thrust of the barbell off the chest is performed by the lower body musculature, it is important to actively press the barbell overhead using the deltoids and the triceps.
8. The barbell should move slightly backward and finish directly overhead, in line or slightly behind the head (d). Athletes may choose to push the head slightly forward to achieve this position.
9. Push up on the barbell to maintain a solid position overhead.
10. Unlock the arms and lower the barbell to the chest.
11. Dip at the hips and knees to absorb the downward descent of the barbell.
12. If using rubber plates to perform single repetitions at heavier loads, the barbell may be dropped to the floor from the overhead position. Keep the hands on the barbell until it reaches waist level to guide it safely to the floor. Take a step backward to allow a clear pathway of return.

Breathing Guidelines

Take a deep breath, inflating the chest before initiating the dipping motion. Hold this Valsalva maneuver during the descent (see chapter 6). Exhale during the forceful extension of the arms overhead.

Figure 5.4 Push press: *(a)* beginning position; *(b)* controlled dip; *(c)* upward drive; *(d)* press overhead.

Exercise Modifications and Variations

Dumbbell Push Press

Football athletes may choose to use dumbbells in place of a barbell. Dumbbells increase the demand for stabilization and they also enable the athlete to choose a variety of grips. As with the barbell push press, hold the dumbbells at shoulder level. Initiate the same controlled dip and explosive drive pattern to propel the dumbbells up and overhead. The dumbbells should be in line with the midline of the body. Exhale while lowering the dumbbells to shoulder level, flexing at the hips and knees to absorb the weight.

Coaching Tips

- The athlete should continue to apply pressure while the weight is overhead by shrugging up on the bar or dumbbells to enhance stability.
- The dumbbell variation can be performed with either one dumbbell or two. When using a single dumbbell, perform the prescribed repetitions on one arm before switching the dumbbell to the other hand and repeating. The athlete could also choose to hold a dumbbell in each hand and alternate arms until the prescribed repetitions are completed.
- The coaching cue "Dip and drive" can help remind the athlete to initiate the movement with the hips and knees and to finish by driving the barbell or dumbbell overhead to a full lockout.

PUSH JERK

Primary Muscles Trained

Gluteus maximus, biceps femoris, semitendinosus, semimembranosus, vastus lateralis, vastus intermedius, vastus medialis, rectus femoris, gastrocnemius, soleus, deltoids, trapezius

Beginning Position

- Place the barbell on a squat rack or squat stand at mid-chest height.
- Face the barbell and take a shoulder-width, pronated grip. Depending on individual comfort, the grip may also be slightly wider than shoulder-width.
- With the barbell balanced across the anterior deltoids, take a few steps back from the rack to allow enough room to safely execute the exercise.
- If a rack or stand is not available, power clean the barbell to set it up in the correct beginning position.
- Assume a hip-width stance, with the balance toward the heels.
- This beginning position should resemble the stance used to set up for a vertical jump.
- Elbows should be positioned underneath the barbell, pointed down toward the floor or slightly up (a).
- The head should be in a neutral position.

Movement Phases

1. Inflate the chest and perform a controlled dip, flexing the knees with a very slight hip hinge (b). Keep the hips in line with the shoulders, with the balance and pressure on the heels.
2. Maintain a rigid trunk during the eccentric dipping motion.
3. Quickly and aggressively reverse the dipping motion, driving the feet into the floor to produce an explosive and rapid extension of the hips, knees, and ankles.
4. Keep the trunk stable with the barbell fixed on the upper chest throughout the dip and initial drive action.
5. Using momentum from the explosive extension of the hips and knees, drive the barbell upward in a straight line (c). Keep the chin tucked in so there is a clear pathway for the barbell.
6. Athletes may choose to pull the head back slightly to allow a more direct path for the barbell.

7. While the initial thrust of the barbell off the chest is performed by the lower body musculature, it is important to use the shoulders and arms to actively drive the body down under the barbell as it is propelled overhead.

8. As the body rapidly moves downward under the rising barbell, quickly move the feet from side to side and land in a position similar to the receiving position of a power clean or front squat. The depth should resemble a quarter squat (d).

9. This repositioning of the feet should occur while the barbell is locked out overhead and the hips and knees re-flex to absorb the landing. The toes can be slightly rotated out at 30- to 45-degree angles.

10. As with the push press, the barbell trajectory moves straight up and slightly back to finish directly overhead, in line with the midline of the body. Athletes may choose to push the head slightly forward to achieve this position (e).

Figure 5.5   Push jerk: (a) beginning position; (b) controlled dip; (c) upward drive; (d) catch; (e) end position.

11. The push jerk is performed in a faster, more explosive fashion than the push press.

12. While both the push press and the push jerk involve a powerful leg drive to propel the weight overhead, the push jerk involves re-flexing the knees and repositioning of the feet to drive under the bar and fix it overhead. Alternatively, the push press involves locking out the knees to complete the exercise.

13. Keeping the barbell securely fixed overhead, reposition the feet and stand up to resume the beginning position stance.

14. Unlock the arms and lower the barbell to the chest. Dip at the hips and knees to absorb the downward descent of the barbell.

15. If using rubber plates to perform single repetitions at heavier loads, the barbell may be dropped to the floor from the overhead position. Keep the hands on the barbell until it reaches waist level to guide it safely to the floor. Take a step backward to allow a clear pathway of return.

Breathing Guidelines

Take a deep breath and inflate the chest before initiating the dipping motion. Hold this Valsalva maneuver during the descent (see chapter 6). Exhale during the forceful extension of the hips, knees, and ankles with the simultaneous propulsion of the barbell overhead.

Exercise Modifications and Variations

Dumbbell Push Jerk

Football athletes may choose to use dumbbells for better stability and variety of hand positioning. Assume the same start position used with the barbell push jerk and proceed to dip and then drive the dumbbells overhead. Re-flex at the hips and knees and move the feet quickly side to side as the dumbbells are locked out overhead. The depth of this receiving position is the same as that used for the barbell version. Keeping the dumbbells fixed overhead, reposition the feet and stand up to return to the start position. Exhale and unlock the arms to lower the dumbbells back to beginning position, flexing at the hips and knees to absorb the weight. One or two dumbbells may be used. When using one dumbbell, perform the prescribed repetitions on one arm before switching the dumbbell to the other hand.

Coaching Tips

- The coaching cue "Dip, drive, and dip again" will remind the athlete to re-flex the knees and shift the feet out to the sides to absorb the force of the weight overhead.

- While moving the feet to their original position, maintain pressure on the barbell by shrugging up to fix it in place overhead.

SPLIT JERK

Primary Muscles Trained

Gluteus maximus, biceps femoris, semitendinosus, semimembranosus, vastus lateralis, vastus intermedius, vastus medialis, rectus femoris, gastrocnemius, soleus, deltoids, trapezius

Beginning Position

- Place the barbell on a squat rack or squat stand at mid-chest height.
- Face the barbell and take a shoulder-width, pronated grip. Depending on individual comfort, the grip may be slightly wider than shoulder-width.
- With the barbell balanced across the anterior deltoids, take a few steps back from the rack to allow enough room to safely execute the exercise.
- If a rack or stand is not available, power clean the barbell to achieve the correct beginning position.
- Assume a hip-width stance, with the balance toward the heels.
- This beginning position should resemble the stance used to set up for a vertical jump.
- Position the elbows underneath the barbell, pointed down toward the floor or slightly up (a).
- Keep the head in a neutral position.

Movement Phases

1. Inflate the chest and perform a controlled dip, flexing the knees with a very slight hip hinge (b). Keep the hips in line with the shoulders, with the balance and pressure on the heels.
2. Maintain a rigid trunk during the eccentric dipping motion.
3. Quickly and aggressively reverse the dipping motion, pushing the feet into the floor to produce an explosive and rapid extension of the hips, knees, and ankles.
4. Keep the trunk stable throughout the dip and drive action.
5. Use momentum from the explosive extension of the hips and thighs to drive the barbell upward in a straight line (c). Keep the chin tucked in so there is a clear pathway for the barbell to travel upward. Athletes may choose to pull the head back slightly to allow a more direct path for the barbell.
6. While the initial thrust of the barbell off the chest is performed by the lower body musculature, it is important to use the shoulders and arms to actively drive the body down under the barbell as it is propelled overhead.
7. As the body rapidly moves downward under the rising barbell, the feet should quickly split, with one leg moving forward and the other moving backward (d).
8. The hips and knees flex to absorb the landing of the feet and the simultaneous locking out of the arms as the barbell is fixed overhead.
9. The repositioning of the legs finishes with the front foot flat and pointed straight ahead. The knee of this front leg is flexed at approximately 90 degrees with the shin perpendicular to the floor.
10. The rear leg is flexed at both the knee and ankle with the ball of the foot in contact with the floor and the heel raised.
11. As with the power jerk, the barbell trajectory moves straight up and slightly back to finish directly overhead, in line with the midline, or hips, of the body. Athletes may choose to push the head slightly forward to achieve this position.
12. Keeping the barbell securely fixed overhead, step back half the distance with the front foot and bring the rear foot forward until both legs are back in the beginning position (e). Finish the exercise by extending the hips and knees to a fully standing position (f).

13. Relax the arms and lower the barbell to the chest. Dip at the hips and knees to absorb the downward descent of the barbell.

14. If using rubber plates to perform single repetitions at heavier loads, the barbell may be dropped to the floor from the overhead position. Hold onto the barbell until it passes waist level to guide it safely to the floor. Take a step backward to allow a clear pathway of return.

Figure 5.6   Split jerk: *(a)* beginning position; *(b)* controlled dip; *(c)* upward drive; *(d)* split feet and lunge; *(e)* bring feet together; *(f)* extend hips and knees to a fully standing position.

Breathing Guidelines

Take a deep breath and inflate the chest before initiating the dipping motion. Hold this Valsalva maneuver during the descent (see chapter 6). Exhale during the forceful extension of the hips, knees, and ankles with the simultaneous propulsion of the barbell overhead.

Exercise Modifications and Variations

Dumbbell Split Jerk

Dumbbells can offer more stability and enable the athlete to choose a variety of hand positions. Hold the dumbbells at shoulder level. Initiate the same controlled dip and explosive drive pattern to propel the dumbbells overhead. As the dumbbells are being driven overhead, drive the body downward with the feet quickly splitting to the front and back. The overhead locking out of the dumbbells occurs simultaneously with the feet contacting the floor. The hips and knees re-flex to eccentrically absorb the force. The dumbbells remain aligned with the body's center of gravity or midline. Keeping the dumbbells locked overhead, reposition the feet and stand up to return to the beginning stance. Exhale and lower the dumbbell back to beginning position, flexing at the hips and knees to absorb the weight. Athletes can also perform a one-arm dumbbell split jerk. With this variation, perform the prescribed repetitions on one arm before switching the dumbbell to the other hand and repeating.

Coaching Tips

- Inflate the chest and maintain an upright posture to create a solid platform for the barbell during the dip and drive phase of the exercise before propelling it overhead.
- The cue "Finish!" may remind the athlete to fully extend the hips and knees during the drive phase of the exercise.
- The cue "Punch under" can encourage the athlete to drive down under the rapidly rising bar, splitting the feet front and back to receive the barbell overhead.

Dylan Buell/Getty Images

Just as cues are used in sport to improve the accuracy of complex tasks, cues can help athletes effectively perform resistance training exercises.

POWER CLEAN COMPLEX

Primary Muscles Trained

Gluteus maximus, biceps femoris, semitendinosus, semimembranosus, vastus lateralis, vastus intermedius, vastus medialis, rectus femoris, soleus, gastrocnemius, trapezius, deltoids, triceps, latissimus dorsi, biceps

Beginning Position

Assume a stance and set-up to perform a power clean (see the power clean description earlier in this chapter).

Movement Phases

1. Perform three power cleans in a consecutive fashion.
2. Reset to a stable beginning position after each repetition.
3. Following the third power clean repetition, keep the barbell on the clavicles and adjust the foot spacing to a front squat stance.
4. Inflate the chest, shift the hips back, and flex the knees to perform a front squat.
5. Keep the trunk upright and elbows held high during a controlled eccentric descent.
6. Maintain this posture during the vigorous concentric action of rising back up.
7. At the completion of the front squat, drop the elbows slightly and use the deltoids and triceps to press the bar to arm's length overhead.
8. The barbell should finish in line with the ears or midline of the body.
9. When working with heavier loads, the athlete may choose to use the explosive action of the leg muscles to initiate the pressing of the barbell overhead.
10. Lower the barbell under control and back to the upper chest area.
11. With heavier loads, flex the knees and hips slightly to absorb the barbell's return.
12. Upon completing three consecutive front squat-to-press movements, place the barbell on the floor and assume a hip-width stance facing the barbell.
13. Take a shoulder-width or wider overhand grip on the barbell.
14. With the knees flexed, flex forward at the waist so that the torso is parallel to the floor or slightly higher.
15. Squeeze the shoulder blades together and perform a bent-over row, bringing the elbows up toward the ceiling and the barbell to the navel.
16. Lower the barbell under control back to the beginning position. Reset and perform a total of three repetitions of the bent-over row.

Breathing Guidelines

Use the same breathing pattern described earlier in the power clean section for this part of the complex. For the front squat-to-press portion, take a deep breath before starting the eccentric descent. Hold the breath, performing a Valsalva maneuver (see chapter 6) during both the descent and the return back up. Exhale through the final quarter of the upward motion. Take a new breath, inflating the chest once again before pressing the bar overhead. Exhale as the barbell is lowered back to the chest. When performing the bent-over row, inhale before starting the movement and exhale as the barbell is drawn to the belly button and then returned to the floor.

Exercise Modifications and Variations

Dumbbell Clean Complex

This variation is a challenging combination of exercises that can be adjusted in terms of volume and duration to suit a variety of football-specific conditioning needs. The athlete begins by performing three consecutive dumbbell power cleans. Upon completion of the third repetition, keep the dumbbells fixed on the upper shoulder and perform three front squats. Following the squats, reposition the dumbbells at mid-thigh and perform three high pulls. At the top of the third high pull, flip the dumbbells back up to the shoulders. From this position, step out with the right foot to perform a lateral lunge. Maintaining an upright torso, return to the start position and then lateral lunge to the left. Perform three repetitions. Set the dumbbells down and perform three bent-over rows. Coaches may choose to substitute upright rows for high pulls and lateral squats or step-ups in place of lateral lunges. Follow the breathing patterns described for each exercise in this book.

Coaching Tips

- During the front squat portion of the complex, keep the trunk upright and the core braced to prevent technique breakdown due to possible fatigue.
- During the bent-over row part of the complex, keep the knees slightly flexed and the trunk fixed slightly above parallel with the floor.
- Pinch the shoulder blades together to prevent rounding of the back into a kyphotic position.

MUSCLE SNATCH

Primary Muscles Trained

Gluteus maximus, biceps femoris, semitendinosus, semimembranosus, vastus lateralis, vastus intermedius, vastus medialis, rectus femoris, soleus, gastrocnemius, deltoids, trapezius, triceps, biceps

Beginning Position

- Assume the same stance and beginning position described for the power snatch.
- Align the barbell over the area where the toes meet the foot, about an inch (2-3 cm) or less from the shins.
- Fully extend the elbows with a snatch-width hand placement.
- A hook grip may be used.
- Set the back in a neutral or slightly lordotic arch, with shoulders ahead of the barbell *(a)*.
- Set the hips higher than the knees and the shoulders higher than the hips.
- Keep balance and foot pressure on the mid-foot and slightly forward.
- Rotate the toes out slightly.
- The arms are rotated inward with the insides of the arms facing the torso.
- Wrists can be cocked in toward the body.
- The head is up, eyes looking straight ahead (unlike what is shown in figure 5.7).

Movement Phases

1. Retract the scapula, pinching the shoulder blades to draw the slack out of the arms.
2. Maintaining a rigid trunk, push hard into the floor with the legs to initiate lift-off of the barbell from the floor *(b)*.

3. Shift the knees slightly back as the barbell rises up and slightly backward, keeping it close to the body at all times.

4. Keep the trunk stable during this first pull.

5. The shoulders remain well ahead of the bar during this first pull, with balance shifting toward the heels.

6. As the barbell passes knee level during the transition phase, raise the chest to allow the hips and knees to re-flex (c). Balance shifts back to mid-foot as the shoulders move slightly backward to a position slightly ahead of or even with the barbell.

Figure 5.7 Muscle snatch: (a) beginning position; (b) lift barbell off the floor; (c) re-flex hips and knees; (d) shrug; (e) drive elbows under barbell; (f) press overhead.

7. Forcefully extend the hips, knees, and ankles, but do not jump off the floor. The bar will brush the upper thigh or higher toward the waist during this action.

8. Shrug the shoulders vigorously, driving the elbows straight up to help guide the pulling motion and keep the trajectory of the barbell close to the body (d). As the elbows near the maximum height of the pull, quickly drive them down and rotate them forward until they are directly under the barbell (e).

9. Immediately begin to press the barbell overhead. The barbell remains close to the body during this phase.

10. Use the trapezius muscles and shoulders to lock the barbell overhead in line with the body's midline (f).

11. Do not re-flex the knees at the end of the movement; lock them out instead.

12. If using rubber bumper plates, release the barbell and let it drop to the floor, as previously described.

13. If using metal plates, lower the barbell as previously described.

Breathing Guidelines

Take a deep breath, inflating the chest before initiating the first pull off the floor. Exhale while performing the aggressive pulling action and quick turnover of the elbows and the subsequent press overhead.

Exercise Modifications and Variations

Narrow Grip Muscle Snatch

Football athletes can also use a narrower grip, similar to a clean grip, to emphasize a quick, full extension of the arms. Keep the barbell close to the body at all times.

Coaching Tip

The cue "Elbows up and under" can help encourage the athlete to execute an aggressive high pull, a quick turnover of the elbows, and an aggressive press up against the barbell to drive it to arm's length overhead.

TWO-ARM KETTLEBELL SWING

Primary Muscles Trained

Gluteus maximus, semimembranosus, semitendinosus, biceps femoris, vastus lateralis, vastus intermedius, vastus medialis, rectus femoris

Beginning Position

- Straddle a kettlebell with the feet placed between hip- and shoulder-width apart and the toes pointed straight ahead.
- Squat down with the arms between the legs and grasp the kettlebell with both hands using a closed, pronated grip.
- Position the body with a flat back, head neutral, shoulders down, chest out, and feet flat on the floor in a quarter-squat position.
- Allow the kettlebell to hang off the floor at arm's length between the thighs.

Movement Phases

1. Begin the exercise by flexing the hips to swing the kettlebell down and backward.
2. Keep the knees in a moderately flexed position with your back flat and elbows extended.

Figure 5.8   Two-arm kettlebell swing: *(a)* swing kettlebell backward; *(b)* swing kettlebell forward.

3. Keep swinging the kettlebell backward until the torso is nearly parallel to the floor *(a)*.
4. Reverse the movement by extending the hips and knees to swing the kettlebell forward and up.
5. Keep the elbows extended throughout the exercise.
6. Allow momentum to raise the kettlebell up to shoulder level *(b)*.
7. After it reaches its highest position, allow the kettlebell to move down and backward, and flex the hips and knees to absorb the weight.

Breathing Guidelines
Inhale during the downward/backward movement and exhale during the upward/forward movement.

Coaching Tip
Focus on a hip extension "pop" to propel the kettlebell forward and up rather than relying only on lumbar extension.

MEDICINE BALL SQUAT-TO-PRESS THROW

Primary Muscles Trained
Gluteus maximus, biceps femoris, semitendinosus, semimembranosus, vastus lateralis, vastus intermedius, vastus medialis, rectus femoris, soleus, gastrocnemius, pectoralis major, deltoids, triceps

Beginning Position
- Hold a medicine ball at chest level and assume a hip-width foot stance, similar to a vertical jump stance. Larger athletes like linemen may choose to use a slightly wider than hip stance to approximate the positions they use on the field.

- Hold the arms close to the body, with the hands in a neutral position on each side of the medicine ball to mimic the arm positioning used during blocking in football.
- Keep the chest up, shift the hips back, and squat down to a position with the thighs parallel to the floor or slightly higher *(a)*.
- Set the back in a neutral or slightly lordotic arch.
- Balance and foot pressure are on the mid-foot and slightly forward.
- Rotate the toes out slightly.
- Keep the head up with eyes looking straight ahead.
- Offensive linemen may choose to hold the squat position for a two count to mimic the static start position on the field.

Movement Phases

1. Maintain a rigid trunk and push hard into the floor with the legs to jump forward.
2. Launch the medicine ball from the chest, using momentum developed from the explosive ascent of the squat and releasing it with a rapid and explosive extension of the arms *(b)*. The action resembles a violent arm punch, similar to blocking on the football field.
3. The athlete may choose to keep the feet planted firmly on the floor during the explosive squatting action or to leap forward to land in an athletic base.
4. The medicine ball may be released at a 45-degree angle, horizontally or vertically.
5. The release point is dependent on the training objective. Defensive linemen may choose a different release point than offensive linemen.
6. This ballistic medicine ball throw can be performed with a partner or against a wall.
7. Distances will depend on the goals of the training plan.

Figure 5.9   Medicine ball squat-to-press throw: *(a)* squat; *(b)* throw.

Breathing Guidelines

Take a deep breath and inflate the chest before beginning the squatting portion of the exercise. Exhale while performing the aggressive medicine ball throw.

Exercise Modifications and Variations

Medicine Ball Squat-to-Press Throw With Hard First Step

The athlete takes a hard step forward with either his right or left foot after rising up from the squat. The deliberate single-leg foot strike should occur as the medicine ball is released. After taking the first step, the athlete should immediately bring the opposite leg forward to a position even with the other leg or slightly offset, depending on the position-specific demands. This finishing stance should be a solid athletic base with good balance and foot spacing. This stepping action can mimic some of the footwork that takes place on the field.

Coaching Tips

- Encourage the athlete to initiate the movement with a powerful leg drive and to finish with an aggressive extension of the arms.
- The cue "Step and punch" may be helpful due to its similarity to football line play terminology.

MEDICINE BALL BLOB THROW (BETWEEN LEGS OVER BACK)

Primary Muscles Trained

Gluteus maximus, biceps femoris, semitendinosus, semimembranosus, vastus lateralis, vastus intermedius, vastus medialis, rectus femoris, soleus, gastrocnemius, erector spinae, latissimus dorsi, deltoids, triceps

Beginning Position

- Hold a medicine ball straight down with fully extended arms and assume a slightly wider than hip-width foot stance, similar to a modified vertical jump stance.
- Hold the arms in front of the body and squat down to a depth with the upper thighs parallel to the floor (a). Depth can be adjusted slightly higher or lower to accommodate individual body segment lengths and mobility issues.
- Hold the medicine ball between the legs with the hands in neutral position on each side of the ball.
- The back should be set in a neutral or slightly lordotic arch.
- Balance and foot pressure should be on the mid-foot.
- Toes may be rotated out slightly.
- The head is up, eyes looking straight ahead.

Movement Phases

1. Initiate movement with the lower extremity musculature and jump upward, tossing the medicine ball up and backward over the head (b).

Figure 5.10 Medicine ball BLOB throw: *(a)* squat; *(b)* throw.

2. Fully extend the hips, knees, and ankles in a manner similar to the triple joint extension that occurs during the second pull of the power clean and power snatch.

3. The arms remain locked during the backward toss.

4. Release the medicine ball at the top of the explosive arm swing, close to 190 to 200 degrees of shoulder flexion.

5. The feet should leave the floor as a result of the explosive jumping action.

6. Regain stable footing after the jumping action.

7. This ballistic medicine ball throw can be performed with a partner or by oneself.

8. Distances will be dependent on the goals of the training plan.

Breathing Guidelines

Take a deep breath, inflating the chest before beginning the squatting portion of the exercise. Exhale while performing the aggressive jumping and throwing action.

Exercise Modifications and Variations

BLOB Throw With Countermovement

Instead of beginning in the squat position, assume a hip-width or slightly wider stance. Hold the medicine ball overhead with arms fully extended. Hinge at the hips by pushing the gluteals back. The knees will be slightly flexed. Take a deep breath and squat down while simultaneously swinging the ball straight down between the legs. Immediately explode up by using the lower extremity muscles to drive into the floor in a vertical jumping action. The arms remain straight as they are swung upward to launch the medicine ball back over the head. Exhale during the jump. The release point of the medicine ball is the same as the non-countermovement version described previously.

Coaching Tips

- Use the legs to initiate the jumping action and not the low back.
- Maintain an upright torso, avoiding trunk flexion during the squatting portion of the exercise.
- Emphasize "squat and jump" to maximize the lower extremity contribution to the exercise.

6

LOWER BODY EXERCISE TECHNIQUE

ANTHONY LOMANDO

The lower body exercises described in this chapter provide the tools needed to develop and maintain lower body strength and stability through all phases of the strength and conditioning program. The primary and secondary lower body exercises develop the pushing, pulling, and single-leg strength needed to be strong in the trenches, explosive in the middle of the field, and fast on the outside. Football is a power-based sport and building the necessary foundation of strength is paramount to developing power and improving on-field performance.

The value of performing the following exercises extends beyond just developing lower body strength. The movement phases for each exercise are described in enough detail and depth to improve movement quality and efficiency. Such improvements can not only enhance performance, they can also make athletes more resistant to injury. A reduction in movement compensations and dysfunctions yields a reduction in the risk of suffering noncontact and soft-tissue injuries.

To develop the foundation of movement needed to build transferable lower body strength gains, coaches must teach proper limb alignment, joint position, and recruitment patterns in all of the lower body exercises prescribed. Too often the emphasis in exercise implementation and execution is on the load lifted rather than on the technique applied. This may lead to gains in strength, but how usable is this strength if it comes at the cost of poorer movement quality and joint health? A technique-driven approach that focuses on improving movement quality in every repetition will more effectively transfer the strength gains to sport. Instead of just developing their lower body strength, athletes will improve their on-field performance.

BREATHING GUIDELINES

Successful and safe execution of the lower body exercises requires giving attention to the involvement of the core musculature in generating intra-abdominal pressure. Intra-abdominal pressure created by activating the deep abdominal muscles and diaphragm helps to support the vertebral column and to manage compressive forces on the discs. Activation of the core musculature helps stabilize and control the trunk and helps to optimize and transmit forces generated in the upper and lower body. There are two main bracing or activation options used to generate intra-abdominal pressure. The **Valsalva maneuver** is a bracing mechanism in which the athlete holds the breath (the glottis is closed) to prevent air from escaping the lungs. This results in abdominal muscle activation, the generation of intra-abdominal pressure, and a rigid torso. This technique does have undesirable side effects on blood pressure and increased compressive forces on the heart. Athletes should only use this method when handling heavier loads, and they should understand and accept the risks involved. The second mechanism, a safer option that is recommended for most resistance training, is elicited by contracting the diaphragm and abdominal muscles without holding the breath. This adds support to the spine and generates intra-abdominal pressure without pressurizing the chest compartment (3).

WEIGHTLIFTING BELTS

The use of a weightlifting belt is another strategy for increasing and maintaining intra-abdominal pressure during resistance training. It is a safe and effective option when used appropriately. The NSCA recommends that a weight belt be worn during exercises that place increased stress on the low back and when performing sets at near-maximal or maximal loads. A weight belt is not needed during lighter sets of exercises that directly stress the low back. Training without a belt for lighter loads helps build strength and proper neuromuscular activation patterns of the deep abdominal muscles. Relying on a weight belt too often can have the unintended consequence of decreasing the natural training stimulus on the abdominal muscles to reflexively contract and stabilize the spine under load (1, 2).

BACK SQUAT

Primary Muscles Trained

Gluteus maximus, semimembranosus, semitendinosus, biceps femoris, vastus lateralis, vastus intermedius, vastus medialis, rectus femoris

Beginning Position

- Start with the barbell resting across the shoulders in either a high-bar back squat or low-bar back squat position. In the high-bar back squat, the bar is placed across the top of the trapezius, above the posterior deltoid at the base of the neck, and it leads to a more upright torso position and slightly more anterior chain muscle recruitment. In the low-bar back squat, the bar rests across the lower/middle trapezius, in contact with the posterior deltoid, and leads to more forward lean and increased posterior chain muscle activity (4).

- In general, grip the bar only slightly wider than shoulder-width if using the high-bar position and definitively wider than shoulder-width if using a low-bar position.

- Grip the bar with strength and pull down as if trying to bend the bar over the shoulders; in turn, the latissimus dorsi and scapular stabilizers contract, causing a bracing of the thoracic spine.

- The head is tilted slightly up at the beginning and will remain this way throughout the repetition to maintain proper cervical and thoracic spine alignment. Excessive extension or flexion at the cervical spine causes a compensation pattern at the thoracic spine.

- Place the feet at shoulder-width or slightly wider than shoulder-width, with the feet rotated out slightly and the weight evenly distributed (a).

Movement Phases

1. Start by unlocking the hips and move down in a sitting-back motion as the hips and knees flex in rhythm *(b)*. Each knee maintains optimal position by tracking the middle of the patella in line with the second and third toes. This ensures that the femurs do not adduct at any point of the lowering phase, so valgus stress on the medial side of knee is avoided.

2. The head maintains a neutral position and the core and upper back musculature brace in order to provide total body stability and strength during the descent. The hips are lowered to a depth just before the moment the pelvis posteriorly tilts and the lumbar spine is forced to flex. For the average athlete, the squat typically ends with the top of the thighs parallel to the floor.

3. During the transition between descent and ascent, it is crucial to maintain the bracing action of the core and upper back musculature. This is the most vulnerable moment of the squat pattern, and trunk stability and femoral alignment are vital for a safe and successful repetition.

4. Now the upward phase begins as the athlete pushes intently through the floor, pressing the weight vertically while maintaining optimal alignment in the lower body *(c)*.

Breathing Guidelines

Under submaximal or moderately loaded squats, inhale as the weight is lowered and exhale as the weight is pushed vertically. Under heavy and maximally loaded squats, inhale before lowering the weight and exhale once the repetition is complete.

Spotting Guidelines

During lighter or submaximal loaded squats, the spotter may stand behind with his arms up and under the arms of the athlete. If needed, the spotter will hold the athlete's upper body and squat vertically, helping the athlete to return to the beginning position. If necessary, this spotting technique should only occur on the last repetition of a set.

During heavier maximal loaded squats, it may be necessary to have two to three spotters, one on either side of the bar and one standing directly behind the athlete. The spotters should squat down with the athlete so if a spot is necessary, they will have proper leverage to help lift the weight out of the hole. The spotters on either side of the bar will have their thumbs crossed, with hands positioned close to but not touching the bar as it descends (1).

Exercise Modifications and Variations

Back Squat Using Chains

A back squat using chains is an example of a chain-supplemented exercise method in the variable-loaded resistance model. This method alters the resistance imposed at the bottom of the movement to maximize force production by decreasing coupling time and increasing acceleration during the concentric phase. The unique loading characteristics felt during chain-supplemented exercise makes this method a suitable option for experienced-, intermediate-, and elite-level athletes who have stable exercise technique.

In using chains for a back squat, the loading profile is changed as a portion of the load is supplemented for chain mass. Two common ways to apply chain mass are (1) letting the chains touch the floor from a fully extended position at the top of the squat or (2) hanging the larger chains from smaller chains, which allows them to only touch the floor upon reaching the bottom of the squat pattern.

Figure 6.1   Back squat: *(a)* beginning position; *(b)* squat; *(c)* return to standing.

Using the second option, apply the chains so they remain off the floor at the top of the squat pattern. As the athlete eccentrically descends to the bottom of the squat pattern, the floor gradually accepts more chain weight until most of its mass now rests on the floor. The reduction in the overall load at the bottom now allows for faster acceleration in the transition (more rapid stretch-shortening cycle) and an enhancement in movement velocity (greater neuromuscular activation) as the athlete moves upward during the concentric phase.

Determining the appropriate resistance when using chains requires quantifying the exact chain mass used because the structure, density, length, and diameter of chains can vary between weight rooms. After determining the chain weight, the offset in chain-to-plate load is found by summing the absolute chain weight at the top and bottom of the movement and calculating the average chain load.

Example: If using a chain that weighs 20 pounds (9 kg) at the top and 0 pounds at the bottom of the squat, the average chain resistance through the repetition is 10 pounds (4.5 kg). This calculated chain resistance is used for any given load prescription as an offset of 10 pounds. Therefore, a back squat with chains set prescribed at 200 pounds (91 kg) would now have 190 pounds (86 kg) of plate and barbell weight plus 10 pounds (4.5 kg) of chain mass (2).

Coaching Tips

- Hand placement on the bar is determined based on the athlete's individual shoulder mobility and individual arm length. Find a width that allows for the proper thoracic spine bracing.

- Individual stance width may vary based on individual mobility and biomechanical factors. As a rule, find a squat-stance width that allows for proper performance of the squat without any discomfort in the lower back, hips, and knees.

FRONT SQUAT

Primary Muscles Trained

Gluteus maximus, semimembranosus, semitendinosus, biceps femoris, vastus lateralis, vastus intermedius, vastus medialis, rectus femoris

Beginning Position

- Differing from the back squat, hold the bar in front of the body across the anterior deltoids and clavicles just below or at the neckline. Grasp the bar slightly wider than shoulder-width with the palms facing up. With the wrists flexed and the elbows facing forward or slightly outward, move the upper arms in a position parallel to the floor (a). This should look very similar to the front rack position when receiving the bar in the power clean.

- Modified beginning position: A modified crossed-arm grip position is used to accommodate an athlete who lacks the needed wrist mobility. Stand next to the bar to position the anterior deltoids and clavicles under the bar. Flex the elbows, cross the arms in front of the chest, and place the hands in an open-grip position on top of the bar. The fingers hold the bar in place as the arms are positioned parallel to the floor.

- Place the feet hip- to shoulder-width apart with both feet slightly turned out.

- Before performing the movement phases, brace the midsection. With the arms lifted, pull the shoulder girdle back and down, bracing the upper back.

Figure 6.2   Front squat: *(a)* beginning position; *(b)* squat.

Movement Phases

1. Unlock the hips and begin lowering the weight under tension, being sure to brace the midsection and maintain a neutral head position. During the downward phase, the hips and knees slowly flex in rhythm, while the torso maintains its positional angle with the floor *(b)*. The athlete maintains a more upright torso position during the front squat than the more forward torso position of the back squat. The torso mechanics differ slightly due to the different bar placement and the resulting shift in center of mass.

2. Similar to the back squat, lower the weight to a depth at which the athlete can maintain proper alignment both in the thoracic and lumbar spine while keeping the elbows high. Keep an even weight distribution on the feet, and at no point should the heels lift off the floor. The typical depth for the average athlete is a position in which the top of the thighs are parallel with the floor.

3. After reaching an adequate squat depth, aggressively press through the floor and begin to push the weight vertically. As this transition occurs, keep the chest up, arms parallel to the floor, and maintain all alignment cues from previous steps. To avoid valgus stress on the knees, avoid excessive femoral adduction throughout the repetition.

Breathing Guidelines

Under submaximal or moderately loaded squats, inhale as the weight is lowered and exhale as the weight is pushed vertically. Under heavy and maximally loaded squats, inhale before lowering the weight and exhale once the repetition is complete.

Spotting Guidelines

During submaximal loaded squats, the spotter stands behind the athlete, placing his arms up and under the athlete with the hands positioned in front of and close to the chest. If needed, the spotter places the hands on the chest and uses the arms to grasp the body as the athlete is assisted vertically. This spotting technique, if necessary, should only occur on the last repetition and should not be used to continue a set. During heavier maximal loaded squats, it may be necessary to have three spotters, one on either side of the bar and one standing directly behind the athlete. The spotters on either side of the bar will have their thumbs crossed, with hands positioned close to but not touching the bar as it descends (1). The spotters squat down with the athlete and maintain proper leverage to help lift the weight should the athlete need assistance.

Coaching Tip

While in the lowering phase, avoid thoracic flexion and upper arm drop at the bottom of the front squat. Doing so avoids unnecessary stress on the lumbar and cervical spine.

OVERHEAD SQUAT

Primary Muscles Trained

Gluteus maximus, semimembranosus, semitendinosus, biceps femoris, vastus lateralis, vastus intermedius, vastus medialis, rectus femoris, erector spinae, intrinsic and extrinsic anterior core musculature, scapular stabilizers

Beginning Position

- Place the feet slightly wider than shoulder-width apart with the feet pointing slightly outward.
- Grip the bar with a snatch grip width (see chapter 5), with the bar resting across the chest. Push the bar vertically overhead (a), and brace the midsection while keeping the shoulder girdle in a strong and stable back and down position.

Movement Phases

1. With a braced midsection, unlock the hips in a sitting-back motion and lower the weight under tension by flexing the hips and knees in rhythm (b). The arms remain locked out in an extended position and align posteriorly with the neutrally positioned head. The athlete works to maintain an upright posture throughout the lowering phase. Also, when viewed from the side during the descent, the bar will remain positioned behind the athlete's ear or behind the entire head, depending on shoulder mobility.
2. Similar to the back squat, continue lowering until just before the moment when the neutral lumbar spine is lost or the trunk flexes forward. The ideal depth occurs as the tops of the thighs reach a position parallel to the floor. This may occur at less depth if mobility or stability deficiencies exist. Optimally, a parallel torso and shin angle is present at the bottom of the squat.
3. After reaching the optimal depth, aggressively push through the floor and lift the body vertically while keeping the arms extended overhead and maintaining trunk control.

Breathing Guidelines

Under submaximal or moderately loaded squats, inhale as the weight is lowered and exhale as the weight is pushed vertically. Under heavy and maximally loaded squats, inhale before lowering the weight and exhale once the repetition is complete.

Spotting Guidelines

A spotter for this exercise is unnecessary and unsafe. The athlete should be taught proper methods of dumping the bar if failure occurs (see chapter 5).

Figure 6.3   Overhead squat: *(a)* beginning position; *(b)* squat.

Coaching Tips

- The width of the grip is too narrow if the shoulder girdle elevates while the bar is in the overhead position.
- Note that stance width may vary based on individual mobility and biomechanical factors. Find a width that allows for proper execution of the squat without causing discomfort in the low back, hips, and knees.
- Inherently, the head will shift slightly forward during the overhead squat, but it is important to avoid excessive forward flexion of the neck. This will result in excessive stress on the cervical spine and can lead to acute and chronic injury.

PISTOL SQUAT

Primary Muscles Trained

Gluteus maximus, semimembranosus, semitendinosus, biceps femoris, vastus lateralis, vastus intermedius, vastus medialis, rectus femoris

Beginning Position

Stand in single-leg stance on the floor or at the edge of a 12- to 24-inch (30-60 cm) plyometric box, with body weight evenly distributed between the ball of the foot and the heel *(a)*.

Movement Phases

1. Begin the motion by unlocking the hips and sitting down into the single-leg squat movement as the up leg extends out in front of the body. More knee flexion must occur earlier in the movement pattern because the torso remains more upright in this exercise than in a standard back squat.

2. At the same time, with elbows extended, the arms begin to flex at the shoulder and act as a counterbalance to the hip and knee flexion that occur during the single-leg squat. The arms extend straight out in front of the torso while the hips flex to maximize the counter-loading action (b). In similar fashion, the up leg acts as a counterbalance as the center of mass shifts.

3. During the lowering phase, the knee must maintain proper alignment without adduction or excessive abduction. To maintain proper trunk control, keep the lumbar and thoracic spine in neutral spine position.

4. At the transition from the downward to the upward phase, begin pushing through the floor and push the body vertically toward the beginning position. The arms flex at the shoulder back to the side as the hip and knee extend and help to generate the force needed to lift vertically into the beginning position.

Breathing Guidelines

Inhale during the lowering phase and exhale during the upward phase of the movement. Depending on loading parameters, the athlete may inhale before the lowering phase and exhale on the upward phase if necessary for optimal force production.

Coaching Tip

A cue of "sitting down" is used as opposed to "sitting back and down." This differs from traditional squat pattern cuing and is important to promote increased knee flexion compared to hip flexion. This difference in hip-to-knee flexion mechanics is needed to keep the torso vertical and to maintain the mechanical advantage needed for the upward phase of the exercise.

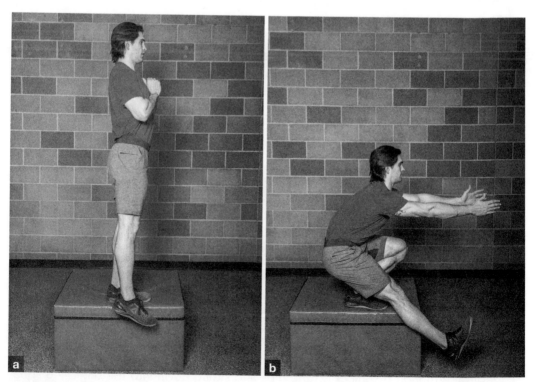

Figure 6.4 Pistol squat: (a) beginning position; (b) squat.

DEADLIFT

Primary Muscles Trained

Gluteus maximus, semimembranosus, semitendinosus, biceps femoris, vastus lateralis, vastus intermedius, vastus medialis, rectus femoris, erector spinae

Beginning Position

- Stand next to the bar with the feet hip- to shoulder-width apart. Position the feet under the bar with the shins no more than 1 inch (2-3 cm) from the bar. The feet should have a slight external rotation outward.
- Tilt forward from the hips and grip the bar with an overhand grip just outside the legs. Pull the hips down toward the bar and create tension in the latissimus dorsi and upper back with the scapulae depressed and retracted and the chest up and out (a). The lower and upper back should be in a flat position without flexion at either the thoracic or the lumbar spine. (A slightly arched back is also acceptable, but excessive arching should be avoided.)
- Viewing from the side, the mid-foot aligns under the bar vertically. Align the shoulders slightly in front of this vertical line extending down through the bar to the mid-foot. The head is neutral, with eyes focused on the floor just out in front of the bar.

Movement Phases

1. Push through the floor and lift the bar vertically by extending the hips and knees with a maximal grip applied to the bar (b). As the bar lifts vertically, maintain tension in the midsection, upper back, and latissimus dorsi. This will allow the torso-to-floor angle to remain constant until the bar clears the knees.
2. Maintain the flat back position as the bar moves vertically. When the bar clears the knees, pull the hips through and extend into a braced upright position (c).
3. During the downward phase, the hips and knees begin to flex, and a retracing of the upward phase takes place. A braced midsection is maintained, keeping the spine neutral so that the torso does not flex forward excessively. The downward phase is completed for every repetition, making sure not to drop the bar after each repetition. However, in cases where maximal or close-to-maximal loads are being lifted, drop the barbell after the pulling phase is complete.

Breathing Guidelines

Inhale before and hold throughout the repetition; exhale when the repetition is complete.

Exercise Modifications and Variations

Trap Bar Deadlift

The trap bar deadlift variation uses a type of bar that makes the deadlift motion more similar biomechanically to a squat. Because the grip of the trap bar deadlift is to the side of the body, the load on the erector spinae that occurs in the barbell deadlift decreases. As a result, when performing the trap bar deadlift, the shoulders will align more vertically with the mid-foot. The width of the feet at the beginning of the exercise and the bracing action remain the same.

Figure 6.5   Deadlift: *(a)* beginning position; *(b)* lift barbell off the floor; *(c)* extend to standing position.

Coaching Tips

- Do not begin with the bar too far away from the shins. Doing so affects the line of pull, puts unnecessary stress on the low back, and affects the efficiency and effectiveness of the exercise.
- Always maintain a braced torso position through all phases of the exercise.

FORWARD STEP LUNGE

Primary Muscles Trained

Gluteus maximus, semimembranosus, semitendinosus, biceps femoris, vastus lateralis, vastus intermedius, vastus medialis, rectus femoris, iliopsoas

Beginning Position

- Start with the barbell resting across the shoulders *(a)*. As a general rule of thumb, grip the bar at a width that allows the shoulders to be pulled back and down into a braced position without the shoulder girdle being elevated or anteriorly tilted from placing the hands too close together.
- Grip the bar with strength and pull down as if trying to bend the bar over the shoulders; this contracts the latissimus dorsi and scapular stabilizers and braces the thoracic spine.
- Feet are together and directly under the hips at the beginning of the exercise.

Movement Phases

1. Maintaining an upright posture, step forward and into a lunge position as the weight is lowered under control by flexing the lead hip and knee *(b)*.

Figure 6.6 Forward step lunge: *(a)* beginning position; *(b)* lunge forward; *(c)* lower deeper into lunge.

2. During the lowering phase, the trunk remains in an upright position, in line with the ear (or shoulder), hip, and the knee of the rear leg. The weight distribution in the foot of the lead leg is evenly distributed and is a crucial component in the lunge. The shin angle should be positive (forward) while maintaining a flat foot, but the lead knee is still directly over the lead foot. Lower the body to a position where the rear knee is about 1 to 2 inches (3-5 cm) from the floor *(c)*. The back foot remains stationary and does not pronate or externally rotate when loaded.

3. The lead leg is the driver as the upward phase begins. Push aggressively at a vertical and slightly backward angle, lifting the body up toward the beginning position. Maintain trunk control, and do not allow for any forward flexion of the torso.

Breathing Guidelines

Inhale during the lowering phase and exhale on the upward phase.

Spotting Guidelines

The spotter steps forward with the same lead leg as the athlete, planting the lead foot 12 to 18 inches (30-46 cm) behind the athlete's lead foot and flexing the lead knee as the athlete's lead knee flexes. The spotter's hands should be near the athlete's hips, waist, or torso, and assistance is only given when necessary to keep the athlete balanced. This spotting technique, if necessary, should only occur on the last repetition and should not be used to continue a set.

Exercise Modifications and Variations

Walking Lunge

Typically, the walking lunge is performed using dumbbells, but kettlebells or a barbell can also be used. The dumbbells are held at the side, and the athlete steps forward into the lunge position. As this occurs, the athlete must decelerate his body to avoid forward trunk flexion and an excessive forward knee position that forces the lead heel off the floor. It is important not to take too big a step; doing so can create an excessive arch in the lower back. The athlete then pushes off the front and back legs (more force production on the lead leg) while maintaining posture. The rear leg steps through as the athlete returns to the top position, and the movement is repeated.

Lateral Lunge

Different primary muscles are trained in the lateral lunge than in the forward step lunge: Hip abductors (gluteus medius, gluteus minimus, tensor fascia latae), hip adductors (gracilis, obturator externus, adductor brevis, adductor longus, and adductor magnus), gluteus maximus, semimembranosus, semitendinosus, biceps femoris, rectus femoris, vastus lateralis, vastus intermedius, vastus medialis, and iliopsoas.

The lateral lunge is loaded using dumbbells, kettlebells, or a barbell with front or back squat bar position. Starting from a tall position, take a lateral step to the side. After completing the step, the downward phase begins as the hip and knee flex in rhythm, lowering the body over a flat foot with even weight distribution. From a side view, the loaded leg takes on similar mechanics to a bilateral squatting motion with the shin and torso angle in a parallel position. From a front view, the knee tracks over the foot, and the midline of the flexed torso is in a vertical or perpendicular alignment with the floor. The athlete begins the upward phase by pushing aggressively through the floor laterally in the opposite direction (toward the beginning position). Enough force is generated to lift the body upward, forcing the foot to lift off the floor and return to the beginning position. The three most common mistakes observed in the lateral squat are (1) the athlete loses the vertical and perpendicular alignment of the torso (as seen from the front), (2) the knee is loaded in a varus fashion, causing excessive joint stress (as seen from the front), and (3) the athlete sits back excessively during the downward phase, causing faulty hip and knee flexion mechanics to minimize the amount of natural knee flexion occurring in the squat pattern, and this results in a poor shin-to-torso angle and excessive stress on the lumbo-pelvic-hip complex (as seen from the side).

Coaching Tips

- The mechanics and timing of flexion in the hip and knee of the forward leg should mimic the same action of both legs in the bilateral squatting motion. Therefore, any excessive heel lift or forward loading of the knee in the front leg of the lunge puts excessive stress on the knee joint and affects joint kinematics in the hip and lumbar spine.

- Poor flexibility of the quadriceps and hip flexor region muscles of the rear leg can affect the performance of the reverse lunge. It is important to maintain optimal pelvic position and to avoid excessive anterior pelvic tilt and lumbar flexion in the hip of the rear leg.

STEP-UP

Primary Muscles Trained

Gluteus maximus, semimembranosus, semitendinosus, biceps femoris, vastus lateralis, vastus intermedius, vastus medialis, rectus femoris

Beginning Position

- Start with the barbell resting across the shoulders. As a general rule of thumb, grip the bar at a width that allows the shoulders to be pulled back and down into a braced position without the shoulder girdle being elevated or anteriorly tilted from placing the hands too close together.

- Grip the bar with strength and pull down as if trying to bend the bar over the shoulders; this contracts the latissimus dorsi and scapular stabilizers and braces the thoracic spine.
- The athlete stands in front of a 12- to 18-inch (30-46 cm) box or high enough to create a 90-degree angle at the knee joint when the foot is placed on the box.

Movement Phases

1. Maintaining an upright posture, lift one leg into hip flexion and step on top of the box (a). The weight is evenly distributed on the foot.
2. The athlete then aggressively pushes the up leg downward into the box by forcefully extending the lead hip and knee, forcing the rear leg to lift off the floor as the body begins to move upward (b).
3. The hip and knee of the step-up leg extend, lifting the body upward until both feet are together on top of the box in an upright posture (c). This same leg starts the downward phase of the repetition by stepping backward off the box.
4. As the leg lowers toward the floor, the step-up leg is now loaded and decelerates the body's descent using the same biomechanical principles as the lead leg in a step-back lunge. The foot remains flat, the shin angle is positive (forward), and the athlete remains upright, minimizing forward flexion of the trunk.
5. When the step-off leg returns to the floor and can accept the majority of the load, the athlete removes the leg from the box and returns to a tall standing position in front of the box.

Breathing Guidelines

Inhale and hold during the movement and exhale once both legs return to the floor. Alternatively, some may find it useful to inhale before stepping up and exhale through the step-up motion.

Figure 6.7 Step-up: (a) step onto box; (b) press into box to lift body; (c) stand on top of box.

Exercise Modifications and Variations

Lateral Step-Up

There are different primary muscles trained in the lateral step-up than in the step-up: Hip abductors (gluteus medius, gluteus minimus, tensor fascia latae), hip adductors (gracilis, obturator externus, adductor brevis, adductor longus and adductor magnus), gluteus maximus, semimembranosus, semitendinosus, biceps femoris, rectus femoris, vastus lateralis, vastus intermedius, vastus medialis, and iliopsoas.

The beginning position for the lateral step-up is the same as the traditional step-up except that the athlete is standing to the side of the box. Maintaining a tall position, the athlete lifts the leg closest to the box into a hip-flexed position and steps laterally onto the box. The athlete pushes through the up leg and drives the body vertically and laterally by forcefully extending the hip and knee. The down leg naturally lifts off the floor and joins the step-up leg on top of the box. The athlete returns to the beginning position by safely stepping off the box and decelerating the body downward in a single-leg squat fashion. Decrease the height of the box when performing the lateral step-up.

Crossover Step-Up

The beginning position for the crossover step-up is the same as the lateral step-up. Maintaining a tall position, the athlete lifts the outside leg into a crossover step and places it flat onto the box. Next, the athlete drives through the leg placed on the box and drives the body vertically and laterally. The hips remain square as the body moves vertically onto the box and the down leg now joins the step-up leg on top of the box. The athlete now steps off to the opposite side of the box, and the crossover motion is repeated with the opposite leg.

Coaching Tip

It is important to maintain a tall position when stepping on the box through all positions. Cue the athlete to imagine trying to touch the top of the head to the ceiling. This ensures that the pelvis remains in the appropriate position and that the lumbar and thoracic spine do not load into a flexed position.

SPLIT SQUAT

Primary Muscles Trained

Gluteus maximus, semimembranosus, semitendinosus, biceps femoris, vastus lateralis, vastus intermedius, vastus medialis, rectus femoris

Beginning Position

- Start with the barbell resting across the shoulders. As a general rule of thumb, grip the bar at a width that allows the shoulders to be pulled back and down into a braced position without the shoulder girdle being elevated or anteriorly tilted from placing the hands too close together.
- Grip the bar with strength and pull down as if trying to bend the bar over the shoulders; this contracts the latissimus dorsi and scapular stabilizers and braces the thoracic spine.
- Step forward into the same split lunge position as the lunge (a).
- The weight distribution between the front and rear leg is a 60/40 front-to-rear-leg ratio.
- The front foot is flat on the floor, facing straight ahead, with even weight distribution across the foot.

Figure 6.8 Split squat: *(a)* beginning position; *(b)* lower into lunge.

Movement Phases

1. Begin lowering the hips, accepting weight on the front and rear legs with a similar 60/40 front-to-rear-leg loading ratio. As the lead leg flexes, the knee aligns with the front foot. The pelvis maintains a stacked position with the shoulders and does not rotate inward or outward.

2. During the lowering phase, maintain the same upright or slightly forward position of the trunk. The key is to keep the ear, hip, and knee of the rear leg in perfect alignment.

3. Lower down until the rear leg is 1 to 2 inches (3-5 cm) from the floor *(b)*.

4. Begin the upward phase by pushing through the lead leg and accelerate the bar vertically. Maintain optimal alignment of the hip, knee, and trunk during the transition phase and throughout the upward phase.

Breathing Guidelines

Inhale through the lowering phase and exhale during the upward phase of the split squat. If heavier loads are used, the athlete may choose to inhale and hold through the lowering phase and exhale on the upward phase of the split squat.

Spotting Guidelines

If heavy loads are used, it is best to use a spotter on either side of the bar. The spotters will squat down with the bar through the lowering phase and move vertically, matching the bar speed, in the upward phase. This places both spotters in an advantageous position to lift the bar vertically should the athlete fail.

Coaching Tip

Poor hip mobility in the rear leg can wreak havoc on the movement quality of this exercise. If the athlete cannot maintain an extended hip position of the rear leg, reduce the range of motion of the repetition. Lower only to a height where proper alignment and movement quality remain high while working on strategies to improve mobility and stability through the hips.

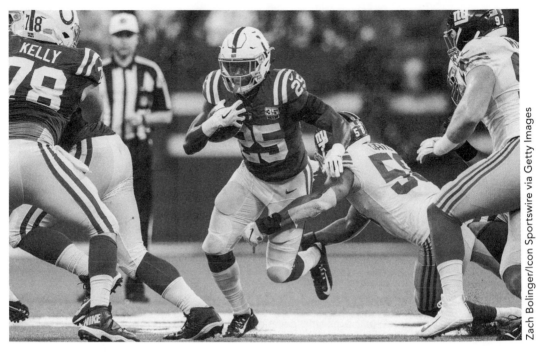

Lower body resistance training exercises develop the pushing, pulling, and single-leg strength needed for optimal on-field performance.

SINGLE-LEG SQUAT

Primary Muscles Trained

Gluteus maximus, semimembranosus, semitendinosus, biceps femoris, vastus lateralis, vastus intermedius, vastus medialis, rectus femoris

Beginning Position

- This exercise is performed using a barbell placed across the shoulders, but dumbbells or kettlebells can be held at the sides instead. If using a barbell, refer to the Beginning Position section of the back squat for proper placement and bracing of the bar on the shoulders. The following description details the movement without reference to the loading modality.
- Start by standing in front of and facing away from a bench, box, or roller pad at a height of 12 to 18 inches (30-46 cm). Step forward into a forward lunge (or split squat) position, but do not lower into the movement. This is done to achieve the proper front-to-rear-foot distance needed to perform the exercise.
- From this optimal split distance, place the rear leg on the box, bench, or roller pad (a). The weight distribution is 60 to 70 percent on the front leg and 30 to 40 percent on the rear leg.

Movement Phases

1. Begin lowering the body toward the floor with the load on the front leg. Maintain proper posture and alignment during the lowering phase. During the lowering phase, there is a slight weight shift backward, but an emphasis of properly loading the lead leg is maintained.
2. Lower the back knee to a height 1 to 2 inches (3-5 cm) from the floor (b). Maintain posture and alignment during this transition phase.

Figure 6.9 Single-leg squat: *(a)* beginning position; *(b)* bottom position.

3. Pushing through the lead foot into the floor in a back and downward fashion, begin to push the weight vertically. The hip and knee begin to extend, lifting the body upward toward the beginning position as a slight forward weight shift occurs. Finish the upward phase of the repetition with a slightly positive shin angle and slight knee flexion.

Breathing Guidelines

Inhale through the lowering phase and exhale during the upward phase of the exercise. If heavier loads are used, the athlete may choose to inhale and hold through the lowering phase and exhale on the upward phase of the movement.

Coaching Tips

- This exercise has many names such as Bulgarian squat, Bulgarian split squat, rear-foot elevated split squat, and rear-foot elevated single-leg squat. Further, a single-leg squat can imply a loaded pistol squat.
- The height of the box, bench, or roller pad is determined by the limb length of the athlete and the flexibility of the quadriceps and hip flexor group. The more restrictions, the lower the height of the box, bench, or roller pad.

LATERAL SQUAT

Primary Muscles Trained

Adductors, gluteus maximus, semimembranosus, semitendinosus, biceps femoris, vastus lateralis, vastus intermedius, vastus medialis, rectus femoris

Beginning Position

- This exercise can be performed using a barbell *(a)*, dumbbells, or kettlebells. (The execution of the exercise is detailed without specific reference to any particular loading modality; if using a barbell, refer to the Beginning Position section of the back squat.)
- To determine the optimal width of the feet for a lateral squat, perform a lateral lunge with perfect technique. Keep the feet at this width for the entire execution of the repetition and set.

Figure 6.10 Lateral squat: *(a)* beginning position; *(b)* side lunge.

Movement Phases

1. The lowering phase starts by bracing the midsection and unlocking the hips and sitting backward into the hips toward one side *(b)*. The same hip and knee flexion timing that is used in the back squat should be used when performing the lateral squat.

2. Stop the lowering phase just before the lumbar and thoracic spine lose neutral position in order to avoid a pelvic posterior tilt.

3. Start the upward phase by pushing downward and laterally into the floor, forcing the body upward and laterally back toward the beginning position.

Breathing Guidelines

Inhale through the lowering phase and exhale during the upward phase of the exercise. If heavier loads are used, the athlete may choose to inhale and hold through the lowering phase and exhale on the upward phase of the lateral squat.

Coaching Tips

- Make sure that as the athlete lowers into the lateral squat position, the torso remains centered with the hips and does not laterally flex at the end of the downward movement phase.

- Observe the lateral weight distribution on the foot at the bottom of the lateral squat. The weight should not shift excessively to the outside of the foot; it should remain balanced between the medial and lateral aspects of the foot.

ROMANIAN DEADLIFT

Primary Muscles Trained

Gluteus maximus, semimembranosus, semitendinosus, biceps femoris, erector spinae

Beginning Position

- Stand next to the bar with the feet hip-width apart. Reach down and grab the bar just outside the thighs. Grip widths will vary by athlete. The wider the grip, the more demanding the exercise will be on the grip and upper back musculature.

- Using the deadlift technique (see page 99), lift the bar to get into the beginning position. Set the knees into a slightly flexed position, with the bar positioned against the thighs (a).

Movement Phases

1. Unlock the hips; maintain a rigid spine and force the center of mass backward as the rigid trunk moves into a forward flexed position (b). Keep the knees slightly flexed as the hips flex. As the bar lowers, it should remain close to or touching the thigh, and the cervical, thoracic, and lumbar spine should remain stabilized. The weight shifts slightly back toward the heel, but the mid-foot and toes continue to remain loaded.

2. The lowering phase ends when the athlete cannot maintain the braced position in the lumbar and thoracic spine or when the hips stop moving backward. Usually this occurs when the torso is just shy of parallel or parallel to the floor.

3. The upward phase is initiated by maintaining the braced position in the upper back and extending the hips and forcing the bar upward, using the hamstrings and gluteus maximus to bring the hips forward. The barbell should maintain contact with the body

Figure 6.11   Romanian deadlift: (a) beginning position; (b) lowering phase.

throughout the movement to achieve the appropriate loading of the posterior chain. The repetition is complete when the bar and athlete return to the beginning position.

Breathing Guidelines

- Inhale through the lowering phase and exhale during the upward phase of the exercise. If heavier loads are used, the athlete may choose to inhale and hold through the lowering phase and exhale on the upward phase.
- Do not allow the knees to fully extend into a straight-legged position. This causes an improper muscle recruitment pattern, excessively loads the hamstrings and erector spinae, and affects optimal gluteus maximus recruitment.

Spotting Guidelines

Ideally, the loading principles used for the Romanian deadlift do not require the use of a spotter. However, if heavier loads are used and there is concern that a repetition might fail, best practices require a spotter on either side of the bar.

Exercise Modifications and Variations

Single-Leg Romanian Deadlift

The single-leg Romanian deadlift is performed using a barbell, dumbbells, or kettlebells. The beginning position is the same as that for the Romanian deadlift, except the athlete lifts one leg off the floor and balances in a single-leg stance with a slightly flexed knee. The lowering phase starts by moving the up leg back as the trunk begins to forward flex at the hip of the support leg. The same biomechanical principles and activation strategies of the Romanian deadlift also hold true for the single-leg Romanian deadlift: Maintain a braced position in the spine as the torso rotates toward the floor. The motion stops when the athlete cannot maintain a stable spine or when the pelvis begins to rotate outward. The upward motion is similar to the Romanian deadlift by extending the hips to return to the beginning position.

Coaching Tips

- Individual differences in mobility, function, and strength dictate the range of motion (depth) of each repetition. Do not perform a full repetition to a trunk parallel position if the athlete cannot maintain a flat-back, braced position.
- Avoid letting the toes lift off the floor during all phases of the exercise. When initiating the upward phase, grip the floor with the toes and push through the floor to maximize drive to the glutes and hamstrings.
- Avoid excessive neck extension during all phases of the repetition. Likewise, avoid excessive extension in the lumbar spine at the beginning and through all phases of the exercise. Doing so appropriately loads the glutes and hamstrings and minimizes stress on the lumbar vertebrae and overload to the erector spinae.
- Turning the toe of the up leg slightly in toward the pelvis can help to maintain hip alignment and prevent excessive hip opening.

BAND TERMINAL KNEE EXTENSION

Primary Muscles Trained

Quadriceps

Beginning Position

- Using a band attached to a stable and heavy object like a squat rack, step through the band so that it rests behind the knee. Step back, creating tension in the band. Make sure the line of pull with the band is directly in front of the center of the patella and slightly downward or parallel to the floor.
- The feet are positioned hip-width apart or slightly narrower. The feet are slightly staggered, with the foot of the nonloaded leg in front (a).

Movement Phases

1. Unlock the hips and sit back into a quarter-squat position, forcing the ankle, knee, and hip into a flexed and loaded position (b). The foot of the working leg remains flat on the floor.
2. Extend the hip and knee by squatting upward (c). When performing the upward phase, the athlete contracts the quadriceps of the banded leg, causing full extension of the knee joint. To further accentuate the quadriceps contraction, hold the contraction for one to three seconds.

Breathing Guidelines

Maintain normal breathing; the exercise is not intense.

Exercise Modifications and Variations

Band Terminal Knee Extension With Heel Lift

If limitations in the ankle joint are present, the heel can lift off the floor as the knee flexes. As the quadriceps contract, bringing the knee into extension, the heel returns to the floor at the terminally extended knee position.

Figure 6.12   Band terminal knee extension: (a) beginning position; (b) quarter-squat; (c) extension.

Coaching Tips

- The foot, knee, and line of pull from the resistance applied must be in alignment to maintain proper biomechanics of ankle and knee flexion.
- Proper tracking of the knee in relation to the foot is vital both to maximize quadriceps activation and to ensure proper neuromuscular activation patterns. Therefore, the athlete should keep the middle of the patella in line with the second and third toes as the knee flexes and extends through the repetition.
- To increase quadriceps activation further, the athlete must finish the repetition in a tall, hip-extended position by contracting the gluteals and maintaining optimal posture from head to toe.

GOOD MORNING

Primary Muscles Trained

Gluteus maximus, semimembranosus, semitendinosus, biceps femoris, erector spinae

Beginning Position

- Start by placing a bar across the back with the bar resting on top of the trapezius muscles. Grip the bar with a firm grip and pull back and down with the arms, activating the latissimus dorsi. Hold the chest up and out, brace the midsection, and prepare for the hip hinge movement (a).
- Place the feet hip-width apart parallel to each other, with weight evenly distributed between the ball of the foot and the heel. The knees are slightly flexed at the beginning position and will remain this way throughout the downward and upward phases.

Figure 6.13 Good morning: (a) beginning position; (b) flex forward.

Movement Phases

1. The first phase of the exercise begins with the hips unlocking and the torso moving into a forward flexion *(b)*. The center of mass shifts backward, and the weight distribution shifts into the heels while maintaining pressure through the mid-foot.

2. As the trunk begins to flex forward, the lumbar, thoracic, and cervical spine remain in a strong and stable neutral position. The torso is fixed as it rotates forward over a fixed lower body. The knees maintain a slight bend without an increase in knee flexion. As a result, the buttocks should move straight back during the descent.

3. The motion stops just before the moment the lumbar spine has a flexion moment due to mobility and the joint kinematics of the lumbo-pelvic hip complex.

4. The upward motion begins as the center of mass starts a shift forward and the athlete extends his hips to get back to the beginning position. The braced upper-back activation is maintained, and the athlete is instructed to "get tall" back into the beginning position.

Breathing Guidelines

Inhale and hold through the lowering phase and exhale on the upward phase of the exercise. If using higher loads, it may be necessary to hold the breath through the upward phase to remain braced through the entire range of motion.

Spotting Guidelines

Ideally, the loading principles used for the good morning exercise do not require the use of a spotter. However, if heavier loads are used, best practices require a spotter on either side of the bar.

Coaching Tip

The good morning exercise improves the strength and function of the posterior chain while grooving the hip hinge pattern. Overloading this exercise and allowing poor technique can have detrimental effects on the spine. Movement quality over quantity of load lifted is vital.

HIP THRUST

Primary Muscles Trained

Gluteus maximus, semimembranosus, semitendinosus, biceps femoris

Beginning Position

- Start by sitting on the floor with the legs extended and leaning back against the long edge of a flat bench.

- Roll a barbell over the hips, then flex the hips and knees to place the feet flat on the floor; the knees will be at approximately a 90-degree angle in this position.

- Adjust the body to line up the upper back (just under the scapulae) with the top edge of the bench pad.

- Grasp the bar with an overhand grip just outside the hips to hold the bar in position over the hips throughout the exercise *(a)*.

Movement Phases

1. The upward phase begins when both feet push into the floor with the weight shifted toward the heels. This causes the hips to extend and the body to rise vertically. The gluteals contract maximally as the hips reach a fully extended position. The shoulders

Figure 6.14 Hip thrust: *(a)* beginning position; *(b)* thrust.

now rest on the bench with the body in a tabletop position *(b)*. The lower legs should be approximately perpendicular to the floor when the hips are in their highest position.

2. The downward phase begins as the hips lower toward the floor. When the hips reach an inch (2-3 cm) from the floor, the repetition is complete.

Breathing Guidelines

Inhale as the hips lower toward the floor and exhale during the upward phase of the hip thrust.

Exercise Modifications and Variations

Single-Leg Hip Thrust

Instead of flexing both hips and knees to place the feet flat on the floor, keep one leg extended out ahead. The leg with the knee flexed to approximately a 90-degree angle with the corresponding foot flat on the floor is the leg that will be used to perform the exercise. During the upward phase, raise and lower the uninvolved leg in tandem with the involved leg to help keep the bar in place and level with the floor.

Coaching Tips

- The knees, hips, and ears must align at the top of the hip thrust motion. If this alignment does not occur because the head or thoracic spine is still flexed at the top of the hip thrust, hip extension decreases and full contraction of the gluteals is affected.
- Do not overextend the hips at the finish position. The torso, hips, and knees should all be aligned in a straight line.

STABILITY BALL TRIPLE THREAT

Primary Muscles Trained

Gluteus maximus/minimus/medius, semimembranosus, semitendinosus, biceps femoris

Beginning Position

- Lying on the floor, face up with arms resting at the sides, place both heels on a stability ball *(a)*.
- The legs are straight with the knees fully extended and the ankles in dorsiflexion.

Figure 6.15   Stability ball triple threat: *(a)* beginning position; *(b)* lift hips; *(c)* roll ball toward body; *(d)* extend knees.

Movement Phases

1. Pushing the heels into the ball, contract the gluteals and raise the hips off the floor *(b)*.

2. Next, simultaneously press the heels into the ball, flex the knees, and use the hamstrings to roll the ball toward the body *(c)*. Once the ball is pulled toward the body, finish the upward phase of the exercise by lifting the hips and contracting the gluteals.

3. The downward phase includes the previous stages but now performed in an eccentric fashion. The hips lower slightly under control. Next, the heels push into the ball, ankles remain flexed as the hamstrings are lengthened under tension, and the knees extend, moving the ball back to the beginning position *(d)*.

Breathing Guidelines

Breathe normally through the set, not paying attention to any specific breathing pattern. The length of each repetition dictates the inhale and exhale patterns and may differ between athletes.

Exercise Modifications and Variations

Stability Ball Triple Threat Eccentric Only

If movement quality during the concentric portion of the exercise is poor due to strength, stability, or mobility concerns, perform only the eccentric portion of the exercise for the prescribed number of repetitions per set. Building a volume of work during the eccentric phase will improve strength, stability, and movement quality.

Coaching Tip

Maintain dorsiflexion in the ankles throughout the movement, specifically paying attention to ankle position during the eccentric (downward) phase of the exercise.

HAMSTRING SLIDE

Primary Muscles Trained

Gluteus maximus, semimembranosus, semitendinosus, biceps femoris

Beginning Position

- In order to perform the exercise, athletes will need to use either a towel on a slick surface or a slideboard.

- Lying on the floor, face up with arms resting at the sides, place both heels on a towel or slideboard. Flex the knees to create roughly 90 degrees of knee flexion. The ankles are dorsiflexed, causing the heels to be the only contact point of the foot on the towel.

- Push the arms into the floor, creating tension in the midsection. Next, lift the hips vertically by contracting the glutes and pushing into the floor through the heels *(a)*. The athlete is now in the beginning position for the exercise.

Movement Phases

1. Slide the heels away from the body and lower the hips toward the floor while maintaining a bridged hip position *(b)*. Keep the ankles dorsiflexed as the hamstrings lengthen

under tension. The lowering phase stops when the knees fully extend and the athlete's hips are 1 to 2 inches (3-5 cm) from the floor.

2. The upward phase begins by contracting the hamstrings and sliding the heels back toward the body, forcing the knees to flex and the hips to rise back vertically *(c)*. When the athlete returns to the beginning position, the motion is repeated without resting the hips on the floor.

Breathing Guidelines

Inhale before the lowering phase and hold until the upward phase begins. Exhale during the upward phase. Many athletes like to maintain a braced position and breathe normally through the entirety of the set.

Exercise Modifications and Variations

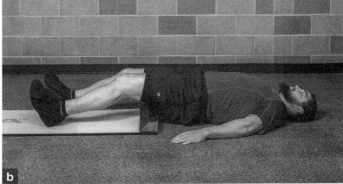

Figure 6.16 Hamstring slide: *(a)* beginning position; *(b)* slide feet out and lower hips; *(c)* slide feet in and lift hips.

Dolly Leg Curl

If available, using a dolly in place of a towel or slideboard is another great way to perform the hamstring slide. It is a good option for heavier athletes, athletes who struggle with resisting hip rotation, or athletes recovering from a hamstring strain.

Coaching Tip

The hips must maintain a level position through the exercise. If the hips rotate, unequal unilateral recruitment of the hamstring muscles occurs, causing an asymmetrical loading pattern.

DUMBBELL HAMSTRING WALK

Primary Muscles Trained

Hamstrings, gluteals, erector spinae

Beginning Position

- The exercise begins with the athlete standing tall with dumbbells held at the sides (a).
- Brace the midsection, pull the shoulders back and down, and start with the head tall, eyes facing forward.

Movement Phases

1. Step forward 6 to 12 inches (15-30 cm) to place the feet in a narrow split position. To start the downward phase, hinge forward from the hips, bringing the trunk into forward flexion (b). Slightly shift the center of mass backward, forcing the hamstrings and gluteals to lengthen under tension. Maintain the flat back and braced position through the entire downward phase.
2. The downward phase stops just before the lumbar or thoracic spine goes into flexion. The upward phase begins as the athlete gets tall and extends the torso over the fixed split-leg position (not shown).
3. Step forward with the rear leg and repeat steps 1 and 2 for the next repetition.

Breathing Guidelines

Inhale during the downward phase and exhale through the upward phase and in between steps.

Coaching Tip

The split position, under a forward-flexing load, is challenging to the lumbar spine. Loading patterns should be moderate and should progress only while movement quality can be maintained.

Figure 6.17   Dumbbell hamstring walk: (a) beginning position; (b) step forward.

NORDIC HAMSTRING CURL

Primary Muscles Trained
Semimembranosus, semitendinosus, biceps femoris

Beginning Position
- The exercise is done using a partner or piece of equipment anchoring the ankle, foot, and lower leg in a fixed position.
- The athlete begins in a double kneeling position with ankles flexed and toes into the floor. A partner or piece of equipment is behind the athlete, pressing down on the heels and forcing the ankles, feet, and lower legs into an anchored position necessary to perform the Nordic hamstring curl.
- At the beginning position, the torso is upright with the hips extended and gluteals contracted. The ear, hip, and knee are in a straight line with the pelvis in a neutral braced position. Next, the shoulders are pulled down and back, stabilizing the thoracic spine (upper back), with the arms resting at the sides (a).

Movement Phases
1. The downward phase begins by bracing the torso as described and allowing the body to slowly fall forward toward the floor (b). The athlete keeps the gluteals contracted and uses the hamstrings and the entire posterior chain to resist the rate at which the body falls toward the floor.

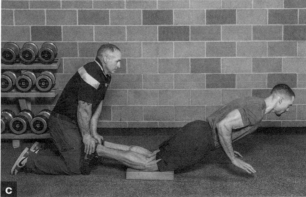

Figure 6.18 Nordic hamstring curl: (a) beginning position; (b) fall forward; (c) catch the body near the floor.

2. The thighs and torso remain in perfect alignment, and the posterior chain remains engaged as the body nears the floor. At this point, reach forward and place the hands on the floor to decelerate the body during the last part of the lowering phase as if doing a push-up *(c)*.

3. Lower the body to within 2 inches (5 cm) of the floor. Next, the upward phase begins as the athlete performs a push-up motion, forcing the body backward toward the beginning position. In the same moment, the hamstrings contract and pull the fixed torso back toward the beginning position. The repetition is complete once the athlete reaches the beginning position.

Breathing Guidelines

Inhale and hold the breath during the lowering phase and exhale during the upward phase.

Exercise Modifications and Variations

Band-Assisted Nordic Hamstring Curl

If the athlete cannot resist his own body weight, banded assistance may be used. The band is attached to a fixed point so that the line of pull is at a 45-degree angle or more to the floor. Place the band around the chest and under the armpit. The band will help to decelerate the body during the lowering phase and to accelerate the body during the upward phase.

Coaching Tip

If the anterior tilt of the pelvis during the concentric (upward) phase is excessive because of a strength deficit or a movement dysfunction, the exercise should be modified. Modify by either performing only the eccentric (lowering) phase of the movement or by adding banded or other external assistance during the concentric phase.

SINGLE-LEG BRIDGE

Primary Muscles Trained

Gluteals

Beginning Position

- Start by lying flat on the floor with both knees flexed to a 90-degree angle, both feet flat on the floor, and arms resting at the sides.
- Bring one leg off the floor into 90 degrees of hip flexion, while maintaining 90 degrees of knee flexion *(a)*.

Movement Phases

1. The upward phase begins by pushing through the grounded leg, forcing the hips to rise off the floor *(b)*. At the same time, the arms press into the floor, activating the core musculature. The upward phase finishes by fully contracting the glute of the down leg as it reaches a fully extended position.

2. After full contraction of the gluteals occurs, the downward phase begins as the hips lower under control toward the floor. The lowering phase ends as the hips reach 1 to 2 inches (3-5 cm) from the floor.

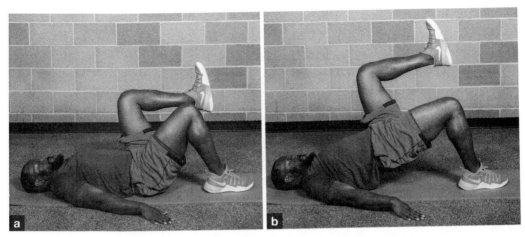

Figure 6.19 Single-leg bridge: *(a)* beginning position; *(b)* upward phase.

Breathing Guidelines

Inhale as the hips lower toward the floor in the downward phase of the exercise. As the hips lift off the floor, exhale through the full range of the upward phase.

Exercise Modifications and Variations

Single-Leg Bridge With Extended Knee

This exercise is performed with the same movement phases as the single-leg bridge with flexed hip and knee, but now the up leg is held in an extended-knee position. The leg is straight out to start the upward phase and finishes aligned with the thigh of the grounded leg.

Coaching Tips

- Pushing through the heel of the grounded leg with the ankle in dorsiflexion may elicit greater glute activation if the athlete does not have any mobility restrictions in the hip.
- Eccentric lowering for athletes who struggle with single-leg bridge. Start in the up position using both legs, shift the weight to a single leg, lower with a one to five count, and repeat.

GLUTE-HAM RAISE

Primary Muscles Trained

Gluteus maximus, semimembranosus, semitendinosus, biceps femoris, erector spinae

Beginning Position

- Using a glute-ham bench, the athlete's body begins in a straight line (parallel to the floor) and shoulders pulled back and down. The ear, shoulder, hip, knee, and ankle form a straight line at the beginning position of the exercise. The arms are crossed and placed on the chest *(a)*.
- The roller pad is positioned at the mid to lower thigh, depending on individual femur and tibia length and the strength of the athlete.

Movement Phases

1. Press the feet into the platform and start the upward phase of the movement by maintaining hip extension while contracting the hamstrings (b). Contracting the hamstrings causes the knees to flex and lifts the body into a vertical position (c). The ear, shoulder, hip, and knee remain aligned through the upward phase.

2. The lowering phase begins as the athlete allows the body to fall forward under tension, using the hamstrings to control the rate of descent. The ear, shoulder, hip, and knee remain aligned as the legs begin to extend through the lowering phase and the body returns to a straight-line position parallel to the floor.

Breathing Guidelines

Exhale during the upward phase and inhale during the lowering phase or inhale before beginning the upward phase and exhale during the lowering phase.

Coaching Tip

Maintain a strong glute contraction through all phases of the movement. This prevents the pelvis from anteriorly tilting, which would cause poor recruitment patterning of the erector spinae and hamstring muscles.

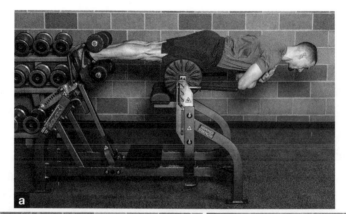

Figure 6.20 Glute-ham raise: (a) beginning position; (b) upward phase; (c) vertical position.

7

UPPER BODY EXERCISE TECHNIQUE

JIM PEAL AND ERIK MYYRA

Because football involves athletes battling each other by pushing and pulling, there is a great demand for upper body strength. When the total mass of a football athlete increases, the force required to take down that athlete increases as well, so increasing the lean mass of a football athlete is critical to training. Creating a comprehensive training program for football athletes will include a mix of pushing and pulling movements that should be completed through full ranges of motion. Making sure that athletes train both of these motions in multiple planes will keep them balanced, which will, in turn, decrease their risk of injury. The exercises can be performed using the equipment that can be found in most weight rooms, and the technique guidelines provided are standard within the strength and conditioning profession (1, 4). Barbells and dumbbells will be used in most of the exercises. This is the best way to increase resistance for each exercise because barbells and dumbbells are easy to use and because weight can be easily tracked or changed.

Exercise Finder

BENCH PRESS

Primary Muscles Trained

Pectoralis major, anterior deltoids, triceps brachii

Beginning Position

- Lie supine on a bench with five points of contact—head, shoulders, and hips on the bench and both feet on the floor—and keep these five points of contact throughout the exercise (a).
- Position the body so that the eyes are directly below the bar.
- Using a closed, pronated grip with hands about shoulder-width apart, move the bar off the supports to above the chest with extended elbows.

Movement Phases

1. While keeping the wrists stiff and the forearms perpendicular to the floor, lower the bar in a controlled motion to the chest at about nipple level (b).
2. Push the bar upward and slightly backward until the elbows are extended (c).
3. Do not raise the chest or hips during the upward movement.
4. Keep the hands on the bar until the bar is fully racked on the supports.

Breathing Guidelines

When using a submaximal load, it is fairly common to inhale on the eccentric phase and exhale on the concentric phase. During heavy submaximal and maximal loads, the Valsalva maneuver is preferred (see chapter 6).

Spotting Guidelines

Spotters should be used at all times during bench pressing. Some racks have platforms so that the spotters can stand elevated above the athlete; use these platforms instead of the staggered stance since it gives the spotter better leverage to pull the bar up. Depending on the load being lifted, an additional two spotters on the sides of the barbell can be used to assist if the athlete needs help. These side spotters will only assist in the lifting of the barbell if the spotter behind the athlete, the primary spotter, gives the command to do so.

When spotting the bench press, the spotter will align behind the athlete and bench with a staggered stance (not shown in figure 7.1). One leg will be to the side of the bench close to the athlete's ear and the other will be behind the bench; this stance gives spotters leverage. The spotter will help the athlete to unrack the bar and position it over the athlete's chest. When the athlete completes the set, the spotter will help the athlete to rack the bar safely. When the athlete can no longer apply enough force to keep the bar moving up, the spotter will help by grabbing the bar between the athlete's hands and pulling it back to the beginning position and then back to the rack position.

Exercise Modifications and Variations

Incline Bench Press

The back of the bench may be raised to change the pushing angle. Spotters should be more aware of their role because the racking and reracking of the bar puts the athlete in a biomechanically inefficient position.

Figure 7.1 Bench press: (a) beginning position; (b) lower barbell to chest; (c) press barbell up.

Close-Grip Bench Press

The hands are placed closer together on the bar to increase the involvement of the triceps. Grip is generally placed inside the knurling (i.e., closer than shoulder-width apart), but not so close that performing the exercise elicits wrist pain.

Dumbbell Bench Press

The exercise is performed using dumbbells instead of a barbell. Keeping the forearms perpendicular to the floor is critical to good technique. The dumbbells can be positioned so that there is a pronated, supinated, or neutral grip. Each of these grips has different benefits; a pronated grip can allow for more weight to be lifted, but a supinated or neutral grip will have more carryover to the football field because of the hand placements used for blocking.

Band or Chain Bench Press

Bands or chains are attached to the barbell to gradually increase the total load of the exercise throughout the concentric range of motion. Note that chains will only create a training effect if they touch the floor at the isometric phase of the exercise; research has shown that most chains should touch the floor as the bar touches the chest in the bottom position of the bench press (3).

Coaching Tips

- The bench press can be tough on the shoulder if it is performed incorrectly, so make sure that the athlete does not press when the shoulders are in an abducted position (a 90-degree angle between the upper arm and torso).
- Using a wider grip will cause the chest to be targeted more than normal, while using a closer grip will involve the triceps more than a normal or wide grip (2).

MEDICINE BALL CHEST PASS

Primary Muscles Trained
Pectoralis major, anterior deltoids, triceps brachii

Beginning Position
- Get into an upright stance with the feet shoulder-width apart.
- Stand facing a partner or wall.
- Hold a medicine ball at chest height with the elbows fully flexed (a).

Movement Phases
1. Explosively push (pass) the medicine ball toward the partner or wall by extending the elbows (b).
2. Fully follow through with the movement; the elbows should be fully extended at the end of the pass.

Breathing Guidelines
Breathe in while performing the eccentric portion of the exercise and exhale during the concentric portion of the exercise.

Figure 7.2   Medicine ball chest pass: *(a)* beginning position; *(b)* push medicine ball to partner.

Coaching Tip

The intensity of the exercise may be increased by standing farther from the partner or the wall or by increasing the weight of the medicine ball.

MEDICINE BALL DROP

Primary Muscles Trained

Pectoralis major, anterior deltoids, triceps brachii

Beginning Position

- Lie supine on the floor with the elbows extended and the arms perpendicular to the floor.
- Position the body so the head is near the base of a box or step.
- A partner stands on the box or step with a medicine ball held over the athlete's hands *(a)*.

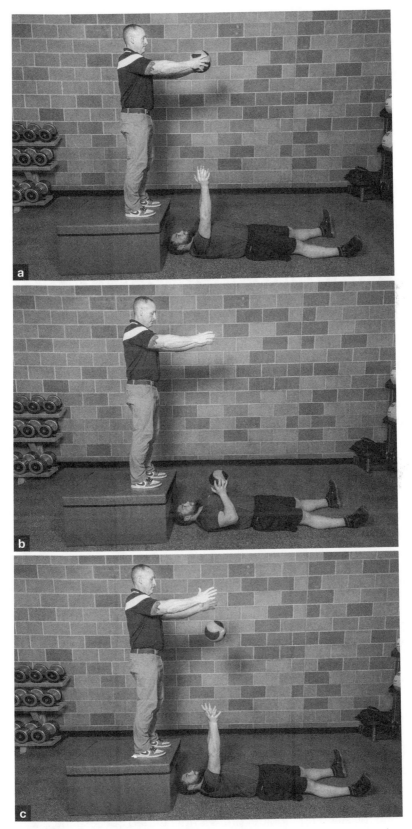

Figure 7.3 Medicine ball drop: *(a)* beginning position; *(b)* catch ball at chest; *(c)* push ball back to partner.

Movement Phases

1. The partner drops the medicine ball into the hands of the athlete, who catches it near the chest *(b)*.
2. Immediately after catching the ball, the athlete explosively throws (pushes) the medicine ball back up to the partner *(c)*.

Breathing Guidelines

Breathe in while performing the eccentric portion of the exercise and exhale during the concentric portion of the exercise.

Coaching Tip

The intensity of the exercise may be increased by placing the partner on a taller box or step or by increasing the weight of the medicine ball.

STANDING SHOULDER PRESS

Primary Muscles Trained

Anterior and medial deltoids, triceps brachii

Beginning Position

- Set up a bar on a rack with J-hooks at shoulder level (not shown in figure 7.4). Set up under the bar so the center of gravity is under the bar. Grasp the bar with a shoulder-width pronated grip *(a)*.
- Position the bar at the clavicles with the forearms perpendicular to the floor.
- In a hip-width standing position, stand upright with knees slightly unlocked.
- Do not use the legs at any time during this movement.

Movement Phases

1. While keeping the forearms perpendicular to the floor, push the bar straight up by extending the elbows and flexing the shoulders *(b)*.
2. Extend the neck slightly backward so that the bar can clear the face and then return the head to the original position when the bar clears the head.
3. Keep a firm grip on the bar, and keep the forearms parallel to each other as the elbows extend completely so that the bar is positioned directly over the head.
4. Lower the bar to the beginning position on the clavicles by flexing at the elbows and extending the shoulders; make sure to retract the neck so the head is out of the bar's path and return it when the bar clears the chin.

Breathing Guidelines

When using a substantially submaximal load, it is fairly common to inhale on the eccentric phase and exhale on the concentric phase. During heavy submaximal and maximal loads, the Valsalva maneuver is preferred (see chapter 6).

Spotting Guidelines

A spotter during the standing shoulder press is not needed because the eccentric portion of the movement is the strongest. An athlete who cannot complete a repetition can just return to the beginning position and then rack the bar.

Figure 7.4 Standing shoulder press: *(a)* beginning position; *(b)* press overhead.

Exercise Modifications and Variations

Seated Shoulder Press

The seated shoulder press will flip-flop the starting and ending positions. Perform the press in reverse order: The arms will begin extended, and the athlete will bring the bar to the clavicles and then back up using the same movements as in the normal shoulder press. A bench with or without a back pad can be used. A slight backward torso lean may be needed to position the head out of the bar's path. A spotter may be used in the seated portion of this exercise if the athlete is facing away from the rack. Use the same technique to spot the seated shoulder press as the bench press.

Behind-the-Neck Shoulder Press

The beginning position changes from the clavicle to behind the neck; the grip may also be slightly wider than shoulder-width. This variation can cause discomfort in the shoulder for some athletes since it requires more range of motion to perform. Athletes with known shoulder injuries should seek other exercises to strengthen the shoulder that do not irritate this area.

Coaching Tip

Make sure that the athlete knows that once the bar clears the head, the head should return to neutral and the torso should remain upright without a backward lean.

SHOULDER SHRUG

Primary Muscle Trained

Trapezius

Beginning Position

- Hold the barbell in a pronated closed grip about shoulder-width (a).
- Retract the shoulders back slightly to prevent rounding in the upper back.
- Knees and hips are slightly flexed and are kept immobile during the movement.

Movement Phases

1. Elevate the shoulders as high as possible so the bar moves straight up (b).
2. Control the barbell back to the beginning position.

Breathing Guidelines

Breathe in while performing the eccentric portion of the exercise and exhale during the concentric portion of the exercise.

Exercise Modifications and Variations

Dumbbell Shrug

Perform the exercise using dumbbells. The beginning position can begin with the dumbbells anterior to the hip or with a neutral grip at the sides of the body.

Power Shrug

Use the same grip type and width and perform the same shrugging movement used for the shoulder shrug, but use an explosive, very short-range-of-motion "dip and drive" effort (see the push press exercise description in chapter 5) from the thighs and calves to shrug the bar up as high as possible (while keeping the elbows fully extended).

Figure 7.5   Shoulder shrug: (a) beginning position; (b) shrug.

Coaching Tips

- Make sure that the legs are not helping with the upward movement.
- If the athlete cannot shrug through a full range of motion, then lower the weight until it can be done with full range of motion and without any lower body assistance.

LATERAL SHOULDER RAISE

Primary Muscle Trained
Middle deltoid

Beginning Position

- Hold a dumbbell in each hand to the side with a neutral grip (a).
- Retract the shoulders back slightly to prevent rounding in the shoulders.
- Slightly flex the elbows (more than what is shown in figure 7.6) and keep them in this position throughout the exercise.
- Knees and hips should be slightly flexed. Keep this position through the entire exercise.

Movement Phases

1. Raise the dumbbells to the side and up (shoulder abduction) until they are approximately parallel to the floor or reach the same height as the shoulder (b); elbows and upper arms should rise at the same pace and should rise slightly ahead of the hands.
2. Resist the urge to swing or kip the body to assist in the dumbbell movement.
3. Reverse the direction; control the dumbbells down to the beginning position.

Coaching Tip
Using a split stance or performing this exercise from a seated position may help prevent swaying or kipping.

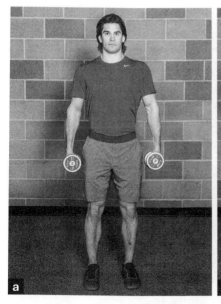 

Figure 7.6 Lateral shoulder raise: (a) beginning position; (b) raise.

FRONT SHOULDER RAISE

Primary Muscle Trained
Anterior deltoid

Beginning Position
- Hold a dumbbell in each hand in front of the thighs with a neutral or pronated grip (a).
- Retract the shoulders back slightly to prevent rounding in the shoulders.
- Slightly flex the elbows (more than what is shown in figure 7.7) and keep them in this position throughout the exercise.
- Knees and hips should be slightly flexed. Keep this position throughout the exercise.

Movement Phases
1. Raise the dumbbells to the front and up (shoulder flexion) until they reach the same height as the shoulder (b).
2. Resist the urge to swing or kip the body to assist in the dumbbell movement.
3. Reverse the direction; control the dumbbells down to the beginning position.

Breathing Guidelines
Breathe in while performing the eccentric portion of the exercise and exhale during the concentric portion of the exercise.

Coaching Tip
Make sure that the weight is being controlled through the entire range of motion; letting the weight drop during the eccentric motion is common.

Figure 7.7   Front shoulder raise: (a) beginning position; (b) raise.

BENT-OVER LATERAL RAISE

Primary Muscle Trained

Posterior deltoid

Beginning Position

- Hold a dumbbell in each hand with a neutral grip.
- While keeping a set back and knees flexed, flex at the hip so that the torso is parallel to the floor.
- Let the arms hang down perpendicular to the floor with the elbows slightly flexed (a).

Movement Phases

1. Raise the dumbbells to the side and up (shoulder horizontal abduction) until they reach the same height as the shoulder (b).
2. Resist the urge to swing or kip the body to assist in the dumbbell movement.
3. Reverse the direction; control the dumbbells down to the beginning position.

Breathing Guidelines

Breathe in while performing the eccentric portion of the exercise and exhale during the concentric portion of the exercise.

Coaching Tips

- The longer the arms are, the harder the motion will be.
- Keeping the same degree of elbow flexion is important if the athlete will be progressing the resistance; if the athlete flexes the elbows more as the resistance increases, then the difficulty of the exercise will be the same.

Figure 7.8 Bent-over lateral raise: (a) beginning position; (b) raise.

FACE PULL (MACHINE)

Primary Muscles Trained
Posterior deltoid, supraspinatus

Beginning Position
- Choose either an even or a split stance with the knees slightly flexed.
- Set up the cable to about forehead level with a rope attachment.
- With a pronated grip, hold the rope at eye level with the arms fully extended (a).

Movement Phases
1. While keeping the elbows high and the hands pronated, pull the rope backward while simultaneously separating the hands to each side of the head, stopping the center of the rope right before the eyes (b).
2. Slowly control the rope back to the beginning position.

Breathing Guidelines
Breathe in while performing the eccentric portion of the exercise and exhale during the concentric portion of the exercise.

Exercise Modifications and Variations

Band Face Pull
Use a band instead of a cable; fix the band at about forehead level, use the same beginning position, and execute as described for the face pull (machine).

Coaching Tip
Keep the torso motionless to allow for greater isolation of targeted muscles.

Figure 7.9 Face pull (machine): (a) beginning position; (b) pull.

PRONE Y, T, I

Primary Muscles Trained

Upper trapezius, middle trapezius, lower trapezius infraspinatus, teres minor/major, mid and low trapezius, rhomboids, posterior deltoids

Prone Y: Beginning Position

- Lie prone on an incline bench or stability ball (20-35 degrees).
- If a bench is used, position the body so the sternum is on the edge or close to the short edge of the bench.
- Hang the arms straight down with dumbbells in a neutral grip (a).

Prone Y: Movement Phases

1. While keeping arms straight and head stationary, slowly flex the shoulders to the end of the range of motion (b).
2. Keep the chest and chin on the bench or stability ball.
3. Slowly control the arms back to the beginning position.

Figure 7.10   Prone Y: (a) beginning position; (b) Y position.

Prone T: Beginning Position

- Lie prone on an incline bench or stability ball (20-35 degrees).
- If a bench is used, position the body so the sternum is on the edge or close to the short edge of the bench.
- Hang the arms straight down with dumbbells in a neutral grip (a).

Figure 7.11 Prone T: *(a)* beginning position; *(b)* T position.

Prone T: Movement Phases

1. While keeping arms straight and head stationary, horizontally abduct the shoulders so that that the arms rise into the air *(b)*. Pinch the shoulder blades together at the top of the movement.
2. Slowly control the arms back to the beginning position.

Prone I: Beginning Position

- Lie prone on an incline bench or stability ball (20-35 degrees).
- If a bench is used, position the body so the sternum is on the edge or close to the short edge of the bench.
- Hang the arms straight down with dumbbells in a neutral grip *(a)*.

Prone I: Movement Phases

1. While keeping the arms straight and the head stationary, fully extend at the shoulder and reach back until the arms hit the end of their range of motion *(b)*.
2. Slowly control the arms back to the beginning position.

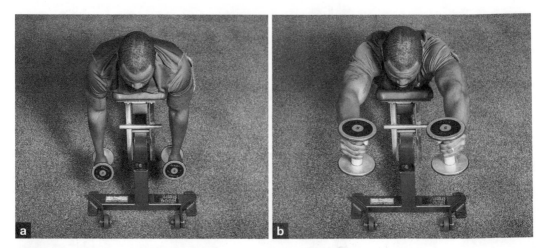

Figure 7.12 Prone I: *(a)* beginning position; *(b)* I position.

Breathing Guidelines

Breathe in while performing the eccentric portion of the exercise and exhale during the concentric portion of the exercise.

Exercise Modifications and Variations

Suspension Y, T, I

Instead of using a stability ball or an incline bench, use a pair of suspension straps that are adjusted to mid-length. To get into the beginning position, lean back until the torso is at a 45-degree angle to the floor with the shoulder blades pulled together. Use the same arm position and range of motion as the stability ball or incline bench versions.

L and W

Use a stability ball, incline bench, or pair of suspension straps and get into the beginning position with the upper arms next to the torso (L's) or at a 45-degree angle to the torso (W's). Keep the elbows flexed to 90 degrees. Perform the movement by externally rotating the arms at the shoulder, keeping the upper arms in the same beginning position.

Coaching Tips

- Head position is critical to this exercise. Keeping it stable will allow the athlete to isolate the movement; if the head starts to lift off the bench, the range of motion comes from the back rather than the shoulder.
- The prone I exercise can be loaded more heavily than the other prone exercises.
- A stability ball or a bench is ideal for this exercise, but if there is not enough equipment, the exercises can be performed on the floor (but the range of motion is much less).

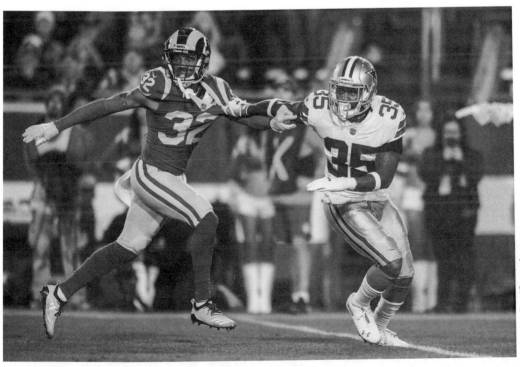

John McCoy/Getty Images

The football athlete's upper body needs to be trained to withstand the many multi-directional forces of the sport.

UPRIGHT ROW

Primary Muscles Trained
Upper trapezius, deltoids

Beginning Position
- Using an even stance and with the feet shoulder-width apart, grasp a barbell with a pronated grip with hands about shoulder-width apart.
- While standing erect, slightly flex the knees and hold the barbell with extended elbows in front of the body (a).

Movement Phases
1. While keeping the barbell close to the body, pull the barbell straight upward until the elbows are even with or slightly higher than shoulder level (b).
2. Control the barbell back down to the beginning position while keeping it close to the body.

Breathing Guidelines
Breathe in while performing the eccentric portion of the exercise and exhale during the concentric portion of the exercise.

Exercise Modifications and Variations

Dumbbell Upright Row

Use dumbbells instead of a barbell.

Figure 7.13   Upright row: (a) beginning position; (b) pull.

Banded Upright Row

Anchor a band to the floor by standing on the band and grip the other end of the band with hands closely together; this is the new beginning position.

Coaching Tip

If the athlete feels pain during the barbell variations, try modifying the exercise to a different variation; the change in grip can be more favorable.

BENT-OVER ROW

Primary Muscles Trained

Latissimus dorsi, teres major, biceps brachii, middle trapezius, posterior deltoids, rhomboids

Beginning Position

- Use a pronated grip on the barbell wider than shoulder-width.
- Flex the knees slightly, keep the torso braced, and hinge at the waist until the torso is slightly above parallel to the floor.
- Allow the arms to hang straight down *(a)*; create a neutral spine position and keep the back set tight for the entire exercise.

Movement Phases

1. Pull the bar upward until it reaches the upper abdomen or lower chest *(b)*.
2. The elbows will move straight back to the side of the body.
3. Control the bar back to the beginning position.

Figure 7.14   Bent-over row: *(a)* beginning position; *(b)* pull.

Breathing Guidelines

Breathe in while performing the eccentric portion of the exercise and exhale during the concentric portion of the exercise. When the load gets heavy, use the Valsalva maneuver (see chapter 6).

Coaching Tip

Keep the torso parallel to the floor so that the exercise continues to be a horizontal row.

ONE-ARM DUMBBELL ROW

Primary Muscles Trained

Latissimus dorsi, teres major, rhomboids, biceps brachii, middle trapezius, posterior deltoids

Beginning Position

- Place one hand firmly on a sturdy surface low enough so that the torso is slightly above parallel to the floor.
- While keeping the spine neutral, hold a dumbbell in the other hand straight down with the elbow fully extended (a).
- The knee of the down hand can be placed on the same surface as the down hand.

Movement Phases

1. Using a neutral grip dumbbell position, pull the dumbbell straight up to the side of the torso (b).
2. The elbow will go straight back and the hand should be about the same level as the bottom of the pectorals or upper abdomen.
3. Control the weight back to the beginning position.
4. Keep a neutral spine and control of the torso.

Figure 7.15   One-arm dumbbell row: (a) beginning position; (b) pull.

Breathing Guidelines

Breathe in while performing the eccentric portion of the exercise and exhale during the concentric portion of the exercise.

Exercise Modifications and Variations

Dumbbell Incline Row

Instead of bracing with the hand, the torso is prone on an incline bench. While keeping the chin placed off the top of the bench, let the dumbbells hang down; this is the new beginning position.

Coaching Tips

- Keep the torso level during the exercise; too much torso motion will target muscles other than those intended.
- Pull the bar against the lower chest.

DUMBBELL PULLOVER

Primary Muscles Trained

Latissimus dorsi, pectoralis major

Beginning Position

- Lie on a bench so that the body is perpendicular to the long edge of a flat bench with the shoulders on the bench.
- Plant the feet firmly on the floor with knees flexed to about 90 degrees.
- Allow the head to be positioned off the bench and held in a neutral position.
- Hold the sides of a dumbbell (so the handle is parallel to the floor) or overlap the hands to cup one end of a dumbbell (so the handle is perpendicular to the floor) and position the dumbbell over the neck or face with the arms perpendicular to the bench (a).
- Keep the elbows unlocked and slightly flexed throughout the entire range of motion.

Movement Phases

1. Allow the dumbbell to lower down and behind the head by flexing at the shoulder (b).
2. After reaching the lowest position, bring the dumbbell back to the beginning position without kipping the body.

Breathing Guidelines

Breathe in while performing the eccentric portion of the exercise and exhale during the concentric portion of the exercise.

Exercise Modifications and Variations

EZ Bar Pullover

Use an EZ bar instead of a dumbbell.

Figure 7.16   Dumbbell pullover: *(a)* beginning position; *(b)* lower dumbbell.

Coaching Tips

- Keep the arms as long as possible with the elbows slightly flexed.
- The pullover can be tough to implement in training with many athletes in the room using multiple benches, so benches may have to be staggered to make more room to account for the many athletes lying perpendicular on benches.

LAT PULLDOWN (MACHINE)

Primary Muscles Trained

Latissimus dorsi, middle trapezius, posterior deltoids, rhomboids, teres major

Beginning Position

- Using a pronated grip, grasp the bar with hands wider than shoulder-width apart.
- Sit down on the seat and position the thighs under the pads to keep the hips on the seat.
- Slightly lean the torso back so that the bar can clear the head and face.
- Extend the elbows so that the arms reach straight up *(a)*.

Movement Phases

1. Pull the bar straight down to the upper chest or clavicles *(b)*.
2. Maintain the torso position. Do not actively lean back during the exercise to assist in the movement.
3. Control the bar back to the beginning position.
4. Maintain the torso position for the entire exercise.

Breathing Guidelines

Breathe in while performing the eccentric portion of the exercise and exhale during the concentric portion of the exercise.

Figure 7.17 Lat pulldown (machine): *(a)* beginning position; *(b)* pull bar down.

Exercise Modifications and Variations

Wide-Grip Lat Pulldown
Grasp the bar with the hands farther apart than in the original beginning position.

Supinated Grip Lat Pulldown
Grasp the bar with a supinated grip instead of a pronated grip.

Neutral Grip Lat Pulldown
Using a V-handle, grasp the attachment with a neutral grip for the beginning position.

Coaching Tip
Perform the exercise as a vertical row; the more the athlete leans back, the more the exercise becomes a horizontal row.

LOW-PULLEY SEATED ROW (MACHINE)

Primary Muscles Trained
Latissimus dorsi, teres major, biceps brachii, middle trapezius, posterior deltoids, rhomboids

Beginning Position
- Sit with the torso upright and feet on the footplate to brace the body.
- Grasp the attachment with a neutral, pronated, or supinated grip.
- Extend the arms straight out with tension in the cable or weight stack *(a)*.

Movement Phases
1. Pull the attachment straight back until it reaches the upper abdomen or lower chest *(b)*.
2. Keep the torso upright. Do not actively lean back during the exercise to assist in the movement.
3. Control the attachment back to the beginning position.

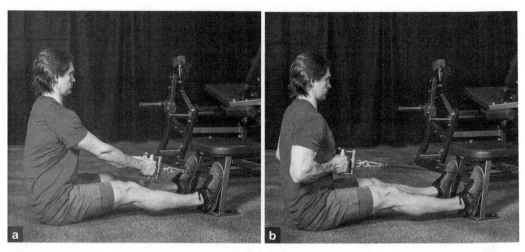

Figure 7.18 Low-pulley seated row (machine): *(a)* beginning position; *(b)* pull handles back.

Breathing Guidelines

Breathe in while performing the eccentric portion of the exercise and exhale during the concentric portion of the exercise.

Coaching Tip

Keeping the chest stable will allow the exercise to remain a horizontal row; using momentum or leaning back too far will change the muscles used and will reduce the stimulus to the targeted muscles.

INVERTED ROW

Primary Muscles Trained

Latissimus dorsi, teres major, rhomboids, biceps brachii, middle trapezius, posterior deltoids

Beginning Position

- Set up a barbell on J-hooks or safety racks at a height just longer than arm's length.
- While grasping the bar with a pronated grip, hang supine with heels on the floor *(a)*; the knees can be fully extended or somewhat flexed.

Movement Phases

1. Pull the body up until the lower chest, sternum, or upper abdomen touches the bar *(b)*.
2. Maintain a straight line from the shoulders to the ankles or the shoulders to the knees (depending on which knee position is used).
3. End with the elbows behind the body.
4. Control the body back down to the beginning position.

Breathing Guidelines

Breathe in while performing the eccentric portion of the exercise and exhale during the concentric portion of the exercise.

Figure 7.19   Inverted row: *(a)* beginning position; *(b)* pull body up.

Exercise Modifications and Variations

Suspension Trainer Row

Instead of using a barbell, use a suspension strap. Set the handles to a height just longer than arm's length.

Coaching Tips

- While performing an inverted row, the athlete must keep the hips from swaying or rocking to assist in the movement. Keeping a tight abdomen will allow the body to move as one straight unit.
- Elevate the heels to make the exercise more difficult.

PULL-UP

Primary Muscles Trained

Latissimus dorsi, teres major, rhomboids, middle trapezius, posterior deltoids

Beginning Position

- Grasp a bar with a pronated grip at or somewhat wider than shoulder-width apart.
- The head should be positioned between the arms.
- Begin from a full hang with the elbows extended and the feet off the floor *(a)*.

Movement Phases

1. Pull the body upward until the chin is over the bar *(b)*.
2. The pull should be controlled without a kip or yanking movement.
3. Control the body back to the beginning position.

Figure 7.20 Pull-up: *(a)* beginning position; *(b)* pull to lift chin over bar.

Breathing Guidelines

Breathe in while performing the eccentric portion of the exercise and exhale during the concentric portion of the exercise.

Exercise Modifications and Variations

Supinated Grip Pull-Up

Use a supinated grip instead of a pronated grip.

Neutral Grip Pull-Up

Using parallel bars, grasp the bars with a neutral grip instead of a pronated grip.

Weighted or Band-Assisted Pull-Up

Increase the resistance of the pull-up with a weighted vest or a weight belt. For those who cannot do a pull-up, use a band between J-hooks in a power rack or tied up to the pull-up bar. Resistance will vary based on the length and width of the band.

Towel Pull-Up

Hang a towel over the bar and grasp each end of the towel with one hand; use this position as the new beginning position.

Coaching Tip

Instruct the athletes to begin and end each repetition with their arms next to their ears so that they perform the exercise through a full range of motion.

TRICEPS PUSHDOWN (MACHINE)

Primary Muscle Trained

Triceps brachii

Beginning Position

- Set up the exercise with a straight bar or rope attachment so that the handles are at shoulder height.
- Grasp the attachment with a pronated grip and the elbows at the sides (a).

Movement Phases

1. While keeping the elbows tucked to the sides, extend the arms at the elbows until the hands are down in front of the torso or hips (b).
2. While keeping the elbows tucked to the sides, control the weight back to the beginning position.

Breathing Guidelines

Breathe in while performing the eccentric portion of the exercise and exhale during the concentric portion of the exercise.

Exercise Modifications and Variations

Rope Triceps Pushdown

Use a rope attachment instead of a straight bar attachment.

Figure 7.21 Triceps pushdown (machine): (a) beginning position; (b) extend elbows.

Band Triceps Pushdown

Hang a band from a high bar and hold a band with a neutral grip at shoulder height; this is the new beginning position. Use the same movement phases as a normal triceps extension.

Coaching Tip

The attachment used to do a triceps pushdown can determine the extent to which the triceps are recruited during this exercise.

LYING TRICEPS EXTENSION

Primary Muscle Trained

Triceps brachii

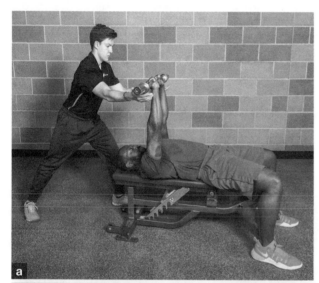

Figure 7.22   Lying triceps extension: *(a)* beginning position; *(b)* lower barbell toward head.

Beginning Position

- Lie supine on a bench with five points of contact—head, shoulders, and hips on the bench and both feet on the floor—and keep these five points of contact throughout the exercise.
- Grasp a straight bar or an EZ bar with a closed, pronated grip to hold the bar above the chest *(a)*.

Movement Phases

1. While keeping the upper arms perpendicular to the body and the elbows in place, flex the elbows to lower the bar toward the head *(b)*. Do not let the upper arms move from the beginning position.
2. Control the bar until it approaches the forehead or the top of the head.
3. Extend the elbows to raise the bar back up to the beginning position.

Breathing Guidelines

Breathe in while performing the eccentric portion of the exercise and exhale during the concentric portion of the exercise.

Spotting Guidelines

The spotter will be positioned behind the athlete's head and will help the athlete if needed during the exercise or when getting into the beginning position.

Exercise Modifications and Variations

Lying Dumbbell Triceps Extension

Use a dumbbell in each hand with a neutral grip position instead of a bar.

Coaching Tips

- Be careful not to hit the forehead with the bar or with a dumbbell on the way down.
- This exercise can produce elbow pain in some athletes, so make sure that there are alternate exercises to target the triceps.

OVERHEAD DUMBBELL TRICEPS EXTENSION

Primary Muscle Trained

Triceps brachii

Beginning Position

- Get into a seated or standing position.
- Hold the sides of a dumbbell (so the handle is parallel to the floor) or overlap the hands to cup one end of a dumbbell (so the handle is perpendicular to the floor).
- Position the dumbbell over the head with the elbows fully extended and the arms perpendicular to the bench.

Figure 7.23   Overhead dumbbell triceps extension: *(a)* lower dumbbell behind head; *(b)* press dumbbell overhead.

Movement Phases

1. While keeping the upper arms vertical, flex the elbows to lower the dumbbell toward the back of the head or neck (a). Do not let the upper arms move from the beginning position.
2. Control the dumbbell until the elbows cannot flex anymore.
3. Extend the elbows to raise the dumbbell back up to the beginning position (b).

Breathing Guidelines

Breathe in while performing the eccentric portion of the exercise and exhale during the concentric portion of the exercise.

Spotting Guidelines

Spotters can be used here to ensure that athletes do not drop the dumbbell on their heads or to help athletes to get the dumbbell into the beginning position. The spotter should stand behind the athlete and assist if the athlete is failing at a repetition.

Coaching Tips

- A seated position will keep the body more stable than a standing position.
- As weight is added, keep the same range of motion.

BARBELL BICEPS CURL

Primary Muscles Trained

Biceps brachii, brachialis, brachioradialis

Beginning Position

Stand erect and hold a bar with a shoulder-width, closed, supinated grip in front of the body with the elbows fully extended (a).

Movement Phases

1. Flex the elbows while keeping the upper arms next to the torso.
2. Raise the bar through the full range of motion only at the elbows, bringing the bar to shoulder level (b).
3. Keep the torso perpendicular to the floor; do not assist the movement by jerking the body backward.
4. Lower the bar under control back to the beginning position.

Breathing Guidelines

Breathe in while performing the eccentric portion of the exercise and exhale during the concentric portion of the exercise.

Exercise Modifications and Variations

EZ Bar Biceps Curl

Use an EZ bar instead of a straight bar.

Figure 7.24   Barbell biceps curl: *(a)* beginning position; *(b)* curl.

Cable Curl

Set up a rope attachment on the cable machine on the lowest level. Grasp the attachment with a neutral grip; this is the new beginning position.

Coaching Tip

For a variation of this exercise, perform the movement with the elbows fixed at different positions, such as by the sides of the torso or raised high up in front of the chest (i.e., with the shoulders flexed).

DUMBBELL BICEPS CURL

Primary Muscles Trained

Biceps brachii, brachialis, brachioradialis

Beginning Position

- Stand in an erect position with the knees slightly flexed.
- Hold a pair of dumbbells with a closed, neutral grip at the sides of the body with the elbows fully extended *(a)*.

Movement Phases

1. Flex the elbows while keeping the upper arms next to the torso.
2. Gradually rotate the dumbbells to a supinated (palms up) position at the top half of the movement until the dumbbells are at shoulder level *(b)*.

Figure 7.25   Dumbbell biceps curl: *(a)* beginning position; *(b)* curl.

3. Raise the dumbbells through a full range of motion (but only at the elbows, not also at the shoulders).
4. Keep the torso perpendicular to the floor; do not assist the movement by jerking the body backward.
5. Lower the dumbbells under control back to the beginning position.

Breathing Guidelines

Breathe in while performing the eccentric portion of the exercise and exhale during the concentric portion of the exercise.

Exercise Modifications and Variations

Hammer Curl

Keep a neutral grip through the entire range of motion.

Coaching Tip

More weight can be lifted using an alternating dumbbell biceps curl.

8

ANATOMICAL CORE EXERCISE TECHNIQUE

TED RATH

An expanded knowledge of proper training and conditioning practices for football athletes includes understanding the value and application of training the muscles of the **anatomical core**. Most recognizable and familiar are the rectus abdominis, transverse abdominis, internal obliques, and external obliques. Because the anatomical core is defined as the axial skeleton and all muscles with proximal attachments on the axial skeleton (1, 2), muscles other than the abdominal muscles and obliques are included, such as the serratus anterior, latissimus dorsi, spinal erectors, quadratus lumborum, and even the gluteals.

The core musculature is especially important to performance in football. The transfer of forces occurs at varying degrees during each play. The core is, in fact, the bridge that connects the many parts of the athlete's anatomy so that the transfer of forces can be powerful and efficient. Force is transferred through the kinetic chain during such common activities as sprinting, kicking, throwing, hitting, punching, and tackling (6). Without adequate core strength, these activities can lose their maximal force.

It is important to understand the difference in terminology when discussing core training. **Core exercises** (sometimes referred to as **ground-based structural exercises**) train the body to effectively transfer forces through the anatomical core regardless of the isolated musculature of the movement. Examples of core exercises are the squat, deadlift, and power clean. These exercises have a targeted musculature that does not single out the anatomical core (e.g., an athlete does not do squats primarily to train the rectus abdominis), but they promote the transfer of force through the anatomical core, and therefore they have a greater application to football than core isolation exercises (2, 4, 5, 6). **Core isolation exercises** commonly include static or dynamic muscle actions that specifically focus on the anatomical core muscles without a significant involvement of the arms or legs (2).

One of the first tasks in designing a training program for the anatomical core is to examine the movement patterns that the athlete will be required to perform (3). Football is complex; the physical stress varies based on the degree and the specific nature of the required movements. A strength and conditioning professional should identify the anatomical areas that are important to train and then develop the program appropriately.

Exercises for the anatomical core can be categorized in several ways; for this chapter, two methods are used, and each type of exercise has a positive training effect on a football athlete.

Movement Category

- *Antirotation exercises* train the athlete to withstand rotation. The goal is to increase stability and strength while the musculature of the internal and external obliques is targeted a majority of the time. *Rotational exercises*, on the other hand, are used to increase the athlete's ability to safely promote rotation through the trunk. These exercises can be very beneficial, but if done incorrectly, rotational exercises cause undue stress to the lumbar spine. Further, *anti-extension exercises* involve movements and holds that require athletes to actively resist lumbar spine extension, and *extension exercises* are those that involve active hip and spine extension. When properly implemented, these two opposing pairs of exercises (i.e., antirotation/rotational and anti-extension/extension) have a place in resistance training programs. Finally, *antilateral flexion exercises* involve movements and holds that the athlete has to perform to resist side bending. Based on the precise technique used for an exercise, a different movement category may apply than what is described in this chapter.

Exercise Category

- The off-season, preseason, in-season, and postseason programs presented in part III label the exercises for the anatomical core as *traditional* (exercises that involve flexion or extension of the spine as the involved muscles contract), *isometric* (exercises that maintain a stiff spine and are statically held for time), *medicine ball* (exercises that use the added resistance of a medicine ball while flexing, twisting, or maintaining a stiff spine), and *functional* (exercises that maintain a stiff spine while doing an activity).

Some of the exercises described in this chapter can be included in more than one category, and many of the exercise modifications or variations can fall within a different category than the primary version. Beyond exercise selection, the most important aspect of a resistance training program is technique. For strength and conditioning professionals, a primary responsibility is to design and implement techniques that will safely enable the athlete to apply a new stimulus to the body that allows for adaptation and improvement. Athletes should perform each exercise in a pain-free manner that induces the best stimulation of the targeted musculature. By adhering to strict control and efficient technique, athletes will develop the anatomical core strength needed to become more functional football athletes.

Exercise Finder

FARMER'S WALK

Figure 8.1 Farmer's walk.

Exercise Type

Antilateral flexion, functional

Primary Muscles Trained

Transverse abdominis, internal oblique, external oblique, rectus abdominis, erector spinae, iliopsoas, gluteals

Beginning Position

- Stand erect and hold one dumbbell in each hand slightly away from the sides of the body.
- Maintain a neutral hand position.

Movement Phases

1. Begin walking with control for the prescribed distance or time.
2. Keep shoulders square and level throughout, while maintaining a normal walking gait.
3. While walking and turning, maintain complete control of the dumbbells, and do not allow momentum to cause them to swing.
4. Engage the abdominals and maintain torso stiffness throughout the exercise.

Breathing Guidelines

Use smooth, controlled breaths that allow intra-abdominal pressure to be maintained throughout the exercise.

Exercise Modifications and Variations

Barbell Farmer's Walk

Perform the exercise using barbells for an increased level of difficulty.

Dumbbell Suitcase Walk

Holding one dumbbell in one hand, walk with control for the prescribed distance or time. Keep the shoulders square and level while maintaining a normal walking gait. Be sure to avoid a flare-out position in the opposite-side hip. Safely transfer the weight into the opposite hand by squatting with good technique to the floor and placing it on the floor during the transition.

Kettlebell Half-Racked Walk

Hold one kettlebell at the top of the chest similar to the arm position of the parallel-arm front squat exercise. Hold the back of the thumb against the top of the mid-chest. Keep the shoulders square and level while maintaining a normal walking gait. Maintain a rib-down position while avoiding a flare-out with the hip. Complete the prescribed distance or time on each side of the body.

Kettlebell Overhead Walk

Hold the kettlebells overhead with the shoulders safely packed down to engage the posterior musculature. Flex the wrists so that the knuckles are pointed directly at the ceiling. Keep the elbows in a locked position. For a variation, hold the kettlebell in a bottoms-up position.

Kettlebell Waiter Carry

Position the elbow and forearm at a 90-degree angle, and hold one kettlebell in a bottoms-up position. Keep the elbow in front of the body and prevent it from flaring out to the side. Keep the shoulders square and level while maintaining a normal walking gait.

Kettlebell Heartbeat Walk

The kettlebell begins at the sternum with both hands holding it. Keep the shoulders square and level in a rib-down position, and maintain a normal walking gait. Slowly press the kettlebell away from the body and return; exhale with each press.

Coaching Tips

- Keep the ribs short and compact.
- Maintain a normal walking stride and gait.

TALL KNEELING PALLOF PRESS

Exercise Type
Antirotation, functional

Primary Muscles Trained
Transverse abdominis, rectus abdominis, internal oblique, external oblique, erector spinae, gluteals

Beginning Position
- Kneel on the floor with both knees with an erect torso position.
- Use the outside hand to support the handle at the sternum (a).

Movement Phases
1. Press the handle away from the sternum in a smooth and controlled manner (b).
2. Apply pressure through the outside arm (the inside pectoral major should not be engaged).
3. Return the handle to the sternum.

Breathing Guidelines
Use strong and powerful breathing, inhaling during the eccentric phase and exhaling throughout the concentric phase.

Figure 8.2 Tall kneeling Pallof press: *(a)* beginning position; *(b)* press.

Exercise Modifications and Variations

Base Position Pallof Press

Stand with feet shoulder-width apart in a neutral foot position. Slightly flex the knees. Engage the glutes and apply pressure through the heels of the feet.

Half-Kneeling Pallof Press

Place the inside knee down. Relax the foot on the kneeling leg side. Contract the glute on the kneeling leg side.

Staggered Stance Pallof Press (Abductor Emphasis)

Stand with the inside foot forward and the toes facing directly forward. Keep the knees slightly flexed. Press the rear foot into the floor while engaging the glute.

Staggered Stance Pallof Press (Groin Emphasis)

Stand with the outside foot forward and the toes facing directly forward. Keep the knees slightly flexed. Press the rear foot into the floor while engaging the glute.

Coaching Tips

- Maintain a rib-down position with the abs contracted and engaged.
- Avoid hip flare-out.
- Stay tall with the hips fully extended over the knees.
- Square and level the shoulders.
- Keep the glutes engaged and contracted throughout.

TALL KNEELING STICK CHOP

Exercise Type
Antirotation, antilateral flexion, functional

Primary Muscles Trained
Transverse abdominis, rectus abdominis, internal oblique, external oblique, erector spinae, gluteals

Beginning Position
- Kneel with both knees on the floor.
- Take an overhand grip on the stick.
- The outside arm is flexed, and the inside arm is extended (a).
- The cable is above the athlete (high to low angle).

Movement Phases
1. Extend the outside arm to a locked-out position (b).
2. Press the inside arm away from the chest into a locked-out position (c).
3. Return the inside arm from a locked-out position to the chest (d).
4. Return the outside arm to a flexed position (e).

Breathing Guidelines
Inhale at the beginning position. Use a smooth, controlled exhale during the concentric and eccentric phases. Use one breath per repetition while maintaining intra-abdominal pressure with steady and smooth breaths.

Figure 8.3 Tall kneeling stick chop: (a) beginning position; (b) extend outside arm. (continued)

Figure 8.3 *(continued)* Tall kneeling stick chop: *(c)* press inside arm away from chest; *(d)* return inside arm to chest; *(e)* flex outside arm.

Exercise Modifications and Variations

Base Position Stick Chop

Stand in a neutral foot position with feet shoulder-width apart. Slightly flex the knees. Engage the glutes, creating pressure through the heels of the feet.

Half-Kneeling Stick Chop

Place the outside knee down. Relax the foot on the kneeling leg side. Contract the glute on the kneeling leg side.

Staggered Stance Stick Chop

Place the inside foot forward with the toes facing straight ahead. Keep the knees slightly flexed. Press the rear foot into the floor while engaging the glute.

Coaching Tips

- Maintain a rib-down position with abs contracted and engaged.
- Avoid hip flare-out.
- Stay tall with the hip(s) fully extended over the knees.
- Square and level the shoulders.
- Keep the glutes engaged and contracted throughout.

TALL KNEELING STICK LIFT

Exercise Type
Antirotation, anti-extension, functional

Primary Muscles Trained
Transverse abdominis, rectus abdominis, internal oblique, external oblique, gluteals

Beginning Position
- Kneel with both knees on the floor.
- Take an overhand grip on the stick.
- The outside arm is flexed, the inside arm is extended (a).
- The cable is below the athlete's hip (a low to a high angle).

Movement Phases
1. Extend the outside arm to a locked-out position (b).
2. Press the inside arm away from the chest using the core into a locked-out position (c).
3. Return the inside arm from a locked-out position to the chest.
4. Return the outside arm to a flexed position.

Figure 8.4   Tall kneeling stick lift: (a) beginning position; (b) extend outside arm; (c) press inside arm away from chest.

Breathing Guidelines

Inhale at the beginning position. Use a smooth, controlled exhale during the concentric and eccentric phases. Use one breath per repetition while maintaining intra-abdominal pressure with steady and smooth breaths.

Exercise Modifications and Variations

Base Position Stick Lift

Stand in a neutral foot position with the feet shoulder-width apart. Slightly flex the knees. Engage the glutes, creating pressure through the heels of the feet.

Half-Kneeling Stick Lift

Place the inside knee down. Relax the foot on the kneeling leg side. Contract the glute on the kneeling leg side.

Staggered Stance Stick Lift

Place the outside foot forward with toes facing directly forward. Keep the knees slightly flexed. Press the rear foot into the floor while engaging the glute.

Coaching Tips

- Maintain a rib-down position with the abs contracted and engaged.
- Avoid hip flare-out.
- Stay tall with the hip(s) fully extended over the knees.
- Square and level the shoulders.
- Keep the glutes engaged and contracted throughout.

SEATED PARTNER OVERHEAD TOSS

Exercise Type

Anti-extension, medicine ball

Primary Muscles Trained

Transverse abdominis, rectus abdominis, external oblique, erector spinae

Beginning Position

- Be seated with the heels touching the floor and the knees flexed *(a)*.
- Engage the abdomen by leaning back.

Movement Phases

1. A partner tosses the medicine ball with an aiming point slightly above the athlete's forehead.
2. Maintain a stiff abdomen when catching the ball.
3. Keep the arms extended with the medicine ball in the hands above the forehead *(b)*.
4. Slowly lean back while pulling in the belly button.
5. Lower until softly tapping the shoulder blades on the floor *(c)*.

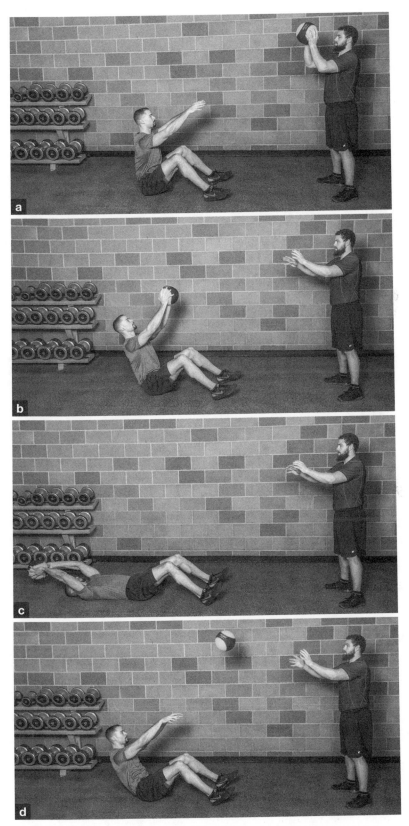

Figure 8.5 Seated partner overhead toss: *(a)* beginning position; *(b)* catch ball; *(c)* lie back; *(d)* sit up and toss ball to partner.

6. Engage the abdominal muscles and lift the shoulder blades off the floor.

7. After a full sit-up, toss the ball to the partner *(d)*.

Breathing Guidelines

Maintain intra-abdominal pressure while using steady and smooth breaths.

Exercise Modifications and Variations

Seated Partner Side-to-Side Toss

The partner stands directly to the side of the athlete. Toss the ball toward the outside arm just below the chest. Maintain a stiff torso when decelerating the medicine ball. Redirect the force into the concentric movement and toss the ball back to the partner. Rotational exercises should only be performed in a pain-free manner.

Coaching Tips

- Maintain a stiff abdomen.
- Pull the belly button into the spine.
- Eliminate momentum from the medicine ball.

FRONT-FACING MEDICINE BALL TOSS

Exercise Type

Anti-rotation, medicine ball

Primary Muscles Trained

Transverse abdominis, rectus abdominis, internal oblique, external oblique, erector spinae, gluteals

Beginning Position

- Stand facing a wall.
- Sit back into a hip-hinge position while loading the posterior chain.
- The medicine ball is loaded outside of the hip on one side of the body *(a)*.
- The athlete should use minimal or no rotation.

Movement Phases

1. Forcefully bring the hips forward while making the arms an extension of the power being generated at the hips.
2. The aiming point is at waist height *(b)*.
3. Muscle action is similar to that of a two-arm kettlebell swing.

Breathing Guidelines

Use powerful breathing techniques while exhaling during the concentric phase and inhaling throughout the eccentric phase of the exercise.

Figure 8.6 Front-facing medicine ball toss: *(a)* beginning position; *(b)* toss ball.

Coaching Tips

- Use a rapid and powerful concentric movement, similar to a two-arm kettlebell swing during the swing phase.
- Reset after each repetition.

LATERAL ROTATION MEDICINE BALL HIP TOSS

Exercise Type

Rotational, medicine ball

Primary Muscles Trained

External oblique, internal oblique, transverse abdominis, rectus abdominis, erector spinae, gluteals

Beginning Position

- Stand perpendicular to the wall that will rebound the ball.
- Sit back into a hip-hinge position while loading the posterior chain, with the wall to the side.
- The medicine ball is loaded by the outside hip away from the wall *(a)*.
- Sit in a balanced position.

Movement Phases

1. Begin to apply pressure through the outside foot away from the wall.
2. Forcefully bring the hips forward while rotating toward the wall.

Figure 8.7 Lateral rotation medicine ball hip toss: *(a)* beginning position; *(b)* finish position.

3. Extend the arms, making them an extension of the power being generated at the hips.
4. Rotate the outside hand over the top as the rotation nears completion, similar to dumping a bucket of water out.
5. Finish with square shoulders with the back foot fully extended and the foot in a plantar flexed position *(b)*.

Breathing Guidelines
Exhale powerfully during the concentric movement of the exercise. Reset and inhale during the eccentric (loading) phase.

Coaching Tips
- Turn the top hand over like dumping out a bucket of water.
- Finish tall and allow all of the force to exit through the hands.

LATERAL ROTATION MEDICINE BALL SHOT PUT

Exercise Type
Rotational, medicine ball

Primary Muscles Trained
External oblique, internal oblique, transverse abdominis, rectus abdominis, erector spinae, gluteals

Beginning Position
- Sit back into a hip-hinge position while loading the posterior chain, with the wall to the side.

- The medicine ball is located on the outside pec away from the wall.
- The outside hand is positioned behind the medicine ball to use as a pushing hand.
- The elbow is raised to just below parallel to the shoulder on the medicine ball side (a).

Movement Phases

1. Begin to press through the outside foot while extending the hips and beginning to rotate toward the wall.
2. The hand becomes an extension of the power being generated from the hips and through the torso.
3. "Squash the bug" with the outside foot while rotating.
4. Finish with square shoulders with the back foot fully extended and the foot in a plantar flexed position (b).

Breathing Guidelines

- Exhale powerfully during the concentric movement of the exercise.
- Reset and inhale during the eccentric (loading) phase.

Exercise Modifications and Variations

Lateral Rotation Medicine Ball Shot Put With Hip Disassociation

This exercise can be executed while using hip disassociation for quarterbacks.

Coaching Tips

- Move from low to high from start to finish.
- Finish tall, allowing the force to transfer from the floor and out through the ball.

Figure 8.8 Lateral rotation medicine ball shot put: (a) beginning position; (b) finish position.

Stan Grossfeld/The Boston Globe via Getty Images

Force is transferred through the anatomical core during sprinting, kicking, throwing, hitting, punching, and tackling.

BARBELL ROLLOUT

Exercise Type
Anti-extension, functional

Primary Muscles Trained
Transverse abdominis, rectus abdominis, latissimus dorsi, erector spinae, gluteals

Beginning Position
- Kneel with the hands on the barbell just below the chest (a).
- Keep the glutes engaged.
- Drive pressure through the hands, and drive the barbell down into the floor.
- Engage the lower abdomen, with the belly button drawn back into the spine.

Movement Phases
1. Using the hips to generate force forward, press and roll the barbell away from the body.
2. Maintain glute contraction throughout.
3. Slowly roll forward and extend the arms to an overhead position (b).
4. Pull the barbell back to the beginning position beneath the chest.

Breathing Guidelines
Inhale at the beginning position. Use a smooth, controlled exhale during the concentric and eccentric phases with one breath per repetition.

Figure 8.9 Barbell rollout: (a) hands on barbell under chest; (b) press barbell out and extend arms overhead.

Coaching Tips

- Maintain a stiff abdomen.
- Maintain a rib-down position for the duration of the exercise.
- This exercise should not cause lower back discomfort.

ABDOMINAL CRUNCH

Exercise Type
Anti-extension, traditional

Primary Muscles Trained
Transverse abdominis, rectus abdominis, external oblique

Beginning Position
- Lie in a supine position on a floor or mat.
- Place the heels on a bench with the hips and knees flexed to about 90 degrees.
- Fold the arms across the chest or abdomen (a).

Movement Phases

1. Flex the neck to move the chin toward the chest.
2. Keeping the buttocks and lower back neutral and stationary on the mat, curl the torso toward the thighs until the upper back is off the mat (b).
3. Uncurl the torso back to the beginning position.
4. Keep the feet, buttocks, lower back, and arms in the same position.

Breathing Guidelines

Exhale during the concentric phase while inhaling throughout the entire eccentric phase.

Exercise Modifications and Variations

Crossover Crunch

Cross one leg over the other. The hand opposite the crossed leg is placed on the head with the elbow pointed out and away from the body. Crunch and make contact between the opposite elbow and knee.

Suitcase Crunch

Place the hands on the head for a landmark only; do not pull the head forward with the arms. The head and heels begin on the floor; elbows and knees meet simultaneously in the middle for a split second and return to the beginning position.

Single-Leg Extended Crunch

Extend one leg and engage the quadriceps. Engage the abdomen. Bring the shoulder blades off the floor and squeeze in the contracted position.

Side Crunch

Begin in a side-lying position with legs slightly flexed. Hands on head.

Coaching Tip

Maintain a rib-down position for the duration of the exercise.

Figure 8.10 Abdominal crunch: (a) beginning position; (b) curl.

FRONT PLANK

Exercise Type

Anti-extension, isometric

Primary Muscles Trained

Transverse abdominis, rectus abdominis, obliques, erector spinae

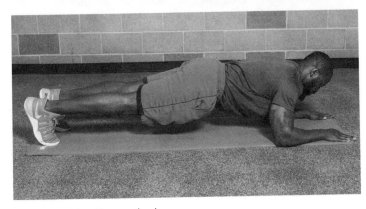

Figure 8.11   Front plank.

Static Position

1. Place the elbows directly underneath the shoulders.
2. Place the hands flat on the floor.
3. Keep the hips parallel to the floor.
4. Actively pull the elbows to the toes in an isometric fashion to ensure engagement from the abdominals and quads.
5. Hold the static position for the prescribed amount of time.

Breathing Guidelines

Use smooth, controlled breathing throughout. Inhale through the nose, and exhale through the mouth in a smooth but forceful manner.

Exercise Modifications and Variations

Side Plank

Position the elbow directly below the shoulder. Keep the shoulder, hip, and ankle in alignment. With hips forward and shoulders back, maintain a straight line throughout.

Front Plank on Hands

Position the hands directly underneath the shoulders. Maintain alignment with the wrist, elbow, and shoulder. Maintain a straight line throughout.

Side Plank on Hand

Position the hand directly under the shoulder. Maintain alignment with the wrist, elbow, and shoulder. Extend the top hand toward the ceiling. With hips forward and shoulders back, maintain a straight line throughout.

Side Plank With Hip Flexion

Raise the top leg. Slowly bring the top knee toward the chest and return to the beginning position for the desired number of repetitions.

Coaching Tips

- Position the elbows directly below the shoulder.
- Maintain a stiff abdomen.
- Maintain a rib-down position for the duration of the exercise.
- Keep the legs locked out (quads engaged).
- Keep the palms up, shoulder blades separated.
- This exercise can be performed for repetitions or for a prescribed amount of time.

SIDE PLANK WITH ISOMETRIC GROIN HOLD

Exercise Type

Antilateral flexion, isometric

Primary Muscles Trained

Obliques, erector spinae, hip adductors

Static Position

1. Lie on the floor on the left side with the left elbow under the left shoulder.
2. Position the left forearm perpendicular to the torso.
3. Stack the lower leg portion of the right leg on top of a bench with the left leg extended underneath the bench. Begin with the majority of the right leg on the bench; over time, place less of the leg on the bench for increased difficulty.
4. The body's weight will be supported by the left arm.
5. Keep the top shoulder, hip, knee, and ankle in alignment.
6. Hold the static position for the prescribed amount of time.

Breathing Guidelines

Use smooth, controlled breathing throughout. Inhale and exhale through the mouth in a smooth but forceful manner.

Exercise Modifications and Variations

Side Plank With Isometric Groin Hold on Stability Ball

Place the top leg on an unstable surface such as a stability ball.

Figure 8.12   Side plank with isometric groin hold.

Coaching Tips

- Maintain a stiff abdomen.
- Maintain a rib-down position for the duration of the exercise.
- Keep the left elbow directly under the left shoulder.

ALTERNATING LEG LOWER

Exercise Type

Anti-extension, functional

Primary Muscles Trained

Transverse abdominis, rectus abdominis

Beginning Position

- Lie on the floor faceup.
- The lower back is pressed into the floor.
- Extend both legs up (a).
- Keep the toes pulled down toward the athlete.

Movement Guidelines

1. Slowly lower one leg down.
2. Maintain flexed quadriceps.
3. Pause just before the heel reaches the floor (b).
4. Slowly return the leg to the beginning position and begin on the opposite side.

Breathing Guidelines

Use smooth, controlled breathing throughout. Inhale and exhale through the mouth in a smooth but forceful manner.

Figure 8.13 Alternating leg lower: (a) beginning position; (b) lower leg.

Exercise Modifications and Variations

Core-Activated Leg Lower

Use a cable pulley or band. The cable is above the athlete, slightly above the forehead. Extend the arms to grasp the handles. Engage the core by pulling the handles to the floor.

Coaching Tips

- Engage and flex the quads throughout the entire exercise.
- Maintain a neutral spine and hips.

SUPINE GLUTE BRIDGE

Exercise Type

Extension, functional

Primary Muscles Trained

Erector spinae, gluteus maximus, hamstrings (semimembranosus, semitendinosus, biceps femoris)

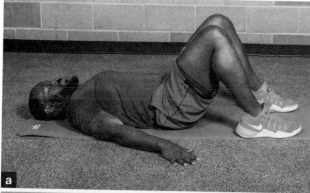

Figure 8.14 Supine glute bridge: *(a)* beginning position; *(b)* lift hips.

Beginning Position

- Lie faceup with the knees flexed and the feet flat on the floor *(a)*.
- The lower back is pressed into the floor.
- Keep the feet shoulder-width apart and close enough to the body that the heels can be touched by the fingers.

Movement Phases

1. Press the feet into the floor.
2. Pressing through the hips, raise the pelvis toward the ceiling *(b)*.
3. Keep a straight line from the shoulder to the knee.
4. Keep the glutes tight, hamstrings loose.
5. Pause in the contracted position.
6. Slowly return the hips to the floor.

Breathing Guidelines

Inhale at the beginning position. Use a smooth, controlled exhale during the concentric and eccentric phases with one breath per repetition.

Exercise Modifications and Variations

Single-Leg Glute Bridge

Lift one knee into the chest. Pull the resting leg into the chest with the arms. Press through the hip while raising the pelvis toward the ceiling.

Single-Leg Glute Bridge With Tennis Ball

Lift one knee into the chest. Place a tennis ball between the abdomen and the resting leg. Press through the hip while raising the pelvis toward the ceiling.

Core-Activated Glute Bridge

Use a cable pulley or band. The cable is above the athlete, slightly above the forehead. Extend the arms to grasp the handles. Engage the core by pulling the handles into the floor.

Mini-Band Glute Bridge

Use a mini-band around the bottom portion of the thigh. Engage the gluteals by pressing the knees out and creating tension on the band. This exercise can be performed while holding a static position or for repetitions.

Glute Bridge on Bench

Place the shoulder blades on a bench. The knees and legs should be at a 90-degree angle in the contracted position.

Coaching Tips

- Maintain a stiff spine during the exercise.
- Maintain a rib-down position for the duration of the exercise.

STABILITY BALL REVERSE BACK EXTENSION

Exercise Type

Extension, traditional

Primary Muscles Trained

Erector spinae

Beginning Position

- Kneel on the floor in front of a stability ball.
- Roll forward onto the ball so that the abdomen rests on the top of the ball in a prone plank position.

Figure 8.15   Stability ball reverse back extension: (a) beginning position; (b) lift legs.

- Place the hands directly underneath or slightly in front of the shoulders on the floor (a).
- Hold the legs together and hold the torso in a rigid position during the exercise with the elbows fully extended.

Movement Phases

1. Keeping the lower body in a rigid position, extend at the hips to raise the legs.
2. Raise the legs until they are in line with the torso (b).
3. Lower the legs back down to the beginning position.

Breathing Guidelines

Inhale at the beginning position. Use a smooth, controlled exhale during the concentric and eccentric phases with one breath per repetition.

Exercise Modifications and Variations

Stability Ball Back Extension

Follow the same guidelines as for the stability ball reverse back extension, but anchor the feet on the floor and raise the upper body until it is in line with the hips and thighs.

Roman Chair Back Extension

Instead of a stability ball, use a Roman chair (bench) with the height of the footplate adjusted so that the hips are aligned with the top of the hip pad. Raise the upper body until it is in line with the legs. Allow the upper body to lower until it is approximately perpendicular to the floor (depending on the design of the chair).

Coaching Tips

- Do not rotate the lower body, hips, or upper body during the movement.
- Do not swing or use any other movements to raise the legs.

PART III

PROGRAM DESIGN GUIDELINES AND SAMPLE PROGRAMS

9

OFF-SEASON PROGRAMMING

JERRY PALMIERI, DARREN KREIN, AND ZAC WOODFIN

This chapter discusses the design of the off-season program for the football athlete, including an explanation of the goals and objectives for this phase of training and the length of training periods that are available for each level of competition (high school, college, and professional). Due to the length of each season and the yearly schedule, each level has a different amount of time that is devoted to off-season training.

Because the off-season training program is usually considered the start of a new yearly cycle of training, it is beneficial to create a training cycle that includes the three common phases of training: Hypertrophy/strength endurance, basic strength, and strength/power. This organization of the training program allows athletes to make good progressions in the off-season as they come out of the postseason training program.

The primary exercises used in the off-season program are provided, followed by the design of a generic (base) resistance training program. Then, to meet the performance needs of the six categories of football positions, the base program is adjusted while still observing the linear volume and intensity progression from medium to medium-heavy to heavy loads.

GOALS AND OBJECTIVES

The off-season provides the greatest opportunity for football athletes to make their biggest physical gains. Since there are no games or formal practices during this time of year, training becomes the priority. Athletes can give their sole attention to making themselves better physically.

One of the primary goals of the off-season program is to develop strength and power. Football is a very physical sport that requires strength and speed to perform at a high level. When one combines strength and speed, power is the result. Because the game involves a significant amount of physical contact, achieving a certain body size is another objective. The formula for force is mass times acceleration. Increasing the mass without decreasing acceleration will yield greater force. The athlete wants to increase lean body mass as much as possible, so long as this increase does not jeopardize speed, agility, or ability to change direction.

Running in football typically consists of three components: Linear, lateral, and reactive. While one needs to run fast, it is imperative to move fast in multiple planes. Furthermore, the athlete must be able to quickly respond to what he sees. Strength and size are valuable characteristics of the football athlete, but if the athlete gains too much mass with little regard to developing more power, the athlete's ability to run will be hindered, and that mass will become less effective. Enhancing one's ability to run and move quickly is another objective of the off-season program. Flexibility facilitates the football athlete's movements on the field;

therefore, flexibility training will improve range of motion and will allow the athlete to move better in the various planes of his position.

Conditioning is the final objective of the off-season. While the ability to endure is a significant factor for the football athlete, it is not as significant as the previous four goals of the off-season program. The season is still several months away, so there is plenty of time to get in peak condition. Putting too much emphasis on conditioning during the off-season could limit progress toward the other goals.

LENGTH OF THE PROGRAM

How long the strength and conditioning professional has to train athletes in the off-season is usually determined by two factors: The football coach and the governing bodies setting the rules for the sport. Some college football coaches will start spring ball later in the semester to allow for the longest continuous training time during the off-season program. Others may want to break the off-season up with two short periods of training before and after spring ball. The National Collegiate Athletic Association (NCAA) establishes certain weeks as "dead weeks" when no organized training can take place. The National Football League (NFL) designates only two weeks that are considered truly off-season training, with another three weeks when the coaches can take the athletes on the field for drills and learning. While training continues during this phase of the off-season, the strength and conditioning professional faces some limitations. After this period are three weeks of organized team activities, which involves full team organized practices. A mandatory minicamp makes up the final week of the off-season program.

The high school football coach probably has the greatest opportunity to organize the longest continuous off-season program; however, some difficulties may arise because high school football athletes may also participate in other sports. One solution for the high school coach is to have an 11-week training cycle followed by a testing week and a transition week. Thirteen weeks is probably about the length of a seasonal sport. The athletes who are not involved in another sport get a significant amount of time to train and then transition into their spring sport, or to begin a new 11-week cycle as stronger athletes. For the athletes who played a winter sport, they can now join their teammates as they all start a new 11-week cycle together.

The sample off-season programs in this chapter are based on an 11-week period. Table 9.1 shows how that sample program can be altered based on the time allotted at the high school, college, and professional levels.

Table 9.1   Program Time Allotment Based on Level of Play

Level of play	Hypertrophy/ strength endurance (phase 1)	Unload/ variation (version 1)	Basic strength (phase 2)	Unload/ variation (version 2)	Strength/ power (phase 3)	Total weeks
High school	3 weeks	1 week	3 weeks	1 week	3 weeks	11 weeks
College	2 weeks	1 week*	3 weeks	1 week*	3 weeks	9 weeks
Professional	2 weeks	—	3 weeks	—	—	5 weeks

* For college, the unload/variation phase can be version 1 or version 2, but not both.

STRUCTURE OF THE PROGRAM

The off-season program is a four-days-per-week split routine with the upper body trained on Monday and Thursday and the lower body trained on Tuesday and Friday. Wednesday is an off day.

The week begins with an upper body training session, since lower body training sessions are likely to be more stressful on the neuromuscular system due to the relatively larger amount of muscle mass involved and the heavier loads typically lifted when training the lower body. Coming off a weekend when it is uncertain what the athletes did or did not do, it is safer to have a workout that will not overly stress the neuromuscular system. Tuesday will be a lower body training session that will put greater stress on the neuromuscular system. Wednesday becomes an off day other than the use of recovery modalities to enhance the recovery process. Thursday and Friday become the second upper and lower body training days, respectively.

Table 9.2 shows a weekly schedule for the four-days-per-week split routine.

Table 9.2 Weekly Schedule: Four-Days-a-Week Split Routine

Day	Focus	Notes
Monday	Upper body	Lower stress day (coming off the weekend)
Tuesday	Lower body	Higher stress day
Wednesday	Off	Recovery day
Thursday	Upper body	Lower stress day
Friday	Lower body	Higher stress day

RECOMMENDED EXERCISES

The off-season resistance training program should be designed to develop the best possible football athlete, not an Olympic lifter, powerlifter, or bodybuilder. Although exercises from these other sports will be used in the program, they are programmed in a way to maximize the performance of the football athlete.

Total Body Exercises

These total body exercises are specific to the off-season and other seasons where noted.

• Dumbbell clean complex involves multiple exercises that together train the entire body with relatively moderate to light weight. It is used in the preparation phase to train the various movements and increase the athlete's work capacity.

• Kettlebell (KB) swings develop the great hip extension that is needed for blocking and tackling. KB swings are also performed during the preseason.

• Muscle snatch is used in the first phase of the program to emphasize the full extension of the hips and knees that is needed to perform the power clean and power snatch.

• Power clean, one-arm dumbbell snatch, and power snatch are all explosive or power exercises that involve a quick generation of force from the hips and legs. Snatch pulls are done in phases 1 and 2, while the one-arm dumbbell snatch is done in the variation week in preparation for the power snatches that will be performed in phase 2. Hang cleans from the mid-thigh position followed by front squats are good technique exercises leading up to the power cleans that will be done in phase 2.

• Power clean complex, power clean combo, and dumbbell clean to push press are all combination exercises that create variation and efficient use of training time. The dumbbell clean to push press is also used in-season.

- Push jerk is an excellent exercise for generating force from the hips and legs into the arms. Since football is a pushing sport, one has to generate force from one's hips and legs while trying to drive the opponent backwards. The push jerk is also incorporated into the preseason program.

- Snatch pulls and clean pulls are shorter pull variations of the power snatch and power clean, allowing the athlete to use heavier loads. These movements are simpler to learn and can be used solely by a coach who is not confident in teaching the power snatch and the power clean. Clean pulls will also be performed during the preseason.

- Clean and jerk is an excellent combination exercise involving two key movements in the program, the power clean and the push jerk. Clean and jerk is done in the preseason as well.

Lower Body Exercises

Because of the value of lower body strength for the football athlete, all of the lower body exercises identified in this list are used during the off-season and in at least one other season as described.

- Back squat is a great developer of strength in the hips and legs. Normally, significant loads can be handled in this exercise, providing a substantial overload to these working muscles. This exercise will be done each week throughout the program. Back squat is also a foundational exercise for the pre- and in-season programs.

- Front squat, whether done with a bar or dumbbells on the shoulders, not only develops the legs but also strengthens the anatomical core, forcing the athlete to maintain a vertical torso. A strong core is beneficial for performing other exercises in the program as well as for keeping the body from collapsing upon contact when blocking and tackling. Front squat is used during the preseason as well.

- Deadlift and trap bar deadlift require the body to generate force from a low beginning position, similar to an offensive or defensive lineman generating force out of his stance. Athletes at these two positions will add the trap bar deadlift to their programs in phases 2 and 3 of the off-season and during phase 2 of the preseason.

- Walking lunge, step-up, split squat, and single-leg squat are designed to develop single-leg strength. Athletes will often find themselves driving off the ground on one leg. They might be cutting, jumping, or landing on one leg. They need single-leg strength to keep themselves from collapsing and also to generate force. These exercises will change with each phase to create variation in the program. Lunge to step-up was added to these exercises during the preseason.

- Band terminal knee extension (TKE), single-leg short arc, and single-leg partial squat develop the vastus medialis, adding stability to the knee. Band TKE is also used in-season.

- Side plank with isometric groin hold, lateral lunge, and isometric groin hold or squeeze develop the groin. Groin strength is critical due to the amount of change of direction that occurs in football. These exercises are done during the preseason and in-season programs as well.

- Hip thrust and single-leg hip thrust are developers of the gluteal muscles. These muscles are very powerful and play a significant role in running. This program introduces the movement with the single-leg hip thrust using body weight only, and it then transitions to both legs with the barbell hip thrust. It is also incorporated during the preseason and in-season.

- Romanian deadlift, stability ball triple threat, glute-ham raise, dumbbell hamstring walk, and hamstring slide develop the hamstrings. Maintaining a good balance of strength between the hamstrings and quadriceps is critical in the prevention of a lower body injury to the thigh. These hamstring developers are used during the preseason and in-season programs as well.

- Ankle rotation on balance disc strengthens the muscles surrounding the ankles. A severe ankle sprain can limit an athlete for up to six weeks, so this area must not be overlooked. This exercise is also programmed for the preseason and in-season.

Upper Body Exercises

Upper body exercises enhance the athlete's ability to push, while also ensuring good anterior to posterior muscular balance. Several of these exercises are done in multiple seasons of training.

- Bench press, incline bench press, dumbbell bench press, dumbbell incline bench press, close-grip bench press, and bench lockout develop the chest, shoulders, and triceps in a pushing movement. Both the bar and dumbbells are used in the bench and incline during the preparation phase to create significant volume in order to enhance the hypertrophy of these muscles. These exercises also add lean body mass to the upper body, which is valuable in protecting the body from the impact of collisions. These pressing movements are also involved in the preseason, yet with less volume.

- Chain bench press is a dynamic exercise that emphasizes pressing the bar with speed. This exercise will be used in phases 2 and 3 for the development of power, while also being incorporated during the preseason and in-season programs.

- Dumbbell shoulder press and shoulder press add significant mass and strength to the shoulders. Dumbbells are used in phase 1 to develop unilateral strength, prior to using a barbell in phase 2. Shoulder press is also prescribed during the preseason.

- Lat pulldown and bent-over row exercises help to create muscular balance between the chest and back muscles. With great emphasis placed upon the pushing exercises, it is not uncommon for an athlete to develop an imbalance between the chest and back muscles. Such an imbalance can lead to injury over time. These exercises are also done throughout the preseason and in-season.

- Power shrugs and neck exercises build up the trapezius and neck muscles, providing protection for the neck area. Power shrugs are done, as opposed to a slow elevation and rolling back of the shoulders, to supplement the pull on the power clean and snatch.

- Assistance exercises for the shoulder are designed to increase the mass of the shoulder region and to create muscular balance between its anterior and posterior muscles.

- Because of the pressing movements performed in the program, there is significant development of the internal shoulder rotation muscles. Therefore, external shoulder rotation exercises must be included in the program to create muscular balance in the shoulder. These exercises are also included in the preseason.

- Medicine ball chest pass and medicine ball drop develop power in the upper body during phases 2 and 3. In phase 3, each set will use decreasing weights to accentuate the power development. These power movements are performed during the preseason as well.

Core Exercises

Exercises that strengthen the anatomical core help to improve the athlete's ability to transfer strength and power from the lower body to the upper body and vice versa. In an off-season program, traditional and medicine ball exercises for the core are performed at the end of the upper body workout on Monday and Thursday, and isometric and functional exercises are performed at the end of the lower body workout on Tuesday and Friday.

POSITIONAL ADJUSTMENTS

When designing an off-season program, a base program (table 9.3 on page 191) must first be created, and then adjustments are made according to positional needs.

Offensive and Defense Linemen (OL and DL)

There are no alterations to the base program for the offensive and defensive linemen in phase 1. In phases 2 and 3, bench lockouts were added to work on the finishing press of close line play. Chain squats replace single-leg exercises for the development of lower body power. Trap bar deadlifts were also added to improve their lower body strength coming out of a stance. In phase 3, the offensive linemen did their medicine ball chest pass out of their stance followed by 3 pass set passes. They do 3 repetitions of 3 pass sets in each set, decreasing the weight of the medicine ball to enhance the power of the pass set. Complex jumps onto a box are done after each set of chain squats for additional power development (table 9.4 on page 196).

- *Phase 1.* No changes
- *Phase 2.* Bench lockouts 3 × 3, chain squats, and trap bar deadlifts 4 × 4
- *Phase 3.*
  - OL: Medicine ball chest pass 3 × 3+3 with decreasing weights for each set
  - DL: Chest pass with decreasing weights, bench lockouts 3 × 2, chain squats with complex jumps onto a box 6 × 2, and trap bar deadlifts 4 × 2

Tight Ends (TE), Fullbacks (FB), and Linebackers (LB)

The tight ends, fullbacks, and linebackers physically fall in between the strong linemen and the fast skill athletes. As with the linemen, chain squats were added to their program in phases 2 and 3 to develop lower body power, yet they still do 2 sets of a single-leg exercise. In phase 3, complex jumps onto a box are done after each set of chain squats for additional power development. Athletes at these positions are vulnerable to a neck and shoulder **burner**, a nerve injury that results from trauma to the neck and shoulder, causing tingling and weakness down the arm. Several exercises are added to the program to strengthen this region and to prevent burners from occurring (table 9.5 on page 201).

- *Phase 1.* Isometric neck stretch
- *Phase 2.* Burner combo, isometric neck stretch, dumbbell neck stretch shrugs, chain squats, and split squats 2 × 6L,R (i.e., 1 set of 6 repetitions with the left leg, then 1 set of 6 repetitions with the right leg, then rest, and repeat)
- *Phase 3.* Burner combo, isometric neck stretch, dumbbell neck stretch shrugs, chain squats with complex jumps onto the box 6 × 2, and single-leg squats 2 × 3L,R

Wide Receivers (WR) and Running Backs (RB)

While wide receivers and running backs need to be strong, they do not want to add too much body mass that may hinder their speed. For their upper back development, which can add significant mass to the upper body, these athletes did weighted pull-ups and weighted inverted rows in phases 1 and 3. In phase 2 they did some traditional back exercises to create variation in their program (table 9.6 on page 207).

- *Phase 1.* Weighted pull-ups 4 × 10 and weighted inverted rows 4 × 10
- *Phase 2.* Close-grip lat pulldowns 3 × 6-8, standing one-arm dumbbell rows 3 × 6-8, and seated rows 5 × 6-8
- *Phase 3.* Weighted pull-ups 5 × 5 and weighted inverted rows 5 × 5

Defensive Backs (DB)

The adjustments to the defensive backs' program are a combination of the WR/RB and TE/FB/LB routines. These athletes are concerned about too much body mass hindering their speed, so they did weighted pull-ups and weighted inverted rows in phases 1 and 3, while doing some traditional back exercises in phase 2 in order to create variation in their program. Defensive backs are also vulnerable to neck and shoulder burners (table 9.7 on page 212).

- *Phase 1.* Weighted pull-ups 4 × 10, weighted inverted rows 4 × 10, and isometric neck stretch
- *Phase 2.* Close-grip lat pulldowns 3 × 6-8, standing one-arm dumbbell rows 3 × 6-8, burner combo 2 × 10L,R, isometric neck stretch, dumbbell neck stretch shrugs, and seated rows 5 × 6-8
- *Phase 3.* Weighted pull-ups 5 × 5, burner combo 2 × 10L,R, isometric neck stretch, dumbbell neck stretch shrugs, and weighted inverted rows 5 × 5

Quarterbacks (QB)

Quarterbacks need to maintain flexibility in their shoulders, so variations of the dumbbell bench press and dumbbell incline bench press replace these movements with the bar, along with some different forms of push-ups. Push-ups are a good exercise that not only strengthen the chest and shoulder but also add stability to that region. Medicine ball chest passes are eliminated from the workout. In phase 1, these athletes do alternating dumbbell bench press and incline bench press, along with stability ball push-ups and weighted push-ups. Grip strength to hold onto the ball, and torso rotation to throw the ball, are factors that must be addressed in the QB's program. Throughout all three phases, extensor bands to strengthen the fingers and 15 seconds of an isometric grip on the football are done after the prescribed grip work of the base program. Half-kneeling stick chops and lifts are done in all three phases for torso rotation. In phase 2, one-arm dumbbell bench presses or incline bench presses are performed instead of the bar, while chain bench is replaced by band push-ups and stability ball push-ups (feet on box). Dumbbell pullovers, which resemble the throwing motion, are done in place of suspension trainer rows. The shoulder press will continue to be performed with dumbbells as opposed to the bar to put less stress on the shoulder joint. Similarly, dumbbells will be used for the snatch exercise as well. To enhance the stretch reflex of the throwing motion, medi ball overhead one-arm quick toss is prescribed. Because the quarterback must decelerate the arm when finishing a throw, medicine ball deceleration throws are included in the workout. Seated partner side-to-side toss and lateral leg raise enhance torso rotation, while medicine ball wood chops assist in developing the power of the throw. In phase 3, two-arm dumbbell bench press or incline bench press are done instead of the bar, while chain push-ups and push-ups (on stability ball) (one foot on box) replace the chain bench. Cable pullovers on a stability ball create variation for the dumbbell pullovers used in phase 2. Medicine ball around the world (decreasing weight) and dumbbell twists develop power in torso rotation, while the kneeling medicine ball blob throw 3 × 5 (decreasing weights) enhances the power of the throw (table 9.8 on page 218).

- *Phase 1.* Alternating dumbbell bench press 3 × 8-10 (in place of bench press); stability ball push-ups 3 × 10 (instead of dumbbell incline bench press); to plate holds, add extensor bands 2 × 10L,R and grip football for 15 seconds; alternating dumbbell incline bench press 3 × 8-10 (in place of incline bench press); weighted push-ups 3 × 8 (instead of dumbbell bench press); half-kneeling stick chops 10L,R; half-kneeling stick lifts 10L,R; and to grip exercises, add extensor bands 2 × 10L,R and grip football for 15 seconds.

- *Phase 2.* One-arm dumbbell bench press or one-arm dumbbell incline bench press 4 × 5 (in place of barbell bench press); dumbbell pullovers 3 × 8 (instead of suspension trainer rows); no medicine ball chest pass; dumbbell shoulder press (as opposed to a barbell); dumbbell snatch (in place of a barbell power snatch); medi ball overhead one-arm quick toss 2 × 10L,R and deceleration throws 2 × 10L,R; seated partner side-to-side toss and lateral leg raise; to plate holds, add extensor bands 2 × 10L,R and grip football for 15 seconds; band push-ups 3 × 6 and stability ball push-ups (feet on box) 3 × 8 (in place of chain bench press); half-kneeling stick chops 10L,R; half-kneeling stick lifts 10L,R; to grip exercises, add extensor bands 2 × 10L,R and grip football for 15 seconds; and medicine ball wood chops.

- *Phase 3.* Dumbbell bench press or dumbbell incline bench press 4 × 5 (instead of a barbell); only 3 sets of close-grip lat pulldowns; stability ball cable pullovers 3 × 6; no medicine ball chest pass; medi ball overhead one-arm quick toss 2 × 10L,R and deceleration throws 2 × 10L,R; medicine ball around the world (decreasing weight) and dumbbell twists 2 × 10L,R; to plate holds, add extensor bands 2 × 10L,R and grip football for 15 seconds; chain push-ups 4 × 3; stability ball push-ups (1 foot on box); half-kneeling stick chops 10L,R; half-kneeling stick lifts 10L,R; to grip, add extensor bands 2 × 10L,R and grip football for 15 seconds; and kneeling medicine ball blob throw 3 × 5 (decreasing weights).

Kickers (K) and Punters (P)

Kickers and punters earn their respect from teammates with their legs. Having a well-developed hip region is critical for these athletes, so the first groin exercise of the week is replaced by the 4-way hip machine (hip flexion, extension, adduction, and abduction). Since upper body power is not as necessary for these athletes, medicine ball chest passes were eliminated (table 9.9 on page 224).

- Add 4-way hip machine for the first groin-focused exercise of the week in each phase.
- Eliminate medicine ball chest passes in phases 2 and 3.

VOLUME AND INTENSITY

The off-season cycle (see table 9.10 on page 229) begins with high volume and low intensity and progresses over the weeks to low volume and high intensity. Phase 1 is programmed to introduce the athlete back to training. Oftentimes the athletes are transitioning into the off-season training program from a period that had a reduction in training. This phase is designed to increase muscular hypertrophy and develop one's work capacity in preparation for the heavier loads to follow in the program. Extra effort is spent on mastering the techniques of the exercises. Phase 2 features a decrease in volume and an increase in intensity. Full power-generating Olympic lifts are incorporated into the program as opposed to the partial, technique-oriented exercises that were done in phase 1. Phase 3 shows a further decrease in volume and an increase in intensity, bringing the training loads to the highest level of the cycle.

After phase 1 and phase 2, there is an unload/variation week. This week is designed to create some variation in the program, while allowing the body to recover. The volume of training is decreased during this week with the load intensity in the medium range. There are only three training days, which promotes the athlete's recovery.

Interpreting the Sample Program Tables

The cycles shown in the sample programs have the specific percentages of the 1RM and the repetitions to be performed for each of the cycled exercises. If a percentage is not listed for a cycled exercise, the athlete should select a weight of the prescribed intensity that can be performed with good technique. The percentage is in the numerator of the fraction, while the number of repetitions is in the denominator. If multiple sets are performed of the same percentage and repetitions, the number of sets will be preceded by ×. For example, 80/5 × 3 means 80% of the 1RM for 3 sets of 5 repetitions. If there is no percentage or intensity assigned, the number of sets is listed first and the number of repetitions is listed second (e.g., 3 × 8 means 3 sets of 8 repetitions).

Gray rows in the programs indicate position-specific changes from the base program (table 9.3 on page 191).

The pattern is a linear cycle of three-week phases that progress in intensity each week from medium to medium heavy to heavy. The unload/variation week follows the week of heavy training before beginning the next phase of training. At the conclusion of phase 3, a week of testing could be conducted to determine new maximums for the cycled exercises.

While the cycle has the specific percentages and repetitions for each cycled exercise, generally speaking, the power-based Olympic lift exercises in phase 1 have an intensity level of 67% to 77% of the 1RM for 4 or 5 repetitions. The non-power core (or primary) exercises (not to be mistaken for exercises that train the anatomical core; see chapter 8) are performed at 65% to 77% of the 1RM for 8 to 10 repetitions. The Olympic lift exercises in phase 2 use loads at 75% to 85% of the 1RM for 3 repetitions. The non-power core exercises are trained at 75% to 87% of the 1RM for 5 repetitions. Phase 3 has the Olympic lift exercises hitting 80% to 92% of the 1RM for sets of 2 repetitions, while the non-power core exercises are prescribed at 80% to 92% of the 1RM for sets of 3 repetitions.

The training percentages, based on the athlete's 1RM, progress over the weeks of each phase in order to reach the intensity prescribed for the repetition maximum for that phase as determined in table 4.1 on page 54. Initially, when doing multiple sets of an exercise, athletes will be unable to complete the repetitions at the percentage prescribed in table 4.1; however, as they increase their strength, they should be able to complete the repetitions at that intensity by the end of the phase. These percentages are programmed from a true 1RM. If the athlete is working from a predicted 1RM, the percentages may need to be slightly decreased.

The assistance exercises typically are trained at 8 to 10 repetitions in phase 1, 6 to 8 repetitions in phase 2, and 4 to 6 repetitions in phase 3.

ORDER OF EXERCISES

It is recommended that the exercises in a training session be ordered in the following manner:

1. Olympic lifts (perform first in a workout),
2. non-power-core exercises,
3. assistance exercises, and
4. anatomical core exercises (to conclude the workout).

The sample workouts in this chapter have some of the exercises paired on a push-to-pull system for time efficiency. While one group of muscles are recovering, an exercise training the antagonistic group of muscles is performed. These exercises should not be trained as a circuit with no rest; instead they should be done with some recovery between sets so significant loads can be handled.

CONCLUSION

This chapter has presented some philosophical guidelines for training football athletes during the off-season. Many different exercises can be used to accomplish the same goals. The programs presented here are only samples. The off-season is a vital training period for football athletes, so strength and conditioning professionals should use the information presented in this chapter to design off-season training programs that best meet their needs.

Warm-Ups

WARM-UP 1

Foam roll, activation, and movement-based warm-up
Warm-up with light weights (5 repetitions each movement)

- Lateral raise
- Front raise
- Rear lateral raise
- Curl to press
- Overhead triceps extension
- External rotation

WARM-UP 2

Foam roll, activation, and movement-based warm-up
Band glute strengthening
Lateral leg step through (1 × 10 each side)
Bar warm-up (45 lb)

- Snatch (5 repetitions)
- Overhead squat (5 repetitions)
- Front squat to press (5 repetitions)

WARM-UP 3

Foam roll, activation, and movement-based warm-up
Band glute strengthening
Lateral step under to over (3-5 repetitions each side)
Bar warm-up (45 lb)

- Snatch (5 repetitions)
- Overhead squat (5 repetitions)
- Front squat to press (5 repetitions)

WARM-UP 4

Foam roll, activation, and movement-based warm-up
Band glute strengthening
Bar warm-up (45 lb)

- Snatch (5 repetitions)
- Overhead squat (5 repetitions)
- Front squat to press (5 repetitions)

Table 9.3 Off-Season Base Program

Preparation (Phase 1)

Monday

	Exercise	Sets × reps		Exercise	Sets × reps
	Warm-up 1				
1a	Snatch pull	4 × 5	4a	Dumbbell shoulder press	3 × 8
1b	Around the world medicine ball slam	3 × 4 each way	4b	Abdominals (medicine ball)	Exercise dependent
2a	Bench press	Cycle*	5a	Dumbbell biceps curl	3 × 10
2b	Wide-grip lat pulldown	3 × 8-10	5b	External shoulder rotation (dumbbell or cable)	2 × 10 each side
3a	Alternating dumbbell incline bench press	3 × 8-10	6a	Plate hold (10 kg) (grip exercise)	Week 1: 30 sec Week 2: 45 sec Week 3: 60 sec
3b	Cable row	3 × 8-10	6b	4-way neck	1 × 8 each way

* For cycle, refer to table 9.10 for details.

Tuesday

	Exercise	Sets × reps		Exercise	Sets × reps
	Warm-up 2				
1	Dumbbell clean complex:	Cycle*	3a	Back extension	Week 1: 2 × 15 Week 2: 2 × 20 Week 3: 2 × 25
	Clean		3b	Rotational disc (shoes off for ankle strengthening)	1 × 20 each way
	Front squat		4a	Stability ball triple threat	Week 1: 3 × 6 Week 2: 3 × 8 Week 3: 3 × 10
	Upright row				
	Lateral squat				
	Bent-over row				
2a	Back squat	Cycle*	4b	Abdominals (functional)	Exercise dependent
2b	Band TKE (hold for a two count)	2 × 10 each side	5	Band flexibility: leg up, leg out, leg over, quad, hip flexor	1 × 10 sec each side

* For cycle, refer to table 9.10 for details.

Thursday

	Exercise	Sets × reps		Exercise	Sets × reps
	Warm-up 1				
1a	Two-arm kettlebell swing	4 × 5	4b	External shoulder rotation: dumbbell shoulder horn (standing, incline, decline)	1 × 10 each position
1b	Lateral rotation medicine ball hip toss	3 × 5 each side			
2a	Incline bench press	Cycle*			
2b	Standing one-arm dumbbell row	3 × 8-10			
3a	Alternating dumbbell bench press	3 × 8-10	5a	Lying triceps extension	3 × 10
3b	Face pull (machine)	3 × 10	5b	Abdominals (medicine ball)	Exercise dependent
4a	Power shrug	3 × 10	6a	Grip work: gripper	2 × 10
			6b	4-way neck	1 × 8 each way

* For cycle, refer to table 9.10 for details.

(continued)

Table 9.3 Off-Season Base Program *(continued)*

Friday

	Exercise	Sets × reps		Exercise	Sets × reps
	Warm-up 3				
1	Muscle snatch	Cycle*	4a	Single-leg short arcs	2 × 10
2	Clean technique (hang clean and front squat)	Cycle*	4b	Glute-ham raise (emphasize eccentric)	Week 1: 2 × 8 Week 2: 2 × 10 Week 3: 2 × 12
			5a	Abdominals (functional)	Exercise dependent
			5b	Rotational disc (shoes off for ankle strengthening)	1 × 20 each way
3a	Walking lunge	3 × 10 each side	6	Band flexibility: leg up, leg out, leg over, quad, hip flexor	1 × 10 sec each side
3b	Side plank with isometric groin hold	2 × 10			

* For cycle, refer to table 9.10 for details.

Unload/Variation (Version 1)

Monday

	Exercise	Sets × reps		Exercise	Sets × reps
	Warm-up 1				
1	Medicine ball slam	3 × 10	3b	Low-pulley seated row (machine)	2 × 8
2a	Close-grip bench press	4 × 5	4a	Dumbbell shrug	3 × 8
2b	Towel pull-up	3 × 8	4b	Reverse grip curl (EZ bar)	3 × 8
3a	Dip	2 × 10	5	4-way neck	1 × 8 each way

Tuesday

	Exercise	Sets × reps		Exercise	Sets × reps
	Warm-up 2				
1	One-arm dumbbell snatch	4 × 3 each arm	3b	Hamstring slide (emphasize eccentric)	2 × 10 each side
2	Back squat (light)	Cycle*	4	Single-leg hip thrust (body weight)	2 × 10 each side
3a	Side plank with isometric groin hold	2 × 30 sec	5	Band flexibility: leg up, leg out, leg over, quad, hip flexor	1 × 10 sec each side

* For cycle, refer to table 9.10 for details.

Thursday

	Exercise	Sets × reps		Exercise	Sets × reps
	Warm-up 4				
1	Power clean complex (barbell):	Cycle*	3b	Shoulder combo (barbell):	2 sets
	Power clean	3 reps		Front raise	6 reps
	Front squat to press	3 reps		Upright row	8 reps
	Bent-over row	3 reps		Shoulder press	8 reps
2a	Dumbbell incline bench press	3 × 8,6,5	4a	Overhead dumbbell triceps extension	3 × 8
2b	Bent-over lateral raise	3 × 8 each side	4b	Abdominals (functional)	Exercise dependent
3a	Step-up (dumbbell or barbell)	3 × 6 each side	5	Band flexibility: leg up, leg out, leg over, quad, hip flexor	1 × 10 sec each side

* For cycle, refer to table 9.10 for details.

Strength (Phase 2)

Monday

	Exercise	Sets × reps		Exercise	Sets × reps
	Warm-up 1				
1	Two-arm dumbbell clean to push press	Cycle*	4b	Abdominals (medicine ball)	Exercise dependent
2a	Bench press or incline bench press	Cycle*	5a	EZ bar biceps curl	3 × 8
2b	Weighted pull-up	3 × 6-8	5b	External shoulder rotation (dumbbell or cable)	2 × 10 each side
3a	Medicine ball chest pass	3 × 10	6a	Plate hold (15 kg) (grip exercise)	Week 1: 30 sec Week 2: 45 sec Week 3: 60 sec
3b	Suspension trainer row	3 × 6-8	6b	4-way neck	1 × 8 each way
4a	Barbell shoulder press	3 × 6			

* For cycle, refer to table 9.10 for details.

Tuesday

	Exercise	Sets × reps		Exercise	Sets × reps
	Warm-up 2				
1	Power snatch (speed)	Cycle*	4b	Lateral squat	2 × 6 each side
2	Back squat	Cycle*	5a	Abdominals (functional)	Exercise dependent
3a	Hip thrust	2 × 8	5b	Rotational disc (shoes off for ankle strengthening)	1 × 25 each way
3b	Single-leg partial squat (weighted)	2 × 10 each side	6	Band flexibility: leg up, leg out, leg over, quad, hip flexor	1 × 10 sec each side
4a	Romanian deadlift	3 × 8			

* For cycle, refer to table 9.10 for details.

Thursday

	Exercise	Sets × reps		Exercise	Sets × reps
	Warm-up 1				
1	Push jerk	Cycle*	4a	Triceps pushdown	3 × 8
2a	Chain bench press	Cycle*	4b	Suspension trainer row	3 × 10
2b	Weighted inverted row	5 × 6-8	5a	Abdominals (medicine ball)	Exercise dependent
3a	Medicine ball drop	3 × 10	5b	Dumbbell hold (grip exercise)	2 × 60 sec each side
3b	Bent-over lateral raise	3 × 8	6	4-way neck	1 × 8 each way

* For cycle, refer to table 9.10 for details.

(continued)

Table 9.3 Off-Season Base Program *(continued)*

Friday

	Exercise	Sets × reps		Exercise	Sets × reps
	Warm-up 3				
1	Power clean	Cycle*	4a	Glute-ham raise (emphasize eccentric)	Week 1: 2 × 8 Week 2: 2 × 10 Week 3: 2 × 12
2	Clean pull	3 × 5	4b	Rotational disc (shoes off for ankle strengthening)	1 × 25 each way
3a	Split squat	3 × 6 each side	5	Abdominals (functional)	Exercise dependent
3b	Side plank with isometric groin hold	2 × 10	6	Band flexibility: leg up, leg out, leg over, quad, hip flexor	1 × 10 sec each side

* For cycle, refer to table 9.10 for details.

Unload/Variation (Version 2)

Monday

	Exercise	Sets × reps		Exercise	Sets × reps
	Warm-up 1				
1	Medicine ball slam	3 × 10	3b	Low-pulley seated row (machine)	2 × 8
2a	Dumbbell bench press	4 × 5	4a	Dumbbell shrug	3 × 8
2b	Towel pull-up	3 × 6	4b	Dumbbell biceps curl	3 × 8
3a	Bench lock out	3 × 3	5	4-way neck	1 × 8 each way

Tuesday

	Exercise	Sets × reps		Exercise	Sets × reps
	Warm-up 2				
1	One-arm dumbbell snatch	4 × 3 each arm	3b	Hamstring slide (emphasize eccentric)	2 × 10 each side
2	Back squat (light)	Cycle*	4	Band flexibility: leg up, leg out, leg over, quad, hip flexor	1 × 10 sec each side
3a	Side plank with isometric groin hold	2 × 30 sec			

* For cycle, refer to table 9.10 for details.

Thursday

	Exercise	Sets × reps		Exercise	Sets × reps
	Warm-up 4				
1	Power clean combo (barbell):	Cycle*	3b	Shoulder combo (barbell):	2 sets
	Power clean	2 reps		Front raise	6 reps
	Push jerk	2 reps		Upright row	8 reps
	Front squat	2 reps		Shoulder press	8 reps
2a	Dumbbell incline bench press	3 × 5	4a	Overhead dumbbell triceps extension	3 × 8
2b	Bent-over lateral raise	3 × 8 each side	4b	Abdominals (functional)	Exercise dependent
3a	Lunge to step-up	3 × 2 each side	5	Band flexibility: leg up, leg out, leg over, quad, hip flexor	1 × 10 sec each side

* For cycle, refer to table 9.10 for details.

Strength and Power (Phase 3)

Monday

	Exercise	Sets × reps		Exercise	Sets × reps
	Warm-up 1				
1	Snatch pull	4 × 3	4b	Hammer curl	3 × 6
2a	Bench press or incline bench press	Cycle*	5a	External shoulder rotation (dumbbell or cable)	2 × 10 each side
2b	Close-grip lat pulldown	5 × 4-6	5b	Abdominals (medicine ball)	Exercise dependent
3a	Medicine ball chest pass	3 × 3 (with a descending load)	6a	Plate hold (20 kg) (grip exercise)	Week 1: 30 sec Week 2: 45 sec Week 3: 60 sec
3b	Dumbbell incline row	3 × 6	6b	4-way neck	1 × 8 each way
4a	Cable lateral raise	3 × 6 each side			

* For cycle, refer to table 9.10 for details.

Tuesday

	Exercise	Sets × reps		Exercise	Sets × reps
	Warm-up 2				
1	Clean and jerk	Cycle*	4a	Lateral lunge	3 × 5 each side
2	Back squat	Cycle*	4b	Abdominals (functional)	Exercise dependent
3a	Romanian deadlift	3 × 5	5	Rotational disc (shoes off for ankle strengthening)	1 × 30 each way
3b	Hip thrust	2 × 5	6	Band flexibility: leg up, leg out, leg over, quad, hip flexor	1 × 10 sec each side

* For cycle, refer to table 9.10 for details.

Thursday

	Exercise	Sets × reps		Exercise	Sets × reps
	Warm-up 1				
1	One-arm dumbbell snatch	4 × 2 each arm	4b	External shoulder rotation: dumbbell shoulder horn (standing, incline, decline)	1 × 10 each position
2a	Chain bench press	Cycle*	5a	Overhead cable triceps extension	3 × 6
2b	One-arm dumbbell row	5 × 4-6	5b	Grip work: pinch gripper	2 × 30 sec each side
3a	Medicine ball drop	3 × 3 (with a descending load)	6a	Abdominals (medicine ball)	Exercise dependent
3b	Reverse-grip lat pulldown	3 × 4-6	6b	4-way neck	1 × 8 each way
4a	Suspension Y, T, I	2 × 8 each way			

* For cycle, refer to table 9.10 for details.

Friday

	Exercise	Sets × reps		Exercise	Sets × reps
	Warm-up 3				
1	Power clean	Cycle*	4b	Dumbbell hamstring walk	3 × 6 each side
2	Clean pull	3 × 3	5a	Abdominals (functional)	Exercise dependent
3	Chain back squat	Cycle*	5b	Rotational disc (shoes off for ankle strengthening)	1 × 30 each way
4a	Single-leg squat	3 × 3 each side	6	Band flexibility: leg up, leg out, leg over, quad, hip flexor	1 × 10 sec each side

* For cycle, refer to table 9.10 for details.

Table 9.4 Off-Season Program for Offensive and Defensive Linemen

Preparation (Phase 1)

Monday

	Exercise	Sets × reps		Exercise	Sets × reps
	Warm-up 1				
1a	Snatch pull	4 × 5	4a	Dumbbell shoulder press	3 × 8
1b	Around the world medicine ball slam	3 × 4 each way	4b	Abdominals (medicine ball)	Exercise dependent
2a	Bench press	Cycle*	5a	Dumbbell biceps curl	3 × 10
2b	Wide-grip lat pulldown	3 × 8-10	5b	External shoulder rotation (dumbbell or cable)	2 × 10 each side
3a	Alternating dumbbell incline bench press	3 × 8-10	6a	Plate hold (10 kg) (grip exercise)	Week 1: 30 sec Week 2: 45 sec Week 3: 60 sec
3b	Cable row	3 × 8-10	6b	4-way neck	1 × 8 each way

* For cycle, refer to table 9.10 for details.

Tuesday

	Exercise	Sets × reps		Exercise	Sets × reps
	Warm-up 2				
1	Dumbbell clean complex:	Cycle*	3a	Back extension	Week 1: 2 × 15 Week 2: 2 × 20 Week 3: 2 × 25
	Clean		3b	Rotational disc (shoes off for ankle strengthening)	1 × 20 each way
	Front squat		4a	Stability ball triple threat	Week 1: 3 × 6
	Upright row				Week 2: 3 × 8
	Lateral squat				Week 3: 3 × 10
	Bent-over row				
2a	Back squat	Cycle*	4b	Abdominals (functional)	Exercise dependent
2b	Band TKE (hold for a two count)	2 × 10 each side	5	Band flexibility: leg up, leg out, leg over, quad, hip flexor	1 × 10 sec each side

* For cycle, refer to table 9.10 for details.

Thursday

	Exercise	Sets × reps		Exercise	Sets × reps
	Warm-up 1				
1a	Two-arm kettlebell swing	4 × 5	4a	Power shrug	3 × 10
1b	Lateral rotation medicine ball hip toss	3 × 5 each side	4b	External shoulder rotation: dumbbell shoulder horn (standing, incline, decline)	1 × 10 each position
2a	Incline bench press	Cycle*	5a	Lying triceps extension	3 × 10
2b	Standing one-arm dumbbell row	3 × 8-10	5b	Abdominals (medicine ball)	Exercise dependent
3a	Alternating dumbbell bench press	3 × 8-10	6a	Grip work: gripper	2 × 10
3b	Face pull (machine)	3 × 10	6b	4-way neck	1 × 8 each way

* For cycle, refer to table 9.10 for details.

Friday

	Exercise	Sets × reps		Exercise	Sets × reps
	Warm-up 3				
1	Muscle snatch	Cycle*	4a	Single-leg short arcs	2 × 10
2	Clean technique (hang clean and front squat)	Cycle*	4b	Glute-ham raise (emphasize eccentric)	Week 1: 2 × 8 Week 2: 2 × 10 Week 3: 2 × 12
			5a	Abdominals (functional)	Exercise dependent
			5b	Rotational disc (shoes off for ankle strengthening)	1 × 20 each way
3a	Walking lunge	3 × 10 each side	6	Band flexibility: leg up, leg out, leg over, quad, hip flexor	1 × 10 sec each side
3b	Side plank with isometric groin hold	2 × 10			

* For cycle, refer to table 9.10 for details.

Unload/Variation (Version 1)

Monday

	Exercise	Sets × reps		Exercise	Sets × reps
	Warm-up 1				
1	Medicine ball slam	3 × 10	3b	Low-pulley seated row (machine)	2 × 8
2a	Close-grip bench press	4 × 5	4a	Dumbbell shrug	3 × 8
2b	Towel pull-up	3 × 8	4b	Reverse grip curl (EZ bar)	3 × 8
3a	Dip	2 × 10	5	4-way neck	1 × 8 each way

Tuesday

	Exercise	Sets × reps		Exercise	Sets × reps
	Warm-up 2				
1	One-arm dumbbell snatch	4 × 3 each arm	3b	Hamstring slide (emphasize eccentric)	2 × 10 each side
2	Back squat (light)	Cycle*	4	Single-leg hip thrust (body weight)	2 × 10 each side
3a	Side plank with isometric groin hold	2 × 30 sec	5	Band flexibility: leg up, leg out, leg over, quad, hip flexor	1 × 10 sec each side

* For cycle, refer to table 9.10 for details.

Thursday

	Exercise	Sets × reps		Exercise	Sets × reps
	Warm-up 3				
1	Power clean complex (barbell):	Cycle*	3b	Shoulder combo (barbell):	2 sets
	Power clean	3 reps		Front raise	6 reps
	Front squat to press	3 reps		Upright row	8 reps
	Bent-over row	3 reps		Shoulder press	8 reps
2a	Dumbbell incline bench press	3 × 8,6,5	4a	Overhead dumbbell triceps extension	3 × 8
2b	Bent-over lateral raise	3 × 8 each side	4b	Abdominals (functional)	Exercise dependent
3a	Step-up (dumbbell or barbell)	3 × 6 each side	5	Band flexibility: leg up, leg out, leg over, quad, hip flexor	1 × 10 sec each side

* For cycle, refer to table 9.10 for details.

(continued)

Strength (Phase 2)

Monday

	Exercise	Sets × reps		Exercise	Sets × reps
	Warm-up 1				
1	Two-arm dumbbell clean to push press	Cycle*	4b	Abdominals (medicine ball)	Exercise dependent
2a	Bench press or incline bench press	Cycle*	5a	EZ bar biceps curl	3 × 8
2b	Weighted pull-up	3 × 6-8	5b	External shoulder rotation (dumbbell or cable)	2 × 10 each side
3a	Medicine ball chest pass	3 × 10	6a	Plate hold (15 kg) (grip exercise)	Week 1: 30 sec Week 2: 45 sec Week 3: 60 sec
3b	Suspension trainer row	3 × 6-8	6b	4-way neck	1 × 8 each way
4a	Barbell shoulder press	3 × 6			

* For cycle, refer to table 9.10 for details.

Tuesday

	Exercise	Sets × reps		Exercise	Sets × reps
	Warm-up 2				
1	Power snatch	Cycle*	4b	Lateral squat	2 × 6 each side
2	Back squat	Cycle*	5a	Abdominals (functional)	Exercise dependent
3a	Hip thrust	2 × 8	5b	Rotational disc (shoes off for ankle strengthening)	1 × 25 each way
3b	Single-leg partial squat (weighted)	2 × 10 each side	6	Band flexibility: leg up, leg out, leg over, quad, hip flexor	1 × 10 sec each side
4a	Romanian deadlift	3 × 8			

* For cycle, refer to table 9.10 for details.

Thursday

	Exercise	Sets × reps		Exercise	Sets × reps
	Warm-up 1				
1	Push jerk	Cycle*	4b	Triceps push-down	3 × 8
2a	Chain bench press	Cycle*	5a	Suspension trainer row	3 × 10
2b	Weighted inverted row	5 × 6-8	5b	Abdominals (medicine ball)	Exercise dependent
3a	Bench lockout	3 × 3	6a	Dumbbell hold (grip exercise)	2 × 60 sec each side
3b	Medicine ball drop	3 × 8	6b	4-way neck	1 × 8 each way
4a	Bent-over lateral raise	3 × 8			

* For cycle, refer to table 9.10 for details.

Friday

	Exercise	Sets × reps		Exercise	Sets × reps
	Warm-up 3				
1	Power clean	Cycle*	5a	Glute-ham raise (10 kg) (emphasize eccentric)	Week 1: 2 × 8 Week 2: 2 × 10 Week 3: 2 × 12
2	Clean pull	3 × 5	5b	Rotational disc (shoes off for ankle strengthening)	1 × 25 each way
3	Chain back squat	Cycle*	6	Abdominals (functional)	Exercise dependent
4a	Trap bar deadlift	4 × 4	7	Band flexibility: leg up, leg out, leg over, quad, hip flexor	1 × 10 sec each side
4b	Side plank with isometric groin hold	2 × 10			

* For cycle, refer to table 9.10 for details.

Unload/Variation (Version 2)

Monday

	Exercise	Sets × reps		Exercise	Sets × reps
	Warm-up 1				
1	Medicine ball slam	3 × 10	3b	Low-pulley seated row (machine)	2 × 8
2a	Dumbbell bench press	4 × 5	4a	Dumbbell shrug	3 × 8
2b	Towel pull-up	3 × 6	4b	Dumbbell biceps curl	3 × 8
3a	Bench lockout	3 × 3	5	4-way neck	1 × 8 each way

Tuesday

	Exercise	Sets × reps		Exercise	Sets × reps
	Warm-up 2				
1	One-arm dumbbell snatch	4 × 3 each arm	3b	Hamstring slide (emphasize eccentric)	2 × 10 each side
2	Back squat (light)	Cycle*	4	Band flexibility: leg up, leg out, leg over, quad, hip flexor	1 × 10 sec each side
3a	Side plank with isometric groin hold	2 × 30 sec			

* For cycle, refer to table 9.10 for details.

Thursday

	Exercise	Sets × reps		Exercise	Sets × reps
	Warm-up 4				
1	Power clean combo (barbell):	Cycle*	3b	Shoulder combo (barbell):	2 sets
	Power clean	2 reps		Front raise	6 reps
	Push jerk	2 reps		Upright row	8 reps
	Front squat	2 reps		Shoulder press	8 reps
2a	Dumbbell incline bench press	3 × 5	4a	Overhead dumbbell triceps extension	3 × 8
2b	Bent-over lateral raise	3 × 8 each side	4b	Abdominals (functional)	Exercise dependent
3a	Lunge to step-up	3 × 2 each side	5	Band flexibility: leg up, leg out, leg over, quad, hip flexor	1 × 10 sec each side

* For cycle, refer to table 9.10 for details.

Strength and Power (Phase 3)

Monday

	Exercise	Sets × reps		Exercise	Sets × reps
	Warm-up 1				
1	Snatch pull	4 × 3	4a	Cable lateral raise	3 × 6 each side
2a	Bench press or incline bench press	Cycle*	4b	Hammer curl	3 × 6
2b	Close-grip lat pulldown	5 × 4-6	5a	External shoulder rotation (dumbbell or cable)	2 × 10 each side
3a	Medicine ball chest pass (with a descending load):		5b	Abdominals (medicine ball)	Exercise dependent
	OL: medicine ball chest pass	3 × 3+3	6a	Plate hold (20 kg) (grip exercise)	Week 1: 30 sec Week 2: 45 sec Week 3: 60 sec
	DL: medicine ball chest pass	3 × 10	6b	4-way neck	1 × 8 each way
3b	Dumbbell incline row	3 × 6			

* For cycle, refer to table 9.10 for details.

(continued)

Table 9.4 Off-Season Program for Offensive and Defensive Linemen *(continued)*

Tuesday

	Exercise	Sets × reps		Exercise	Sets × reps
	Warm-up 2				
1	Clean and jerk	Cycle*	4a	Lateral lunge	3 × 5 each leg
2	Back squat	Cycle*	4b	Abdominals (functional)	Exercise dependent
3a	Romanian deadlift	3 × 5	5	Rotational disc (shoes off for ankle strengthening)	1 × 30 each way
3b	Hip thrust	2 × 5	6	Band flexibility: leg up, leg out, leg over, quad, hip flexor	1 × 10 sec each side

* For cycle, refer to table 9.10 for details.

Thursday

	Exercise	Sets × reps		Exercise	Sets × reps
	Warm-up 1				
1	One-arm dumbbell snatch	4 × 2 each arm	4b	Suspension Y, T, I	2 × 8 each way
2a	Chain bench press	Cycle*	5a	External shoulder rotation: dumbbell shoulder horn (standing, incline, decline)	1 × 10 each position
2b	One-arm dumbbell row	5 × 4-6	5b	Overhead cable triceps extension	3 × 6
3a	DL: Bench lockout	3 × 2	6a	Grip work: pinch gripper	2 × 30 sec each side
3b	Medicine ball drop	3 × 3 (with a descending load)	6b	Abdominals (medicine ball)	Exercise dependent
4a	Reverse grip lat pulldown	3 × 4-6	7	4-way neck	1 × 8 each way

* For cycle, refer to table 9.10 for details.

Friday

	Exercise	Sets × reps		Exercise	Sets × reps
	Warm-up 3				
1	Power clean	Cycle*	5a	Dumbbell hamstring walk	3 × 6 each side
2	Clean pull	3 × 3	5b	Abdominals (functional)	Exercise dependent
3	DL: Chain back squat	Cycle*	6	Rotational disc (shoes off for ankle strengthening)	1 × 30 each way
	DL: Complex jump onto a box (after each set of chain back squats)	6 × 2	7	Band flexibility: leg up, leg out, leg over, quad, hip flexor	1 × 10 sec each side
4	DL: Trap bar deadlift	4 × 2			

* For cycle, refer to table 9.10 for details.

Table 9.5   Off-Season Program for Tight Ends, Fullbacks, and Linebackers

Preparation (Phase 1)

Monday

	Exercise	Sets × reps		Exercise	Sets × reps
	Warm-up 1				
1a	Snatch pull	4 × 5	4b	Abdominals (medicine ball)	Exercise dependent
1b	Around the world medicine ball slam	3 × 4 each way	5a	Dumbbell biceps curl	3 × 10
2a	Bench press	Cycle*	5b	External shoulder rotation (dumbbell or cable)	2 × 10 each side
2b	Wide-grip lat pulldown	3 × 8-10	6a	Plate hold (10 kg) (grip exercise)	Week 1: 30 sec Week 2: 45 sec Week 3: 60 sec
3a	Alternating dumbbell incline bench press	3 × 8-10	6b	4-way neck	1 × 8 each way
3b	Cable row	3 × 8-10		Isometric neck stretch	2 × 5 for 30 sec each way
4a	Dumbbell shoulder press	3 × 8			

* For cycle, refer to table 9.10 for details.

Tuesday

	Exercise	Sets × reps		Exercise	Sets × reps
	Warm-up 2				
1	Dumbbell clean complex:	Cycle*	3b	Rotational disc (shoes off for ankle strengthening)	1 × 20 each way
	Clean		4a	Stability ball triple threat	Week 1: 3 × 6 Week 2: 3 × 8 Week 3: 3 × 10
	Front squat				
	Upright row				
	Lateral squat				
	Bent-over row				
2a	Back squat	Cycle*	4b	Abdominals (functional)	Exercise dependent
2b	Band TKE (hold for a two count)	2 × 10 each side	5	Band flexibility: leg up, leg out, leg over, quad, hip flexor	1 × 10 sec each side
3a	Back extension	Week 1: 2 × 15 Week 2: 2 × 20 Week 3: 2 × 25			

* For cycle, refer to table 9.10 for details.

Thursday

	Exercise	Sets × reps		Exercise	Sets × reps
	Warm-up 1				
1a	Two-arm kettlebell swing	4 × 5	4b	External shoulder rotation: dumbbell shoulder horn (standing, incline, decline)	1 × 10 each position
1b	Lateral rotation medicine ball hip toss	3 × 5 each side	5a	Lying triceps extension	3 × 10
2a	Incline bench press	Cycle*	5b	Abdominals (medicine ball)	Exercise dependent

(continued)

Thursday *(continued)*

	Exercise	Sets × reps		Exercise	Sets × reps
2b	Standing one-arm dumbbell row	3 × 8-10	6a	Grip work: gripper	2 × 10
3a	Alternating dumbbell bench press	3 × 8-10	6b	4-way neck	1 × 8 each way
3b	Face pull (machine)	3 × 10		Isometric neck stretch	2 × 5 for 30 sec each way
4a	Power shrug	3 × 10			

* For cycle, refer to table 9.10 for details.

Friday

	Exercise	Sets × reps		Exercise	Sets × reps
	Warm-up 3				
1	Muscle snatch	Cycle*	4a	Single-leg short arcs	2 × 10
2	Clean technique (hang clean and front squat)	Cycle*	4b	Glute-ham raise (emphasize eccentric)	Week 1: 2 × 8 Week 2: 2 × 10 Week 3: 2 × 12
			5a	Abdominals (functional)	Exercise dependent
			5b	Rotational disc (shoes off for ankle strengthening)	1 × 20 each way
3a	Walking lunge	3 × 10 each side	6	Band flexibility: leg up, leg out, leg over, quad, hip flexor	1 × 10 sec each side
3b	Side plank with isometric groin hold	2 × 10			

* For cycle, refer to table 9.10 for details.

Unload/Variation (Version 1)

Monday

	Exercise	Sets × reps		Exercise	Sets × reps
	Warm-up 1				
1	Medicine ball slam	3 × 10	4a	Dumbbell shrug	3 × 8
2a	Close-grip bench press	4 × 5	4b	Reverse-grip curl (EZ bar)	3 × 8
2b	Towel pull-up	3 × 8	5	4-way neck	1 × 8 each way
3a	Dip	2 × 10		Isometric neck stretch	2 × 5 for 30 sec each way
3b	Low-pulley seated row (machine)	2 × 8			

Tuesday

	Exercise	Sets × reps		Exercise	Sets × reps
	Warm-up 2				
1	One-arm dumbbell snatch	4 × 3 each arm	3b	Hamstring slide (emphasize eccentric)	2 × 10 each side
2	Back squat (light)	Cycle*	4	Single-leg hip thrust (body weight)	2 × 10 each side
3a	Side plank with isometric groin hold	2 × 30 sec	5	Band flexibility: leg up, leg out, leg over, quad, hip flexor	1 × 10 sec each side

* For cycle, refer to table 9.10 for details.

	Exercise	Sets × reps		Exercise	Sets × reps
	Warm-up 4				
1	Power clean complex (barbell):	Cycle*	3b	Shoulder combo (barbell):	2 sets
	Power clean	3 reps		Front raise	6 reps
	Front squat to press	3 reps		Upright row	8 reps
	Bent-over row	3 reps		Shoulder press	8 reps
2a	Dumbbell incline bench press	3 × 8,6,5	4a	Overhead dumbbell triceps extension	3 × 8
2b	Bent-over lateral raise	3 × 8 each side	4b	Abdominals (functional)	Exercise dependent
3a	Step-up (dumbbell or barbell)	3 × 6 each side	5	Band flexibility: leg up, leg out, leg over, quad, hip flexor	1 × 10 sec each side

* For cycle, refer to table 9.10 for details.

Strength (Phase 2)

Monday

	Exercise	Sets × reps		Exercise	Sets × reps
	Warm-up 1				
1	Two-arm dumbbell clean to push press	Cycle*	5a	EZ bar biceps curl	3 × 8
2a	Bench press or incline bench press	Cycle*	5b	Burner combo	2 × 10 each way
2b	Weighted pull-up	3 × 6-8	6a	External shoulder rotation (dumbbell or cable)	2 × 10 each way
3a	Medicine ball chest pass	3 × 10	6b	Plate hold (15 kg) (grip exercise)	Week 1: 30 sec Week 2: 45 sec Week 3: 60 sec
3b	Suspension trainer row	3 × 6-8	7	4-way neck	1 × 8 each way
4a	Barbell shoulder press	3 × 6		Isometric neck stretch	2 × 5 for 30 sec each way
4b	Abdominals (medicine ball)	Exercise dependent			

* For cycle, refer to table 9.10 for details.

Tuesday

	Exercise	Sets × reps		Exercise	Sets × reps
	Warm-up 2				
1	Power snatch	Cycle*	4b	Lateral squat	2 × 6 each side
2	Back squat	Cycle*	5a	Abdominals (functional)	Exercise dependent
3a	Hip thrust	2 × 8	5b	Dumbbell neck stretch shrug	2 × 10 each way
3b	Single-leg partial squat (weighted)	2 × 10 each side	6	Rotational disc (shoes off for ankle strengthening)	1 × 25 each way
4a	Romanian deadlift	3 × 8	7	Band flexibility: leg up, leg out, leg over, quad, hip flexor	1 × 10 each side

* For cycle, refer to table 9.10 for details.

(continued)

Thursday

	Exercise	Sets × reps		Exercise	Sets × reps
	Warm-up 1				
1	Push jerk	Cycle*	4b	Suspension trainer row	3 × 10
2a	Chain bench press	Cycle*	5a	Abdominals (medicine ball)	Exercise dependent
2b	Weighted inverted row	5 × 6-8	5b	Dumbbell hold (grip exercise)	2 × 60 sec each side
3a	Medicine ball drop	3 × 8	6	4-way neck	1 × 8 each way
3b	Bent-over lateral raise	3 × 8		Isometric neck stretch	2 × 5 for 30 sec each way
4a	Triceps pushdown	3 × 8			

* For cycle, refer to table 9.10 for details.

Friday

	Exercise	Sets × reps		Exercise	Sets × reps
	Warm-up 3				
1	Power clean	Cycle*	5a	Glute-ham raise (10 kg) (emphasize eccentric)	Week 1: 2 × 8 Week 2: 2 × 10 Week 3: 2 × 12
2	Clean pull	3 × 5	5b	Rotational disc (shoes off for ankle strengthening)	1 × 25 each way
3	Chain back squat	Cycle*	6	Abdominals (functional)	Exercise dependent
4a	Split squat	2 × 6 each side	7	Band flexibility: leg up, leg out, leg over, quad, hip flexor	1 × 10 sec each side
4b	Side plank with isometric groin hold	2 × 10			

* For cycle, refer to table 9.10 for details.

Unload/Variation (Version 2)

Monday

	Exercise	Sets × reps		Exercise	Sets × reps
	Warm-up 1				
1	Medicine ball slam	3 × 10	4a	Dumbbell shrug	3 × 8
2a	Dumbbell bench press	4 × 5	4b	Dumbbell biceps curl	3 × 8
2b	Towel pull-up	3 × 6	5	4-way neck	1 × 8 each way
3a	Bench lockout	3 × 3		Isometric neck stretch	2 × 5 for 30 sec each way
3b	Low-pulley seated row (machine)	2 × 8			

Tuesday

	Exercise	Sets × reps		Exercise	Sets × reps
	Warm-up 2				
1	One-arm dumbbell snatch	4 × 3 each arm	3b	Hamstring slide (emphasize eccentric)	2 × 10 each side
2	Back squat (light)	Cycle*	4	Band flexibility: leg up, leg out, leg over, quad, hip flexor	1 × 10 sec each side
3a	Side plank with isometric groin hold	2 × 30 sec			

* For cycle, refer to table 9.10 for details.

Thursday

	Exercise	Sets × reps		Exercise	Sets × reps
	Warm-up 4				
1	Power clean combo (barbell):	Cycle*	3b	Shoulder combo (barbell):	2 sets
	Power clean	2 reps		Front raise	6 reps
	Push jerk	2 reps		Upright row	8 reps
	Front squat	2 reps		Shoulder press	8 reps
2a	Dumbbell incline bench press	3 × 5	4a	Overhead dumbbell triceps extension	3 × 8
2b	Bent-over lateral raise	3 × 8 each side	4b	Abdominals (functional)	Exercise dependent
3a	Lunge to step-up	3 × 2 each side	5	Band flexibility: leg up, leg out, leg over, quad, hip flexor	1 × 10 sec each side

* For cycle, refer to table 9.10 for details.

Strength and Power (Phase 3)

Monday

	Exercise	Sets × reps		Exercise	Sets × reps
	Warm-up 1				
1	Snatch pull	4 × 3	5a	Burner combo	2 × 10 each way
2a	Bench press or incline bench press	Cycle*	5b	External shoulder rotation (dumbbell or cable)	2 × 10 each side
2b	Close-grip lat pulldown	5 × 4-6	6a	Abdominals (medicine ball)	Exercise dependent
3a	Medicine ball chest pass	3 × 3 (with a descending load)	6b	Plate hold (20 kg) (grip exercise)	Week 1: 30 sec / Week 2: 45 sec / Week 3: 60 sec
3b	Dumbbell incline row	3 × 6	7	4-way neck	1 × 8 each way
4a	Hammer curl	3 × 6		Isometric neck stretch	2 × 5 for 30 sec each way
4b	Cable lateral raise	2 × 6 each side			

* For cycle, refer to table 9.10 for details.

Tuesday

	Exercise	Sets × reps		Exercise	Sets × reps
	Warm-up 2				
1	Clean and jerk	Cycle*	4b	Dumbbell neck stretch shrug	2 × 10 each side
2	Back squat	Cycle*	5a	Abdominals (functional)	Exercise dependent
3a	Romanian deadlift	3 × 5	5b	Rotational disc (shoes off for ankle strengthening)	1 × 30 each way
3b	Hip thrust	2 × 5	6	Band flexibility: leg up, leg out, leg over, quad, hip flexor	1 × 10 sec each side
4a	Lateral lunge	3 × 5 each leg			

* For cycle, refer to table 9.10 for details.

Thursday

	Exercise	Sets × reps		Exercise	Sets × reps
	Warm-up 1				
1	One-arm dumbbell snatch	4 × 2 each arm	4b	External shoulder rotation: dumbbell shoulder horn (standing, incline, decline)	1 × 10 each position
2a	Chain bench press	Cycle*	5a	Overhead cable triceps extension	3 × 6
2b	One-arm dumbbell row	5 × 4-6	5b	Grip work: pinch gripper	2 × 30 sec each side
3a	Medicine ball drop	3 × 3 (with a descending load)	6a	Abdominals (medicine ball)	Exercise dependent
3b	Reverse-grip lat pulldown	3 × 4-6	6b	4-way neck	1 × 8 each way
4a	Suspension Y, T, I	2 × 8 each way		Isometric neck stretch	2 × 5 for 30 sec each way

* For cycle, refer to table 9.10 for details.

Friday

	Exercise	Sets × reps		Exercise	Sets × reps
	Warm-up 3				
1	Power clean	Cycle*	4b	Dumbbell hamstring walk	3 × 6 each side
2	Clean pull	3 × 3	5a	Abdominals (functional)	Exercise dependent
3	Chain back squat	Cycle*	5b	Rotational disc (shoes off for ankle strengthening)	1 × 30 each way
	Complex jump onto a box (after each set of chain back squats)	6 × 2	6	Band flexibility: leg up, leg out, leg over, quad, hip flexor	1 × 10 sec each side
4a	Single-leg squat	2 × 3 each side			

* For cycle, refer to table 9.10 for details.

Table 9.6 Off-Season Program for Wide Receivers and Running Backs

Preparation (Phase 1)

Monday

	Exercise	Sets × reps		Exercise	Sets × reps
	Warm-up 1				
1a	Snatch pull	4 × 5	4a	Dumbbell shoulder press	3 × 8
1b	Around the world medicine ball slam	3 × 4 each way	4b	Abdominals (medicine ball)	Exercise dependent
2a	Bench press	Cycle*	5a	Dumbbell biceps curl	3 × 10
2b	Weighted pull-up	4 × 10	5b	External shoulder rotation (dumbbell or cable)	2 × 10 each side
3a	Alternating dumbbell incline bench press	3 × 8-10	6a	Plate hold (10 kg) (grip exercise)	Week 1: 30 sec Week 2: 45 sec Week 3: 60 sec
3b	Cable row	3 × 8-10	6b	4-way neck	1 × 8 each way

* For cycle, refer to table 9.10 for details.

Tuesday

	Exercise	Sets × reps		Exercise	Sets × reps
	Warm-up 2				
1	Dumbbell clean complex:	Cycle*	3a	Back extension	Week 1: 2 × 15 Week 2: 2 × 20 Week 3: 2 × 25
	Clean		3b	Rotational disc (shoes off for ankle strengthening)	1 × 20 each way
	Front squat		4a	Stability ball triple threat	Week 1: 3 × 6 Week 2: 3 × 8 Week 3: 3 × 10
	Upright row				
	Lateral squat				
	Bent-over row				
2a	Back squat	Cycle*	4b	Abdominals (functional)	Exercise dependent
2b	Band TKE (hold for a two count)	2 × 10 each side	5	Band flexibility: leg up, leg out, leg over, quad, hip flexor	1 × 10 sec each side

* For cycle, refer to table 9.10 for details.

Thursday

	Exercise	Sets × reps		Exercise	Sets × reps
	Warm-up 1				
1a	Two-arm kettlebell swing	4 × 5	4a	Power shrug	3 × 10
1b	Lateral rotation medicine ball hip toss	3 × 5 each side	4b	External shoulder rotation: dumbbell shoulder horn (standing, incline, decline)	1 x 10 each position
2a	Incline bench press	Cycle*	5a	Lying triceps extension	3 × 10
2b	Weighted inverted row	4 × 10	5b	Abdominals (medicine ball)	Exercise dependent
3a	Alternating dumbbell bench press	3 × 8-10	6a	Grip work: gripper	2 × 10
3b	Face pull (machine)	3 × 10	6b	4-way neck	1 × 8 each way

* For cycle, refer to table 9.10 for details.

(continued)

Friday

	Exercise	Sets × reps		Exercise	Sets × reps
	Warm-up 3				
1	Muscle snatch	Cycle*	4a	Single-leg short arcs	2 × 10
2	Clean technique (hang clean and front squat)	Cycle*	4b	Glute-ham raise (emphasize eccentric)	Week 1: 2 × 8 Week 2: 2 × 10 Week 3: 2 × 12
			5a	Abdominals (functional)	Exercise dependent
			5b	Rotational disc (shoes off for ankle strengthening)	1 × 20 each way
3a	Walking lunge	3 × 10 each side	6	Band flexibility: leg up, leg out, leg over, quad, hip flexor	1 × 10 sec each side
3b	Side plank with isometric groin hold	2 × 10			

* For cycle, refer to table 9.10 for details.

Unload/Variation (Version 1)

Monday

	Exercise	Sets × reps		Exercise	Sets × reps
	Warm-up 1				
1	Medicine ball slam	3 × 10	3b	Low-pulley seated row (machine)	2 × 8
2a	Close-grip bench press	4 × 5	4a	Dumbbell shrug	3 × 8
2b	Towel pull-up	3 × 8	4b	Reverse-grip curl (EZ bar)	3 × 8
3a	Dip	2 × 10	5	4-way neck	1 × 8 each way

Tuesday

	Exercise	Sets × reps		Exercise	Sets × reps
	Warm-up 2				
1	One-arm dumbbell snatch	4 × 3 each arm	3b	Hamstring slide (emphasize eccentric)	2 × 10 each side
2	Back squat (light)	Cycle*	4	Single-leg hip thrust (body weight)	2 × 10 each side
3a	Side plank with isometric groin hold	2 × 30 sec	5	Band flexibility: leg up, leg out, leg over, quad, hip flexor	1 × 10 sec each side

* For cycle, refer to table 9.10 for details.

Thursday

	Exercise	Sets × reps		Exercise	Sets × reps
	Warm-up 4				
1	Power clean complex (barbell):	Cycle*	3b	Shoulder combo (barbell):	2 sets
	Power clean	3 reps		Front raise	6 reps
	Front squat to press	3 reps		Upright row	8 reps
	Bent-over row	3 reps		Shoulder press	8 reps
2a	Dumbbell incline bench press	3 × 8,6,5	4a	Overhead dumbbell triceps extension	3 × 8
2b	Bent-over lateral raise	3 × 8 each side	4b	Abdominals (functional)	Exercise dependent
3a	Step-up (dumbbell or barbell)	3 × 6 each side	5	Band flexibility: leg up, leg out, leg over, quad, hip flexor	1 × 10 sec each side

* For cycle, refer to table 9.10 for details.

Strength (Phase 2)

Monday

	Exercise	Sets × reps		Exercise	Sets × reps
	Warm-up 1				
1	Two-arm dumbbell clean to push press	Cycle*	4b	Abdominals (medicine ball)	Exercise dependent
2a	Bench press or incline bench press	Cycle*	5a	EZ bar biceps curl	3 × 8
2b	Close-grip lat pulldown	3 × 6-8	5b	External shoulder rotation (dumbbell or cable)	2 × 10 each side
3a	Medicine ball chest pass	3 × 10	6a	Plate hold (15 kg) (grip exercise)	Week 1: 30 sec Week 2: 45 sec Week 3: 60 sec
3b	Standing one-arm dumbbell row	3 × 6-8	6b	4-way neck	1 × 8 each way
4a	Barbell shoulder press	3 × 6			

* For cycle, refer to table 9.10 for details.

Tuesday

	Exercise	Sets × reps		Exercise	Sets × reps
	Warm-up 2				
1	Power snatch	Cycle*	4b	Lateral squat	2 × 6 each side
2	Back squat	Cycle*	5a	Abdominals (functional)	Exercise dependent
3a	Hip thrust	2 × 8	5b	Rotational disc (shoes off for ankle strengthening)	1 × 25 each way
3b	Single-leg partial squat (weighted)	2 × 10 each side	6	Band flexibility: leg up, leg out, leg over, quad, hip flexor	1 × 10 sec each side
4a	Romanian deadlift	3 × 8			

* For cycle, refer to table 9.10 for details.

Thursday

	Exercise	Sets × reps		Exercise	Sets × reps
	Warm-up 1				
1	Push jerk	Cycle*	4b	Suspension trainer row	3 × 10
2a	Chain bench press	Cycle*	5a	Abdominals (medicine ball)	Exercise dependent
2b	Seated row	5 × 6-8	5b	Grip work	
3a	Medicine ball drop	3 × 8		Dumbbell hold (grip exercise)	2 × 60 sec each side
3b	Bent-over lateral raise	3 × 8	6	4-way neck	1 × 8 each way
4a	Triceps pushdown	3 × 8			

* For cycle, refer to table 9.10 for details.

Friday

	Exercise	Sets × reps		Exercise	Sets × reps
	Warm-up 3				
1	Power clean	Cycle*	4a	Glute-ham raise (10 kg) (emphasize eccentric)	Week 1: 2 × 8 Week 2: 2 × 10 Week 3: 2 × 12
2	Clean pull	3 × 5	4b	Rotational disc (shoes off for ankle strengthening)	1 × 25 each way
3a	Split squat	3 × 6 each side	5	Abdominals (functional)	Exercise dependent
3b	Side plank with isometric groin hold	2 × 10	6	Band flexibility: leg up, leg out, leg over, quad, hip flexor	1 × 10 sec each side

* For cycle, refer to table 9.10 for details.

(continued)

Unload/Variation (Version 2)

Monday

	Exercise	Sets × reps		Exercise	Sets × reps
	Warm-up 1				
1	Medicine ball slam	3 × 10	3b	Low-pulley seated row (machine)	2 × 8
2a	Dumbbell bench press	4 × 5	4a	Dumbbell shrug	3 × 8
2b	Towel pull-up	3 × 6	4b	Dumbbell biceps curl	3 × 8
3a	Bench lock out	3 × 3	5	4-way neck	1 × 8 each way

Tuesday

	Exercise	Sets × reps		Exercise	Sets × reps
	Warm-up 2				
1	One-arm dumbbell snatch	4 × 3 each arm	3b	Hamstring slide (emphasize eccentric)	2 × 10 each side
2	Back squat (light)	Cycle*	4	Band flexibility: leg up, leg out, leg over, quad, hip flexor	1 × 10 sec each side
3a	Side plank with isometric groin hold	2 × 30 sec			

* For cycle, refer to table 9.10 for details.

Thursday

	Exercise	Sets × reps		Exercise	Sets × reps
	Warm-up 4				
1	Power clean combo (barbell):	Cycle*	3b	Shoulder combo (barbell):	2 sets
	Power clean	2 reps		Front raise	6 reps
	Push jerk	2 reps		Upright row	8 reps
	Front squat	2 reps		Shoulder press	8 reps
2a	Dumbbell incline bench press	3 × 5	4a	Overhead dumbbell triceps extension	3 × 8
2b	Bent-over lateral raise	3 × 8 each side	4b	Abdominals (functional)	Exercise dependent
3a	Lunge to step-up	3 × 2 each side	5	Band flexibility: leg up, leg out, leg over, quad, hip flexor	1 × 10 sec each side

* For cycle, refer to table 9.10 for details.

Strength and Power (Phase 3)

Monday

	Exercise	Sets × reps		Exercise	Sets × reps
	Warm-up 1				
1	Snatch pull	4 × 3	4b	Hammer curl	3 × 6
2a	Bench press or incline bench press	Cycle*	5a	External shoulder rotation (dumbbell or cable)	2 × 10 each side
2b	Weighted pull-up	5 × 5	5b	Abdominals (medicine ball)	Exercise dependent
3a	Medicine ball chest pass	3 × 3 (with a descending load)	6a	Plate hold (20 kg) (grip exercise)	Week 1: 30 sec Week 2: 45 sec Week 3: 60 sec
3b	Dumbbell incline row	3 × 6	6b	4-way neck	1 × 8 each way
4a	Cable lateral raise	3 × 6 each side			

* For cycle, refer to table 9.10 for details.

Tuesday

	Exercise	Sets × reps		Exercise	Sets × reps
	Warm-up 2				
1	Clean and jerk	Cycle*	4a	Lateral lunge	3 × 5 each leg
2	Back squat	Cycle*	4b	Abdominals (functional)	Exercise dependent
3a	Romanian deadlift	3 × 5	5	Rotational disc (shoes off for ankle strengthening)	1 × 30 each way
3b	Hip thrust	2 × 5	6	Band flexibility: leg up, leg out, leg over, quad, hip flexor	1 × 10 sec each side

* For cycle, refer to table 9.10 for details.

Thursday

	Exercise	Sets × reps		Exercise	Sets × reps
	Warm-up 1				
1	One-arm dumbbell snatch	4 × 2 each arm	4b	External shoulder rotation: dumbbell shoulder horn (standing, incline, decline)	1 × 10 each position
2a	Chain bench press	Cycle*	5a	Overhead cable triceps extension	3 × 6
2b	Weighted inverted row	5 × 5	5b	Grip work: pinch gripper	2 × 30 sec each side
3a	Medicine ball drop	3 × 3 (with a descending load)	6a	Abdominals (medicine ball)	Exercise dependent
3b	Reverse-grip lat pulldown	3 × 4-6	6b	4-way neck	1 × 8 each way
4a	Suspension Y, T, I	2 × 8 each way			

* For cycle, refer to table 9.10 for details.

Friday

	Exercise	Sets × reps		Exercise	Sets × reps
	Warm-up 3				
1	Power clean	Cycle*	4a	Abdominals (functional)	Exercise dependent
2	Clean pull	3 × 3	4b	Rotational disc (shoes off for ankle strengthening)	1 × 30 each way
3a	Single-leg squat	3 × 3 each side	5	Band flexibility: leg up, leg out, leg over, quad, flexor	1 × 10 sec each side
3b	Dumbbell hamstring walk	3 × 6 each side			

* For cycle, refer to table 9.10 for details.

Table 9.7 Off-Season Program for Defensive Backs

Preparation (Phase 1)

Monday

	Exercise	Sets × reps		Exercise	Sets × reps
	Warm-up 1				
1a	Snatch pull	4 × 5	4b	Abdominals (medicine ball)	Exercise dependent
1b	Around the world medicine ball slam	3 × 4 each way	5a	Dumbbell biceps curl	3 × 10
2a	Bench press	Cycle*	5b	External shoulder rotation (dumbbell or cable)	2 × 10 each side
2b	Weighted pull-up	4 × 10	6a	Plate hold (10 kg) (grip exercise)	Week 1: 30 sec Week 2: 45 sec Week 3: 60 sec
3a	Alternating dumbbell incline bench press	3 × 8-10	6b	4-way neck	1 × 8 each way
3b	Cable row	3 × 8-10		Isometric neck stretch	2 × 5 for 30 sec each way
4a	Dumbbell shoulder press	3 × 8			

* For cycle, refer to table 9.10 for details.

Tuesday

	Exercise	Sets × reps		Exercise	Sets × reps
	Warm-up 2				
1	Dumbbell clean complex:	4 sets	3a	Back extension	Week 1: 2 × 15 Week 2: 2 × 20 Week 3: 2 × 25
	Clean		3b	Rotational disc (shoes off for ankle strengthening)	1 × 20 each way
	Front squat		4a	Stability ball triple threat	Week 1: 3 × 6 Week 2: 3 × 8 Week 3: 3 × 10
	Upright row				
	Lateral squat				
	Bent-over row				
2a	Back squat	Cycle*	4b	Abdominals (functional)	Exercise dependent
2b	Band TKE (hold for a two count)	2 × 10 each side	5	Band flexibility: leg up, leg out, leg over, quad, hip flexor	1 × 10 sec each side

* For cycle, refer to table 9.10 for details.

Thursday

	Exercise	Sets × reps		Exercise	Sets × reps
	Warm-up 1				
1a	Two-arm kettlebell swing	4 × 5	4b	External shoulder rotation: dumbbell shoulder horn (standing, incline, decline)	1 × 10 each position
1b	Lateral rotation medicine ball hip toss	3 × 5 each side	5a	Lying triceps extension	3 × 10
2a	Incline bench press	Cycle*	5b	Abdominals (medicine ball)	Exercise dependent

	Exercise	Sets × reps		Exercise	Sets × reps
2b	Weighted inverted row	4 × 10	6a	Grip work: gripper	2 × 10
3a	Alternating dumbbell bench press	3 × 8-10	6b	4-way neck	1 × 8 each way
3b	Face pull (machine)	3 × 10		Isometric neck stretch	2 × 5 for 30 sec each way
4a	Power shrug	3 × 10			

* For cycle, refer to table 9.10 for details.

Friday

	Exercise	Sets × reps		Exercise	Sets × reps
	Warm-up 3				
1	Muscle snatch	Cycle*	4a	Single-leg short arcs	2 × 10
2	Clean technique (hang clean and front squat)	Cycle*	4b	Glute-ham raise (emphasize eccentric)	Week 1: 2 × 8 Week 2: 2 × 10 Week 3: 2 × 12
			5a	Abdominals (functional)	Exercise dependent
			5b	Rotational disc (shoes off for ankle strengthening)	1 × 20 each way
3a	Walking lunge	3 × 10 each side	6	Band flexibility: leg up, leg out, leg over, quad, hip flexor	1 × 10 sec each side
3b	Side plank with isometric groin hold	2 × 10			

* For cycle, refer to table 9.10 for details.

Unload/Variation (Version 1)

Monday

	Exercise	Sets × reps		Exercise	Sets × reps
	Warm-up 1				
1	Medicine ball slam	3 × 10	4a	Dumbbell shrug	3 × 8
2a	Close-grip bench press	4 × 5	4b	Reverse-grip curl (EZ bar)	3 × 8
2b	Towel pull-up	3 × 8	5	4-way neck	1 × 8 each way
3a	Dip	2 × 10		Isometric neck stretch	2 × 5 for 30 sec each way
3b	Low-pulley seated row (machine)	2 × 8			

Tuesday

	Exercise	Sets × reps		Exercise	Sets × reps
	Warm-up 2				
1	One-arm dumbbell snatch	4 × 3 each arm	3b	Hamstring slide (emphasize eccentric)	2 × 10 each side
2	Back squat (light)	Cycle*	4	Single-leg hip thrust (body weight)	2 × 10 each side
3a	Side plank with isometric groin hold	2 × 30 sec	5	Band flexibility: leg up, leg out, leg over, quad, hip flexor	1 × 10 sec each side

* For cycle, refer to table 9.10 for details.

(continued)

Table 9.7 Off-Season Program for Defensive Backs *(continued)*

Thursday

	Exercise	Sets × reps		Exercise	Sets × reps
	Warm-up 4				
1	Power clean complex (barbell):	Cycle*	3b	Shoulder combo (barbell):	2 sets
	Power clean	3 reps		Front raise	6 reps
	Front squat to press	3 reps		Upright row	8 reps
	Bent-over row	3 reps		Shoulder press	8 reps
2a	Dumbbell incline bench press	3 × (8,6,5)	4a	Overhead dumbbell triceps extension	3 × 8
2b	Bent-over lateral raise	3 × 8 each side	4b	Abdominals (functional)	Exercise dependent
3a	Step-up (dumbbell or barbell)	3 × 6 each side	5	Band flexibility: leg up, leg out, leg over, quad, hip flexor	1 × 10 sec each side

* For cycle, refer to table 9.10 for details.

Strength (Phase 2)

Monday

	Exercise	Sets × reps		Exercise	Sets × reps
	Warm-up 1				
1	Two-arm dumbbell clean to push press	Cycle*	5a	EZ bar curl	3 × 8
2a	Bench press or incline bench press	Cycle*	5b	Burner combo	2 × 10 each way
2b	Close-grip lat pulldown	3 × 6-8	6a	External shoulder rotation (dumbbell or cable)	2 × 10 each way
3a	Medicine ball chest pass	3 × 10	6b	Plate hold (15 kg) (grip exercise)	Week 1: 30 sec Week 2: 45 sec Week 3: 60 sec
3b	Standing one-arm dumbbell row	3 × 6-8	7	4-way neck	1 × 8 each way
4a	Barbell shoulder press	3 × 6		Isometric neck stretch	2 × 5 for 30 sec each way
4b	Abdominals (medicine ball)	Exercise dependent			

* For cycle, refer to table 9.10 for details.

Tuesday

	Exercise	Sets × reps		Exercise	Sets × reps
	Warm-up 2				
1	Power snatch	Cycle*	4b	Lateral squat	2 × 6 each side
2	Back squat	Cycle*	5a	Abdominals (functional)	Exercise dependent
3a	Hip thrust	2 × 8	5b	Dumbbell neck stretch shrug	2 × 10 each way
3b	Single-leg partial squat (weighted)	2 × 10 each side	6	Rotational disc (shoes off for ankle strengthening)	1 × 25 each way
4a	Romanian deadlift	3 × 8	7	Band flexibility: leg up, leg out, leg over, quad, hip flexor	1 × 10 sec each side

* For cycle, refer to table 9.10 for details.

Thursday

	Exercise	Sets × reps		Exercise	Sets × reps
	Warm-up 1				
1	Push jerk	Cycle*	4b	Suspension trainer row	3 × 10
2a	Chain bench press	Cycle*	5a	Abdominals (medicine ball)	Exercise dependent
2b	Seated row	5 × 6-8	5b	Dumbbell hold (grip exercise)	2 × 60 sec each side
3a	Medicine ball drop	3 × 8	6	4-way neck	1 × 8 each way
3b	Bent-over lateral raise	3 × 8		Isometric neck stretch	2 × 5 for 30 sec each way
4a	Triceps pushdown	3 × 8			

* For cycle, refer to table 9.10 for details.

Friday

	Exercise	Sets × reps		Exercise	Sets × reps
	Warm-up 3				
1	Power clean	Cycle*	4a	Glute-ham raise (10 kg) (emphasize eccentric)	Week 1: 2 × 8 Week 2: 2 × 10 Week 3: 2 × 12
2	Clean pull	3 × 5	4b	Rotational disc (shoes off for ankle strengthening)	1 × 25 each way
3a	Split squat	3 × 6 each side	5	Abdominals (functional)	Exercise dependent
3b	Side plank with isometric groin hold	2 × 10	6	Band flexibility: leg up, leg out, leg over, quad, hip flexor	1 × 10 sec each side

* For cycle, refer to table 9.10 for details.

Unload/Variation (Version 2)

Monday

	Exercise	Sets × reps		Exercise	Sets × reps
	Warm-up 1				
1	Medicine ball slam	3 × 10	4a	Dumbbell shrug	3 × 8
2a	Dumbbell bench press	4 × 5	4b	Dumbbell biceps curl	3 × 8
2b	Towel pull-up	3 × 6	5	4-way neck	1 × 8 each way
3a	Bench lockout	3 × 3		Isometric neck stretch	2 × 5 for 30 sec each way
3b	Low-pulley seated row (machine)	2 × 8			

Tuesday

	Exercise	Sets × reps		Exercise	Sets × reps
	Warm-up 2				
1	One-arm dumbbell snatch	4 × 3 each arm	3b	Hamstring slide (emphasize eccentric)	2 × 10 each side
2	Back squat (light)	Cycle*	4	Band flexibility: leg up, leg out, leg over, quad, hip flexor	1 × 10 sec each side
3a	Side plank with isometric groin hold	2 × 30 sec			

* For cycle, refer to table 9.10 for details.

(continued)

Table 9.7   Off-Season Program for Defensive Backs *(continued)*

Thursday

	Exercise	Sets × reps		Exercise	Sets × reps
	Warm-up 4				
1	Power clean combo (barbell):	Cycle*	3b	Shoulder combo (barbell):	2 sets
	Power clean	2 reps		Front raise	6 reps
	Push jerk	2 reps		Upright row	8 reps
	Front squat	2 reps		Shoulder press	8 reps
2a	Dumbbell incline bench press	3 × 5	4a	Overhead dumbbell triceps extension	3 × 8
2b	Bent-over lateral raise	3 × 8 each side	4b	Abdominals (functional)	Exercise dependent
3a	Lunge to step-up	3 × 2 each side	5	Band flexibility: leg up, leg out, leg over, quad, hip flexor	1 × 10 sec each side

* For cycle, refer to table 9.10 for details.

Strength and Power (Phase 3)

Monday

	Exercise	Sets × reps		Exercise	Sets × reps
	Warm-up 1				
1	Snatch pull	4 × 3	5a	Burner combo	2 × 10 each way
2a	Bench press or incline bench press	Cycle*	5b	External shoulder rotation (dumbbell or cable)	2 × 10 each side
2b	Weighted pull-up	5 × 5	6	Abdominals (medicine ball)	Exercise dependent
3a	Medicine ball chest pass	3 × 3 (with a descending load)	7a	Plate hold (20 kg) (grip exercise)	Week 1: 30 sec / Week 2: 45 sec / Week 3: 60 sec
3b	Dumbbell incline row	3 × 6	7b	4-way neck	1 × 8 each way
4a	Hammer curl	3 × 6		Isometric neck stretch	2 × 5 for 30 sec each way
4b	Cable lateral raise	2 × 6 each side			

* For cycle, refer to table 9.10 for details.

Tuesday

	Exercise	Sets × reps		Exercise	Sets × reps
	Warm-up 2				
1	Clean and jerk	Cycle*	4b	Dumbbell neck stretch shrug	2 × 10 each side
2	Back squat	Cycle*	5a	Abdominals (functional)	Exercise dependent
3a	Romanian deadlift	3 × 5	5b	Rotational disc (shoes off for ankle strengthening)	1 × 30 each way
3b	Hip thrust	2 × 5	6	Band flexibility: leg up, leg out, leg over, quad, hip flexor	1 × 10 sec each side
4a	Lateral lunge	3 × 5 each leg			

* For cycle, refer to table 9.10 for details.

Thursday

	Exercise	Sets × reps		Exercise	Sets × reps
	Warm-up 1				
1	One-arm dumbbell snatch	4 × 2 each arm	4b	External shoulder rotation: dumbbell shoulder horn (standing, incline, decline)	1 × 10 each position
2a	Chain bench press	Cycle*	5a	Overhead cable triceps extension	3 × 6
2b	Weighted inverted row	5 × 5	5b	Grip work: pinch gripper	2 × 30 sec each side
3a	Medicine ball drop	3 × 3 (with a descending load)	6a	Abdominals (medicine ball)	Exercise dependent
3b	Reverse-grip lat pulldown	3 × 4-6	6b	4-way neck	1 × 8 each way
4a	Suspension Y, T, I	2 × 8 each way		Isometric neck stretch	2 × 5 for 30 sec each way

* For cycle, refer to table 9.10 for details.

Friday

	Exercise	Sets × reps		Exercise	Sets × reps
	Warm-up 3				
1	Power clean	Cycle*	4a	Dumbbell hamstring walk	3 × 6 each side
2	Clean pull	3 × 3	4b	Abdominals (functional)	Exercise dependent
3a	Chain back squat	Cycle*	5	Rotational disc (shoes off for ankle strengthening)	1 × 30 each way
3b	Single-leg squat	3 × 3 each side	6	Band flexibility: leg up, leg out, leg over, quad, hip flexor	1 × 10 sec each side

* For cycle, refer to table 9.10 for details.

Table 9.8 Off-Season Program for Quarterbacks

Preparation (Phase 1)

Monday

	Exercise	Sets × reps		Exercise	Sets × reps
	Warm-up 1				
1a	Snatch pull	4 × 5	4b	Abdominals (medicine ball)	Exercise dependent
1b	Around the world medicine ball slam	3 × 4 each way	5a	Dumbbell biceps curl	3 × 10
2a	Alternating dumbbell bench press	3 × 8-10	5b	External shoulder rotation (dumbbell or cable)	2 × 10 each side
2b	Wide-grip lat pulldown	3 × 8-10	6a	Plate hold (10 kg) (grip exercise)	Week 1: 30 sec Week 2: 45 sec Week 3: 60 sec
3a	Push-up (on stability ball)	3 × 10		Finger extensor band (grip exercise)	2 × 10 each way
3b	Cable row	3 × 8-10		Grip football	15 sec
4a	Dumbbell shoulder press	3 × 8	6b	4-way neck	1 × 8 each way

Tuesday

	Exercise	Sets × reps		Exercise	Sets × reps
	Warm-up 2				
1	Dumbbell clean complex:	Cycle*	3a	Back extension	Week 1: 2 × 15 Week 2: 2 × 20 Week 3: 2 × 25
	Clean		3b	Rotational disc (shoes off for ankle strengthening)	1 × 20 each way
	Front squat		4a	Stability ball triple threat	Week 1: 3 × 6 Week 2: 3 × 8 Week 3: 3 × 10
	Upright row				
	Lateral squat				
	Bent-over row				
2a	Back squat	Cycle*	4b	Abdominals (functional)	Exercise dependent
2b	Band TKE (hold for a two count)	2 × 10 each side	5	Band flexibility: leg up, leg out, leg over, quad, hip flexor	1 × 10 sec each side

* For cycle, refer to table 9.10 for details.

Thursday

	Exercise	Sets × reps		Exercise	Sets × reps
	Warm-up 1				
1a	Two-arm kettlebell swing	4 × 5	5a	Lying triceps extension	3 × 10
1b	Lateral rotation medicine ball hip toss	3 × 5 each side	5b	Half-kneeling stick chop	10 each side
2a	Alternating dumbbell incline bench press	3 × 8-10		Half-kneeling stick lift	10 each side
2b	Standing one-arm dumbbell row	3 × 8-10	6a	Gripper	2 × 10

	Exercise	Sets × reps		Exercise	Sets × reps
3a	Weighted push-up	3 × 8		Finger extension band	2 × 10 each side
3b	Face pull (machine)	3 × 10		Grip football	15 sec
4a	Power shrug	3 × 10	6b	4-way neck	1 × 8 each way
4b	External shoulder rotation: dumbbell shoulder horn (standing, incline, decline)	1 × 10 each position			

Friday

	Exercise	Sets × reps		Exercise	Sets × reps
	Warm-up 3				
1	Muscle snatch	Cycle*	4a	Single-leg short arcs	2 × 10
2	Clean technique (hang clean and front squat)	Cycle*	4b	Glute-ham raise (emphasize eccentric)	Week 1: 2 × 8 Week 2: 2 × 10 Week 3: 2 × 12
			5a	Abdominals (functional)	Exercise dependent
			5b	Rotational disc (shoes off for ankle strengthening)	1 × 20 each way
3a	Walking lunge	3 × 10 each side	6	Band flexibility: leg up, leg out, leg over, quad, hip flexor	1 × 10 sec each side
3b	Side plank with isometric groin hold	2 × 10			

* For cycle, refer to table 9.10 for details.

Unload/Variation (Version 1)

Monday

	Exercise	Sets × reps		Exercise	Sets × reps
	Warm-up 1				
1	Medicine ball slam	3 × 10	3b	Low-pulley seated row (machine)	2 × 8
2a	Dumbbell bench press	3 × 8,6,5	4a	Dumbbell shrug	3 × 8
2b	Towel pull-up	3 × 8	4b	Reverse-grip curl (EZ bar)	3 × 8
3a	Dip	2 × 10	5	4-way neck	1 × 8 each way

Tuesday

	Exercise	Sets × reps		Exercise	Sets × reps
	Warm-up 2				
1	One-arm dumbbell snatch	4 × 3 each arm	3b	Hamstring slide (emphasize eccentric)	2 × 10 each side
2	Back squat (light)	Cycle*	4	Single-leg hip thrust (body weight)	2 × 10 each side
3a	Side plank with isometric groin hold	2 × 30 sec	5	Band flexibility: leg up, leg out, leg over, quad, hip flexor	1 × 10 sec each side

* For cycle, refer to table 9.10 for details.

(continued)

Table 9.8   Off-Season Program for Quarterbacks *(continued)*

Thursday

	Exercise	Sets × reps		Exercise	Sets × reps
	Warm-up 4				
1	Power clean complex (barbell):	Cycle*	3b	Shoulder combo (barbell):	2 sets
	Power clean	3 reps		Front raise	6 reps
	Front squat to press	3 reps		Upright row	8 reps
	Bent-over row	3 reps		Shoulder press	8 reps
2a	Dumbbell incline bench press	3 × 8,6,5	4a	Overhead dumbbell triceps extension	3 × 8
2b	Bent-over lateral raise	3 × 8 each side	4b	Abdominals (functional)	Exercise dependent
3a	Step-up (dumbbell or barbell)	3 × 6 each side	5	Band flexibility: leg up, leg out, leg over, quad, hip flexor	1 × 10 sec each side

* For cycle, refer to table 9.10 for details.

Strength (Phase 2)

Monday

	Exercise	Sets × reps		Exercise	Sets × reps
	Warm-up 1				
1	Two-arm dumbbell clean to push press	Cycle*	4b	Seated partner side-to-side toss	2 × 10 each way
2a	One-arm dumbbell bench press or one-arm dumbbell incline bench press	4 × 5 each arm		Lateral leg raise	2 × 8 each side
2b	Weighted pull-up	3 × 6-8	5a	EZ bar biceps curl	3 × 8
3a	Dumbbell pullover	3 × 6-8	5b	External shoulder rotation (dumbbell or cable)	2 × 10 each side
3b	Dumbbell shoulder press	3 × 6	6a	Plate hold (15 kg) (grip exercise)	Week 1: 30 sec Week 2: 45 sec Week 3: 60 sec
4a	Medi ball overhead one-arm quick toss	2 × 10 each way		Finger extensor band (grip exercise)	2 × 10 each way
	Medi ball overhead one-arm deceleration throw	2 × 10 each way		Grip football	15 sec
			6b	4-way neck	1 × 8 each way

* For cycle, refer to table 9.10 for details.

Tuesday

	Exercise	Sets × reps		Exercise	Sets × reps
	Warm-up 2				
1	One-arm dumbbell snatch	4 × 3 each arm	4b	Lateral squat	2 × 6 each side
2	Back squat	Cycle*	5a	Abdominals (functional)	Exercise dependent
3a	Hip thrust	2 × 8	5b	Rotational disc (shoes off for ankle strengthening)	1 × 25 each way
3b	Single-leg partial squat (weighted)	2 × 10 each side	6	Band flexibility: leg up, leg out, leg over, quad, hip flexor	1 × 10 sec each side
4a	Romanian deadlift	3 × 8			

* For cycle, refer to table 9.10 for details.

Thursday

	Exercise	Sets × reps		Exercise	Sets × reps
	Warm-up 1				
1	Push jerk	Cycle*	5a	Half-kneeling stick chop	10 each side
2a	Band push-up	3 × 6		Half-kneeling stick lift	10 each side
2b	Weighted inverted row	5 × 6-8	5b	Dumbbell hold (grip exercise)	2 × 60 sec each side
3a	Push-up (on stability ball) (feet on box)	3 × 8		Finger extensor band (grip exercise)	2 × 10 each side
3b	Bent-over lateral raise	3 × 8		Grip football	15 sec
4a	Triceps pushdown	3 × 8	6	4-way neck	1 × 8 each way
4b	Suspension trainer row	3 × 10			

* For cycle, refer to table 9.10 for details.

Friday

	Exercise	Sets × reps		Exercise	Sets × reps
	Warm-up 3				
1	Power clean	Cycle*	4a	Glute-ham raise (10 kg) (emphasize eccentric)	Week 1: 2 × 8 / Week 2: 2 × 10 / Week 3: 2 × 12
2	Clean pull	3 × 5	4b	Rotational disc (shoes off for ankle strengthening)	1 × 25 each way
3a	Split squat	3 × 6 each side	5	Medicine ball wood chop	3 × 5
3b	Side plank with isometric groin hold	2 × 10	6	Band flexibility: leg up, leg out, leg over, quad, hip flexor	1 × 10 sec each side

* For cycle, refer to table 9.10 for details.

Unload/Variation (Version 2)

Monday

	Exercise	Sets × reps		Exercise	Sets × reps
	Warm-up 1				
1	Medicine ball slam	3 × 10	3b	Low-pulley seated row (machine)	2 × 8
2a	Dumbbell bench press	4 × 5	4a	Dumbbell shrug	3 × 8
2b	Towel pull-up	3 × 6	4b	Dumbbell biceps curl	3 × 8
3a	Chain push-up	3 × 3	5	4-way neck	1 × 8 each way

Tuesday

	Exercise	Sets × reps		Exercise	Sets × reps
	Warm-up 2				
1	One-arm dumbbell snatch	4 × 3 each arm	3b	Hamstring slide (emphasize eccentric)	2 × 10 each side
2	Back squat (light)	Cycle*	4	Band flexibility: leg up, leg out, leg over, quad, hip flexor	1 × 10 sec each side
3a	Side plank with isometric groin hold	2 × 30 sec			

* For cycle, refer to table 9.10 for details.

(continued)

Table 9.8 Off-Season Program for Quarterbacks *(continued)*

Thursday

	Exercise	Sets × reps		Exercise	Sets × reps
	Warm-up 4				
1	Power clean combo (barbell):	Cycle*	3b	Shoulder combo (barbell):	2 sets
	Power clean	2 reps		Front raise	6 reps
	Push jerk	2 reps		Upright row	8 reps
	Front squat	2 reps		Shoulder press	8 reps
2a	Dumbbell incline bench press	3 × 5	4a	Overhead dumbbell triceps extension	3 × 8
2b	Bent-over lateral raise	3 × 8 each side	4b	Abdominals (functional)	Exercise dependent
3a	Lunge to step-up	3 × 2 each side	5	Band flexibility: leg up, leg out, leg over, quad, hip flexor	1 × 10 sec each side

* For cycle, refer to table 9.10 for details.

Strength and Power (Phase 3)

Monday

	Exercise	Sets × reps		Exercise	Sets × reps
	Warm-up 1				
1	Snatch pull	4 × 3	4b	Medicine ball around the world	2 × 10 each way (with a descending load)
2a	Dumbbell bench press or dumbbell incline bench press	4 × 4		Dumbbell twist	2 × 10 each way
2b	Close-grip lat pulldown	3 × 4-6	5a	Hammer curl	3 × 6
3a	Cable pullover (on stability ball)	3 × 6	5b	External shoulder rotation (dumbbell or cable)	2 × 10 each side
3b	Cable lateral raise	3 × 6 each side	6a	Plate hold (20 kg) (grip exercise)	Week 1: 30 sec Week 2: 45 sec Week 3: 60 sec
4a	Medi ball overhead one-arm quick toss	2 × 10 each side		Finger extensor band (grip exercise)	2 × 10 each way
	Medi ball overhead one-arm deceleration throw	2 × 10 each side		Grip football	15 sec
			6b	4-way neck	1 × 8 each way

Tuesday

	Exercise	Sets × reps		Exercise	Sets × reps
	Warm-up 2				
1	Clean and jerk	Cycle*	4a	Lateral lunge	3 × 5 each leg
2	Back squat	Cycle*	4b	Abdominals (functional)	Exercise dependent
3a	Romanian deadlift	3 × 5	5	Rotational disc (shoes off for ankle strengthening)	1 × 30 each way
3b	Hip thrust	2 × 5	6	Band flexibility: leg up, leg out, leg over, quad, hip flexor	1 × 10 sec each side

* For cycle, refer to table 9.10 for details.

Thursday

	Exercise	Sets × reps		Exercise	Sets × reps
	Warm-up 1				
1	One-arm dumbbell snatch	4 × 2 each arm	5a	Overhead cable triceps extension	3 × 6
2a	Chain push-up	4 × 3	5b	Half-kneeling stick chop	10 each side
2b	One-arm dumbbell row	4 × 4-6		Half-kneeling stick lift	10 each side
3a	Push-up (on stability ball) (one foot on box)	3 × 6	6a	Pinch gripper	2 × 30 sec each side
3b	Reverse-grip lat pulldown	3 × 4-6		Finger extensor band (grip exercise)	2 × 10 each side
4a	Suspension Y, T, I	2 × 8 each way		Grip football	15 sec
4b	External shoulder rotation: dumbbell shoulder horn (standing, incline, decline)	1 × 10 each position	6b	4-way neck	1 × 8 each way

Friday

	Exercise	Sets × reps		Exercise	Sets × reps
	Warm-up 3				
1	Power clean	Cycle*	4b	Dumbbell hamstring walk	3 × 6 each side
2	Clean pull	3 × 3	5a	Kneeling medicine ball blob throw	3 × 5 (with a descending load)
3	Chain back squat	Cycle*	5b	Rotational disc (shoes off for ankle strengthening)	1 × 30 each way
4a	Single-leg squat	3 × 3 each side	6	Band flexibility: leg up, leg out, leg over, quad, hip flexor	1 × 10 sec each side

* For cycle, refer to table 9.10 for details.

Table 9.9 Off-Season Program for Kickers and Punters

Preparation (Phase 1)

Monday

	Exercise	Sets × reps		Exercise	Sets × reps
	Warm-up 1				
1a	Snatch pull	4 × 5	4a	Dumbbell shoulder press	3 × 8
1b	Around the world medicine ball slam	3 × 4 each way	4b	Abdominals (medicine ball)	Exercise dependent
2a	Bench press	Cycle*	5a	Dumbbell biceps curl	3 × 10
2b	Wide-grip lat pulldown	3 × 8-10	5b	External shoulder rotation (dumbbell or cable)	2 × 10 each way
3a	Alternating dumbbell incline bench press	3 × 8-10	6a	Plate hold (10 kg) (grip exercise)	Week 1: 30 sec Week 2: 45 sec Week 3: 60 sec
3b	Cable row	3 × 8-10	6b	4-way neck	1 × 8 each way

* For cycle, refer to table 9.10 for details.

Tuesday

	Exercise	Sets × reps		Exercise	Sets × reps
	Warm-up 2				
1	Dumbbell clean complex:	Cycle*	3b	Rotational disc (shoes off for ankle strengthening)	1 × 20 each way
	Clean		4a	4-way hip machine	10 each way
	Front squat		4b	Stability ball triple threat	Week 1: 6
	Upright row				Week 2: 8
	Lateral squat				Week 3: 10
	Bent-over row				
2a	Back squat	Cycle*	5	Abdominals (functional)	Exercise dependent
2b	Band TKE (hold for a two count)	2 × 10 each side	6	Band flexibility: leg up, leg out, leg over, quad, hip flexor	1 × 10 sec each side
3a	Back extension	Week 1: 2 × 15 Week 2: 2 × 20 Week 3: 2 × 25			

* For cycle, refer to table 9.10 for details.

Thursday

	Exercise	Sets × reps		Exercise	Sets × reps
	Warm-up 1				
1a	Two-arm kettlebell swing	4 × 5	4a	Power shrug	3 × 10
1b	Lateral rotation medicine ball hip toss	3 × 5 each side	4b	External shoulder rotation: dumbbell shoulder horn (standing, incline, decline)	1 × 10 each position
2a	Incline bench press	Cycle*	5a	Lying EZ-bar triceps extension	3 × 10
2b	Standing one-arm dumbbell row	3 × 8-10	5b	Abdominals (medicine ball)	Exercise dependent
3a	Alternating dumbbell bench press	3 × 8-10	6a	Grip work: gripper	2 × 10
3b	Face pull (machine)	3 × 10	6b	4-way neck	1 × 8 each way

* For cycle, refer to table 9.10 for details.

	Exercise	Sets × reps		Exercise	Sets × reps
	Warm-up 3				
1	Muscle snatch	Cycle*	4a	Single-leg short arcs	2 × 10
2	Clean technique (hang clean and front squat)	Cycle*	4b	Glute-ham raise (emphasize eccentric)	Week 1: 2 × 8 Week 2: 2 × 10 Week 3: 2 × 12
			5a	Abdominals (functional)	Exercise dependent
			5b	Rotational disc (shoes off for ankle strengthening)	1 × 20 each way
3a	Walking lunge	3 × 10 each side	6	Band flexibility: leg up, leg out, leg over, quad, hip flexor	1 × 10 sec each side
3b	Side plank with isometric groin hold	2 × 10			

* For cycle, refer to table 9.10 for details.

Unload/Variation (Version 1)

Monday

	Exercise	Sets × reps		Exercise	Sets × reps
	Warm-up 1				
1	Medicine ball slam	3 × 10	3b	Low-pulley seated row (machine)	2 × 8
2a	Close-grip bench press	4 × 5	4a	Dumbbell shrug	3 × 8
2b	Towel pull-up	3 × 8	4b	Reverse-grip curl (EZ-bar)	3 × 8
3a	Dip	2 × 10	5	4-way neck	1 × 8 each way

Tuesday

	Exercise	Sets × reps		Exercise	Sets × reps
	Warm-up 2				
1	One-arm dumbbell snatch	4 × 3 each arm	3b	Hamstring slide (emphasize eccentric)	2 × 10 each side
2	Back squat (light)	Cycle*	4	Single-leg hip thrust (body weight)	2 × 10 each side
3a	Side plank with isometric groin hold	2 × 30 sec	5	Band flexibility: leg up, leg out, leg over, quad, hip flexor	1 × 10 sec each side

* For cycle, refer to table 9.10 for details.

Thursday

	Exercise	Sets × reps		Exercise	Sets × reps
	Warm-up 4				
1	Power clean complex (barbell):	Cycle*	3b	Shoulder combo (barbell):	2 sets
	Power clean	3 reps		Front raise	6 reps
	Front squat to press	3 reps		Upright row	8 reps
	Bent-over row	3 reps		Shoulder press	8 reps
2a	Dumbbell incline bench press	3 × (8,6,5)	4a	Overhead dumbbell triceps extension	3 × 8
2b	Bent-over lateral raise	3 × 8 each side	4b	Abdominals (functional)	Exercise dependent
3a	Step-up (dumbbell or barbell)	3 × 6 each side	5	Band flexibility: leg up, leg out, leg over, quad, hip flexor	1 × 10 sec each side

* For cycle, refer to table 9.10 for details.

(continued)

Table 9.9 Off-Season Program for Kickers and Punters *(continued)*

Strength (Phase 2)

Monday

	Exercise	Sets × reps		Exercise	Sets × reps
	Warm-up 1				
1	Two-arm dumbbell clean to push press	Cycle*	4a	Abdominals (medicine ball)	Exercise dependent
2a	Bench press or incline bench press	Cycle*	4b	EZ-bar curl	3 × 8
2b	Weighted pull-up	3 × 6-8	5a	External shoulder rotation (dumbbell or cable)	2 × 10 each side
3a	Barbell shoulder press	3 × 6	5b	Plate hold (15 kg) (grip exercise)	Week 1: 30 sec Week 2: 45 sec Week 3: 60 sec
3b	Suspension trainer row	3 × 6-8	6	4-way neck	1 × 8 each way

* For cycle, refer to table 9.10 for details.

Tuesday

	Exercise	Sets × reps		Exercise	Sets × reps
	Warm-up 2				
1	Power snatch	Cycle*	4b	4-way hip machine	10 each way
2	Back squat	Cycle*	5a	Abdominals (functional)	Exercise dependent
3a	Hip thrust	2 × 8	5b	Rotational disc (shoes off for ankle strengthening)	1 × 25 each way
3b	Single-leg partial squat (weighted)	2 × 10 each side	6	Band flexibility: leg up, leg out, leg over, quad, hip flexor	1 × 10 sec each side
4a	Romanian deadlift	3 × 8			

* For cycle, refer to table 9.10 for details.

Thursday

	Exercise	Sets × reps		Exercise	Sets × reps
	Warm-up 1				
1	Push jerk	Cycle*	4a	Suspension trainer row	3 × 10
2a	Chain bench press	Cycle*	4b	Abdominals (medicine ball)	Exercise dependent
2b	Weighted inverted row	5 × 6-8	5a	Dumbbell hold (grip exercise)	2 × 60 sec each side
3a	Bent-over lateral raise	3 × 8	6	4-way neck	1 × 8 each way
3b	Triceps push-down	3 × 8			

* For cycle, refer to table 9.10 for details.

	Exercise	Sets × reps		Exercise	Sets × reps
	Warm-up 3				
1	Power clean	Cycle*	4a	Glute-ham raise (10 kg) (emphasize eccentric)	Week 1: 2 × 8 Week 2: 2 × 10 Week 3: 2 × 12
2	Clean pull	3 × 5	4b	Rotational disc (shoes off for ankle strengthening)	1 × 25 each way
3a	Split squat	3 × 6 each side	5	Abdominals (functional)	Exercise dependent
3b	Side plank with isometric groin hold	2 × 10	6	Band flexibility: leg up, leg out, leg over, quad, hip flexor	1 × 10 sec each side

* For cycle, refer to table 9.10 for details.

Unload/Variation (Version 2)

Monday

	Exercise	Sets × reps		Exercise	Sets × reps
	Warm-up 1				
1	Medicine ball slam	3 × 10	3b	Low-pulley seated row (machine)	2 × 8
2a	Dumbbell bench press	4 × 5	4a	Dumbbell shrug	3 × 8
2b	Towel pull-up	3 × 6	4b	Dumbbell biceps curl	3 × 8
3a	Bench lockout	3 × 3	5	4-way neck	1 × 8 each way

Tuesday

	Exercise	Sets × reps		Exercise	Sets × reps
	Warm-up 2				
1	One-arm dumbbell snatch	4 × 3 each arm	3b	Hamstring slide (emphasize eccentric)	2 × 10 each way
2	Back squat (light)	Cycle*	4	Band flexibility: leg up, leg out, leg over, quad, hip flexor	1 × 10 sec each side
3a	Side plank with isometric groin hold	2 × 30 sec			

* For cycle, refer to table 9.10 for details.

Thursday

	Exercise	Sets × reps		Exercise	Sets × reps
	Warm-up 4				
1	Power clean combo (barbell):	Cycle*	3b	Shoulder combo (barbell):	2 sets
	Power clean	2 reps		Front raise	6 reps
	Push jerk	2 reps		Upright row	8 reps
	Front squat	2 reps		Shoulder press	8 reps
2a	Dumbbell incline bench press	3 × 5	4a	Overhead dumbbell triceps extension	3 × 8
2b	Bent-over lateral raise	3 × 8 each side	4b	Abdominals (functional)	Exercise dependent
3a	Lunge to step-up	3 × 2 each side	5	Band flexibility: leg up, leg out, leg over, quad, hip flexor	1 × 10 sec each side

* For cycle, refer to table 9.10 for details.

(continued)

Table 9.9 Off-Season Program for Kickers and Punters *(continued)*

Strength and Power (Phase 3)

Monday

	Exercise	Sets × reps		Exercise	Sets × reps
	Warm-up 1				
1	Snatch pull	4 × 3	4a	Hammer curl	3 × 6
2a	Bench press or incline bench press	Cycle*	4b	External shoulder rotation (dumbbell or cable)	2 × 10 each side
2b	Close-grip lat pulldown	5 × 4-6	5a	Abdominals (medicine ball)	Exercise dependent
3a	Cable lateral raise	3 × 6 each side	5b	Plate hold (20 kg) (grip exercise)	Week 1: 30 sec / Week 2: 45 sec / Week 3: 60 sec
3b	Dumbbell incline row	3 × 6	6	4-way neck	1 × 8 each way

* For cycle, refer to table 9.10 for details.

Tuesday

	Exercise	Sets × reps		Exercise	Sets × reps
	Warm-up 2				
1	Clean and jerk	Cycle*	4a	4-way hip machine	10 each way
2	Back squat	Cycle*	4b	Abdominals (functional)	Exercise dependent
3a	Romanian deadlift	3 × 5	5	Rotational disc (shoes off for ankle strengthening)	1 × 30 each way
3b	Hip thrust	2 × 5	6	Band flexibility: leg up, leg out, leg over, quad, hip flexor	1 × 10 sec each side

* For cycle, refer to table 9.10 for details.

Thursday

	Exercise	Sets × reps		Exercise	Sets × reps
	Warm-up 1				
1	One-arm dumbbell snatch	4 × 2 each arm	4a	External shoulder rotation: dumbbell shoulder horn (standing, incline, decline)	1 × 10 each position
2a	Chain bench press	Cycle*	4b	Overhead cable triceps extension	3 × 6
2b	One-arm dumbbell row	5 × 4-6	5a	Grip work: pinch gripper	2 × 30 sec each side
3a	Suspension Y, T, I	2 × 8 each way	5b	Abdominals (medicine ball)	Exercise dependent
3b	Reverse-grip lat pulldown	3 × 4-6	6	4-way neck	1 × 8 each way

* For cycle, refer to table 9.10 for details.

Friday

	Exercise	Sets × reps		Exercise	Sets × reps
	Warm-up 3				
1	Power clean	Cycle*	4a	Abdominals (functional)	Exercise dependent
2	Clean pull	3 × 3	4b	Rotational disc (shoes off for ankle strengthening)	1 × 30 each way
3a	Single-leg squat	4 × 3 each side	5	Band flexibility: leg up, leg out, leg over, quad, hip flexor	1 × 10 sec each side
3b	Dumbbell hamstring walk	3 × 6 each side			

* For cycle, refer to table 9.10 for details.

Table 9.10 Off-Season Cycle

Phase number	Phase name	Week	Intensity	Exercise	Scheme*
1	Preparation	1	Medium	Muscle snatch	4 × 5
				Dumbbell clean complex	4 × 3
				Clean technique	52/4, 60/4, 67/4, 70/4, 72/4
				Back squat	50/5, 57/5, 65/10, 67/10, 70/10
				Bench press/incline bench press	50/5, 57/5, 65/10, 67/10, 70/10
1	Preparation	2	Medium heavy	Muscle snatch	4 × 4
				Dumbbell clean complex	4 × 4
				Clean technique	55/4, 62/4, 70/4, 72/4, 75/4
				Back squat	55/5, 62/5, 70/10, 72/10, 75/8
				Bench press/incline bench press	55/5, 62/5, 70/10, 72/10, 75/8
1	Preparation	3	Heavy	Muscle snatch	4 × 3
				Dumbbell clean complex	4 × 5
				Clean technique	57/4, 65/4, 72/4, 75/4, 77/4
				Back squat	57/5, 65/5, 72/10, 75/8, 77/8
				Bench press/incline bench press	55/3, 62/3, 70/4, 72/4, 75/4
	Unload/ variation (Version 1)	4		Back squat (light)	57/5, 65/5, 72/10, 75/8, 77/8
				Power clean complex	57/3, 65/3, 67/3, 70/3
2	Strength	5	Medium	Two-arm dumbbell clean to push press	4 × 5
				Bench press	60/3, 67/3, 75/5, 77/5, 80/5, 82/5
				Chain bench press	135 × 8, 135CH × 3, 50CH/3 × 6, 70/1, 80/1
				Power snatch	50/3, 57/3, 65/3, 67/3, 70/3
				Back squat	60/3, 67/3, 75/5, 77/5, 80/5, 82/5
				Push jerk/power clean	60/3, 67/3, 75/3, 77/3, 80/3
2	Strength	6	Medium heavy	Two-arm dumbbell clean to push press	4 × 4
				Incline bench press	62/3, 70/3, 77/5, 80/5, 82/5, 85/5
				Chain bench press	135 × 8, 135CH × 3, 50CH/3 × 6, 72/1, 82/1
				Power snatch	52/3, 60/3, 67/3, 70/3, 72/3
				Back squat	62/3, 70/3, 77/5, 80/5, 82/5, 85/5
				Push jerk/power clean	62/3, 70/3, 77/3, 80/3, 82/3

(continued)

Table 9.10 Off-Season Cycle *(continued)*

Phase number	Phase name	Week	Intensity	Exercise	Scheme*
2	Strength	7	Heavy	Two-arm dumbbell clean to push press	4 × 3
				Bench press	57/3, 65/3, 80/5, 82/5, 85/5, 87/5
				Chain bench press	135 × 8, 135CH × 3, 50CH/3 × 6, 75/1, 85/1
				Power snatch	55/3, 62/3, 70/3, 72/3, 75/3
				Back squat	57/3, 65/3, 80/5, 82/5, 85/5, 87/5
				Push jerk/power clean	65/3, 72/3, 80/3, 82/3, 85/3
	Unload/ variation (Version 2)	8		Back squat (light)	60/3, 67/3, 75/3, 77/3, 80/3
				Power clean combo	60/2, 67/2, 70/2, 72/2
3	Strength and power	9	Medium	Bench press	62/3, 70/3, 77/3, 80/3, 82/3, 85/3, 87/3
				Chain bench press	135 × 8, 135CH × 3, 50CH/3 × 6, 75/1, 85/1
				Clean and jerk	65/2, 72/2, 75/2, 77/2
				Back squat	62/3, 70/3, 77/3, 80/3, 82/3, 85/3, 87/3
				Chain back squat	135 × 8, 135CH × 3, 50CH/3 × 4
				Power clean	67/2, 75/2, 82/2, 85/2, 87/2
3	Strength and power	10	Medium heavy	Incline bench press	65/3, 72/3, 80/3, 82/3, 85/3, 87/3, 90/3
				Chain bench press	135 × 8, 135CH × 3, 50CH/3 × 6, 77/1, 87/1
				Clean and jerk	67/2, 75/2, 77/2, 80/2
				Back squat	65/3, 72/3, 80/3, 82/3, 85/3, 87/3, 90/3
				Chain back squat	135 × 8, 135CH × 3, 50CH/3 × 4
				Power clean	70/2, 77/2, 85/2, 87/2, 90/2
3	Strength and power	11	Heavy	Bench press	65/3, 72/3, 82/3, 85/3, 87/3, 90/3, 92/3
				Chain bench press	135 × 8, 135CH × 3, 50CH/3 × 6, 80/1, 90/1
				Clean and jerk	70/2, 77/2, 80/2, 82/2
				Back squat	65/3, 72/3, 82/3, 85/3, 87/3, 90/3, 92/3
				Chain back squat	135 × 8, 135CH × 3, 50CH/3 × 4
				Power clean	72/2, 80/2, 87/2, 90/2, 92/2

*The cycles shown have the specific percentages of the 1RM and the repetitions to be performed for each of the cycled exercises. The percentage is in the numerator of the fraction, while the number of repetitions is in the denominator. If a percentage is not listed, the athlete should select a weight of the prescribed intensity that can be performed with good technique (the number of sets is listed first and the number of repetitions is listed second; e.g., 3 × 8 means 3 sets of 8 repetitions). If multiple sets are performed of the same percentage and repetitions, the number of sets will be preceded by ×. For example, 80/5 × 3 means 80% of the 1RM for 3 sets of 5 repetitions. For the chain back squat and chain bench press, 135 × 8 refers to 135 pounds (61 kg) × 8 repetitions and 135CH × 3 is 135 pounds (61 kg) plus the chains × 3 repetitions (those are warm-up sets). For chain back squat and chain bench press training sets, the %1RM comes before "CH" and the chains are added to that load. For example, 50CH/3 × 4 means 50% of the 1RM plus the chains × 3 repetitions for 4 sets.

10

PRESEASON PROGRAMMING

JERRY PALMIERI, DARREN KREIN, AND ZAC WOODFIN

The preseason training program for the football athlete is similar to the off-season program described in chapter 9. As a result, very few new exercises are introduced, but there are recommended variations for the six categories of football positions. Due to the shorter training period, the program only has two phases: A basic strength phase and a strength/power phase.

GOALS AND OBJECTIVES

For the purposes of this book, the preseason is the period of training leading up to the time when athletes report to training camp. It is an extension of the off-season that must provide a smooth transition of preparation to the upcoming season. The goals of the preseason are similar to those of the off-season but differ slightly in emphasis.

As the athlete approaches the season, conditioning becomes a significant priority. All the strength and power gains obtained in the off-season program will be useless if the athlete cannot overcome fatigue to use those attributes. That being said, strength and power still must be developed during the preseason, yet to a lesser degree than it was emphasized during the off-season. The football athlete must go into the season generating as much power as possible. Assuming the athlete put on quality lean body mass in his off-season training, it would be important for him to maintain that size with the increased demands of conditioning. Going into the season at a body weight that withstood the demands of extensive conditioning is a good sign that the football athlete will be able to maintain his lean body mass through the rigors of a long playing season.

As athletes get closer to the season, lateral change of direction and reactive movements in multiple planes must be emphasized over linear movements. Football is played in multiple directions, often while reacting to opponents' movements. The closer one gets to the season, the more specific the training becomes, especially in movement and conditioning. Flexibility training must continue to improve the athlete's range of motion.

LENGTH OF THE PROGRAM

The length of the preseason may vary depending on the coach's discretion or on the time allotted based on schedules. In a college setting, summer school may be an eight-week semester that leads right up to the start of training camp, so that preseason would be eight weeks. Usually, the NFL schedule has five weeks between the end of the off-season program or mandatory mini-camp until the reporting date of training camp. The high school program will typically begin six to seven weeks before the start of training camp.

The sample preseason programs in this chapter are based on a six-week period. Regardless of the length of the preseason period, the program will consist of two phases: A strength phase (phase 1) and a strength and power phase (phase 2). Table 10.1 shows how the sample program can be altered for the high school, college, and professional levels.

Table 10.1 Program Time Allotment Based on Level of Play

Level of play	Basic strength	Unload/ variation	Strength/ power	Unload/ variation	Total weeks
High school	2 weeks	—	3 weeks	1 week	6 weeks
College	3 weeks	1 week	3 weeks	1 week	8 weeks
Professional	2 weeks	—	2 weeks	1 week	5 weeks

STRUCTURE OF THE PROGRAM

The preseason program begins with a four-days-per-week split routine with the upper body trained on Monday and Thursday and the lower body trained on Tuesday and Friday. Wednesday is an off day. This split routine is similar to the program that was recommended for the strength phase in the off-season program.

In the second phase, the program switches to a three-days-per-week total body program. Each workout includes an Olympic lift, an upper body pressing movement, and some assistance exercises. The resistance training workouts are scheduled for Monday, Wednesday, and Friday. There is a reduction of resistance training to accommodate the increased emphasis on conditioning that occurs during this phase of training.

RECOMMENDED EXERCISES

The preseason resistance training program should be designed to prepare the athlete for the upcoming season.

Total Body Exercises

The total body exercises used during the preseason were identified in chapter 9. Although these exercises were presented as a part of off-season programming, they have specific uses during the preseason. The power clean, one-arm dumbbell snatch, and power snatch are all explosive or power exercises that involve a quick generation of force from the hips and legs. The one-arm dumbbell snatch is done in the unload/variation week as a changeup from the power snatch. The power clean combo is a combination exercise that provides efficient use of training time during the unload/variation week.

Lower Body Exercises

All of the lower body exercises that are a part of the preseason program were described in chapter 9.

Upper Body Exercises

With one exception, the preseason upper body exercises were covered in chapter 9. The upright row strengthens the shoulders and the trapezius to complement the neck exercises to add protection to the neck and reduce the incidence of burners.

Core Exercises

In a preseason program, traditional and medicine ball exercises for the anatomical core are performed at the end of the upper body workout on Monday and Thursday in phase 1 and on Wednesday in phase 2, and isometric and functional exercises are performed at the end of the lower body workout on Tuesday and Friday in phase 1 and on Monday and Friday in phase 2.

POSITIONAL ADJUSTMENTS

When designing a preseason program, first create a base program (table 10.2 on page 238) and then make adjustments according to the needs of the position groups.

Offensive and Defense Linemen (OL and DL)

There are no adjustments to the base program for the offensive and defensive linemen in phase 1. In phase 2, medicine ball drop with descending weights is added for power development. The trap bar deadlift is also added to improve their lower body strength coming out of a stance. The offensive linemen do their medicine ball chest pass out of their stance followed by 3 pass set passes. They do 3 repetitions of 3 pass sets in each set, decreasing the weight of the medicine ball to enhance the power of the pass set (table 10.3 on page 241).

- *Phase 1.* No changes
- *Phase 2.* Medicine ball drop with descending weight for each set; trap bar deadlift 4 × 3; the OL does the medicine ball chest pass 3 × 3+3 with decreasing weight in each set, and the DL does the medicine ball chest pass 3 × 10

Tight Ends (TE), Fullbacks (FB), and Linebackers (LB)

Because of the violent collisions these athletes are involved in at their positions and on special teams, the tight ends, fullbacks, and linebackers are vulnerable to neck and shoulder burners; therefore, a number of exercises are added to the program to strengthen this region and reduce the risk of this injury (table 10.4 on page 244).

Wide Receivers (WR) and Running Backs (RB)

Wide receivers and running backs need to be strong without extra body mass to affect their speed. These athletes do traditional back exercises only in phase 1. Weighted pull-ups and weighted inverted rows are prescribed for the three training weeks of phase 2 (table 10.5 on page 247).

- *Phase 1.* No changes
- *Phase 2.* Weighted inverted rows 4 × 5 (in place of the suspension trainer row) and weighted pull-ups 4 × 5 (instead of the close-grip lat pulldown)

Defensive Backs (DB)

The defensive back–specific program is a combination of the wide receivers/running backs and tight ends/fullbacks/linebackers programs. To avoid gaining too much muscle mass, these athletes only do traditional back exercises in phase 1. Weighted pull-ups and weighted inverted rows are prescribed for the three training weeks of phase 2. Because of the violent hits associated with the position and their involvement on special teams, defensive backs are vulnerable to neck and shoulder burners, so isometric neck stretch, burner combo, and dumbbell neck stretch shrugs are added to the program to reduce the risk of burners (table 10.6 on page 250).

- *Phase 1.* Burner combo, isometric neck stretch, and dumbbell neck stretch shrugs
- *Phase 2.* Weighted inverted rows 4 × 5 (in place of the suspension trainer row), weighted pull-ups 4 × 5 (instead of the close-grip lat pulldown), burner combo, isometric neck stretch, and dumbbell neck stretch shrugs

Quarterbacks (QB)

In order to maintain shoulder flexibility, variations of the dumbbell bench press and incline bench press replace barbell movement. Different forms of push-ups are included as well. Not only do push-ups strengthen the chest and shoulders, they also add stability to that region. The medicine ball chest passes are removed from the workout.

In phase 1, quarterbacks perform alternating dumbbell bench presses and incline bench presses plus stability ball push-ups (with feet on the box) and band push-ups. To improve torso rotation, quarterbacks perform half-kneeling stick chops and lifts during both phases. Instead of lat pulldowns, quarterbacks perform dumbbell pullovers, which resemble the throwing motion. To minimize stress on the shoulders, quarterbacks use dumbbells instead of a barbell for the power snatch during both phases. The medi ball overhead one-arm quick toss enhances the stretch reflex of the throwing motion. Since the quarterback decelerates the arm when finishing a throw, medicine ball deceleration throws are included in the workout. The seated partner side-to-side toss and lateral leg raise enhance torso rotation, and medicine ball wood chops improve throwing power. Exercises with extensor bands strengthen the fingers, and a 15-second isometric grip of the football is added to the dumbbell hold to prepare the quarterback to hold onto the ball.

In phase 2, quarterbacks perform two arm dumbbell (not barbell) bench presses or incline bench presses, while chain push-ups and stability ball push-ups (one foot on box) replace the chain bench press. The stability ball cable pullovers replace the dumbbell pullovers used in phase 1 to add variation. The dumbbell shoulder horn is added to further strengthen the external rotator cuff muscles. The medicine ball around the world (decreasing weight) and dumbbell twist exercises enhance power during torso rotation. The kneeling medicine ball blob throw 3 × 5 (with decreasing weight) enhances throwing power. As with the snatch, the shoulder press is performed with dumbbells instead of a barbell to put less stress on the shoulder joints. A pinch gripper and extensor band exercises are added to strengthen the fingers, and a 15-second isometric grip on the football is included to get an extra session of grip work (table 10.7 on page 253).

- *Phase 1.* Alternating dumbbell bench press 4 × 5 (instead of bench press); stability ball push-ups (feet on box) 3 × 8 (in place of medicine ball chest pass); dumbbell pullovers 3 × 6-8 (instead of wide-grip lat pulldown); dumbbell snatch (as opposed to bar power snatch); medi ball overhead one-arm quick toss 2 × 10L,R and deceleration throws 2 ×

10L,R; seated partner side-to-side toss and lateral leg raise; alternating dumbbell incline bench press 4 × 5 (instead of incline bench press); band push-ups 3 × 6 (in place of medicine ball drop); half-kneeling stick chops 10L,R; half-kneeling stick lifts 10L,R; medicine ball wood chops 3 × 5; and to dumbbell hold, add extensor bands 2 × 10L,R and grip football for 15 seconds.

- *Phase 2.* Dumbbell bench press or dumbbell incline bench press 4 × 4 (instead of a barbell); stability ball cable pullovers 3 × 6; medi ball overhead one-arm quick toss 2 × 10L,R and deceleration throws 2 × 10L,R; medicine ball around the world (decreasing weight) and dumbbell twist 2 × 10L,R; dumbbell shoulder press (as opposed to the bar); chain push-ups 4 × 3 and stability ball push-ups (1 foot on box); 3 × 6 for chain bench and medicine chest pass; half-kneeling stick chops 10L,R; half-kneeling stick lifts 10L,R; kneeling overhead max medicine ball toss 3 × 5 (decreasing weights); dumbbell twists 2 × 10L,R; dumbbell shoulder horn was added to get another day of shoulder external rotation; and add pinch gripper 2 × 30 second L,R, extensor bands 2 × 10L,R, and grip football for 15 seconds.

Kickers (K) and Punters (P)

Kickers and punters need a well-trained hip musculature, so the 4-way hip machine is a priority exercise (and the medicine ball chest pass is not needed) (table 10.8 on page 256).

- Add 4-way hip machine as the targeted groin exercise in both phases.
- Eliminate medicine ball chest passes in both phases.

VOLUME AND INTENSITY

Because the preseason program follows an off-season program, the athletes have a significant training base going into this training period; therefore, the cycle (see table 10.9 on page 259) begins with moderate intensity and moderate volume progressing to high intensity and low volume. Phase 1 is a strength phase similar to phase 2 of the off-season program. Phase 2 shows a decrease in volume not only due to lower repetitions, but also because of one less training day and fewer exercises. Such a reduction is necessary as the running volume increases in the conditioning program.

The off-season cycle schedules an unload/variation week after each phase of three training weeks, which creates a three-to-one ratio of training weeks to the unload week. During shorter cycles of six weeks or less, more training weeks can be done consecutively, and the unload week can be pushed to the end of the cycle. Such is the case during the preseason program. The unload week is at the end of the cycle, giving the athletes some recovery going into training camp.

The cycle is linear, progressing in intensity each week within each phase. Since phase 1 is only a two-week phase, the intensity goes from medium to medium heavy. The second phase of lower repetitions has three weeks with the intensity progressing from medium to medium heavy to heavy for the non-power-core (or primary) exercises (not to be misidentified as exercises for the anatomical core; see chapter 8). The second back squat and bench press workouts of the week are done dynamically using chains. The bar is moved very quickly with less weight than earlier in the week to promote power development. Furthermore, complex jumps onto a box are done after each set of chain squats for additional power development. The Olympic lift exercises keep similar percentages to those that were used in phase 1, with a reduction of repetitions from

Interpreting the Sample Program Tables

The cycles shown in the sample programs have the specific percentages of the 1RM and the repetitions to be performed for each of the cycled exercises. If a percentage is not listed for a cycled exercise, the athlete should select a weight of the prescribed intensity that can be performed with good technique. The percentage is in the numerator of the fraction, while the number of repetitions is in the denominator. If multiple sets are performed of the same percentage and repetitions, the number of sets will be preceded by ×. For example, 80/5 × 3 means 80% of the 1RM for 3 sets of 5 repetitions. If there is no percentage or intensity assigned, the number of sets is listed first and the number of repetitions is listed second (e.g., 3 × 8 means 3 sets of 8 repetitions).

Gray rows in the programs indicate position-specific changes from the base program (table 10.2 on page 238).

3 to 2, allowing more emphasis to be placed on bar speed and power production. The unload/variation week, which follows the five training weeks, has low volume and moderate intensity.

Although the program provides certain percentages and repetitions for each cycled exercise, in general the Olympic lift exercises in phase 1 have an intensity level of 75% to 82% of the 1RM for 3 repetitions. The non-power-core exercises are performed at 75% to 85% of the 1RM for 5 repetitions. In phase 2, the snatch and the clean and jerk are done for speed using 72% to 82% of the 1RM for 2 repetitions, while the clean pull will use heavier loads for repetitions of 3. The non-power-core exercises are trained at 80% to 92% of the 1RM for 3 repetitions.

The training percentages are based on the athlete's 1RM, and they increase during the phase until they reach the intensity prescribed for the maximum number of repetitions, as seen in table 4.1 on page 54. In the beginning it is unlikely that athletes will be able to complete the number of repetitions at the assigned percentages seen in table 4.1, especially for multiple sets. As their strength increases, they should be able to complete the repetitions at the assigned intensities by the end of the phase. Note that the prescribed percentages are programmed from a true 1RM. If athletes are working with a predicted 1RM, the percentages may need to be slightly decreased.

The assistance exercises are commonly assigned 6 to 8 repetitions in phase 1 and 4 to 6 repetitions in phase 2.

ORDER OF EXERCISES

The strength and conditioning professional should follow this sequence for ordering the resistance training exercises in a workout session:

1. Olympic lifts (do in the initial part of a workout),
2. non-power-core exercises,
3. assistance exercises, and
4. anatomical core exercises (to finish the workout).

Some sample workouts have exercises arranged in a push-to-pull order; the antagonist muscle or muscle group is resting while the agonist is active. The strength and conditioning professional should not sequence the exercises as a circuit with no rest between sets or exercises, but instead should permit enough recovery so that sufficient loads can be lifted.

CONCLUSION

While preseason training is similar philosophically to the off-season program, it is important that coaches and athletes recognize the need for the preseason training to be more specific to the demands of football. With training camp practices and games soon to begin, athletes must be prepared physically to perform at their highest level while remaining healthy enough to compete.

Warm-Ups

WARM-UP 1

Foam roll, activation, and movement-based warm-up
Warm-up with light weights (5 repetitions each movement)

- Lateral raise
- Front raise
- Rear lateral raise
- Curl to press
- Overhead triceps extension
- External rotation

WARM-UP 2

Foam roll, activation, and movement-based warm-up
Band glute strengthening
Lateral leg step-through (1 × 10 each side)
Bar warm-up (45 lb)

- Snatch (5 repetitions)
- Overhead squat (5 repetitions)
- Front squat to press (5 repetitions)

WARM-UP 3

Foam roll, activation, and movement-based warm-up
Band glute strengthening
Lateral step under to over: 3 to 5 repetitions each side
Bar warm-up (45 lb)

- Snatch (5 repetitions)
- Overhead squat (5 repetitions)
- Front squat to press (5 repetitions)

WARM-UP 4

Foam roll, activation, and movement-based warm-up
Band glute strengthening
Bar warm-up (45 lb)

- Snatch (5 repetitions)
- Overhead squat (5 repetitions)
- Front squat to press (5 repetitions)

Table 10.2 Preseason Base Program

Strength Phase

Monday

	Exercise	Sets × reps		Exercise	Sets × reps
	Warm-up 1				
1	Two-arm kettlebell swing	4 × 5	5a	Dumbbell hammer curl	3 × 8
2a	Bench press	Cycle*	5b	External shoulder rotation: dumbbell shoulder horn (standing, incline, decline)	1 × 10 each position
2b	Wide-grip lat pulldown	5 × 6-8			
3	Medicine ball chest pass	3 × 10			
4a	Upright row	3 × 6			
4b	Abdominals (medicine ball)	Exercise dependent	6	4-way neck	1 × 8 each way

* For cycle, refer to table 10.9 for details.

Tuesday

	Exercise	Sets × reps		Exercise	Sets × reps
	Warm-up 2				
1	Power snatch	Cycle*	4a	Romanian deadlift	3 × 6
2	Back squat	Cycle*	4b	Abdominals (functional)	Exercise dependent
3a	Hip thrust	2 × 8	5	Band flexibility: leg up, leg out, leg over, quad, hip flexor	1 × 10 sec each side
3b	Lateral squat	2 × 6 each side			

* For cycle, refer to table 10.9 for details.

Thursday

	Exercise	Sets × reps		Exercise	Sets × reps
	Warm-up 1				
1	Push jerk	Cycle*	4a	Triceps pushdown	3 × 8
2a	Incline bench press	Cycle*	4b	Abdominals (medicine ball)	Exercise dependent
2b	Standing one-arm dumbbell row	5 × 6-8	5a	Dumbbell hold (grip exercise)	2 × 60 sec each side
3a	Medicine ball drop	3 × 10	5b	4-way neck	1 × 8 each way
3b	Suspension trainer row	3 × 8			

* For cycle, refer to table 10.9 for details.

Friday

	Exercise	Sets × reps		Exercise	Sets × reps
	Warm-up 2				
1	Power clean	Cycle*	4a	Rotational disc (shoes off for ankle strengthening)	1 × 30 each way
2	Clean pull	3 × 5	4b	Abdominals (functional)	Exercise dependent
3a	Lunge to step-up	3 × 3 each side	5	Band flexibility: leg up, leg out, leg over, quad, hip flexor	1 × 10 sec each side
3b	Reverse back extension	Week 1: 2 × 15 Week 2: 2 × 20			

* For cycle, refer to table 10.9 for details.

Strength and Power Phase

Monday

	Exercise	Sets × reps		Exercise	Sets × reps
	Warm-up 2				
1	Clean pull	5 × 3	4a	Dumbbell hamstring walk	2 × 5 each side
2	Back squat	Cycle*	4b	Abdominals (functional)	Exercise dependent
3a	Bench press or incline bench press	Cycle*	5	4-way neck	1 × 8 each way
3b	Suspension trainer row	4 × 4-6	6	Band flexibility: leg up, leg out, leg over, quad, hip flexor	1 × 10 sec each side

* For cycle, refer to table 10.9 for details.

Wednesday

	Exercise	Sets × reps		Exercise	Sets × reps
	Warm-up 3				
1	Power snatch	Cycle*	4a	External shoulder rotation (dumbbell or cable)	2 × 10 each way
2a	Step-up	3 × 5 each leg	4b	Abdominals (medicine ball)	Exercise dependent
2b	Barbell shoulder press	4 × 5	5	Rotational disc (shoes off for ankle strengthening)	1 × 30 each way
3a	Hip thrust	2 × 5	6	Band flexibility: leg up, leg out, leg over, quad, hip flexor	1 × 10 sec each side
3b	Lateral lunge	2 × 5 each leg			

* For cycle, refer to table 10.9 for details.

Friday

	Exercise	Sets × reps		Exercise	Sets × reps
	Warm-up 2				
1	Clean and jerk	Cycle*	4	Medicine ball chest pass	3 sets of descending weight: 20/3, 15/3, 10/3
2	Chain back squat	Cycle*	5a	Reverse back extension (10 lb)	Week 1: 2 × 15 Week 2: 2 × 20 Week 3: 2 × 25
	Complex jump onto a box (after each set of chain back squats)	4 × 2	5b	Abdominals (functional)	Exercise dependent
3a	Chain bench press	Cycle*	6	4-way neck	1 × 8 each way
3b	Close-grip lat pulldown	4 × 4-6	7	Band flexibility: leg up, leg out, leg over, quad, hip flexor	1 × 10 sec each side

* For cycle, refer to table 10.9 for details.

(continued)

Table 10.2 Preseason Base Program *(continued)*

Unload Variation Phase

Monday

	Exercise	Sets × reps		Exercise	Sets × reps
	Warm-up 1				
1	Two-arm kettlebell swing	4 × 5	3b	Prone T, Y, I	2 × 5 each way
2a	Incline bench press (light)	Cycle*	4a	Hammer curl	3 × 6
2b	Pull-up	4 × 8	4b	4-way neck	1 × 8 each way
3a	Dumbbell shrug	3 × 10			

* For cycle, refer to table 10.9 for details.

Tuesday

	Exercise	Sets × reps		Exercise	Sets × reps
	Warm-up 2				
1	One-arm dumbbell snatch	4 × 2 each arm	3b	Hamstring slide	2 × 10 each side
2	Back squat (light)	Cycle*	4	Band flexibility: leg up, leg out, leg over, quad, hip flexor	1 × 10 sec each side
3a	Side plank with isometric groin hold	2 × 30 sec			

* For cycle, refer to table 10.9 for details.

Thursday

	Exercise	Sets × reps		Exercise	Sets × reps
	Warm-up 4				
1	Power clean combo (barbell):	Cycle*	3	Shoulder combo (barbell):	2 sets
	Power clean	2 reps		Front raise	6 reps
	Push jerk	2 reps		Upright row	8 reps
	Front squat	2 reps		Shoulder press	8 reps
2a	Dumbbell bench press	3 × 5	4a	Overhead dumbbell triceps extension	3 × 8
2b	Lunge to step-up	3 × 2 each side	4b	Abdominals (functional)	Exercise dependent
			5	Band flexibility: leg up, leg out, leg over, quad, hip flexor	1 × 10 sec each side

* For cycle, refer to table 10.9 for details.

Table 10.3 Preseason Program for Offensive and Defensive Linemen

Strength (Phase 1)

Monday

	Exercise	Sets × reps		Exercise	Sets × reps
	Warm-up 1				
1	Two-arm kettlebell swing	4 × 5	5a	Dumbbell hammer curl	3 × 8
2a	Bench press	Cycle*	5b	External shoulder rotation: dumbbell shoulder horn (standing, incline, decline)	1 × 10 each position
2b	Wide-grip lat pulldown	5 × 6-8			
3	Medicine ball chest pass	3 × 10			
4a	Upright row	3 × 6			
4b	Abdominals (medicine ball)	Exercise dependent	6	4-way neck	1 × 8 each way

* For cycle, refer to table 10.9 for details.

Tuesday

	Exercise	Sets × reps		Exercise	Sets × reps
	Warm-up 2				
1	Power snatch	Cycle*	4a	Romanian deadlift	3 × 6
2	Back squat	Cycle*	4b	Abdominals (functional)	Exercise dependent
3a	Double leg hip thrust	2 × 8	5	Band flexibility: leg up, leg out, leg over, quad, hip flexor	1 × 10 sec each side
3b	Lateral squat	2 × 6 each side			

* For cycle, refer to table 10.9 for details.

Thursday

	Exercise	Sets × reps		Exercise	Sets × reps
	Warm-up 1				
1	Push jerk	Cycle*	4a	Triceps pushdown	3 × 8
2a	Incline bench press	Cycle*	4b	Abdominals (medicine ball)	Exercise dependent
2b	Standing one-arm dumbbell row	5 × 6-8	5a	Dumbbell hold (grip exercise)	2 × 60 sec each side
3a	Medicine ball drop	3 × 10	5b	4-way neck	1 × 8 each way
3b	Suspension trainer row	3 × 8			

* For cycle, refer to table 10.9 for details.

Friday

	Exercise	Sets × reps		Exercise	Sets × reps
	Warm-up 3				
1	Power clean	Cycle*	4a	Rotational disc (shoes off for ankle strengthening)	1 × 30 each way
2	Clean pull	3 × 5	4b	Abdominals (functional)	Exercise dependent
3a	Lunge to step-up	3 × 3 each side	5	Band flexibility: leg up, leg out, leg over, quad, hip flexor	1 × 10 sec each side
3b	Reverse back extension	Week 1: 2 × 15 Week 2: 2 × 20			

* For cycle, refer to table 10.9 for details.

(continued)

Strength and Power (Phase 2)

Monday

	Exercise	Sets × reps		Exercise	Sets × reps
	Warm-up 2				
1	Clean pull	5 × 3	4b	Dumbbell hamstring walk	2 × 5 each side
2	Back squat	Cycle*	5a	Abdominals (functional)	Exercise dependent
3a	Bench press or incline bench press	Cycle*	5b	4-way neck	1 × 8 each way
3b	Suspension trainer row	4 × 4-6	6	Band flexibility: leg up, leg out, leg over, quad, hip flexor	1 × 10 sec each side
4a	Medicine ball drop	3 × 3 (with a descending load)			

* For cycle, refer to table 10.9 for details.

Wednesday

	Exercise	Sets × reps		Exercise	Sets × reps
	Warm-up 3				
1	Power snatch	Cycle*	4a	External shoulder rotation (dumbbell or cable)	2 × 10 each way
2a	Trap bar deadlift	4 × 3	4b	Abdominals (medicine ball)	Exercise dependent
2b	Barbell shoulder press	4 × 5	5	Rotational disc (shoes off for ankle strengthening)	1 × 30 each way
3a	Hip thrust	2 × 5	6	Band flexibility: leg up, leg out, leg over, quad, hip flexor	1 × 10 sec each side
3b	Lateral lunge	2 × 5 each leg			

* For cycle, refer to table 10.9 for details.

Friday

	Exercise	Sets × reps		Exercise	Sets × reps
	Warm-up 2				
1	Clean-and-jerk	Cycle*	4	Medicine ball chest pass (with a descending load):	
2	Chain back squat	Cycle*		OL: medicine ball chest pass	3 × 3+3
	Complex jump onto a box (after each set of chain back squats)	4 × 2		DL: medicine ball chest pass	3 × 10
3a	Chain bench press	Cycle*	5a	Reverse back extension (10 lb)	Week 1: 2 × 15 Week 2: 2 × 20 Week 3: 2 × 25
3b	Close-grip lat pulldown	4 × 4-6	5b	Abdominals (functional)	Exercise dependent
			6	4-way neck	1 × 8 each way
			7	Band flexibility: leg up, leg out, leg over, quad, hip flexor	1 × 10 sec each side

* For cycle, refer to table 10.9 for details.

Unload/Variation

Monday

	Exercise	Sets × reps		Exercise	Sets × reps
	Warm-up 1				
1	Two-arm kettlebell swing	4 × 5	3b	Prone T, Y, I	2 × 5 each way
2a	Incline bench press (light)	Cycle*	4a	Hammer curl	3 × 6
2b	Pull-up	4 × 8	4b	4-way neck	1 × 8 each way
3a	Dumbbell shrug	3 × 10			

* For cycle, refer to table 10.9 for details.

Tuesday

	Exercise	Sets × reps		Exercise	Sets × reps
	Warm-up 2				
1	One-arm dumbbell snatch	4 × 2 each arm	3b	Hamstring slide	2 × 10 each side
2	Back squat (light)	Cycle*	4	Band flexibility: leg up, leg out, leg over, quad, hip flexor	1 × 10 sec each side
3a	Side plank with isometric groin hold	2 × 30 sec			

* For cycle, refer to table 10.9 for details.

Thursday

	Exercise	Sets × reps		Exercise	Sets × reps
	Warm-up 4				
1	Power clean combo (barbell):	Cycle*	3	Shoulder combo (barbell):	2 sets
	Power clean	2 reps		Front raise	6 reps
	Push jerk	2 reps		Upright row	8 reps
	Front squat	2 reps		Shoulder press	8 reps
2a	Dumbbell bench press	3 × 5	4a	Overhead dumbbell triceps extension	3 × 8
2b	Lunge to step-up	3 × 2 each side	4b	Abdominals (functional)	Exercise dependent
			5	Band flexibility: leg up, leg out, leg over, quad, hip flexor	1 × 10 sec each side

* For cycle, refer to table 10.9 for details.

Table 10.4 Preseason Program for Tight Ends, Fullbacks, and Linebackers

Strength (Phase 1)

Monday

	Exercise	Sets × reps		Exercise	Sets × reps
	Warm-up 1				
1	Two-arm kettlebell swing	4 × 5	5b	Burner combo	2 × 10 each way
2a	Bench press	Cycle*	6	External shoulder rotation: dumbbell shoulder horn (standing, incline, decline)	1 × 10 each position
2b	Wide-grip lat pulldown	5 × 6-8			
3	Medicine ball chest pass	3 × 10			
4a	Upright row	3 × 6			
4b	Abdominals (medicine ball)	Exercise dependent	7	4-way neck	1 × 8 each way
5a	Dumbbell hammer curl	3 × 8		Isometric neck stretch	2 × 5 for 30 sec each way

* For cycle, refer to table 10.9 for details.

Tuesday

	Exercise	Sets × reps		Exercise	Sets × reps
	Warm-up 2				
1	Power snatch	Cycle*	4a	Romanian deadlift	3 × 6
2	Back squat	Cycle*	4b	Dumbbell neck stretch shrug	2 × 10 each way
3a	Hip thrust	2 × 8	5	Abdominals (functional)	Exercise dependent
3b	Lateral squat	2 × 6 each side	6	Band flexibility: leg up, leg out, leg over, quad, hip flexor	1 × 10 sec each side

* For cycle, refer to table 10.9 for details.

Thursday

	Exercise	Sets × reps		Exercise	Sets × reps
	Warm-up 1				
1	Push jerk	Cycle*	4a	Triceps pushdown	3 × 8
2a	Incline bench press	Cycle*	4b	Abdominals (medicine ball)	Exercise dependent
2b	Standing one-arm dumbbell row	5 × 6-8	5a	Dumbbell hold (grip exercise)	2 × 60 sec each side
3a	Medicine ball drop	3 × 10	5b	4-way neck	1 × 8 each way
3b	Suspension trainer row	3 × 8		Isometric neck stretch	2 × 5 for 30 sec each way

* For cycle, refer to table 10.9 for details.

Friday

	Exercise	Sets × reps		Exercise	Sets × reps
	Warm-up 3				
1	Power clean	Cycle*	4a	Rotational disc (shoes off for ankle strengthening)	1 × 30 each way
2	Clean pull	3 × 5	4b	Abdominals (functional)	Exercise dependent

	Exercise	Sets × reps		Exercise	Sets × reps
3a	Lunge to step-up	3 × 3 each side	5	Band flexibility: leg up, leg out, leg over, quad, hip flexor	1 × 10 sec each side
3b	Reverse back extension	Week 1: 2 × 15 Week 2: 2 × 20			

* For cycle, refer to table 10.9 for details.

Strength and Power (Phase 2)

Monday

	Exercise	Sets × reps		Exercise	Sets × reps
	Warm-up 2				
1	Clean pull	5 × 3	4b	Dumbbell hamstring walk	2 × 5 each side
2	Back squat	Cycle*	5a	Abdominals (functional)	Exercise dependent
3a	Bench press or incline bench press	Cycle*	5b	4-way neck	1 × 8 each way
3b	Suspension trainer row	4 × 4-6		Isometric neck stretch	2 × 5 for 30 sec each way
4a	Burner combo	2 × 10 each way	6	Band flexibility: leg up, leg out, leg over, quad, hip flexor	1 × 10 sec each side

* For cycle, refer to table 10.9 for details.

Wednesday

	Exercise	Sets × reps		Exercise	Sets × reps
	Warm-up 3				
1	Power snatch	Cycle*	4a	Dumbbell neck stretch shrug	2 × 10 each way
2a	Step-up	3 × 5 each leg	4b	External shoulder rotation (dumbbell or cable)	2 × 10 each way
2b	Barbell shoulder press	4 × 5	5a	Abdominals (medicine ball)	Exercise dependent
3a	Hip thrust	2 × 5	5b	Rotational disc (shoes off for ankle strengthening)	1 × 30 each way
3b	Lateral lunge	2 × 5 each leg	6	Band flexibility: leg up, leg out, leg over, quad, hip flexor	1 × 10 sec each side

* For cycle, refer to table 10.9 for details.

Friday

	Exercise	Sets × reps		Exercise	Sets × reps
	Warm-up 2				
1	Clean and jerk	Cycle*	5a	Reverse back extension (10 lb)	Week 1: 2 × 15 Week 2: 2 × 20 Week 3: 2 × 25
2	Chain back squat	Cycle*	5b	Abdominals (functional)	Exercise dependent
	Complex jump onto a box (after each set of chain back squats)	4 × 2	6	4-way neck	1 × 8 each way

(continued)

Table 10.4 Preseason Program for Tight Ends, Fullbacks, and Linebackers *(continued)*

Friday *(continued)*

	Exercise	Sets × reps		Exercise	Sets × reps
3a	Chain bench press	Cycle*		Isometric neck stretch	2 × 5 for 30 sec each way
3b	Close-grip lat pulldown	4 × 4-6	7	Band flexibility: leg up, leg out, leg over, quad, hip flexor	1 × 10 sec each side
4	Medicine ball chest pass	3 sets of descending weight: 20/3, 15/3, 10/3			

* For cycle, refer to table 10.9 for details.

Unload/Variation

Monday

	Exercise	Sets × reps		Exercise	Sets × reps
	Warm-up 1				
1	Two-arm kettlebell swing	4 × 5	3b	Prone T, Y, I	2 × 5 each way
2a	Incline bench press (light)	Cycle*	4a	Hammer curl	3 × 6
2b	Pull-up	4 × 8	4b	4-way neck	1 × 8 each way
3a	Dumbbell shrug	3 × 10		Isometric neck stretch	2 × 5 for 30 sec each way

* For cycle, refer to table 10.9 for details.

Tuesday

	Exercise	Sets × reps		Exercise	Sets × reps
	Warm-up 2				
1	One-arm dumbbell snatch	4 × 2 each arm	3b	Hamstring slide	2 × 10 each side
2	Back squat (light)	Cycle*	4	Band flexibility: leg up, leg out, leg over, quad, hip flexor	1 × 10 sec each side
3a	Side plank with isometric groin hold	2 × 30 sec			

* For cycle, refer to table 10.9 for details.

Thursday

	Exercise	Sets × reps		Exercise	Sets × reps
	Warm-up 4				
1	Power clean combo (barbell):	Cycle*	3	Shoulder combo (barbell):	2 sets
	Power clean	2 reps		Front raise	6 reps
	Push jerk	2 reps		Upright row	8 reps
	Front squat	2 reps		Shoulder press	8 reps
2a	Dumbbell bench press	3 × 5	4a	Overhead dumbbell triceps extension	3 × 8
2b	Lunge to step-up	3 × 2 each side	4b	Abdominals (functional)	Exercise dependent
			5	Band flexibility: leg up, leg out, leg over, quad, hip flexor	1 × 10 sec each side

* For cycle, refer to table 10.9 for details.

Table 10.5 Preseason Program for Wide Receivers and Running Backs

Strength (Phase 1)

Monday

	Exercise	Sets × reps		Exercise	Sets × reps
	Warm-up 1				
1	Two-arm kettlebell swing	4 × 5	5a	Dumbbell hammer curl	3 × 8
2a	Bench press	Cycle*	5b	External shoulder rotation: dumbbell shoulder horn (standing, incline, decline)	1 × 10 each position
2b	Wide-grip lat pulldown	5 × 6-8			
3	Medicine ball chest pass	3 × 10			
4a	Upright row	3 × 6			
4b	Abdominals (medicine ball)	Exercise dependent	6	4-way neck	1 × 8 each way

* For cycle, refer to table 10.9 for details.

Tuesday

	Exercise	Sets × reps		Exercise	Sets × reps
	Warm-up 2				
1	Power snatch	Cycle*	4a	Romanian deadlift	3 × 6
2	Back squat	Cycle*	4b	Abdominals (functional)	Exercise dependent
3a	Hip thrust	2 × 8	5	Band flexibility: leg up, leg out, leg over, quad, hip flexor	1 × 10 sec each side
3b	Lateral squat	2 × 6 each side			

* For cycle, refer to table 10.9 for details.

Thursday

	Exercise	Sets × reps		Exercise	Sets × reps
	Warm-up 1				
1	Push jerk	Cycle*	4a	Triceps pushdown	3 × 8
2a	Incline bench press	Cycle*	4b	Abdominals (medicine ball)	Exercise dependent
2b	Standing one-arm dumbbell row	5 × 6-8	5a	Dumbbell hold (grip exercise)	2 × 60 sec each side
3a	Medicine ball drop	3 × 10	5b	4-way neck	1 × 8 each way
3b	Suspension trainer row	3 × 8			

* For cycle, refer to table 10.9 for details.

Friday

	Exercise	Sets × reps		Exercise	Sets × reps
	Warm-up 2				
1	Power clean	Cycle*	4a	Rotational disc (shoes off for ankle strengthening)	1 × 30 each way
2	Clean pull	3 × 5	4b	Abdominals (functional)	Exercise dependent
3a	Lunge to step-up	3 × 3 each side	5	Band flexibility: leg up, leg out, leg over, quad, hip flexor	1 × 10 sec each side
3b	Reverse back extension	Week 1: 2 × 15 Week 2: 2 × 20			

* For cycle, refer to table 10.9 for details.

(continued)

Strength and Power (Phase 2)

Monday

	Exercise	Sets × reps		Exercise	Sets × reps
	Warm-up 2				
1	Clean pull	5 × 3	4a	Dumbbell hamstring walk	2 × 5 each side
2	Back squat	Cycle*	4b	Abdominals (functional)	Exercise dependent
3a	Bench press or incline bench press	Cycle*	5	4-way neck	1 × 8 each way
3b	Weighted inverted row	4 × 5	6	Band flexibility: leg up, leg out, leg over, quad, hip flexor	1 × 10 sec each side

* For cycle, refer to table 10.9 for details.

Wednesday

	Exercise	Sets × reps		Exercise	Sets × reps
	Warm-up 3				
1	Power snatch	Cycle*	4a	External shoulder rotation (dumbbell or cable)	2 × 10 each way
2a	Step-up	3 × 5 each leg	4b	Abdominals (medicine ball)	Exercise dependent
2b	Barbell shoulder press	4 × 5	5	Rotational disc (shoes off for ankle strengthening)	1 × 30 each way
3a	Hip thrust	2 × 5	6	Band flexibility: leg up, leg out, leg over, quad, hip flexor	1 × 10 sec each side
3b	Lateral lunge	2 × 5 each leg			

* For cycle, refer to table 10.9 for details.

Friday

	Exercise	Sets × reps		Exercise	Sets × reps
	Warm-up 2				
1	Clean and jerk	Cycle*	4	Medicine ball chest pass	3 × 3 (with a descending load)
2	Chain back squat	Cycle*	5a	Reverse back extension (10 lb)	Week 1: 2 × 15 Week 2: 2 × 20 Week 3: 2 × 25
	Complex jump onto a box (after each set of chain back squats)	4 × 2	5b	Abdominals (functional)	Exercise dependent
3a	Chain bench press	Cycle*	6	4-way neck	1 × 8 each way
3b	Weighted pull-up	4 × 5	7	Band flexibility: leg up, leg out, leg over, quad, hip flexor	1 × 10 sec each side

* For cycle, refer to table 10.9 for details.

Unload/Variation

Monday

	Exercise	Sets × reps		Exercise	Sets × reps
	Warm-up 1				
1	Two-arm kettlebell swing	4 × 5	3b	Prone T, Y, I	2 × 5 each way
2a	Incline bench press (light)	Cycle*	4a	Hammer curl	3 × 6
2b	Pull-up	4 × 8	4b	4-way neck	1 × 8 each way
3a	Dumbbell shrug	3 × 10			

* For cycle, refer to table 10.9 for details.

Tuesday

	Exercise	Sets × reps		Exercise	Sets × reps
	Warm-up 2				
1	One-arm dumbbell snatch	4 × 2 each arm	3b	Hamstring slide	2 × 10 each side
2	Back squat (light)	Cycle*	4	Band flexibility: leg up, leg out, leg over, quad, hip flexor	1 × 10 sec each side
3a	Side plank with isometric groin hold	2 × 30 sec			

* For cycle, refer to table 10.9 for details.

Thursday

	Exercise	Sets × reps		Exercise	Sets × reps
	Warm-up 4				
1	Power clean combo (barbell):	Cycle*	3	Shoulder combo (barbell):	2 sets
	Power clean	2 reps		Front raise	6 reps
	Push jerk	2 reps		Upright row	8 reps
	Front squat	2 reps		Shoulder press	8 reps
2a	Dumbbell bench press	3 × 5	4a	Overhead dumbbell triceps extension	3 × 8
2b	Lunge to step-up	3 × 2 each side	4b	Abdominals (functional)	Exercise dependent
			5	Band flexibility: leg up, leg out, leg over, quad, hip flexor	1 × 10 sec each side

* For cycle, refer to table 10.9 for details.

Table 10.6 Preseason Program for Defensive Backs

Strength (Phase 1)

Monday

	Exercise	Sets × reps		Exercise	Sets × reps
	Warm-up 1				
1	Two-arm kettlebell swing	4 × 5	5b	Burner combo	2 × 10 each way
2a	Bench press	Cycle*	6	External shoulder rotation: dumbbell shoulder horn (standing, incline, decline)	1 × 10 each position
2b	Wide-grip lat pulldown	5 × 6-8			
3	Medicine ball chest pass	3 × 10			
4a	Upright row	3 × 6			
4b	Abdominals (medicine ball)	Exercise dependent	7	4-way neck	1 × 8 each way
5a	Dumbbell hammer curl	3 × 8		Isometric neck stretch	2 × 5 for 30 sec each way

* For cycle, refer to table 10.9 for details.

Tuesday

	Exercise	Sets × reps		Exercise	Sets × reps
	Warm-up 2				
1	Power snatch	Cycle*	4a	Romanian deadlift	3 × 6
2	Back squat	Cycle*	4b	Dumbbell neck stretch shrug	2 × 10 each way
3a	Hip thrust	2 × 8	5	Abdominals (functional)	Exercise dependent
3b	Lateral squat	2 × 6 each side	6	Band flexibility: leg up, leg out, leg over, quad, hip flexor	1 × 10 sec each side

* For cycle, refer to table 10.9 for details.

Thursday

	Exercise	Sets × reps		Exercise	Sets × reps
	Warm-up 1				
1	Push jerk	Cycle*	4a	Triceps pushdown	3 × 8
2a	Incline bench press	Cycle*	4b	Abdominals (medicine ball)	Exercise dependent
2b	Standing one-arm dumbbell row	5 × 6-8	5a	Dumbbell hold (grip exercise)	2 × 60 sec each side
3a	Medicine ball drop	3 × 10	5b	4-way neck	1 × 8 each way
3b	Suspension trainer row	3 × 8		Isometric neck stretch	2 × 5 for 30 sec each way

* For cycle, refer to table 10.9 for details.

Friday

	Exercise	Sets × reps		Exercise	Sets × reps
	Warm-up 2				
1	Power clean	Cycle*	4a	Rotational disc (shoes off for ankle strengthening)	1 × 30 each way
2	Clean pull	3 × 5	4b	Abdominals (functional)	Exercise dependent

	Exercise	Sets × reps		Exercise	Sets × reps
3a	Lunge to step-up	3 × 3 each side	5	Band flexibility: leg up, leg out, leg over, quad, hip flexor	1 × 10 sec each side
3b	Reverse back extension	Week 1: 2 × 15 Week 2: 2 × 20			

* For cycle, refer to table 10.9 for details.

Strength and Power (Phase 2)

Monday

	Exercise	Sets × reps		Exercise	Sets × reps
	Warm-up 2				
1	Clean pull	5 × 3	5a	Abdominals (functional)	Exercise dependent
2	Back squat	Cycle*	5b	4-way neck	1 × 8 each way
3a	Bench press or incline bench press	Cycle*		Isometric neck stretch	2 × 5 for 30 sec each way
3b	Weighted inverted row	4 × 5	6	Band flexibility: leg up, leg out, leg over, quad, hip flexor	1 × 10 sec each side
4a	Burner combo	2 × 10 each way			
4b	Dumbbell hamstring walk	2 × 5 each side			

* For cycle, refer to table 10.9 for details.

Wednesday

	Exercise	Sets × reps		Exercise	Sets × reps
	Warm-up 3				
1	Power snatch	Cycle*	4a	Dumbbell neck stretch shrug	2 × 10 each way
2a	Step-up	3 × 5 each leg	4b	External shoulder rotation (dumbbell or cable)	2 × 10 each way
2b	Barbell shoulder press	4 × 5	5a	Abdominals (medicine ball)	Exercise dependent
3a	Hip thrust	2 × 5	5b	Rotational disc (shoes off for ankle strengthening)	1 × 30 each way
3b	Lateral lunge	2 × 5 each leg	6	Band flexibility: leg up, leg out, leg over, quad, hip flexor	1 × 10 sec each side

* For cycle, refer to table 10.9 for details.

Friday

	Exercise	Sets × reps		Exercise	Sets × reps
	Warm-up 2				
1	Clean and jerk	Cycle*	4	Medicine ball chest pass	3 × 3 (with a descending load)
2	Chain back squat	Cycle*	5a	Reverse back extension (10 lb)	Week 1: 2 × 15 Week 2: 2 × 20 Week 3: 2 × 25

(continued)

Table 10.6 Preseason Program for Defensive Backs *(continued)*

Friday *(continued)*

	Exercise	Sets × reps		Exercise	Sets × reps
	Complex jump onto a box (after each set of chain back squats)	4 × 2	5b	Abdominals (functional)	Exercise dependent
3a	Chain bench press	Cycle*	6	4-way neck	1 × 8 each way
3b	Weighted pull-up	4 × 5		Isometric neck stretch	2 × 5 for 30 sec each way
			7	Band flexibility: leg up, leg out, leg over, quad, hip flexor	1 × 10 sec each side

* For cycle, refer to table 10.9 for details.

Unload/Variation

Monday

	Exercise	Sets × reps		Exercise	Sets × reps
	Warm-up 1				
1	Two-arm kettlebell swing	4 × 5	3b	Prone T, Y, I	2 × 5 each way
2a	Incline bench press (light)	Cycle*	4a	Hammer curl	3 × 6
2b	Pull-up	4 × 8	4b	4-way neck	1 × 8 each way
3a	Dumbbell shrug	3 × 10		Isometric neck stretch	2 × 5 for 30 sec each way

* For cycle, refer to table 10.9 for details.

Tuesday

	Exercise	Sets × reps		Exercise	Sets × reps
	Warm-up 2				
1	One-arm dumbbell snatch	4 × 2 each arm	3b	Hamstring slide	2 × 10 each side
2	Back squat (light)	Cycle*	4	Band flexibility: leg up, leg out, leg over, quad, hip flexor	1 × 10 sec each side
3a	Side plank with isometric groin hold	2 × 30 sec			

* For cycle, refer to table 10.9 for details.

Thursday

	Exercise	Sets × reps		Exercise	Sets × reps
	Warm-up 4				
1	Power clean combo (barbell):	Cycle*	3	Shoulder combo (barbell):	2 sets
	Power clean	2 reps		Front raise	6 reps
	Push jerk	2 reps		Upright row	8 reps
	Front squat	2 reps		Shoulder press	8 reps
2a	Dumbbell bench press	3 × 5	4a	Overhead dumbbell triceps extension	3 × 8
2b	Lunge to step-up	3 × 2 each side	4b	Abdominals (functional)	Exercise dependent
			5	Band flexibility: leg up, leg out, leg over, quad, hip flexor	1 × 10 sec each side

* For cycle, refer to table 10.9 for details.

Table 10.7 Preseason Program for Quarterbacks

Strength (Phase 1)

Monday

	Exercise	Sets × reps		Exercise	Sets × reps
	Warm-up 1				
1	Two-arm kettlebell swing	4 × 5	4b	Seated partner side-to-side toss	2 × 10 each way
2a	Alternating dumbbell bench press	4 × 5		Lateral leg raise	2 × 8 each side
2b	Dumbbell pullover	3 × 6-8	5a	Dumbbell hammer curl	3 × 8
3a	Push-up (on stability ball) (feet on box)	3 × 8	5b	External shoulder rotation: dumbbell shoulder horn (standing, incline, decline)	1 × 10 each position
3b	Upright row	3 × 6	6	4-way neck	1 × 8 each way
4a	Medi ball overhead one-arm quick toss	2 × 10 each way			
	Medi ball overhead one-arm deceleration throw	2 × 10 each way			

Tuesday

	Exercise	Sets × reps		Exercise	Sets × reps
	Warm-up 2				
1	One-arm dumbbell snatch	4 × 3 each arm	4a	Romanian deadlift	3 × 6
2	Back squat	Cycle*	4b	Abdominals (functional)	Exercise dependent
3a	Hip thrust	2 × 8	5	Band flexibility: leg up, leg out, leg over, quad, hip flexor	1 × 10 sec each side
3b	Lateral squat	2 × 6 each side			

* For cycle, refer to table 10.9 for details.

Thursday

	Exercise	Sets × reps		Exercise	Sets × reps
	Warm-up 1				
1	Push jerk	Cycle*	4a	Triceps pushdown	3 × 8
2a	Alternating dumbbell incline bench press	4 × 5	4b	Half-kneeling stick chop	10 each side
2b	Standing one-arm dumbbell row	5 × 6-8		Half-kneeling stick lift	10 each side
3a	Band push-up	3 × 6	5a	Dumbbell hold (grip exercise)	2 × 60 sec each side
3b	Suspension trainer row	3 × 8		Finger extensor band (grip exercise)	2 × 10 each way
				Grip football	15 sec
			6	4-way neck	1 × 8 each way

* For cycle, refer to table 10.9 for details.

Friday

	Exercise	Sets × reps		Exercise	Sets × reps
	Warm-up 2				
1	Power clean	Cycle*	4a	Rotational disc (shoes off for ankle strengthening)	1 × 30 each way
2	Clean pull	3 × 5	4b	Medicine ball wood chop	3 × 5
3a	Lunge to step-up	3 × 3 each side	5	Band flexibility: leg up, leg out, leg over, quad, hip flexor	1 × 10 sec each side
3b	Reverse back extension	Week 1: 2 × 15 Week 2: 2 × 20			

* For cycle, refer to table 10.9 for details.

(continued)

Table 10.7 Preseason Program for Quarterbacks *(continued)*

Strength and Power (Phase 2)

Monday

	Exercise	Sets × reps		Exercise	Sets × reps
	Warm-up 2				
1	Clean pull	5 × 3	5	External shoulder rotation: dumbbell shoulder horn (standing, incline, decline)	1 × 10 each position
2	Back squat	Cycle*	6a	Pinch gripper	2 × 30 sec each side
3a	Dumbbell bench press or incline dumbbell bench press	4 × 4		Finger extensor band (grip exercise)	2 × 10 each side
3b	Cable pullover (on stability ball)	3 × 6		Grip football	15 sec
4a	Dumbbell hamstring walk	2 × 5 each side	6	4-way neck	1 × 8 each way
4b	Half-kneeling stick chop	10 each side	7	Band flexibility: leg up, leg out, leg over, quad, hip flexor	1 × 10 sec each side
	Half-kneeling stick lift	10 each side			

* For cycle, refer to table 10.9 for details.

Wednesday

	Exercise	Sets × reps		Exercise	Sets × reps
	Warm-up 3				
1	One-arm dumbbell snatch	4 × 2 each arm	4a	Medi ball overhead one-arm quick toss	2 × 10 each way
2a	Step-up	3 × 5 each leg		Medi ball overhead one-arm deceleration throw	2 × 10 each way
2b	Dumbbell shoulder press	4 × 5	4b	Medicine ball around the world	2 × 10 each way (with a descending load)
3a	Hip thrust	2 × 5		Dumbbell twist	2 × 10 each way
3b	Lateral lunge	2 × 5 each leg	5	Rotational disc (shoes off for ankle strengthening)	1 × 30 each way
			6	Band flexibility: leg up, leg out, leg over, quad, hip flexor	1 × 10 sec each side

* For cycle, refer to table 10.9 for details.

Friday

	Exercise	Sets × reps		Exercise	Sets × reps
	Warm-up 2				
1	Clean and jerk	Cycle*	4	Push-up (on stability ball) (one foot on box)	3 × 6
2	Chain back squat	Cycle*	5a	Reverse back extension	Week 1: 2 × 15 Week 2: 2 × 20 Week 3: 2 × 25
	Complex jump onto a box (after each set of chain back squats)	4 × 2	5b	Kneeling medicine ball blob throw	3 × 5 (with a descending load)
3a	Chain push-up	4 × 3	6a	External shoulder rotation (dumbbell or cable)	2 × 10 each side
3b	Close-grip lat pulldown	4 × 4-6	6b	4-way neck	1 × 8 each way
			7	Band flexibility: leg up, leg out, leg over, quad, hip flexor	1 × 10 sec each side

* For cycle, refer to table 10.9 for details.

Unload/Variation

Monday

	Exercise	Sets × reps		Exercise	Sets × reps
	Warm-up 1				
1	Two-arm kettlebell swing	4 × 5	3b	Prone T, Y, I	2 × 5 each way
2a	Incline dumbbell bench press	4 × 4	4a	Hammer curl	3 × 6
2b	Pull-up	4 × 8	4b	4-way neck	1 × 8 each way
3a	Dumbbell shrug	3 × 10			

Tuesday

	Exercise	Sets × reps		Exercise	Sets × reps
	Warm-up 2				
1	One-arm dumbbell snatch	4 × 2 each arm	3b	Hamstring slide	2 × 10 each side
2	Back squat (light)	Cycle*	4	Band flexibility: leg up, leg out, leg over, quad, hip flexor	1 × 10 sec each side
3a	Side plank with isometric groin hold	2 × 30 sec			

* For cycle, refer to table 10.9 for details.

Thursday

	Exercise	Sets × reps		Exercise	Sets × reps
	Warm-up 4				
1	Power clean combo (barbell):	Cycle*	3	Shoulder combo (barbell):	2 sets
	Power clean	2 reps		Front raise	6 reps
	Push jerk	2 reps		Upright row	8 reps
	Front squat	2 reps		Shoulder press	8 reps
2a	Band push-up	3 × 5	4a	Overhead dumbbell triceps extension	3 × 8
2b	Lunge to step-up	3 × 2 each side	4b	Abdominals (functional)	Exercise dependent
			5	Band flexibility: leg up, leg out, leg over, quad, hip flexor	1 × 10 sec each side

* For cycle, refer to table 10.9 for details.

Table 10.8 Preseason Program for Kickers and Punters

Strength (Phase 1)

Monday

	Exercise	Sets × reps		Exercise	Sets × reps
	Warm-up 1				
1	Two-arm kettlebell swing	4 × 5	4a	Dumbbell hammer curl	3 × 8
2a	Bench press	Cycle*	4b	External shoulder rotation: dumbbell shoulder horn (standing, incline, decline)	1 × each position
2b	Wide-grip lat pulldown	5 × 6-8	5	4-way neck	1 × 8 each way
3a	Upright row	3 × 6			
3b	Abdominals (medicine ball)	Exercise dependent			

* For cycle, refer to table 10.9 for details.

Tuesday

	Exercise	Sets × reps		Exercise	Sets × reps
	Warm-up 2				
1	Power snatch	Cycle*	4a	Romanian deadlift	3 × 6
2	Back squat	Cycle*	4b	Abdominals (functional)	Exercise dependent
3a	Hip thrust	2 × 8	5	Band flexibility: leg up, leg out, leg over, quad, hip flexor	1 × 10 sec each side
3b	4-way hip machine	10 each way			

* For cycle, refer to table 10.9 for details.

Thursday

	Exercise	Sets × reps		Exercise	Sets × reps
	Warm-up 1				
1	Push jerk	Cycle*	3b	Triceps pushdown	3 × 8
2a	Incline bench press	Cycle*	4a	Abdominals (medicine ball)	Exercise dependent
2b	Standing one-arm dumbbell row	5 × 6-8	4b	Dumbbell hold (grip exercise)	2 × 60 sec each side
3a	Suspension trainer row	3 × 8	5	4-way neck	1 × 8 each way

* For cycle, refer to table 10.9 for details.

Friday

	Exercise	Sets × reps		Exercise	Sets × reps
	Warm-up 2				
1	Power clean	Cycle*	4a	Rotational disc (shoes off for ankle strengthening)	1 × 30 each way
2	Clean pull	3 × 5	4b	Abdominals (functional)	Exercise dependent
3a	Lunge to step-up	3 × 3 each side	5	Band flexibility: leg up, leg out, leg over, quad, hip flexor	1 × 10 sec each side
3b	Reverse back extension	Week 1: 2 × 15 Week 2: 2 × 20			

* For cycle, refer to table 10.9 for details.

Strength and Power (Phase 2)

Monday

	Exercise	Sets × reps		Exercise	Sets × reps
	Warm-up 2				
1	Clean pull	5 × 3	4a	Dumbbell hamstring walk	2 × 5 each side
2	Back squat	Cycle*	4b	Abdominals (functional)	Exercise dependent
3a	Bench press or incline bench press	Cycle*	5	4-way neck	1 × 8 each way
3b	Suspension trainer row	4 × 4-6	6	Band flexibility: leg up, leg out, leg over, quad, hip flexor	1 × 10 sec each side

* For cycle, refer to table 10.9 for details.

Wednesday

	Exercise	Sets × reps		Exercise	Sets × reps
	Warm-up 3				
1	Power snatch	Cycle*	4a	External shoulder rotation (dumbbell or cable)	2 × 10 each way
2a	Step-up	3 × 5 each leg	4b	Abdominals (medicine ball)	Exercise dependent
2b	Barbell shoulder press	4 × 5	5	Rotational disc (shoes off for ankle strengthening)	1 × 30 each way
3a	Hip thrust	2 × 5	6	Band flexibility: leg up, leg out, leg over, quad, hip flexor	1 × 10 sec each side
3b	4-way hip machine	10 each way			

* For cycle, refer to table 10.9 for details.

Friday

	Exercise	Sets × reps		Exercise	Sets × reps
	Warm-up 2				
1	Clean and jerk	Cycle*	4a	Reverse back extension (10 lb)	Week 1: 2 × 15 Week 2: 2 × 20 Week 3: 2 × 25
2	Chain back squat	Cycle*	4b	Abdominals (functional)	Exercise dependent
	Complex jump onto a box (after each set of chain back squats)	4 × 2	5	4-way neck	1 × 8 each way
3a	Chain bench press	Cycle*	6	Band flexibility: leg up, leg out, leg over, quad, hip flexor	1 × 10 sec each side
3b	Close-grip lat pulldown	4 × 4-6			

* For cycle, refer to table 10.9 for details.

(continued)

Table 10.8 Preseason Program for Kickers and Punters *(continued)*

Unload/Variation

Monday

	Exercise	Sets × reps		Exercise	Sets × reps
	Warm-up 1				
1	Two-arm kettlebell swing	4 × 5	3b	Prone T, Y, I	2 × 5 each way
2a	Incline bench press (light)	Cycle*	4a	Hammer curl	3 × 6
2b	Pull-up	4 × 8	4b	4-way neck	1 × 8 each way
3a	Dumbbell shrug	3 × 10			

* For cycle, refer to table 10.9 for details.

Tuesday

	Exercise	Sets × reps		Exercise	Sets × reps
	Warm-up 2				
1	One-arm dumbbell snatch	4 × 2 each arm	3b	Hamstring slide	2 × 10 each side
2	Back squat (light)	Cycle*	4	Band flexibility: leg up, leg out, leg over, quad, hip flexor	1 × 10 sec each side
3a	Side plank with isometric groin hold	2 × 30 sec			

* For cycle, refer to table 10.9 for details.

Thursday

	Exercise	Sets × reps		Exercise	Sets × reps
	Warm-up 4				
1	Power clean combo (barbell):	Cycle*	3	Shoulder combo (barbell):	2 sets
	Power clean	2 reps		Front raise	6 reps
	Push jerk	2 reps		Upright row	8 reps
	Front squat	2 reps		Shoulder press	8 reps
2a	Dumbbell bench press	3 × 5	4a	Overhead dumbbell triceps extension	3 × 8
2b	Lunge to step-up	3 × 2 each side	4b	Abdominals (functional)	Exercise dependent
			5	Band flexibility: leg up, leg out, leg over, quad, hip flexor	1 × 10 sec each side

* For cycle, refer to table 10.9 for details.

Table 10.9 Preseason Cycle

Phase number	Phase name	Week	Intensity	Exercise	Scheme*
1	Strength	1	Medium	Power snatch	50/3, 57/3, 65/3, 67/3, 70/3
				Back squat	60/3, 67/3, 75/5, 77/5, 80/5, 82/5
				Push jerk/power clean	60/3, 67/3, 75/3, 77/3, 80/3
				Bench press/incline bench press	60/3, 67/3, 75/5, 77/5, 80/5, 82/5
1	Strength	2	Medium heavy	Power snatch	52/3, 60/3, 67/3, 70/3, 72/3
				Back squat	62/3, 70/3, 77/5, 80/5, 82/5, 85/5
				Push jerk/power clean	62/3, 70/3, 77/3, 80/3, 82/3
				Bench press/incline bench press	62/3, 70/3, 77/5, 80/5, 82/5, 85/5
2	Strength and power	3	Medium	Power snatch	57/2, 65/2, 72/2, 75/2, 77/2
				Back squat	62/3, 70/3, 77/3, 80/3, 82/3, 85/3, 87/3
				Chain back squat	135 × 8, 135CH × 3, 50CH/3 × 4
				Clean and jerk	57/2, 65/2, 72/2, 75/2, 77/2
				Bench press	62/3, 70/3, 77/3, 80/3, 82/3, 85/3, 87/3
				Chain bench press	135 × 8, 135CH × 3, 50CH/3 × 4
2	Strength and power	4	Medium heavy	Power snatch	60/2, 67/2, 75/2, 77/2, 80/2
				Back squat	65/3, 72/3, 80/3, 82/3, 85/3, 87/3, 90/3
				Chain back squat	135 × 8, 135CH × 3, 50CH/3 × 4
				Clean and jerk	60/2, 67/2, 75/2, 77/2, 80/2
				Incline bench press	65/3, 72/3, 80/3, 82/3, 85/3, 87/3, 90/3
				Chain bench press	135 × 8, 135CH × 3, 50CH/3 × 4
2	Strength and power	5	Heavy	Power snatch	62/2, 70/2, 77/2, 80/2, 82/2
				Back squat	65/3, 72/3, 82/3, 85/3, 87/3, 90/3, 92/3
				Chain back squat	135 × 8, 135CH × 3, 50CH/3 × 4
				Clean and jerk	62/2, 70/2, 77/2, 80/2, 82/2
				Bench press	65/3, 72/3, 82/3, 85/3, 87/3, 90/3, 92/3
				Chain bench press	135 × 8, 135CH × 3, 50CH/3 × 4
	Unload/variation	6		Incline bench press	62/3, 70/3, 77/3, 80/2, 82/2
				Back squat	62/3, 70/3, 77/3, 80/2, 82/2
				Power clean combo	60/2, 67/2, 70/2, 72/2

*The cycles shown have the specific percentages of the 1RM and the repetitions to be performed for each of the cycled exercises. The percentage is in the numerator of the fraction, while the number of repetitions is in the denominator. If a percentage is not listed, the athlete should select a weight of the prescribed intensity that can be performed with good technique (the number of sets is listed first and the number of repetitions is listed second; e.g., 3 × 8 means 3 sets of 8 repetitions). If multiple sets are performed of the same percentage and repetitions, the number of sets will be preceded by ×. For example, 80/5 × 3 means 80% of the 1RM for 3 sets of 5 repetitions. For the chain back squat and chain bench press, 135 × 8 refers to 135 pounds (61 kg) × 8 repetitions and 135CH × 3 is 135 pounds (61 kg) plus the chains × 3 repetitions (those are warm-up sets). For chain back squat and chain bench press training sets, the %1RM comes before "CH" and the chains are added to that load. For example, 50CH/3 × 4 means 50% of the 1RM plus the chains × 3 repetitions for 4 sets.

11

IN-SEASON PROGRAMMING

JERRY PALMIERI, DARREN KREIN, AND ZAC WOODFIN

This chapter discusses the design of the in-season program for the football athlete from training camp until the end of the season, and it is presented in a manner similar to chapters 9 and 10. Most of the exercises used during the in-season program were presented in chapters 9 and 10, and the specific position adjustments are similar to the off-season and preseason programs. There is a discussion of in-season training volume and intensity, but the strength and conditioning professional must have the wisdom to adjust these intensities depending on the health and fatigue of the athletes due to the stresses of the season.

GOALS AND OBJECTIVES

In-season is the time when the football athlete must be able to perform at his highest level. The hard work invested in the off-season and preseason training programs enables the athlete to be at his best during the season. However, the season is long, and athletes must still be performing well at the end of it. The primary objective of the in-season program is to maintain the physical qualities developed during the previous training cycles. The football athlete must be strong and powerful throughout the season because the game is very physical. Strength and power are needed to put the force into the ground that enables athletes to run fast, jump high, change direction, and move the opponent. A good indicator that the athlete is maintaining his strength and power is his ability to maintain his lean body mass. Failure to maintain one's body weight usually leads to a decrease in strength and in the ability to generate force. Because of the physical collisions that occur in football, athletes must maintain their body weight not only for performance, but also for injury prevention.

Training the athletes during the season will require great skill by the coach. There must be enough work done in the weight room to maintain the physical qualities of the athlete, but not to the point that such training will hinder the athlete's performance on the field. Such a task will require wise management of the training loads and volume and will include variations between athletes depending on playing time and overall workload in practice. For example, a wide receiver who also plays on many special teams may need a greater reduction in training volume to accommodate for the on-the-field workload than an athlete who does not play on any special teams. It is imperative that coaches and strength and conditioning professionals remain alert to the possible need to make individual adjustments.

Conditioning is a critical training component of the in-season program. Since many games are won or lost in the final minutes, the team must be able to perform well at both the beginning and the end of the game. Practicing at a high speed with a good tempo will be the best conditioning the athletes can experience.

Football teams have many members. Because of these large team sizes, some members may not compete in the games. Often college programs will redshirt an underclassman, making him ineligible to compete in games so that he can have another year of eligibility for competition when he is older and physically more mature. In the NFL, teams have a certain number of athletes designated as practice squad athletes. These men practice with the team and run the plays of the upcoming opponent, but they do not play in the games. Since these redshirt and practice squad athletes are not competing, their in-season goals and objectives will differ from those of other athletes. These athletes can train harder on a modified off-season program that will enable them to target physical improvement rather than maintenance.

LENGTH OF THE PROGRAM

The length of the in-season resistance training program varies significantly between the three levels of competition as well as within the levels, depending on where a school is located and whether it is on a semester or quarter system. A high school strength and conditioning professional in the Northeast, where school starts later than in other parts of the country, may have a four-week training camp followed by a nine-week in-season. Southern schools that start earlier in August may have a two-week training camp and an 11-week in-season. Colleges on the semester system may only have two weeks of training camp, while a school on the quarter system may have three or more weeks. For most colleges, the regular season is 13 weeks long. The professional teams typically have a six-week training camp, but with the exception of adjustments for preseason games, the latter two weeks resemble more of an in-season schedule. The NFL regular season is 17 weeks long.

At the end of the high school and professional seasons, athletes will follow the post-season training guidelines presented in chapter 12. However, another phase of training may be needed for college teams that have a significant amount of time from the end of the regular season to a playoff or bowl game (table 11.1). Depending on when the final regular season game was played and when the playoff or bowl game is scheduled, this period may be up to five or six weeks. Practice time is usually reduced, giving the athletes more time to devote to resistance training. During this time, athletes can recover from any injuries they suffered during the season while also regaining the strength and speed levels they had at the beginning of the season. Because of the variability between and within levels, table 11.1 should be viewed as one possible example (coaches can make adjustments based on their own team's schedule).

Table 11.1 Sample Extra Training Phase*

Active rest	3-days-per-week total body routine	Modified 3-days-per-week total body routine (with practice)	Modified 2-days-per-week total body routine (with practice)
1 week	2 or 3 weeks	1 week	1 week

*When there is time between the end of the regular season and the playoff or bowl game.

Immediately after the regular season, there should be a week of recovery and rejuvenation featuring rest and low activity. Over the next two to three weeks, there will be little if any practice time, so the athletes can return to training that is more aggressive, similar to the three-days-per-week total body routine that was recommended for the latter portion of the preseason phase. When practice resumes, the resistance training routine can continue with the three-days-per-week total body routine. However, depending on practice volume and intensity, the volume and intensity of the program will need adjustment. For those teams involved in postseason play, the week of the playoff or bowl game is often filled with activities and athlete appearances. A two-days-per-week total body routine may be more realistic during this final week of preparation.

The sample in-season programs displayed in this chapter are based on a four-week training camp and then a 15-week in-season period.

STRUCTURE OF THE PROGRAM

During training camp, there are four total body workouts. Each session consists of a total body power exercise, a lower body exercise, an upper body exercise, and some assistance exercises and exercises for the anatomical core. The workouts are similar in design but use different exercises to create variation. These routines should be rotated with each training session. There should be at least two training sessions a week, with a maximum of three. As training camp winds down, the training program should transition into the in-season program.

The in-season program is a three-days-per-week routine consisting of a lower body day, a total body day, and an upper body with a total body power movement day. The lower body day should be scheduled as early as possible in the week between games. Depending on the team's weekly schedule, the legs will be trained the day after the game, or if that day is an off day, they will be trained the second day after the game. In either case, a dynamic mobility routine consisting of foam rolling and band activation, hurdle overs and unders, dynamic flexibility, and tempo runs should be performed prior to the first exercise. This dynamic mobility routine will enhance blood flow, elevate the core body temperature, and bring some relief to tight, sore muscles in preparation for the first workout of the week. The second workout of the week will include a total body power movement and low-volume lower body and upper body exercises. This training day will follow the off day, or, if the off day was immediately after the game, it will be done on the day after the lower body day. The third workout will be performed two days before the next game.

There are two in-season workout programs (designated as Workout 1 and Workout 2 in the in-season program tables). Both workouts have the same goals but use different exercises to create variation in the program. Each workout is designed to be performed on a three-week cycle separated by an unload/variation week, and then repeated for the third and fourth three-week training periods (table 11.2).

Table 11.2   Three-Week Cycles

Number of weeks	Phase
4 weeks	Training camp
3 weeks	Workout 1
1 week	Unload/variation
3 weeks	Workout 2
1 week	Unload/variation
3 weeks	Workout 1
1 week	Unload/variation
3 weeks	Workout 2

This rotation of workouts will keep the athletes from becoming stale over the long in-season period. If the coach believes that a three-days-per-week in-season program requires too much time in the weight room, the training can be reduced to a two-days-per-week program using the first two workouts of the week. Table 11.3 shows the weekly training schedules for the three levels of competition.

Table 11.3   Weekly In-Season Training Schedules for High School, College, and Professional Football Athletes

High school		
Day of the week	**3-days-per-week routine**	**2-days-per-week routine**
Friday	Game day	Game day
Saturday or Sunday	Lower body	Lower body
Monday	Total body	—
Tuesday	—	Total body
Wednesday	Total body power movement and upper body	—
College		
Day of the week	**3-days-per-week routine**	**2-days-per-week routine**
Saturday	Game day	Game day
Sunday or Monday	Lower body	Lower body
Tuesday	Total body	—
Wednesday	—	Total body
Thursday	Total body power movement and upper body	—
Professional		
Day of the week	**3-days-per-week routine**	**2-days-per-week routine**
Sunday	Game day	Game day
Monday or Tuesday	Lower body	Lower body
Wednesday	Total body	—
Thursday	—	Total body
Friday	Total body power movement and upper body	—

RECOMMENDED EXERCISES

The in-season resistance training program should be designed to maintain the strength, power, size, and mobility that was attained through the off-season and preseason programs. Exercises from those training phases will be used throughout the in-season program to enable the athlete to maintain the physical qualities that will help him to be the best football athlete possible.

Total Body Exercises

Since the entire body is involved in performing these exercises, they promote efficient training, which is valuable during an in-season program. Some types of total body movement will be performed in two of the three training sessions. The total body exercises specific to the in-season program are described in the next paragraph.

The snatch pull, clean pull, clean high pull, and one-arm dumbbell snatch are all power exercises involving a quick, explosive generation of force from the hips and legs. These movements are preferred to the full Olympic lifts (e.g., snatch or power clean) because they are somewhat less demanding on the body. Due to the physical nature of football, the elbows and wrists can become sore, and that can make it difficult to rack the bar onto the shoulders or put it in the overhead position. The recommended alternative exercises put less stress on these vulnerable joints.

Lower Body Exercises

Many of the lower body exercises used in-season were discussed in chapter 9; some adjustments specific to the in-season include the following:

- The chain back squat is done as a variation of the back squat and for power development during the unload/variation week.
- The lunge, step-up, and single-leg squat help maintain single-leg strength. Lunge and step-up are done with low volume as secondary leg exercises in the training week. The single-leg squat replaces the back squat in the second prescribed routine for all the athletes except the offensive linemen and defensive linemen. Like the back squat, the single-leg squat is trained with greater intensity than the other single-leg movements. Rotating the back squat and the single-leg squat is necessary for these athletes to be certain that they are building enough single-leg strength.

Upper Body Exercises

Most of the upper body exercises of the in-season were covered in chapter 9. Exercise adjustments for the in-season include the following:

- The bench press, incline bench press, dumbbell bench press, and dumbbell incline bench press are exercises with value that were discussed in chapter 9. During the season, each week will include a barbell pressing movement and a dumbbell for the other pressing movement. If the barbell is used for the bench press, dumbbells will be used for incline bench press. In the next phase, the exercises will switch the barbell and dumbbell.
- The dumbbell shrug and neck exercises build up the trapezius and neck muscles, providing protection for the neck area to reduce the risk of burners.
- Assistance exercises for the shoulders, such as the upright row, lateral shoulder raise, face pull (machine), and bent-over lateral raise, are designed to maintain the mass of the shoulder region and to create muscular balance between its anterior and posterior muscles.

Core Exercises

During the in-season program, exercises for the anatomical core using a medicine ball are excluded in lieu of traditional isometric and functional exercises that are performed once a week.

POSITIONAL ADJUSTMENTS

There are two phases to the in-season program: Training camp and in-season. A base program was established for both phases (table 11.4 and table 11.5 on pages 270-272), and then adjustments were made to those base programs according to positional needs. After the base programs for training camp and in-season are shown, there is a description of the modifications that are needed for each position group.

Offensive and Defensive Linemen (OL and DL)

There are no changes to the base program for the offensive and defensive linemen with the exception of continuing to do back squats as opposed to single-leg squats in the second in-season routine. Because of the physical nature of the position, it is believed that these athletes must continue to back squat and handle significant loads (table 11.6 and table 11.7 on pages 273-275).

Tight Ends (TE), Fullbacks (FB), and Linebackers (LB)

The tight ends, fullbacks, and linebackers are susceptible to neck and shoulder burners, so it is important to add exercises such as isometric neck stretch, burner combo, and dumbbell neck stretch shrugs to strengthen this area (table 11.8 and table 11.9 on pages 276-278).

- *Training camp 1.* Isometric neck stretch and dumbbell neck stretch shrugs
- *Training camp 2.* Burner combo and isometric neck stretch
- *Training camp 3.* Isometric neck stretch and dumbbell neck stretch shrugs
- *Training camp 4.* Burner combo and isometric neck stretch
- *In-season program, workout 1, day 2.* Burner combo and isometric neck stretch
- *In-season program, workout 1, day 3.* Dumbbell neck stretch shrugs and isometric neck stretch
- *In-season program, unload/variation, day 2.* Isometric neck stretch
- *In-season program, workout 2, day 2.* Burner combo and isometric neck stretch
- *In-season program, workout 2, day 3.* Dumbbell neck stretch shrugs and isometric neck stretch

Wide Receivers (WR) and Running Backs (RB)

Wide receivers and running backs need to be strong and fast without an excess of mass, so these athletes do weighted pull-ups or weighted inverted rows in place of one traditional back exercise a week (table 11.10 and table 11.11 on pages 279-281).

- *In-season program, workout 1, day 2.* Weighted pull-up instead of close-grip lat pulldown
- *In-season program, workout 2, day 2.* Weighted inverted row in place of suspension trainer row
- *In-season program, workout 2, day 3.* Wide-grip lat pulldown instead of suspension trainer row

Defensive Backs (DB)

The in-season training programs for wide receivers/running backs and tight ends/fullbacks/linebackers are combined in the defensive backs' program. For example, they do weighted pull-ups or weighted inverted rows in place of one traditional back exercise a week. Defensive backs are also at risk of neck and shoulder burners, so isometric neck stretch, burner combo, and dumbbell neck stretch shrugs are added to reduce that risk (table 11.12 and table 11.13 on pages 282-285).

- *Training camp 1.* Isometric neck stretch and dumbbell neck stretch shrugs
- *Training camp 2.* Burner combo and isometric neck stretch

- *Training camp 3.* Isometric neck stretch and dumbbell neck stretch shrugs
- *Training camp 4.* Burner combo and isometric neck stretch
- *In-season program, workout 1, day 2.* Isometric neck stretch, burner combo, and weighted pull-up instead of close-grip lat pulldown
- *In-season program, workout 1, day 3.* Isometric neck stretch and dumbbell neck stretch shrugs
- *In-season program, unload/variation, day 2.* Isometric neck stretch
- *In-season program, workout 2, day 2.* Isometric neck stretch, burner combo, weighted inverted row in place of suspension trainer row
- *In-season program, workout 2, day 3.* Isometric neck stretch, dumbbell neck stretch shrugs, and wide-grip lat pulldown instead of suspension trainer row

Quarterbacks (QB)

To maintain shoulder flexibility, quarterbacks use dumbbell variations of the bench press and incline bench press instead of barbell variations. Chain push-ups are performed during the unload/variation week. Push-ups not only strengthen the chest and shoulders but also improve stability in that region. Quarterbacks add external shoulder rotation with a cable or dumbbell to maintain the strength of the external rotators of the shoulders. The medicine ball around the world exercise maintains power during torso rotation, and the medicine ball wood chop maintains throwing power (table 11.14 and table 11.15 on pages 286-288).

- *Training camp 1.* Alternating dumbbell bench press (instead of bench press) and external shoulder rotation (cable or dumbbell)
- *Training camp 3.* External shoulder rotation (cable or dumbbell)
- *Training camp 4.* Alternating dumbbell incline bench press (in place of incline bench press)
- *In-season program, workout 1, day 2.* Dumbbell bench press (instead of bench press), medicine ball around the world (in place of dumbbell shrugs), and external shoulder rotation (cable or dumbbell)
- *In-season program, workout 1, day 3.* Alternating dumbbell incline bench press (in place of dumbbell incline bench press) and medicine ball wood chop for abdominals (function)
- *In-season program, unload/variation, day 2.* Chain push-ups (in place of chain bench press), medicine ball around the world (instead of dumbbell shrugs), and external shoulder rotation (cable or dumbbell)
- *In-season program, workout 2, day 2.* Dumbbell incline bench press for incline, medicine ball around the world for dumbbell shrugs, external shoulder rotation cable or dumbbell
- *In-season program, workout 2, day 3.* Alternating dumbbell bench press (instead of dumbbell bench press) and medicine ball wood chop for abdominals (function)

Kickers (K) and Punters (P)

A well-developed hip is very important for the success of kickers and punters. Therefore, the groin exercises performed during training camp workouts 2 and 4 are replaced by the 4-way hip machine. During the season, the exercises for the groin in workouts 1 and 2 are replaced by the 4-way hip machine. There is no change to the groin exercises in the unload/variation workout to create variation (table 11.16 and table 11.17 on pages 289-291).

- *Training camp 2.* 4-way hip machine in place of side plank with isometric groin hold
- *Training camp 4.* 4-way hip machine in place of side plank with isometric groin hold

- *In-season program, workout 1, day 1.* 4-way hip machine (rather than side plank with isometric groin hold)
- *In-season program, workout 2, day 1.* 4-way hip machine (instead of dumbbell goblet lateral squat)

VOLUME AND INTENSITY

The training camp and in-season cycles (table 11.18 on page 292) must be addressed separately. The former is for a shorter period when there is a greater weekly volume of practice time. The latter extends over many weeks, which involves less weekly practice time but includes a competitive game most weeks.

Due to the high volume of training devoted to practice time during training camp, the volume and intensity of lower body resistance training must be low. Some may suggest that since the practice volume is so high, there is no need to resistance train the legs. There is no doubt that too much fatigue will yield diminishing returns; however, failure to do any lower body training will lead to extensive soreness when lower body training is resumed after training camp. To avoid such soreness and to maintain lower body strength, total body exercises are done for 4 sets of 3 repetitions, while squats and step-ups are prescribed at 2 to 3 sets of 3 repetitions. The intensity on the squats is at 40% to 57% of the 1RM. Squat loads begin low and increase as the athletes adapt to the workload in practice.

The upper body can be trained a little more aggressively because the chest and shoulders do not experience as much fatigue as the legs. The bench press and incline bench press can be trained up to a medium intensity using work percentages of 62% to 80% of the 1RM for 3 sets of 2 to 5 repetitions. The volume of the dumbbell bench press and incline bench press is a little bit higher than the bar, with the work sets ranging from 4 to 6 repetitions.

The in-season cycle works on three-week blocks. While the athlete's perceived exertion remains the same, the weight will increase as the repetitions decrease during the phase. At the conclusion of each block, there is an unload/variation week that includes an overall reduction in training volume, some reduction in intensity, and the use of different exercises to create some variation in the program. The next three-week block will have some different exercises than the previous three-week block to keep the athlete stimulated.

Squats are progressed conservatively in phase 1 coming off training camp, but beginning with phase 2, they are trained using 15 percent lighter loads, while the loads for the bench

Interpreting the Sample Program Tables

The cycles shown in the sample programs have the specific percentages of the 1RM and the repetitions to be performed for each of the cycled exercises. If a percentage is not listed for a cycled exercise, the athlete should select a weight of the prescribed intensity that can be performed with good technique. The percentage is in the numerator of the fraction, while the number of repetitions is in the denominator. If multiple sets are performed of the same percentage and repetitions, the number of sets will be preceded by ×. For example, 80/5 × 3 means 80% of the 1RM for 3 sets of 5 repetitions. If there is no percentage or intensity assigned, the number of sets is listed first and the number of repetitions is listed second (e.g., 3 × 8 means 3 sets of 8 repetitions).

Gray rows in the programs indicate position-specific changes from the base program (table 11.4 and table 11.5).

press and incline bench press are approximately 10 percent less than the prescribed repetitions based on table 4.1. Regardless of the load, the athlete should move the weight as fast as possible. These percentages are programmed with a true 1RM. If the athlete is working from a predicted 1RM, the percentages may need to be slightly decreased.

The assistance exercises typically are trained in the 8 to 10 repetition range throughout the cycle.

ORDER OF EXERCISES

As explained in chapters 9 and 10, there is a recommended order of exercises within a workout that produces optimal results:

1. Olympic lifts (always first in a workout),
2. non-power core exercises,
3. assistance exercises, and
4. anatomical core exercises (at the end of the workout).

Similar to the off-season and preseason sample programs, time can be saved by alternating push and pull exercises (with a rest period still included; the pairings are not intended to be performed as a continuous circuit).

CONCLUSION

In-season training is a critical period of the yearly training cycle. For a team to be successful, its members must be prepared to compete for the entire season. It is not uncommon to see a team begin the season with a run of victories, only to fall off as the playoffs approach. It is important for teams to play their best football at the end of the season, when championships are on the line. Aim to finish strong.

Warm-Ups

WARM-UP 1
Three-station postgame recovery and regeneration
- Foam roll or band activation
- Hurdle over/under range of motion
- Dynamic flexibility

Tempo runs

WARM-UP 2
Dynamic warm-up
Band side-lying leg raise (2 × 15 each side)

WARM-UP 3
Dynamic warm-up
Band hip extension (2 × 15 each side)

WARM-UP 4
Dynamic warm-up
Band side-lying clam shell (2 × 15 each side)

Table 11.4 Training Camp Base Program

Workout 1

	Exercise	Sets × reps		Exercise	Sets × reps
	Warm-up 2				
1	Snatch pull	4 × 3	5	Dumbbell Romanian deadlift	1 × 6
2	Back squat	Cycle*	6	4-way neck	1 × 6 each way
3a	Bench press	Cycle*	7	Rotational disc (shoes off for ankle strengthening)	1 × 20 each way
3b	Inverted row	3 × 8	8	Band flexibility: leg up, leg out, leg over, quad, hip flexor	1 × 10 sec each side
4	Lateral squat	1 × 6 each leg			

* For cycle, refer to table 11.18 for details.

Workout 2

	Exercise	Sets × reps		Exercise	Sets × reps
	Warm-up 3				
1	Clean pull	4 × 3	4	Side plank with isometric groin hold	1 × 20 sec
2	Hip thrust	2 × 5	5	Reverse back extension	1 × 15
3a	Dumbbell incline bench press	Cycle*	6	4-way neck	1 × 6 each way
3b	Wide-grip lat pulldown	3 × 8	7	Band flexibility: leg up, leg out, leg over, quad, hip flexor	1 × 10 sec each side

* For cycle, refer to table 11.18 for details.

Workout 3

	Exercise	Sets × reps		Exercise	Sets × reps
	Warm-up 2				
1	One-arm dumbbell snatch	4 × 3 each arm	5	Physio ball leg curl	1 × 6
2	Back squat	Cycle*	6	4-way neck	1 × 6 each way
3a	Dumbbell bench press	Cycle*	7	Rotational disc (shoes off for ankle strengthening)	1 × 20 each way
3b	Close-grip lat pulldown	3 × 8	8	Band flexibility: leg up, leg out, leg over, quad, hip flexor	1 × 10 sec each side
4	Lateral lunge	1 × 6 each leg			

* For cycle, refer to table 11.18 for details.

Workout 4

	Exercise	Sets × reps		Exercise	Sets × reps
	Warm-up 4				
1	Clean high pull	4 × 3	4b	Side plank with isometric groin hold	1 × 10
2	Dumbbell step-up	2 × 3 each side	4c	Back extension	1 × 15
3a	Incline bench press	Cycle*	5	4-way neck	1 × 6 each way
3b	Pull-up	3 × 8	6	Band flexibility: leg up, leg out, leg over, quad, hip flexor	1 × 10 sec each side
4a	Abdominals (functional)	Exercise dependent			

* For cycle, refer to table 11.18 for details.

Table 11.5 In-Season Base Program

Workout 1

Day 1: Lower Body

	Exercise	Sets × reps		Exercise	Sets × reps
	Warm-up 1				
1	Back squat	Cycle*	3b	Physio ball leg curl	2 × 8
2a	Band TKE	2 × 10 each side	4	Rotational disc (shoes off for ankle strengthening)	1 × 20 each way
2b	Side plank with isometric groin hold	2 × 10	5	Band flexibility: leg up, leg out, leg over, quad, hip flexor	1 × 10 sec each side
3a	Back extension	2 × 10			

* For cycle, refer to table 11.18 for details.

Day 2: Total Body

	Exercise	Sets × reps		Exercise	Sets × reps
	Warm-up 2				
1	Snatch pull	Cycle*	4a	Dumbbell lateral shoulder raise	2 × 8
2a	Hip thrust	2 × 5	4b	Dumbbell shrug	2 × 10
2b	Step-up	2 × 3 each leg	5	4-way neck	1 × 6 each way
3a	Bench press	Cycle*	6	Band flexibility: leg up, leg out, leg over, quad, hip flexor	1 × 10 sec each side
3b	Close-grip lat pulldown	3 × 8			

* For cycle, refer to table 11.18 for details.

Day 3: Upper Body with a Total Body Power Movement

	Exercise	Sets × reps		Exercise	Sets × reps
	Warm-up 3				
1	Clean high pull	Cycle*	3a	Face pull (machine)	3 × 10
2a	Dumbbell incline bench press	Cycle*	3b	Abdominals (functional)	Exercise dependent
2b	Standing one-arm dumbbell row	3 × 8	4	4-way neck	1 × 6 each way

* For cycle, refer to table 11.18 for details.

Unload/Variation

Day 1

	Exercise	Sets × reps		Exercise	Sets × reps
	Warm-up 1				
1	Chain back squat	Cycle*	3	Rotational disc (shoes off for ankle strengthening)	1 × 20 each way
2a	Side plank with isometric groin hold	2 × 30 sec	4	Band flexibility: leg up, leg out, leg over, quad, hip flexor	1 × 10 sec each side
2b	Glute-ham raise	2 × 8			

* For cycle, refer to table 11.18 for details.

(continued)

Table 11.5 In-Season Base Program *(continued)*

Day 2

	Exercise	Sets × reps		Exercise	Sets × reps
	Warm-up 2				
1	Two-arm dumbbell clean to push press	4 × 3	3b	Dumbbell shrug	2 × 10
2a	Chain bench press	Cycle*	4	4-way neck	1 × 6 each way
2b	Pull-up	3 × 8	5	Band flexibility: leg up, leg out, leg over, quad, hip flexor	1 × 10 sec each side
3a	Upright row	2 × 8			

* For cycle, refer to table 11.18 for details.

Workout 2

Day 1: Lower Body

	Exercise	Sets × reps		Exercise	Sets × reps
	Warm-up 1				
1	Single-leg squat	Cycle*	3b	Dumbbell Romanian deadlift	2 × 6
2a	Band TKE	2 × 10 each side	4	Rotational disc (shoes off for ankle strengthening)	1 × 20 each way
2b	Dumbbell goblet lateral squat	2 × 6 each side	5	Band flexibility: leg up, leg out, leg over, quad, hip flexor	1 × 10 sec each side
3a	Reverse back extension	2 × 10			

* For cycle, refer to table 11.18 for details.

Day 2: Total Body

	Exercise	Sets × reps		Exercise	Sets × reps
	Warm-up 2				
1	One-arm dumbbell snatch	Cycle*	4a	Cable lateral shoulder raise	2 × 8
2a	Hip thrust	2 × 5	4b	Dumbbell shrug	2 × 10
2b	Lunge	2 × 3 each leg	5	4-way neck	1 × 6 each way
3a	Incline bench press	4 × cycle*	6	Band flexibility: leg up, leg out, leg over, quad, hip flexor	1 × 10 sec each side
3b	Wide-grip lat pulldown	3 × 8			

* For cycle, refer to table 11.18 for details.

Day 3: Upper Body with a Total Body Power Movement

	Exercise	Sets × reps		Exercise	Sets × reps
	Warm-up 4				
1	Clean pull	Cycle*	3a	Bent-over lateral raise	3 × 10
2a	Dumbbell bench press	Cycle*	3b	Abdominals (functional)	Exercise dependent
2b	Suspension trainer row	3 × 8	4	4-way neck	1 × 6 each way

* For cycle, refer to table 11.18 for details.

Table 11.6 Training Camp Program for Offensive and Defensive Linemen

Workout 1

	Exercise	Sets × reps		Exercise	Sets × reps
	Warm-up 2				
1	Snatch pull	4 × 3	5	Dumbbell Romanian deadlift	1 × 6
2	Back squat	Cycle*	6	4-way neck	1 × 6 each way
3a	Bench press	Cycle*	7	Rotational disc (shoes off for ankle strengthening)	1 × 20 each way
3b	Inverted row	3 × 8	8	Band flexibility: leg up, leg out, leg over, quad, hip flexor	1 × 10 sec each side
4	Lateral squat	1 × 6 each way			

* For cycle, refer to table 11.18 for details.

Workout 2

	Exercise	Sets × reps		Exercise	Sets × reps
	Warm-up 3				
1	Clean pull	4 × 3	4	Side plank with isometric groin hold	1 × 20 sec
2	Hip thrust	2 × 5	5	Reverse back extension	1 × 15
3a	Dumbbell incline bench press	Cycle*	6	4-way neck	1 × 6 each way
3b	Wide-grip lat pulldown	3 × 8	7	Band flexibility: leg up, leg out, leg over, quad, hip flexor	1 × 10 sec each side

* For cycle, refer to table 11.18 for details.

Workout 3

	Exercise	Sets × reps		Exercise	Sets × reps
	Warm-up 2				
1	One-arm dumbbell snatch	4 × 3 each arm	5	Dolly leg curl	1 × 6
2	Back squat	Cycle*	6	4-way neck	1 × 6 each way
3a	Dumbbell bench press	Cycle*	7	Rotational disc (shoes off for ankle strengthening)	1 × 20 each way
3b	Close-grip lat pulldown	3 × 8	8	Band flexibility: leg up, leg out, leg over, quad, flexor	1 × 10 sec each side
4	Lateral lunge	1 × 6 each leg			

* For cycle, refer to table 11.18 for details.

Workout 4

	Exercise	Sets × reps		Exercise	Sets × reps
	Warm-up 4				
1	Clean high pull	4 × 3	4b	Side plank with isometric groin hold	1 × 10
2	Dumbbell step-up	2 × 3 each side	4c	Back extension	1 × 15
3a	Incline bench press	Cycle*	5	4-way neck	1 × 6 each way
3b	Pull-up	3 × 8	6	Band flexibility: leg up, leg out, leg over, quad, hip flexor	1 × 10 sec each side
4a	Abdominals (functional)	Exercise dependent			

* For cycle, refer to table 11.18 for details.

Table 11.7 In-Season Program for Offensive and Defensive Linemen

Workout 1

Day 1: Lower Body

	Exercise	Sets × reps		Exercise	Sets × reps
	Warm-up 1				
1	Back squat	Cycle*	3b	Dolly leg curl	2 × 8
2a	Band TKE	2 × 10 each side	4	Rotational disc (shoes off for ankle strengthening)	1 × 20 each way
2b	Side plank with isometric groin hold	2 × 10	5	Band flexibility: leg up, leg out, leg over, quad, hip flexor	1 × 10 sec each side
3a	Back extension	2 × 10			

* For cycle, refer to table 11.18 for details.

Day 2: Total Body

	Exercise	Sets × reps		Exercise	Sets × reps
	Warm-up 2				
1	Snatch pull	Cycle*	4a	Lateral shoulder raise	2 × 8
2a	Hip thrust	2 × 5	4b	Dumbbell shrug	2 × 10
2b	Step-up	2 × 3 each leg	5	4-way neck	1 × 6 each way
3a	Bench press	Cycle*	6	Band flexibility: leg up, leg out, leg over, quad, hip flexor	1 × 10 sec each side
3b	Close-grip lat pulldown	3 × 8			

* For cycle, refer to table 11.18 for details.

Day 3: Upper Body with a Total Body Power Movement

	Exercise	Sets × reps		Exercise	Sets × reps
	Warm-up 3				
1	Clean high pull	Cycle*	3a	Face pull (machine)	3 × 10
2a	Dumbbell incline bench press	Cycle*	3b	Abdominals (functional)	Exercise dependent
2b	Standing one-arm dumbbell row	3 × 8	4	4-way neck	1 × 6 each way

* For cycle, refer to table 11.18 for details.

Unload/Variation

Day 1

	Exercise	Sets × reps		Exercise	Sets × reps
	Warm-up 1				
1	Chain back squat	Cycle*	3	Rotational disc (shoes off for ankle strengthening)	1 × 20 each way
2a	Side plank with isometric groin hold	2 × 30 sec	4	Band flexibility: leg up, leg out, leg over, quad, hip flexor	1 × 10 sec each side
2b	Glute-ham raise	2 × 8			

* For cycle, refer to table 11.18 for details.

	Exercise	Sets × reps		Exercise	Sets × reps
	Warm-up 2				
1	Two-arm dumbbell clean to push press	4 × 3	3b	Dumbbell shrug	2 × 10
2a	Chain bench press	Cycle*	4	4-way neck	1 × 6 each way
2b	Pull-up	3 × 8	5	Band flexibility: leg up, leg out, leg over, quad, hip flexor	1 × 10 sec each side
3a	Upright row	2 × 8			

* For cycle, refer to table 11.18 for details.

Workout 2

Day 1: Lower Body

	Exercise	Sets × reps		Exercise	Sets × reps
	Warm-up 1				
1	Back squat	Cycle*	3b	Dumbbell Romanian deadlift	2 × 6
2a	Band TKE	2 × 10 each side	4	Rotational disc (shoes off for ankle strengthening)	1 × 20 each way
2b	Dumbbell goblet lateral squat	2 × 6 each side	5	Band flexibility: leg up, leg out, leg over, quad, hip flexor	1 × 10 sec each side
3a	Reverse back extension	2 × 10			

* For cycle, refer to table 11.18 for details.

Day 2: Total Body

	Exercise	Sets × reps		Exercise	Sets × reps
	Warm-up 2				
1	One-arm dumbbell snatch	Cycle*	4a	Cable lateral shoulder raise	2 × 8
2a	Hip thrust	2 × 5	4b	Dumbbell shrug	2 × 10
2b	Lunge	2 × 3 each leg	5	4-way neck	1 × 6 each way
3a	Incline bench press	4 × cycle*	6	Band flexibility: leg up, leg out, leg over, quad, hip flexor	1 × 10 sec each side
3b	Wide-grip lat pulldown	3 × 8			

* For cycle, refer to table 11.18 for details.

Day 3: Upper Body with a Total Body Power Movement

	Exercise	Sets × reps		Exercise	Sets × reps
	Warm-up 4				
1	Clean pull	Cycle*	3a	Bent-over lateral raise	3 × 10
2a	Dumbbell bench press	Cycle*	3b	Abdominals (functional)	Exercise dependent
2b	Suspension trainer row	3 × 8	4	4-way neck	1 × 6 each way

* For cycle, refer to table 11.18 for details.

Table 11.8 Training Camp Program for Tight Ends, Fullbacks, and Linebackers

Workout 1

	Exercise	Sets × reps		Exercise	Sets × reps
	Warm-up 2				
1	Snatch pull	4 × 3	4c	Dumbbell Romanian deadlift	1 × 6
2	Back squat	Cycle*	5	4-way neck	1 × 6 each way
3a	Bench press	Cycle*		Isometric neck stretch	2 × 5 for 30 sec each way
3b	Inverted row	3 × 8	6	Rotational disc (shoes off for ankle strengthening)	1 × 20 each way
4a	Dumbbell neck stretch shrug	2 × 10 each way	7	Band flexibility: leg up, leg out, leg over, quad, hip flexor	1 × 10 sec each side
4b	Lateral squat	1 × 6 each way			

* For cycle, refer to table 11.18 for details.

Workout 2

	Exercise	Sets × reps		Exercise	Sets × reps
	Warm-up 3				
1	Clean pull	4 × 3	4b	Side plank with isometric groin hold	1 × 20 sec
2	Hip thrust	2 × 5	4c	Reverse back extension	1 × 15
3a	Dumbbell incline bench press	Cycle*	5	4-way neck	1 × 6 each way
3b	Wide-grip lat pulldown	3 × 8		Isometric neck stretch	2 × 5 for 30 sec each way
4a	Burner combo	2 × 10 each way	6	Band flexibility: leg up, leg out, leg over, quad, hip flexor	1 × 10 sec each side

* For cycle, refer to table 11.18 for details.

Workout 3

	Exercise	Sets × reps		Exercise	Sets × reps
	Warm-up 2				
1	One-arm dumbbell snatch	4 × 3 each arm	4c	Dolly leg curl	1 × 6
2	Back squat	Cycle*	5	4-way neck	1 × 6 each way
3a	Dumbbell bench press	Cycle*		Isometric neck stretch	2 × 5 for 30 sec each way
3b	Close-grip lat pulldown	3 × 8	6	Rotational disc (shoes off for ankle strengthening)	1 × 20 each way
4a	Dumbbell neck stretch shrug	2 × 10 each way	7	Band flexibility: leg up, leg out, leg over, quad, hip flexor	1 × 10 sec each side
4b	Lateral lunge	1 × 6 each leg			

* For cycle, refer to table 11.18 for details.

Workout 4

	Exercise	Sets × reps		Exercise	Sets × reps
	Warm-up 4				
1	Clean high pull	4 × 3	5	Side plank with isometric groin hold	1 × 10
2	Dumbbell step-up	2 × 3 each side	6	Back extension	1 × 15
3a	Incline bench press	Cycle*	7	4-way neck	1 × 6 each way
3b	Pull-up	3 × 8		Isometric neck stretch	2 × 5 for 30 sec each way
4a	Burner combo	2 × 10 each way	8	Band flexibility: leg up, leg out, leg over, quad, hip flexor	1 × 10 sec each side
4b	Abdominals (functional)	Exercise dependent			

* For cycle, refer to table 11.18 for details.

Table 11.9 In-Season Program for Tight Ends, Fullbacks, and Linebackers

Workout 1

Day 1: Lower Body

	Exercise	Sets × reps		Exercise	Sets × reps
	Warm-up 1				
1	Back squat	Cycle*	3b	Dolly leg curl	2 × 8
2a	Band TKE	2 × 10 each side	4	Rotational disc (shoes off for ankle strengthening)	1 × 20 each way
2b	Side plank with isometric groin hold	2 × 10	5	Band flexibility: leg up, leg out, leg over, quad, hip flexor	1 × 10 sec each side
3a	Back extension	2 × 10			

* For cycle, refer to table 11.18 for details.

Day 2: Total Body

	Exercise	Sets × reps		Exercise	Sets × reps
	Warm-up 2				
1	Snatch pull	Cycle*	4b	Dumbbell shrug	2 × 10
2a	Hip thrust	2 × 5	5a	Burner combo	2 × 10 each way
2b	Step-up	2 × 3 each leg	5b	4-way neck	1 × 6 each way
3a	Bench press	Cycle*		Isometric neck stretch	2 × 5 for 30 sec each way
3b	Close-grip lat pulldown	3 × 8	6	Band flexibility: leg up, leg out, leg over, quad, hip flexor	1 × 10 sec each side
4a	Lateral shoulder raise	2 × 8			

* For cycle, refer to table 11.18 for details.

Day 3: Upper Body with a Total Body Power Movement

	Exercise	Sets × reps		Exercise	Sets × reps
	Warm-up 3				
1	Clean high pull	Cycle*	3b	Dumbbell neck stretch shrug	2 × 10 each way
2a	Dumbbell incline bench press	Cycle*	4a	Abdominals (functional)	Exercise dependent
2b	Standing one-arm dumbbell row	3 × 8	4b	4-way neck	1 × 6 each way
3a	Cable face pull	3 × 10		Isometric neck stretch	2 × 5 for 30 sec each way

* For cycle, refer to table 11.18 for details.

Unload/Variation

Day 1

	Exercise	Sets × reps		Exercise	Sets × reps
	Warm-up 1				
1	Chain back squat	Cycle*	3	Rotational disc (shoes off for ankle strengthening)	1 × 20 each way
2a	Side plank with isometric groin hold	2 × 30 sec	4	Band flexibility: leg up, leg out, leg over, quad, hip flexor	1 × 10 sec each side
2b	Glute–ham extension	2 × 8			

* For cycle, refer to table 11.18 for details.

(continued)

Day 2

	Exercise	Sets × reps		Exercise	Sets × reps
	Warm-up 2				
1	Two-arm dumbbell clean to push press	4 × 3	3b	Dumbbell shrug	2 × 10
2a	Chain bench press	Cycle*	4	4-way neck	1 × 6 each way
2b	Pull-up	3 × 8		Isometric neck stretch	2 × 5 for 30 sec each way
3a	Upright row	2 × 8	5	Band flexibility: leg up, leg out, leg over, quad, hip flexor	1 × 10 sec each side

* For cycle, refer to table 11.18 for details.

Workout 2

Day 1: Lower Body

	Exercise	Sets × reps		Exercise	Sets × reps
	Warm-up 1				
1	Single-leg squat	Cycle*	3b	Dumbbell Romanian deadlift	2 × 6
2a	Band TKE	2 × 10 each side	4	Rotational disc (shoes off for ankle strengthening)	1 × 20 each way
2b	Dumbbell goblet lateral squat	2 × 6 each side	5	Band flexibility: leg up, leg out, leg over, quad, hip flexor	1 × 10 sec each side
3a	Reverse back extension	2 × 10			

* For cycle, refer to table 11.18 for details.

Day 2: Total Body

	Exercise	Sets × reps		Exercise	Sets × reps
	Warm-up 2				
1	One-arm dumbbell snatch	Cycle*	4b	Dumbbell shrug	2 × 10
2a	Hip thrust	2 × 5	5a	Burner combo	2 × 10 each way
2b	Lunge	2 × 3 each leg	5b	4-way neck	1 × 6 each way
3a	Incline bench press	4 × cycle*		Isometric neck stretch	2 × 5 for 30 sec each way
3b	Wide-grip lat pulldown	3 × 8	6	Band flexibility: leg up, leg out, leg over, quad, hip flexor	1 × 10 sec each side
4a	Cable lateral shoulder raise	2 × 8			

* For cycle, refer to table 11.18 for details.

Day 3: Upper Body with a Total Body Power Movement

	Exercise	Sets × reps		Exercise	Sets × reps
	Warm-up 4				
1	Clean pull	Cycle*	3b	Dumbbell neck stretch shrug	2 × 10 each way
2a	Dumbbell bench press	Cycle*	4a	Abdominals (functional)	Exercise dependent
2b	Suspension trainer row	3 × 8	4b	4-way neck	1 × 6 each way
3a	Bent-over lateral raise	3 × 10		Isometric neck stretch	2 × 5 for 30 sec each way

* For cycle, refer to table 11.18 for details.

Table 11.10 Training Camp Program for Wide Receivers and Running Backs

Workout 1

	Exercise	Sets × reps		Exercise	Sets × reps
	Warm-up 2				
1	Snatch pull	4 × 3	5	Dumbbell Romanian deadlift	1 × 6
2	Back squat	Cycle*	6	4-way neck	1 × 6 each way
3a	Bench press	Cycle*	7	Rotational disc (shoes off for ankle strengthening)	1 × 20 each way
3b	Inverted row	3 × 8	8	Band flexibility: leg up, leg out, leg over, quad, hip flexor	1 × 10 sec each side
4	Lateral squat	1 × 6 each way			

* For cycle, refer to table 11.18 for details.

Workout 2

	Exercise	Sets × reps		Exercise	Sets × reps
	Warm-up 3				
1	Clean pull	4 × 3	4	Side plank with isometric groin hold	1 × 20 sec
2	Hip thrust	2 × 5	5	Reverse back extension	1 × 15
3a	Dumbbell incline bench press	Cycle*	6	4-way neck	1 × 6 each way
3b	Wide-grip lat pulldown	3 × 8	7	Band flexibility: leg up, leg out, leg over, quad, hip flexor	1 × 10 sec each side

* For cycle, refer to table 11.18 for details.

Workout 3

	Exercise	Sets × reps		Exercise	Sets × reps
	Warm-up 2				
1	One-arm dumbbell snatch	4 × 3 each arm	5	Dolly leg curl	1 × 6
2	Back squat	Cycle*	6	4-way neck	1 × 6 each way
3a	Dumbbell bench press	Cycle*	7	Rotational disc (shoes off for ankle strengthening)	1 × 20 each way
3b	Close-grip lat pulldown	3 × 8	8	Band flexibility: leg up, leg out, leg over, quad, hip flexor	1 × 10 sec each side
4	Lateral lunge	1 × 6 each leg			

* For cycle, refer to table 11.18 for details.

Workout 4

	Exercise	Sets × reps		Exercise	Sets × reps
	Warm-up 4				
1	Clean high pull	4 × 3	4b	Side plank with isometric groin hold	1 × 10
2	Dumbbell step-up	2 × 3 each side	4c	Back extension	1 × 15
3a	Incline bench press	Cycle*	5	4-way neck	1 × 6 each way
3b	Pull-up	3 × 8	6	Band flexibility: leg up, leg out, leg over, quad, hip flexor	1 × 10 sec each side
4a	Abdominals (functional)	Exercise dependent			

* For cycle, refer to table 11.18 for details.

Table 11.11 In-Season Program for Wide Receivers and Running Backs

Workout 1

Day 1: Lower Body

	Exercise	Sets × reps		Exercise	Sets × reps
	Warm-up 1				
1	Back squat	Cycle*	3b	Dolly leg curl	2 × 8
2a	Band TKE	2 × 10 each side	4	Rotational disc (shoes off for ankle strengthening)	1 × 20 each way
2b	Side plank with isometric groin hold	2 × 10	5	Band flexibility: leg up, leg out, leg over, quad, hip flexor	1 × 10 sec each side
3a	Back extension	2 × 10			

* For cycle, refer to table 11.18 for details.

Day 2: Total Body

	Exercise	Sets × reps		Exercise	Sets × reps
	Warm-up 2				
1	Snatch pull	Cycle*	4a	Lateral shoulder raise	2 × 8
2a	Hip thrust	2 × 5	4b	Dumbbell shrug	2 × 10
2b	Step-up	2 × 3 each leg	5	4-way neck	1 × 6 each way
3a	Bench press	Cycle*	6	Band flexibility: leg up, leg out, leg over, quad, hip flexor	1 × 10 sec each side
3b	Weighted pull-up	3 × 8			

* For cycle, refer to table 11.18 for details.

Day 3: Upper Body with a Total Body Power Movement

	Exercise	Sets × reps		Exercise	Sets × reps
	Warm-up 3				
1	Clean high pull	Cycle*	3a	Face pull (machine)	3 × 10
2a	Dumbbell incline bench press	Cycle*	3b	Abdominals (functional)	Exercise dependent
2b	Standing one-arm dumbbell row	3 × 8	4	4-way neck	1 × 6 each way

* For cycle, refer to table 11.18 for details.

Unload/Variation

Day 1

	Exercise	Sets × reps		Exercise	Sets × reps
	Warm-up 1				
1	Chain back squat	Cycle*	3	Rotational disc (shoes off for ankle strengthening)	1 × 20 each way
2a	Side plank with isometric groin hold	2 × 30 sec	4	Band flexibility: leg up, leg out, leg over, quad, hip flexor	1 × 10 sec each side
2b	Glute-ham raise	2 × 8			

* For cycle, refer to table 11.18 for details.

Day 2

	Exercise	Sets × reps		Exercise	Sets × reps
	Warm-up 2				
1	Two-arm dumbbell clean to push press	4 × 3	3b	Dumbbell shrug	2 × 10
2a	Chain bench press	Cycle*	4	4-way neck	1 × 6 each way
2b	Pull-up	3 × 8	5	Band flexibility: leg up, leg out, leg over, quad, hip flexor	1 × 10 sec each side
3a	Upright row	2 × 8			

* For cycle, refer to table 11.18 for details.

Workout 2

Day 1: Lower Body

	Exercise	Sets × reps		Exercise	Sets × reps
	Warm-up 1				
1	Single-leg squat	Cycle*	3b	Dumbbell Romanian deadlift	2 × 6
2a	Band TKE	2 × 10 each side	4	Rotational disc (shoes off for ankle strengthening)	1 × 20 each way
2b	Dumbbell goblet lateral squat	2 × 6 each side	5	Band flexibility: leg up, leg out, leg over, quad, hip flexor	1 × 10 sec each side
3a	Reverse back extension	2 × 10			

* For cycle, refer to table 11.18 for details.

Day 2: Total Body

	Exercise	Sets × reps		Exercise	Sets × reps
	Warm-up 2				
1	One-arm dumbbell snatch	Cycle*	4a	Cable lateral shoulder raise	2 × 8
2a	Hip thrust	2 × 5	4b	Dumbbell shrug	2 × 10
2b	Lunge	2 × 3 each leg	5	4-way neck	1 × 6 each way
3a	Incline bench press	4 × cycle*	6	Band flexibility: leg up, leg out, leg over, quad, hip flexor	1 × 10 sec each side
3b	Weighted inverted row	3 × 8			

* For cycle, refer to table 11.18 for details.

Day 3: Upper Body with a Total Body Power Movement

	Exercise	Sets × reps		Exercise	Sets × reps
	Warm-up 4				
1	Clean pull	Cycle*	3a	Lateral shoulder raise	3 × 10
2a	Dumbbell bench press	Cycle*	3b	Abdominals (functional)	Exercise dependent
2b	Wide-grip lat pulldown	3 × 8	4	4-way neck	1 × 6 each way

* For cycle, refer to table 11.18 for details.

Table 11.12 Training Camp Program for Defensive Backs

Workout 1

	Exercise	Sets × reps		Exercise	Sets × reps
	Warm-up 2				
1	Snatch pull	4 × 3	5	Dumbbell Romanian deadlift	1 × 6
2	Back squat	Cycle*	6	4-way neck	1 × 6 each way
3a	Bench press	Cycle*		Isometric neck stretch	2 × 5 for 30 sec each way
3b	Inverted row	3 × 8	7	Rotational disc (shoes off for ankle strengthening)	1 × 20 each way
4a	Dumbbell neck stretch shrug	2 × 10 each way	8	Band flexibility: leg up, leg out, leg over, quad, hip flexor	1 × 10 sec each side
4b	Lateral squat	1 × 6 each way			

* For cycle, refer to table 11.18 for details.

Workout 2

	Exercise	Sets × reps		Exercise	Sets × reps
	Warm-up 3				
1	Clean pull	4 × 3	4b	Side plank with isometric groin hold	1 × 20 sec
2	Hip thrust	2 × 5	4c	Reverse back extension	1 × 15
3a	Dumbbell incline bench press	Cycle*	5	4-way neck	1 × 6 each way
3b	Wide-grip lat pulldown	3 × 8		Isometric neck stretch	2 × 5 for 30 sec each way
4a	Burner combo	2 × 10 each way	6	Band flexibility: leg up, leg out, leg over, quad, hip flexor	1 × 10 sec each side

* For cycle, refer to table 11.18 for details.

Workout 3

	Exercise	Sets × reps		Exercise	Sets × reps
	Warm-up 2				
1	One-arm dumbbell snatch	4 × 3 each arm	4c	Dolly leg curl	1 × 6
2	Back squat	Cycle*	5	4-way neck	1 × 6 each way
3a	Dumbbell bench press	Cycle*		Isometric neck stretch	2 × 5 for 30 sec each way
3b	Close-grip lat pulldown	3 × 8	6	Rotational disc (shoes off for ankle strengthening)	1 × 20 each way
4a	Dumbbell neck stretch shrug	2 × 10 each way	7	Band flexibility: leg up, leg out, leg over, quad, hip flexor	1 × 10 sec each side
4b	Lateral lunge	1 × 6 each leg			

* For cycle, refer to table 11.18 for details.

Workout 4

	Exercise	Sets × reps		Exercise	Sets × reps
	Warm-up 4				
1	Clean high pull	4 × 3	5	Side plank with isometric groin hold	1 × 10
2	Dumbbell step-up	2 × 3 each side	6	Back extension	1 × 15
3a	Incline bench press	Cycle*	7	4-way neck	1 × 6 each way
3b	Pull-up	3 × 8		Isometric neck stretch	2 × 5 for 30 sec each way
4a	Burner combo	2 × 10 each way	8	Band flexibility: leg up, leg out, leg over, quad, hip flexor	1 × 10 sec each side
4b	Abdominals (functional)	Exercise dependent			

* For cycle, refer to table 11.18 for details.

Table 11.13　In-Season Program for Defensive Backs

Workout 1

Day 1: Lower Body

	Exercise	Sets × reps		Exercise	Sets × reps
	Warm-up 1				
1	Back squat	Cycle*	3b	Physio ball leg curl	2 × 8
2a	Band TKE	2 × 10 each side	4	Rotational disc (shoes off for ankle strengthening)	1 × 20 each way
2b	Side plank with isometric groin hold	2 × 10	5	Band flexibility: leg up, leg out, leg over, quad, hip flexor	1 × 10 sec each side
3a	Back extension	2 × 10			

* For cycle, refer to table 11.18 for details.

Day 2: Total Body

	Exercise	Sets × reps		Exercise	Sets × reps
	Warm-up 2				
1	Snatch pull	Cycle*	4b	Dumbbell shrug	2 × 10
2a	Hip thrust	2 × 5	5a	Burner combo	2 × 10 each way
2b	Step-up	2 × 3 each leg	5b	4-way neck	1 × 6 each way
3a	Bench press	Cycle*		Isometric neck stretch	2 × 5 for 30 sec each way
3b	Weighted pull-up	3 × 8	6	Band flexibility: leg up, leg out, leg over, quad, hip flexor	1 × 10 sec each side
4a	Dumbbell lateral shoulder raise	2 × 8			

* For cycle, refer to table 11.18 for details.

Day 3: Upper Body with a Total Body Power Movement

	Exercise	Sets × reps		Exercise	Sets × reps
	Warm-up 3				
1	Clean high pull	Cycle*	3b	Dumbbell neck stretch shrug	2 × 10 each side
2a	Dumbbell incline bench press	Cycle*	4a	Abdominals (functional)	Exercise dependent
2b	Standing one-arm dumbbell row	3 × 8	4b	4-way neck	1 × 6 each way
3a	Face pull (machine)	3 × 10		Isometric neck stretch	2 × 5 for 30 sec each way

* For cycle, refer to table 11.18 for details.

Unload/Variation

Day 1

	Exercise	Sets × reps		Exercise	Sets × reps
	Warm-up 1				
1	Chain back squat	Cycle*	3	Rotational disc (shoes off for ankle strengthening)	1 × 20 each way
2a	Side plank with isometric groin hold	2 × 30 sec	4	Band flexibility: leg up, leg out, leg over, quad, hip flexor	1 × 10 sec each side
2b	Glute–ham extension	2 × 8			

* For cycle, refer to table 11.18 for details.

Day 2

	Exercise	Sets × reps			Exercise	Sets × reps
	Warm-up 2					
1	Two-arm dumbbell clean to push press	4 × 3		3b	Dumbbell shrug	2 × 10
2a	Chain bench press	Cycle*		4	4-way neck	1 × 6 each way
2b	Pull-up	3 × 8			Isometric neck stretch	2 × 5 for 30 sec each way
3a	Upright row	2 × 8		5	Band flexibility: leg up, leg out, leg over, quad, hip flexor	1 × 10 sec each side

* For cycle, refer to table 11.18 for details.

Workout 2

Day 1: Lower Body

	Exercise	Sets × reps			Exercise	Sets × reps
	Warm-up 1					
1	Single-leg squat	Cycle*		3b	Dumbbell Romanian deadlift	2 × 6
2a	Band TKE	2 × 10 each side		4	Rotational disc (shoes off for ankle strengthening)	1 × 20 each way
2b	Dumbbell goblet lateral squat	2 × 6 each side		5	Band flexibility: leg up, leg out, leg over, quad, hip flexor	1 × 10 sec each side
3a	Reverse back extension	2 × 10				

* For cycle, refer to table 11.18 for details.

Day 2: Total Body

	Exercise	Sets × reps			Exercise	Sets × reps
	Warm-up 2					
1	One-arm dumbbell snatch	Cycle*		4b	Dumbbell shrug	2 × 10
2a	Hip thrust	2 × 5		5a	Burner combo	2 × 10 each way
2b	Lunge	2 × 3 each leg		5b	4-way neck	1 × 6 each way
3a	Incline bench press	4 × cycle*			Isometric neck stretch	2 × 5 for 30 sec each way
3b	Weighted inverted row	3 × 8		6	Band flexibility: leg up, leg out, leg over, quad, hip flexor	1 × 10 sec each side
4a	Cable lateral shoulder raise	2 × 8				

* For cycle, refer to table 11.18 for details.

Day 3: Upper Body with a Total Body Power Movement

	Exercise	Sets × reps			Exercise	Sets × reps
	Warm-up 4					
1	Clean pull	Cycle*		3b	Dumbbell neck stretch shrug	2 × 10 each side
2a	Dumbbell bench press	Cycle*		4a	Abdominals (functional)	Exercise dependent
2b	Wide-grip lat pulldown	3 × 8		4b	4-way neck	1 × 6 each way
3a	Bent-over lateral raise	3 × 10			Isometric neck stretch	2 × 5 for 30 sec each way

* For cycle, refer to table 11.18 for details.

Table 11.14 Training Camp Program for Quarterbacks

Workout 1

	Exercise	Sets × reps		Exercise	Sets × reps
	Warm-up 2				
1	Snatch pull	4 × 3	4b	Lateral squat	1 × 6 each way
2	Back squat	Cycle*	4c	Dumbbell Romanian deadlift	1 × 6
3a	Alternating dumbbell bench press	Cycle*	5	4-way neck	1 × 6 each way
3b	Inverted row	3 × 8	6	Rotational disc (shoes off for ankle strengthening)	1 × 20 each way
4a	External shoulder rotation (dumbbell or cable)	2 × 10 each side	7	Band flexibility: leg up, leg out, leg over, quad, hip flexor	1 × 10 sec each side

* For cycle, refer to table 11.18 for details.

Workout 2

	Exercise	Sets × reps		Exercise	Sets × reps
	Warm-up 3				
1	Clean pull	4 × 3	4	Side plank with isometric groin hold	1 × 20 sec
2	Hip thrust	2 × 5	5	Reverse back extension	1 × 15
3a	Dumbbell incline bench press	Cycle*	6	4-way neck	1 × 6 each way
3b	Wide-grip lat pulldown	3 × 8	7	Band flexibility: leg up, leg out, leg over, quad, hip flexor	1 × 10 sec each side

* For cycle, refer to table 11.18 for details.

Workout 3

	Exercise	Sets × reps		Exercise	Sets × reps
	Warm-up 2				
1	One-arm dumbbell snatch	4 × 3 each arm	4b	Lateral lunge	1 × 6 each leg
2	Back squat	Cycle*	4c	Dolly leg curl	1 × 6
3a	Dumbbell bench press	Cycle*	5	4-way neck	1 × 6 each way
3b	Close-grip lat pulldown	3 × 8	6	Rotational disc (shoes off for ankle strengthening)	1 × 20 each way
4a	External shoulder rotation (dumbbell or cable)	2 × 10 each side	7	Band flexibility: leg up, leg out, leg over, quad, hip flexor	1 × 10 sec each side

* For cycle, refer to table 11.18 for details.

Workout 4

	Exercise	Sets × reps		Exercise	Sets × reps
	Warm-up 4				
1	Clean high pull	4 × 3	4b	Side plank with isometric groin hold	1 × 10
2	Dumbbell step-up	2 × 3 each side	4c	Back extension	1 × 15
3a	Alternating dumbbell incline bench press	Cycle*	5	4-way neck	1 × 6 each way
3b	Pull-up	3 × 8	6	Band flexibility: leg up, leg out, leg over, quad, hip flexor	1 × 10 sec each side
4a	Abdominals (functional)	Exercise dependent			

* For cycle, refer to table 11.18 for details.

Table 11.15 In-Season Program for Quarterbacks

Workout 1

Day 1: Lower Body

	Exercise	Sets × reps		Exercise	Sets × reps
	Warm-up 1				
1	Back squat	Cycle*	3b	Dolly leg curl	2 × 8
2a	Band TKE	2 × 10 each side	4	Rotational disc (shoes off for ankle strengthening)	1 × 20 each way
2b	Side plank with isometric groin hold	2 × 10	5	Band flexibility: leg up, leg out, leg over, quad, hip flexor	1 × 10 sec each side
3a	Back extension	2 × 10			

* For cycle, refer to table 11.18 for details.

Day 2: Total Body

	Exercise	Sets × reps		Exercise	Sets × reps
	Warm-up 2				
1	Snatch pull	Cycle*	4a	Lateral shoulder raise	2 × 8
2a	Hip thrust	2 × 5	4b	External shoulder rotation (dumbbell or cable)	2 × 10 each arm
2b	Step-up	2 × 3 each leg	5a	Medicine ball around the world	1 × 2 each way
3a	Dumbbell bench press	Cycle*	5b	4-way neck	1 × 6 each way
3b	Close-grip lat pulldown	3 × 8	6	Band flexibility: leg up, leg out, leg over, quad, hip flexor	1 × 10 sec each side

* For cycle, refer to table 11.18 for details.

Day 3: Upper Body with a Total Body Power Movement

	Exercise	Sets × reps		Exercise	Sets × reps
	Warm-up 3				
1	Clean high pull	Cycle*	3a	Face pull (machine)	3 × 10
2a	Alternating dumbbell incline bench press	Cycle*	3b	Medicine ball wood chop	2 × 5
2b	Standing one-arm dumbbell row	3 × 8	4	4-way neck	1 × 6 each way

* For cycle, refer to table 11.18 for details.

Unload/Variation

Day 1

	Exercise	Sets × reps		Exercise	Sets × reps
	Warm-up 1				
1	Chain back squat	Cycle*	3	Rotational disc (shoes off for ankle strengthening)	1 × 20 each way
2a	Side plank with isometric groin hold	2 × 30 sec	4	Band flexibility: leg up, leg out, leg over, quad, hip flexor	1 × 10 sec each side
2b	Glute-ham raise	2 × 8			

* For cycle, refer to table 11.18 for details.

(continued)

Table 11.15 In-Season Program for Quarterbacks *(continued)*

Day 2

	Exercise	Sets × reps		Exercise	Sets × reps
	Warm-up 2				
1	Two-arm dumbbell clean to push press	4 × 3	3b	External shoulder rotation (dumbbell or cable)	2 × 10 each arm
2a	Chain push-up	4 × 3	4a	Medicine ball around the world	1 × 2 each way
2b	Pull-up	3 × 8	4b	4-way neck	1 × 6 each way
3a	Upright row	2 × 8	5	Band flexibility: leg up, leg out, leg over, quad, hip flexor	1 × 10 sec each side

Workout 2

Day 1: Lower Body

	Exercise	Sets × reps		Exercise	Sets × reps
	Warm-up 1				
1	Single-leg squat	Cycle*	3b	Dumbbell Romanian deadlift	2 × 6
2a	Band TKE	2 × 10 each side	4	Rotational disc (shoes off for ankle strengthening)	1 × 20 each way
2b	Dumbbell goblet lateral squat	2 × 6 each side	5	Band flexibility: leg up, leg out, leg over, quad, hip flexor	1 × 10 sec each side
3a	Reverse back extension	2 × 10			

* For cycle, refer to table 11.18 for details.

Day 2: Total Body

	Exercise	Sets × reps		Exercise	Sets × reps
	Warm-up 2				
1	One-arm dumbbell snatch	Cycle*	4a	Cable lateral shoulder raise	2 × 8
2a	Hip thrust	2 × 5	4b	External shoulder rotation (dumbbell or cable)	2 × 10 each arm
2b	Lunge	2 × 3 each leg	5a	Medicine ball around the world	1 × 2 each way
3a	Dumbbell incline bench press	4 × cycle*	5b	4-way neck	1 × 6 each way
3b	Wide-grip lat pulldown	3 × 8	6	Band flexibility: leg up, leg out, leg over, quad, hip flexor	1 × 10 sec each side

* For cycle, refer to table 11.18 for details.

Day 3: Upper Body with a Total Body Power Movement

	Exercise	Sets × reps		Exercise	Sets × reps
	Warm-up 4				
1	Clean pull	Cycle*	3a	Lateral shoulder raise	3 × 10
2a	Alternating dumbbell bench press	Cycle*	3b	Medicine ball wood chop	2 × 5
2b	Suspension trainer row	3 × 8	4	4-way neck	1 × 6 each way

* For cycle, refer to table 11.18 for details.

Table 11.16 Training Camp Program for Kickers and Punters

Workout 1

	Exercise	Sets × reps		Exercise	Sets × reps
	Warm-up 2				
1	Snatch pull	4 × 3	5	Dumbbell Romanian deadlift	1 × 6
2	Back squat	Cycle*	6	4-way neck	1 × 6 each way
3a	Bench press	Cycle*	7	Rotational disc (shoes off for ankle strengthening)	1 × 20 each way
3b	Inverted row	3 × 8	8	Band flexibility: leg up, leg out, leg over, quad, hip flexor	1 × 10 sec each side
4	Lateral squat	1 × 6 each way			

* For cycle, refer to table 11.18 for details.

Workout 2

	Exercise	Sets × reps		Exercise	Sets × reps
	Warm-up 3				
1	Clean pull	4 × 3	4	4-way hip machine	10 each way, each leg
2	Hip thrust	2 × 5	5	Reverse back extension	1 × 15
3a	Dumbbell incline bench press	Cycle*	6	4-way neck	1 × 6 each way
3b	Wide-grip lat pulldown	3 × 8	7	Band flexibility: leg up, leg out, leg over, quad, hip flexor	1 × 10 sec each side

* For cycle, refer to table 11.18 for details.

Workout 3

	Exercise	Sets × reps		Exercise	Sets × reps
	Warm-up 2				
1	One-arm dumbbell snatch	4 × 3 each arm	5	Dolly leg curl	1 × 6
2	Back squat	Cycle*	6	4-way neck	1 × 6 each way
3a	Dumbbell bench press	Cycle*	7	Rotational disc (shoes off for ankle strengthening)	1 × 20 each way
3b	Close-grip lat pulldown	3 × 8	8	Band flexibility: leg up, leg out, leg over, quad, hip flexor	1 × 10 sec each way
4	Lateral lunge	1 × 6 each leg			

* For cycle, refer to table 11.18 for details.

Workout 4

	Exercise	Sets × reps		Exercise	Sets × reps
	Warm-up 4				
1	Clean high pull	4 × 3	4b	4-way hip machine	10 each way, each leg
2	Dumbbell step-up	2 × 3 each side	4c	Back extension	1 × 15
3a	Incline bench press	Cycle*	5	4-way neck	1 × 6 each way
3b	Pull-up	3 × 8	6	Band flexibility: leg up, leg out, leg over, quad, hip flexor	1 × 10 sec each side
4a	Abdominals (functional)	Exercise dependent			

* For cycle, refer to table 11.18 for details.

Table 11.17 In-Season Program for Kickers and Punters

Workout 1

Day 1: Lower Body

	Exercise	Sets × reps		Exercise	Sets × reps
	Warm-up 1				
1	Back squat	Cycle*	3b	Dolly leg curl	2 × 8
2a	Band TKE	2 × 10 each side	4	Rotational disc (shoes off for ankle strengthening)	1 × 20 each way
2b	4-way hip machine	10 each way, each leg	5	Band flexibility: leg up, leg out, leg over, quad, hip flexor	1 × 10 sec each side
3a	Back extension	2 × 10			

* For cycle, refer to table 11.18 for details.

Day 2: Total Body

	Exercise	Sets × reps		Exercise	Sets × reps
	Warm-up 2				
1	Snatch pull	Cycle*	4a	Lateral shoulder raise	2 × 8
2a	Hip thrust	2 × 5	4b	Dumbbell shrug	2 × 10
2b	Step-up	2 × 3 each leg	5	4-way neck	1 × 6 each way
3a	Bench press	Cycle*	6	Band flexibility: leg up, leg out, leg over, quad, hip flexor	1 × 10 sec each side
3b	Close-grip lat pulldown	3 × 8			

* For cycle, refer to table 11.18 for details.

Day 3: Upper Body with a Total Body Power Movement

	Exercise	Sets × reps		Exercise	Sets × reps
	Warm-up 3				
1	Clean high pull	Cycle*	3a	Face pull (machine)	3 × 10
2a	Dumbbell incline bench press	Cycle*	3b	Abdominals (functional)	Exercise dependent
2b	Standing one-arm dumbbell row	3 × 8	4	4-way neck	1 × 6 each way

* For cycle, refer to table 11.18 for details.

Unload/Variation

Day 1

	Exercise	Sets × reps		Exercise	Sets × reps
	Warm-up 1				
1	Chain back squat	Cycle*	3	Rotational disc (shoes off for ankle strengthening)	1 × 20 each way
2a	Side plank with isometric groin hold	2 × 30 sec	4	Band flexibility: leg up, leg out, leg over, quad, hip flexor	1 × 10 sec each side
2b	Glute-ham raise	2 × 8			

* For cycle, refer to table 11.18 for details.

Day 2

	Exercise	Sets × reps		Exercise	Sets × reps
	Warm-up 2				
1	Two-arm dumbbell clean to push press	4 × 3	3b	Dumbbell shrug	2 × 10
2a	Chain bench press	Cycle*	4	4-way neck	1 × 6 each way
2b	Pull-up	3 × 8	5	Band flexibility: leg up, leg out, leg over, quad, hip flexor	1 × 10 sec each side
3a	Upright row	2 × 8			

* For cycle, refer to table 11.18 for details.

Workout 2

Day 1: Lower Body

	Exercise	Sets × reps		Exercise	Sets × reps
	Warm-up 1				
1	Single-leg squat	Cycle*	3b	Dumbbell Romanian deadlift	2 × 6
2a	Band TKE	2 × 10 each side	4	Rotational disc (shoes off for ankle strengthening)	1 × 20 each way
2b	4-way hip machine	10 each way, each leg	5	Band flexibility: leg up, leg out, leg over, quad, hip flexor	1 × 10 sec each side
3a	Reverse back extension	2 × 10			

* For cycle, refer to table 11.18 for details.

Day 2: Total Body

	Exercise	Sets × reps		Exercise	Sets × reps
	Warm-up 2				
1	One-arm dumbbell snatch	Cycle*	4a	Cable lateral shoulder raise	2 × 8
2a	Hip thrust	2 × 5	4b	Dumbbell shrug	2 × 10
2b	Lunge	2 × 3 each leg	5	4-way neck	1 × 6 each way
3a	Incline bench press	4 × cycle*	6	Band flexibility: leg up, leg out, leg over, quad, hip flexor	1 × 10 sec each side
3b	Wide-grip lat pulldown	3 × 8			

* For cycle, refer to table 11.18 for details.

Day 3: Upper Body with a Total Body Power Movement

	Exercise	Sets × reps		Exercise	Sets × reps
	Warm-up 4				
1	Clean pull	Cycle*	3a	Bent-over lateral raise	3 × 10
2a	Dumbbell bench press	Cycle*	3b	Abdominals (functional)	Exercise dependent
2b	Suspension trainer row	3 × 8	4	4-way neck	1 × 6 each way

* For cycle, refer to table 11.18 for details.

Table 11.18 Training Camp and In-Season Cycle

Training camp			
Overall week	**Workout**	**Exercise**	**Scheme***
1	1, 2, 3, 4	Back squat	40/3, 42/3
		Bench press/incline bench press	55/3, 62-72/5 × 3
		Dumbbell bench press/dumbbell incline bench press	8, 6, 5, 5
2	1, 2, 3, 4	Back squat	42/3, 47/3
		Bench press/incline bench press	57/3, 65-75/4 × 3
		Dumbbell bench press/dumbbell incline bench press	8, 5, 5, 5
3	1, 2, 3, 4	Back squat	42/3, 47/3, 52/3
		Bench press/incline bench press	60/3, 67-77/3 × 3
		Dumbbell bench press/dumbbell incline bench press	8, 6, 5, 4
4	1, 2, 3, 4	Back squat	45/3, 52/3, 57/3
		Bench press/incline bench press	62/3, 70/4, 75/3, 80/2
		Dumbbell bench press/dumbbell incline bench press	6, 5, 4, 4

In-season			
Overall week	**Workout**	**Exercise**	**Scheme***
5	1	Back squat	50/3, 55/3, 60/3, 65/3
		Snatch pull	4 × 3
		Bench press	57/3, 65/5, 70/5, 75/5
		Clean high pull	4 × 3
		Dumbbell bench press/dumbbell incline bench press	8, 5, 5, 5
6	1	Back squat	52/3, 60/3, 65/2, 70/2
		Snatch pull	3, 3, 2, 2
		Bench press	60/3, 67/4, 72/4, 77/4
		Clean high pull	3, 3, 2, 2
		Dumbbell bench press/dumbbell incline bench press	8, 5, 4, 4
7	1	Back squat	57/3, 65/2, 70/2, 75/1
		Snatch pull	4 × 2
		Bench press	62/3, 70/3, 75/3, 80/3
		Clean high pull	4 × 2
		Dumbbell bench press/dumbbell incline bench press	8, 5, 4, 3
8	Unload/ variation	Chain back squat	135 × 8, 135CH × 3, 45CH/3 × 3
		Chain bench press	135 × 8, 135CH × 3, 50CH/3 × 4
9	2	Back squat	57/3, 65/3, 70/3, 75/3
		Single-leg squat	57/3, 65/3, 70/3, 75/3 (each leg)
		One-arm dumbbell snatch	4 × 3 (each arm)
		Incline bench press	57/3, 65/5, 70/5, 75/5
		Clean pull	4 × 3
		Dumbbell bench press/dumbbell incline bench press	8, 5, 5, 5

In-season			
Overall week	**Workout**	**Exercise**	**Scheme***
10	2	Back squat	62/3, 70/3, 75/2, 80/2
		Single-leg squat	62/3, 70/3, 75/2, 80/2 (each leg)
		One-arm dumbbell snatch	3, 3, 2, 2 (each arm)
		Incline bench press	60/3, 67/4, 72/4, 77/4
		Clean pull	3, 3, 2, 2
		Dumbbell bench press/dumbbell incline bench press	8, 5, 4, 4
11	2	Back squat	67/3, 75/3, 80/2, 85/1
		Single-leg squat	67/3, 75/3, 80/2, 85/1 (each leg)
		One-arm dumbbell snatch	4 × 2 (each arm)
		Incline bench press	62/3, 70/3, 75/3, 80/3
		Clean pull	4 × 2
		Dumbbell bench press/dumbbell incline bench press	8, 5, 4, 3
12	Unload/ variation	Chain back squat	135 × 8, 135CH × 3, 45CH/3 × 3
		Chain bench press	135 × 8, 135CH × 3, 50CH/3 × 4
13	1	Back squat	57/3, 65/3, 70/3, 75/3
		Snatch pull	4 × 3
		Bench press	60/3, 67/4, 72/4, 77/4
		Clean high pull	4 × 3
		Dumbbell bench press/dumbbell incline bench press	8, 5, 5, 5
14	1	Back squat	62/3, 70/3, 75/2, 80/2
		Snatch pull	3, 3, 2, 2
		Bench press	62/3, 70/3, 75/3, 80/3
		Clean high pull	3, 3, 2, 2
		Dumbbell bench press/dumbbell incline bench press	8, 5, 4, 4
15	1	Back squat	67/3, 75/3, 80/2, 85/1
		Snatch pull	4 × 2
		Bench press	65/3, 72/4, 77/3, 82/2
		Clean high pull	4 × 2
		Clean high pull	8, 5, 4, 3
16	Unload/ variation	Chain back squat	135 × 8, 135CH × 3, 45CH/3 × 3
		Chain bench press	135 × 8, 135CH × 3, 50CH/3 × 4
17	2	Back squat	57/3, 65/3, 70/3, 75/3
		Single-leg squat	57/3, 65/3, 70/3, 75/3 (each leg)
		One-arm dumbbell snatch	4 × 3 (each arm)
		Incline bench press	60/3, 67/4, 72/4, 77/4
		Clean pull	4 × 3
		Dumbbell bench press/dumbbell incline bench press	8, 5, 5, 5

(continued)

Table 11.18 Training Camp and In-Season Cycle *(continued)*

		In-season	
Overall week	**Workout**	**Exercise**	**Scheme***
18	2	Back squat	62/3, 70/3, 75/2, 80/2
		Single-leg squat	62/3, 70/3, 75/2, 80/2 (each leg)
		One-arm dumbbell snatch	3, 3, 2, 2 (each arm)
		Incline bench press	62/3, 70/3, 75/3, 80/3
		Clean pull	3, 3, 2, 2
		Dumbbell bench press/dumbbell incline bench press	8, 5, 4, 4
19	2	Back squat	67/3, 75/3, 80/2, 85/1
		Single-leg squat	67/3, 75/3, 80/2, 85/1 (each leg)
		One-arm dumbbell snatch	4 × 2 (each arm)
		Incline bench press	65/3, 72/4, 77/3, 82/2
		Clean pull	4 × 2
		Dumbbell bench press/dumbbell incline bench press	8, 5, 4, 3

*The cycles shown have the specific percentages of the 1RM and the repetitions to be performed for each of the cycled exercises. The percentage is in the numerator of the fraction, while the number of repetitions is in the denominator. If a percentage is not listed, the athlete should select a weight of the prescribed intensity that can be performed with good technique (the number of sets is listed first and the number of repetitions is listed second; e.g., 3 × 8 means 3 sets of 8 repetitions). If multiple sets are performed of the same percentage and repetitions, the number of sets will be preceded by ×. For example, 80/5 × 3 means 80% of the 1RM for 3 sets of 5 repetitions. For the chain back squat and chain bench press, 135 × 8 refers to 135 pounds (61 kg) × 8 repetitions and 135CH × 3 is 135 pounds (61 kg) plus the chains × 3 repetitions (those are warm-up sets). For chain back squat and chain bench press training sets, the %1RM comes before "CH" and the chains are added to that load. For example, 50CH/3 × 4 means 50% of the 1RM plus the chains × 3 repetitions for 4 sets.

12

POSTSEASON PROGRAMMING

DARREN KREIN, JERRY PALMIERI, AND ZAC WOODFIN

The design of the postseason program for football athletes will include a discussion of the program's goals, objectives, and variations of training time for the three primary levels of athletes: High school, college, and professional. While it is true that different football positions have unique resistance training needs, those needs become more specific to the individual athlete the further he gets away from the season and into the off-season program. During this phase, after the end of a rigorous season, there is no need to be specific with the positional workouts. All positions can work through the **general preparatory phase** (GPP) and the strength phase of postseason training. There is little specificity in this phase; only the quarterback position needs some adjustments (which are not needed in the GPP, only in the strength phase).

GOALS AND OBJECTIVES

The goals of the postseason program include the following:

- Allow the body to rest, recover, and be restored to a good level of health.
- Maintain control of body weight and body fat percentage.
- Maintain an average level of strength, cardiovascular conditioning, and flexibility.
- Maintain abdominal and lower back strength.
- Prepare the body for the beginning of the off-season workout program.

As athletes conclude the in-season training program, practice, and weekly games, shifting gears toward general physical preparation and movement quality becomes the top priority. It is common for athletes to enter this phase of training having suffered a drop in strength levels (seemingly coordinated to the number of games played and the length of the season) and general deconditioning and fatigue from overuse on the field. Injury-related weakness is also common. Thus, the challenge during the postseason training program is to accommodate the needs of individual athletes and still train as a team. Ideally, these individual needs should be specific and simple, and athletes should be encouraged to take some ownership of their postseason programs. They can be advised to set aside time for personal reflection or self-assessment in order to identify the areas that they can improve upon for next year. Coaches, strength and conditioning professionals, and other support staff can help athletes by providing insights based on their data on recent and past injuries, body weight or body composition, flexibility, and strength and power performance.

Lastly, it is important that athletes understand the importance of body composition in the postseason. Many athletes relax at the end of a long season. It is vital that they continue with healthy eating habits. The biggest stresses on the body can come from a decrease in lean body mass and an increase in body fat percentage during this transition period. Athletes should remain within a small percentage of their in-season body weight, lean body mass, and fat mass. This will make for more productive postseason training as well less overall stress on the body.

Football is a strength- and power-based sport. The beginning of the postseason program presents an opportunity to focus on returning to good physical health and using good body mechanics. This includes challenging athletes to proficiently control their body weight through basic exercises. Body weight movements (e.g., push-ups, pull-ups, planks, jumping jacks, jump rope, squats, lunges, and step-ups) focused on the full range of motion of the concentric and eccentric phases of an exercise will help increase overall flexibility and anatomical core strength (2). Placing the focus on body weight exercises and gradually building into loaded resistance training exercises will enable athletes to respond better to the heavier resistance training to follow and to be at their best when the off-season program begins.

LENGTH OF THE PROGRAM

The length of the postseason will vary depending on many factors, including level of play, when the season ends, how much time is given for holidays, and when the athletes must report back to work or school. High school and college settings can be similar and yet very different. Most high school programs finish their season in early to mid-November, but if they make it to the playoffs their season may end in late November or early December. Likewise, a college football season may end in mid-November, but if they participate in a bowl game or playoff system, their season may extend to mid-January. NFL teams not involved in the playoffs conclude their season the last week of December or the first week in January. High schools and colleges may have six to eight weeks before beginning their off-season programs, but professional teams may only have 3-1/2 months before the start of voluntary training at the facility. In this chapter we will suggest sample programs for all three levels.

The sample postseason programs displayed in this chapter are based on an eight-week period. Regardless of the length of the postseason period, the program will typically be made up of two phases: A GPP and a strength phase. Table 12.1 shows how the sample program can be altered based on the time allotted at the high school, college, and professional levels.

Table 12.1   Program Time Allotment Based on Level of Play

Level of play	Rest	GPP	Strength	Rest	Total weeks
High school	1 week	3 weeks	3 weeks	1 week	8 weeks
College	1 week	3 weeks	3 weeks	1 week	8 weeks
Professional	2 weeks	3 weeks	4 weeks	1 week	10 weeks

STRUCTURE OF THE PROGRAM

The postseason program begins with the GPP: A three-days-per-week total body routine with an emphasis on movement quality and rest in between sets to build up general physical preparedness. Monday, Wednesday, and Friday is the preferred format. However, a Monday, Wednesday, and Thursday routine will also work to allow for activity conflicts or long weekends.

The second phase of the postseason training is the strength phase, which includes a split routine similar to the training program recommended for the off-season. This routine involves training the upper body on Monday and Thursday and the lower body on Tuesday and Friday. Wednesday is an off day. The program will continue to increase in volume and intensity each week. Cardiovascular conditioning should also be progressively increased, but it is not the most important aspect during this phase.

RECOMMENDED EXERCISES

The postseason resistance training program includes an explosive type of movement that involves triple extension of the ankles, knees, and hips. This power exercise is followed by an upper body pressing and pulling movement and some assistance exercises on the upper body days. On the lower body training days, the explosive movement is followed by a triple extension lower body exercise and assistance exercises.

Total Body Exercises

During this phase, the total body exercises are centered on developing a baseline fitness level and gradually building the body up to handle heavier loads. Football requires a combination of strength and power, but it is important to build up the athletes gradually, especially at the end of the season and the beginning of a new training phase. The total body exercises used during the first half of this phase will be exercises that stress all areas, including the upper body, lower body, core, and to some extent, the cardiovascular system. After the GPP, training will switch to more conventional exercises in the strength phase of the postseason program. These exercises are very similar to the start of an off-season program (i.e., exercises that are explosive, relate to movements on the field, and require triple extension).

The following are GPP total body exercises:

- Jumping jacks, jump rope, and quick feet are all exercises geared toward getting the body moving and back into shape. These exercises improve overall fitness and cardiovascular levels rather than developing specific muscles.
- Inchworms and in-place inchworms both work on overall fitness while incorporating flexibility and stressing the muscles of the core.

The following are strength phase total body exercises:

- Hang clean high pulls and barbell snatch pulls are explosive exercises requiring triple extension that stress the muscles of the hips, the quadriceps, and the gluteal muscles while also working in conjunction with the upper body. These exercises also force the central nervous system to activate and work in a similar fashion to what takes place on the field. Both exercises provide a segue to exercises that will be used in the off-season training phase.
- Box jumps, dumbbell quarter-squat jumps, front-facing medicine ball hip toss, and medicine ball slams are all exercises that relate to football. These exercises force a hip hinge while activating the upper and lower body systems together and placing stress on the central nervous system.

Lower Body Exercises

Lower body strength is crucial to success on the field. Lower body exercises also help athletes to maintain and increase lean body mass levels.

- Back squat and front squat are often considered the best exercises for developing the lower body. These movements are similar to those on the football field, and they require a significant response from the body, especially as volume and intensity increase. Both exercises stress the hips, quadriceps, low back, core, and glutes. However, the front squat has been shown to recruit the vastus medialis (3), rectus abdominis, and erector spinae more than the back squat (1).

- The step-up, walking lunge, reverse lunge, split squat, and single-leg squat are all designated movements to help athletes to improve single-leg strength and also to develop symmetry, coordination, and balance. Often football athletes will find themselves forced into situations where it is vital to have good single-leg strength. These include motions that require driving off the floor on one leg, cutting, jumping, or landing on one leg.

- Lateral squat, lateral lunge on slideboard, 90-90 lateral lunge, slideboard abduction and adduction, lateral lunge, cable adduction, and isometric groin hold or squeeze develop the groin. Groin strength is critical due to the amount of multiple-direction work that occurs in football, and it also may aid in injury prevention.

- Stability ball leg curls and slideboard leg curls develop the hamstrings. In addition, other exercises (squats, step-ups, and lunges) use the hamstring muscles as co-contractors. It is important to have a good balance of strength and symmetry between the hamstrings and quadriceps because this aids in the prevention of lower body injuries.

- Reverse back extension strengthens the muscles of the lower back. There is a strong crossover to the hip joint during this exercise, thereby strengthening it as well.

- Heel and toe walks provide mobility, coordination, and stabilization while strengthening the muscles surrounding the ankles. Often this area is overlooked in training due to time constraints and the focus on larger muscle groups. Training these muscles may help prevent or limit the severity of an ankle injury.

Upper Body Exercises

Football is a violent, collision-based sport that requires tackling, blocking, ripping, and swimming moves that place strong demands on upper body strength.

- Bench press, incline bench press, and all dumbbell bench press exercises are very similar to the pushing aspects of football. These exercises mainly develop the chest, shoulders, and triceps, which are all areas that help with the impact of collisions in football.

- Overhead pressing is a natural movement with application to most positions in football. These exercises are important for maintaining a properly functioning shoulder joint. They also aid in the development of mass and strength in the shoulder region while providing an extra layer of protection from the impacts of football.

- Pull-ups and all pulling and rowing movements both in vertical and horizontal planes mimic the pulling techniques required on the football field. These exercises play an important part in posture and proper placement of the shoulder joint. The pectoral muscles are usually easier to develop and more popular with athletes, often creating a significant imbalance. Emphasis should be placed on the vertical and horizontal pull exercises to prevent imbalance and symmetry issues and to aid in injury prevention.

- Neck exercises are an important part of any sport that involves contact with the head. Most Olympic lifts will build the trap and neck muscles that protect the neck and head. A properly trained body area from the shoulders up can help to reduce injuries such as concussions.

Core Exercises

In the GPP, exercises for the core are included within the circuits. When the GPP switches to the strength phase, the traditional and medicine ball exercises for the core are performed on Mondays and Thursdays; isometric core exercises are performed on Tuesdays, Thursdays, and Fridays; and functional exercises are performed on Tuesdays and Fridays—all at the tail end of each workout.

POSITIONAL ADJUSTMENTS

When designing a postseason program, a base program (table 12.2 on page 301) focused on body weight exercises should be established first to set a foundation for training. After approximately three weeks of the GPP, the program will shift to a strength phase (table 12.3 on page 302), which will lead up to the start of the off-season program. Most postseason training does not require specific position training adjustments. The exception may be the quarterback position, which may need some adjustments regarding pressing exercises.

VOLUME AND INTENSITY

The postseason training phase marks the beginning of a new year of football training. A foundational base needs to be set during this time to further develop the athlete's general physical preparedness. It is also an opportunity to begin to build a foundation in preparation for the off-season training phase. Since athletes will be coming off a long season and should have had at least a week of downtime, it is important for them to set their minds toward slowly getting themselves healthy, fit, and back into football shape.

The GPP circuits are designed for body weight training using a higher volume. The goal is to keep the athletes moving from one exercise to the next. For each exercise, athletes should try to go through a full range of motion while focusing on using good technique. Athletes do not need to run from one exercise to the next, but they should keep moving at a good pace. During the three weeks of the GPP, the athletes should slowly begin to get into better shape, which will be noticeable at the end of each week. The goal for athletes is to use good technique and movement patterns and to eventually increase the number of sets for each circuit. It may be useful for some athletes to add a weighted vest, starting out with a light load (6-10 lb [3-5 kg]) and increasing over time.

Each circuit during week 1 should be completed at least twice through with no rest at the end of each circuit set. After week 1, if an athlete is able, the volume can be increased by doing the circuit three to four times. It is more important for athletes to focus on technique and movement quality than it is for them to focus on getting through the circuit as quickly as possible or as many times as possible.

After the three weeks of general preparation training, athletes will shift to a strength phase. The volume will remain high but lower than what they experienced during the GPP. Adding traditional resistance exercise and an increase in intensity will significantly affect the athletes. The volume will decrease in weeks 2 and 3 of the strength phase, and the intensity should increase as the athletes near the start of the official off-season training phase. The strength phase should be a transitional point in training where technique and movement quality should continue to receive great emphasis.

ORDER OF EXERCISES

The order of exercises during the GPP is irrelevant, other than mixing up the order to make sure all the upper or lower body exercises are not one after the other. When switching to the strength phase, it is recommended that the training session exercises be ordered in the following way:

1. Olympic lifts (completed first in a workout),
2. non-power-core exercises,
3. assistance exercises, and
4. anatomical core exercises (to finish the workout).

Similar to the other three seasons' sample training program, there are some paired push-pull exercises (or a group of exercises focused on an isolated area) in the strength phase. Between-exercise rest is still needed, however; those pairings or groups are not intended to be performed as an unbroken circuit.

CONCLUSION

Postseason training can be viewed from many different perspectives. A strength and conditioning professional needs to factor in the level of the athletes' play, what exercises work best for the team, the length of the season and number of games played, the actual age and training age of the athletes and, most importantly, what is in the athletes' best interest. The guidelines presented in this chapter are just that—guidelines. Mix and match what works best.

Warm-Up

WARM-UP 1

Foam roll and dynamic warm-up

WARM-UP 2

Foam roll, activation, and movement-based warm-up
Mini-band wall clock, 2 × 5 each side

- *Right arm.* 1, 3, 5 o'clock
- *Left arm.* 11, 9, 7 o'clock

Straight-arm plank shoulder tap, 2 × 10 each arm

WARM-UP 3

Foam roll, activation, and movement-based warm-up
Mini-band walk

- *Lateral (5 yd).* 2 × 3 down and back
- *Forward and backward (10 yd).* 2 × 2 down and back

Table 12.2 General Preparatory Phase

Monday

	Exercise	Sets × reps		Exercise	Sets × reps
	Warm-up 1				
1	Squat	15	7	Inverted row	12-15
2	Push-up	12	8	Lateral lunge on slideboard	8 each leg
3	Alternating leg lower	30-50 sec	9	Bench dip	12-20
4	Front plank	40-65 sec	10	Barbell rollout	15
5	Reverse lunge and reach	8 each leg	11	Jumping jack	25
6	Dead hang	30-60 sec	12	Straight-arm shoulder tap	10 each arm

Perform the circuit 2-4 times continuously with no rest between sets.

Wednesday

	Exercise	Sets × reps		Exercise	Sets × reps
	Warm-up 1				
1	Uneven push-up	8 each side	7	In-place inchworm	8
2	Walking lunge	8 each leg	8	Lateral lunge	8 each leg
3	Abdominal crunch	15	9	Stability ball triple threat	40-70 sec
4	Single-leg squat	8 each leg	10	Medicine ball or stability ball groin squeeze	15
5	Pull-up	6-15	11	Jump rope	70
6	Prone snow angel	25	12	Half roll (same side elbow to knee)	5 each side

Perform the circuit 2-4 times continuously with no rest between sets.

Friday

	Exercise	Sets × reps		Exercise	Sets × reps
	Warm-up 1				
1	Side plank	10 sec each side, twice per side	7	Lateral squat	10 each leg
2	Quick feet (use 3-6 in. [7-15 cm] box)	10 right foot first, 10 left foot first	8	Reverse hyperextension	15
3	Dip	8-15	9	Suspension Y and T	10 each exercise
4	Single-leg squat	8 each leg	10	Slideboard abduction and adduction	12
5	Crossover crunch	25 each side	11	Step-up	10 each leg
6	Inchworm (moving)	8	12	Suspension inverted row	12-15

Perform the circuit 2-4 times continuously with no rest between sets.

Table 12.3 Strength Phase

Monday (Upper Body)

	Exercise	Sets × reps		Exercise	Sets × reps
	Warm-up 2				
1	Box jump	Week 1: 3 × 8 Week 2: 2 × 6 Week 3: 2 × 5	4a	Stability ball push-up	3 × 12-15
2a	Dumbbell bench press	Week 1: 3 × 10 Week 2: 2 × 8 Week 3: 2 × 6	4b	Suspension L	3 × 12
2b	Pull-up	3 × 10-15	5a	Abdominals (medicine ball)	Exercise dependent
3a	Standing barbell shoulder press (QBs use dumbbells)	3 × 8-10	5b	Suspension W	3 × 12
3b	Straight-arm plank dumbbell row	3 × 10	6	4-way neck	1 × 8 each way

Tuesday (Lower Body)

	Exercise	Sets × reps		Exercise	Sets × reps
	Warm-up 3				
1a	Dumbbell quarter-squat jump	2 × 6, 2 × 8	3b	Reverse back extension	Week 1: 3 × 12 Week 2: 3 × 15 Week 3: 3 × 20
1b	Front-facing medicine ball toss	3 × 8 each side	4a	Stability ball leg curl	Week 1: 2 × 10 + 8 Week 2: 2 × 15 + 10 Week 3: 2 × 15 + 12
2a	Front or back squat	Week 1: 3 × 8 Week 2: 2 × 6 Week 3: 2 × 5	4b	Abdominals (functional)	Exercise dependent
2b	Medicine ball or stability ball groin squeeze	Week 1: 3 × 15 sec Week 2: 3 × 20 sec Week 3: 3 × 25 sec	4c	Toe and heel walk	3 × 20 yards each foot
3a	Lateral squat	3 × 8 each side	5	Band flexibility: leg up, leg out, leg over, quad, hip flexor	1 × 10 sec each side

Thursday (Upper Body)

	Exercise	Sets × reps		Exercise	Sets × reps
	Warm-up 2				
1	Snatch pull	Week 1: 3 × 6 Week 2: 2 × 5 Week 3: 2 × 4	4a	Standing dumbbell or kettlebell windmill	3 × 8 each side
2a	Incline bench press (QBs use dumbbells)	Week 1: 3 × 10 Week 2: 2 × 8 Week 3: 2 × 6	4b	Prone incline 20-degree bench shoulder combo: L, T, W, Y	2 × 15 each exercise
2b	Inverted row (barbell or suspension)	4 × 10-15	5a	Lying dumbbell triceps extension	3 × 12
3a	Alternating dumbbell bench press	3 × 10-12	5b	Abdominals (isometric)	Exercise dependent
3b	20-degree prone dumbbell row	3 × 10	6	4-way neck	1 × 8 each way

Friday (Lower Body)

	Exercise	Sets × reps		Exercise	Sets × reps
	Warm-up 3				
1a	Hang clean high pull	Week 1: 3 × 5 Week 2: 3 × 5 Week 3: 2 × 5	3b	Cable pull-through	3 × 15
1b	Medicine ball slam	3 × 10	4a	Dolly leg curl	2 × 15 sec + 8 reps
2a	Single-leg squat	Week 1: 3 × 8 Week 2: 2 × 6 Week 3: 2 × 5	4c	Abdominals (functional)	Exercise dependent
2b	Band or cable adduction and hip flexion	3 × 10 each leg	5	Band flexibility: leg up, leg out, leg over, quad, hip flexor	1 × 10 sec each side
3a	Step-up	3 × 8, 7, 6 each leg			

Chapter 1

1. Anderson, LL, and Aagaard, P. Influence of maximal muscle strength and intrinsic muscle contractile properties on contractile rate of force development. *Eur J Appl Physiol* 96(4):46-52, 2006.

2. Baker, D. A series of studies on the training of high-intensity muscle power in rugby league football players. *J Strength Cond Res* 15(2):198-209, 2001.

3. Blazevich, AJ, and Jenkins, DG. Effect of the movement of resistance training exercises on sprint and strength performance in concurrently training elite junior sprinters. *J Sports Sci* 20:981-990, 2002.

4. Brown, SR, Feldman, ER, Cross, MR, Helms, ER, Marrier, B, Samozino, P, and Morin, JB. The potential for a target strength-training program to decrease asymmetry and increase performance: A proof of concept in sprinting. *Intl J Sports Physiol and Perf* 12(10):1392-1395, 2017.

5. Bilsborough, JC, Kempton, T, Greenway, K, Cordy, J, and Coutts, AJ. Longitudinal changes and seasonal variation in body composition in professional Australian football players. *Inter J Sports Physiol and Perf* 12:10-17, 2017.

6. Caterisano, A, Hutchison, R, Parker, C, James, S, and Opskar, S. Improved functional power over a 5-week period: Comparison of combined weight-training to flexible barbell training. *J Strength Cond Res* 32(8):2109-2115, 2018.

7. Chelly, MS, Hermassi, S, Aouadi, R, and Shepard, RJ. Effects of 8-week in-season plyometric training on upper and lower limb performance of elite adolescent handball players. *J Strength Cond Res* 28(5):1401-1410, 2014.

8. Collins, CL, Fletcher, EN, Fields, SK, Kluchurosky, L, Rohrkemper, MK, Comstock, and Cantu, R. Neck strength: A protective factor reducing risk for concussion in high school sports. *J Primary Prevent* 35:309-319, 2014.

9. Colquhoun, RJ, Tomko, PM, Magrini, MA, Muddle, TWD, and Jenkins, NDM. The influence of input excitation on the inter- and intra-day reliability of the motor unit firing rate versus recruitment threshold relationship. *J Neurophysiol* 120:3131-3139, 2018.

10. de Hoyo, M, Pozzo, M, Sanudo, B, Carrasco, L, Gonzalo-Skok, O, Dominguez-Cobo, S, and Moran-Camacho, E. Effects of a 10-week in-season eccentric-overload training program on muscle-injury prevention and performance in junior elite soccer players. *Intl J Sports Physiol and Perf* 10(1):46-52, 2015.

11. Del Vecchio, A, Negro, F, Falla, D, Bazzucchi, I, Farina, D and Felici, F. Higher muscle fiber conduction velocity and early rate of torque development in chronically strength trained individuals. *J Appl Physiol* 125(4):1218-1226, 2018.

12. Gentry, M, and Caterisano, A. *The Ultimate Guide to Physical Training for Football.* New York: Sports Publishing, 6-18, 2013.

13. Goolsby, MA, and Boniquit, N. Bone health in athletes: The role of exercise, nutrition, and hormones. *Sports Health* 9(2):108-117, 2017.

14. Goode, AP, Reiman, MP, Harris, L, DeLisa, L, Kauffman, A, Beltramo, D, Poole, C, Ledbetter, L, and Taylor, AB. Eccentric training for prevention of hamstring injuries may depend on intervention and compliance: A systematic review and meta-analysis. *Brit J Sports Med* 49(6):349-356, 2015.

15. Haff, GG, and Nimphius, S. Training principles for power. *Strength Cond J* 34(1):2-12, 2012.

16. Haff, GG, and Triplett, NT. *Essentials of Strength Training and Conditioning.* 4th ed. Champaign, IL: Human Kinetics, 25, 261, 522-523, 2016.

17. Hislop, MD, Stokes, KA, Williams, S, McKay, CD, England, ME, Kemp, SPT, and Trewartha, G. Reducing musculoskeletal injury and concussion risk in schoolboy rugby players with pre-activity movement control exercise program: A cluster randomized controlled trial. *Brit J Sports Med* 51(15):1473-1480, 2017.

18. Hodgson, M, Docherty, D, and Robbins, D. Post-activation potentiation: Underlying physiology and implications for motor performance. *Sports Med* 35(7):585-595, 2005.

19. Hutchison, R, and Caterisano, A. Electromyographic and kinetic comparison of a flexible and steel barbell. *J of Human Sport and Exer* 12:380-385, 2017.

20. Jakobsen, JR, Jakobsen, NR, Mackey, AL, Knudsen, AB, Koch, M, Kjaer, M, and Krogsgaard, MR. Composition and adaptation of human myotendinous junction and neighboring muscle fibers to heavy resistance training. *Scand J Med Sci Sports* 27(12):1547-1559, 2016.

21. Jakobsen, JR, Mackey, AL, Koch, M, Kjaer, M, and Krogsgaard, MR. Remodeling of muscle fibers approaching the human myotendinous junction. *Scand J Med Sci Sports* 28(6):1-13, 2018.

22. Kelly, JS, and Metcalfe, J. Validity and reliability of body composition analysis using the Tanita BC418-MA. *J Exer Physiol* 15(6):74-83, 2012.

23. Knuttgen, HG, and Kraemer, WJ. Terminology and measurement in exercise performance. *J Appl Sport Sci Res* 1:1-10, 1987.

24. Mehl, J, Diermieir, T, Herbst, E, Imhoff, AB, Stoffels, T, Zantop, T, Petersen, W, and Achtnich, A. Evidence-based concepts for prevention of knee and ACL injuries. 2017 guidelines of the ligament committee of the German Knee Society (DKG). *Arthro Sports Med* 138:51-61, 2018.

25. McBride, JM. Nature of power. In *NSCA Sport Performance Series: Developing Power.* McGuigan, M, ed. Champaign, IL: Human Kinetics, 2017.

26. McBride, JM, Blow, D, Kirby, TJ, Haines, TL, Dayne, AM, and Triplett, NT. Relationship between maximal squat strength and five, ten, and forty-yard sprint times. *J Strength Cond Res* 23(6):1633-1636, 2009.

27. Muller, W, Furhapter-Rieger, A, Kainz, P, Kropfl, JM, Maughan, RJ, and Ahammer, H. Body composition in sport: A comparison of a novel ultrasound imaging technique to measure subcutaneous fat tissue compared with skinfold measurement. *Brit J Sports Med* 47(16):1028-1035, 2013.

28. Owen, A, Dunlop, G, Chtara, M, Zouhal, H, and Wong P. The relationship between lower-limb strength and match-related muscle damage in elite level professional European soccer players. *J Sports Sci* 33(20):2100-2105, 2015.

29. Ramos, VR, Requena, B, Suarez-Arrones, L, Newton, RU, and Saez de Villareal, E. Effects of an 18-week in-season heavy-resistance and power training on throwing velocity, strength, jumping and maximal sprint swim performance of elite male water polo players. *J Strength Cond Res* 28(4):1007-1014, 2014.

30. Ratamess, NA, Hoffman, JR, Faigenbaum, AD, Mangine, GT, Falvo, MJ, and Kang, J. The combined effect of protein intake and resistance training on serum osteocalcin concentrations in strength and power athletes. *J Strength Cond Res* 21(4):1197-1207, 2007.

31. Rector, RS, Rogers, R, Ruebel, M, Widzer, MO, and Hinton, PS. Lean body mass and weight-bearing activity in the prediction of bone mineral density in physically active men. *J Strength Cond Res* 23(2):427-435, 2009.

32. Rodriguez-Rosell, D, Franco-Marquez, F, Pareja-Blanco, F, Mora-Custodio, R, Yanez-Garcia, JM, Gonzalez-Suarez, JM, and Gonzalez-Badillo, JJ. Effects of 6 weeks resistance training combined with plyometric and speed exercises on physical performance of pre-peak-height-velocity soccer players. *Intl J Sports Physiol* 11:240-246, 2016.

33. Sale, D. Post-activation potentiation: Role in human performance. *Exer Sport Sci Rev* 30:138-143, 2002.

34. Seitz, LB, and Haff, GG. Factors modulating post-activation potentiation of jump, sprint, throw, and upper-body ballistic performances: A systemic review with meta-analysis. *Sports Med* 46:231-240, 2016.

35. Serpell, BG, and Young, WB. Are the perceptual and decision making components of agility trainable? A preliminary investigation. *J Strength Cond Res* 25(5):1240-1248, 2011.

36. Soomro, N, Sanders, R, Hackett, D, Hubka, T, Ebrahimi, S, Freeston, J, and Cobley, S. The efficacy of injury prevention programs in adolescent team sports. *Am J Sports Med* 44(9):2415-2424, 2015.

37. Speirs, DE, Bennett, MA, Finn, CV, and Turner, AP. Unilateral and bilateral squat training for strength, sprints, and agility in academy rugby players. *J Strength Cond Res* 30(2):386-392, 2016.

38. Stodden, DF, and Galitsky, M. Longitudinal effects of a collegiate strength and conditioning program in American football. *J Strength Cond Res* 24(9):2300-2308, 2010.

39. Stone, MH, Collins, D, Plisk, S, Haff, GG, and Stone, ME. Training principles: Evaluation of modes and methods of training. *NSCA Journal* 22(3):65-76, 2000.

40. Suchomel, T, Nimphius, S, and Stone, MH. The importance of muscular strength in athletic performance. *Sports Med* 46(10):1419-1431, 2016.

41. Sugiura, Y, Sakuma, K, Sakuraba, K, and Sato, Y. Prevention of hamstring injuries in collegiate sprinters. *Ortho J Sports Med* 5(1):1-6, 2017.

42. Thomas, K, French, D, and Hayes, PR. The effect of two plyometric training techniques on muscular power and agility in youth soccer players. *J Strength Cond Res* 23(1):332-335, 2009.

43. Tucker, LA, Lecheminant, JD, and Bailey, BW. Test-retest reliability of the Bod Pod: The effect of multiple assessments. *Percep Motor Skills* 118(2):563-570, 2014.

44. Van der Horst, N, Smits, DW, Petersen, J, Goedhart, EA, and Backx, FJ. The preventative effect of the Nordic hamstring exercise on hamstring injuries in amateur soccer players: Study protocol for a randomized controlled trial. *J Int Soc Child Adol Inj Prevent* 20(4):e8, 2013.

45. Zatsiorsky, VM, and Kraemer, WJ. *Science and Practice of Strength Training.* 2nd ed. Champaign, IL: Human Kinetics, 26-27, 61-65, 2006.

Chapter 2

1. Aagaard, P, Simonsen, EB, Andersen, JL, Magnusson, P, and Dyhre-Poulsen, P. Increased rate of force development and neural drive of human skeletal muscle following resistance training. *J Appl Physiol* 93(4):1318-1326, 2002.

2. Anderson, T, and Kearney, JT. Effects of three resistance training programs on muscular strength and absolute and relative endurance. *Res Q Exerc Sport*, 53(1):1-7, 1982.

3. Angelino, D, McCabe, TJ, and Earp, JE. Comparing acceleration and change of direction ability between backpedal and cross-over run techniques for use in American football. *J Strength Cond Res*, 2018. https://doi.org/10.1519/JSC.0000000000002626.

4. Arthur, RC, Liotta, FJ, Klootwyk, TE, Porter, DA, and Mieling, P. Potential risk of rerupture in primary Achilles tendon repair in athletes younger than 30 years of age. *Am J Sports Med* 33:119-123, 2005.

5. Baker, D. Comparison of upper-body strength and power between professional and college-aged rugby league players. *J Strength Cond Res* 15(1):30-35, 2001.

6. Bernstein, N. *The Coordination and Regulation of Movements.* Oxford, England: Pergamon Press, 1967.

7. Cormie, P, McGuigan, MR, and Newton, RU. Developing maximal neuromuscular power. *Sports Med* 41(2):125-146, 2011.

8. DeWeese, B, and Nimphius, S. Speed and agility program design and technique. In *Essentials of Strength Training and Conditioning.* Triplett, NT, and Haff, GG, eds. Champaign, IL: Human Kinetics, 521-557, 2016.

9. Flynn, TW, and Soutas-Little, RW. Mechanical power and muscle action during forward and backward running. *J Orthop Sports Phys Ther* 17:108-112, 1993.

10. Haff, GG, and Nimphius, S. Training principles for power. *Strength Cond J* 34:2-12, 2012.

11. Hoff, J, Støren, Ø, Finstad, A, Wang, E, and Helgerud, J. Increased blood lactate level deteriorates running economy in world class endurance athletes. *J Strength Cond Res* 30(5):1373-1378, 2016.

12. Howe, LP, Read, P, and Waldron, M. Muscle hypertrophy. *Strength Cond J* 39(5):72-81, 2017.

13. Järvinen, TA, Järvinen, TL, Kääriäinen, M, Aärimaa, V, Vaittinen, S, Kalimo, H, and Järvinen, M. Muscle injuries: Optimising recovery. *Best Pract Res Clin Rheumatol* 21:317-331, 2007.

14. Kraemer, WJ. A series of studies—the physiological basis for strength training in American football. *J Strength Cond Res* 11(3):131-142, 1997.

15. Komi, PV. Physiological and biomechanical correlates of muscle function: Effects of muscle structure and stretch-shortening cycle on force and speed. *Exerc Sport Sci Rev* 12:81-121, 1984.

16. Lacquaniti, F, Ivanenko, YP, and Zago, M. Patterned control of human locomotion. *J Physiol* 590:2189-2199, 2012.

17. Novacheck, TF. The biomechanics of running. *Gait Posture* 7:77-95, 1998.

18. Peterson, MD, Alvar, BA, and Rhea, MR. The contribution of maximal force production to explosive movement among young collegiate athletes. *J Strength Cond Res* 20:867-873, 2006.

19. Pincivero, DM, and Bompa, TO. A physiological review of American football. *Sports Med* 23(4):247-260, 1997.

20. Rhea, MR, Hunter, RL, and Hunter, TJ. Competition modeling of American football. *J Strength Cond Res* 20(1):58-61, 2006.

21. Sheppard, JM, and Young, WB. Agility literature review: classifications, training and testing. *J Sports Sci* 24(9):919-932, 2006.

22. Siff M. Biomechanical foundations of strength and power training. In *Biomechanics in Sport.* Zatsiorsky, V, ed. London: Blackwell Scientific Ltd, 103-139, 2001.

23. Sparrow, WA. Measuring changes in coordination and control. In *Approaches to the study of motor control and learning.* Summers, J.J., ed. North Holland: Elsevier Science Publishers, 147-162, 1992.

24. Stone, MH. Position statement: Explosive exercises and training. *J Strength Cond Res* 15(3):7-15, 1993.

25. Stone MH, Moir, G, Glaister, M, and Sanders, R. How much strength is necessary? *Phys Ther Sport* 3:88-96, 2002.

26. Suchomel, TJ, Nimphius, S, and Stone, MH. The importance of muscular strength in athletic performance. *Sports Med* 46(10):1419-1449, 2016.

27. Turvey, MT. Coordination. *Am Psychol* 45:938-953, 1990.

28. Ward, PA, Ramsden, S, Coutts, AJ, Hulton, AT, and Drust, B. Positional differences in running and non-running activities during elite American football training. *J Strength Cond Res* 32(7):2072-2084, 2018.

29. Wellman, AD, Coad, SC, Goulet, GC, and McLellan, CP. Quantification of competitive game demands of NCAA Division I college football players using global positioning systems. *J Strength Cond Res* 30(1):11-19, 2016.

30. Wellman, AD, Coad, SC, Goulet, GC, Coffey, VG, and McLellan, CP. Quantification of accelerometer derived impacts associated with competitive games in NCAA Division I college football players. *J Strength Cond Res* 31(2):330-338, 2016.

31. Weyand, PG, Sternlight, DB, Bellizzi, MJ, and Wright, S. Faster top running speeds are achieved with greater ground forces, not more rapid leg movements. *J Appl Physiol* 89(5):1991-1999, 2000.

32. Wickkiser, JD, and Kelly, JM. The body composition of a college football team. *Med Sci Sports Exerc* 7(3):199-202, 1975.

33. Young, WB, Dawson, B, and Henry, GJ. Agility and change-of-direction speed are independent skills: Implications for training for agility in invasion sports. *Int J Sports Sci Coach* 10(1):159-169, 2015.

34. Zamparo, P, Minetti AM, and Prampero, PD. Interplay among the changes of muscle strength, cross-sectional area and maximal explosive power: Theory and facts. *Eur J Appl Physiol* 88(3):193-202, 2002.

Chapter 3

1. Earle, RW. Weight training exercise prescription. In *Essentials of Personal Training Symposium Workbook.* Lincoln, NE: NSCA Certification Commission, 3-39, 2006.

2. Haff, GG, and Triplett, NT. Principles of test selection and administration; Administration, scoring, and interpretation of selected tests. In *Essentials of Strength Training and Conditioning.* 4th ed. Champaign, IL: Human Kinetics, 249-316, 2016.

3. Hopkins WG, Schabort EJ, and Hawley JA. Reliability of power in physical performance tests. *Sports Med* 31: 211-234, 2001.

4. Ivey, P, and Stoner, J. *Complete Conditioning for Football.* Champaign, IL: Human Kinetics, 15, 20, 69, 103-186, 2012.

5. McBride, MJ. Nature of power. In *Developing Power.* McGuigan, M, ed. Champaign, IL: Human Kinetics, 11-12, 2017.

6. McGuigan, M. Principles of test selection and administration. In *Essentials of Strength Training and Conditioning.* 4th ed. Haff, GG, and Triplett, NT, eds. Champaign, IL: Human Kinetics, 250-252, 2016.

7. Sheppard, MJ. Lower body power exercises. In *Developing Power.* McGuigan, M, ed. Champaign, IL: Human Kinetics, 113-114, 2017.

Chapter 4

1. Colquhoun, RJ, Gai, CM, Aguilar, D, Bove, D, Dolan, J, Vargas, A, Couvillion, K, Jenkins, ND, and Campbell, BI. Training volume, not frequency, indicative of maximal strength adaptations to resistance training. *J Strength Cond Res* 32:1207-1213, 2018.

2. DeLorme, TL. Restoration of muscle power by heavy-resistance exercises. *J Bone Joint Surg* 27:645, 1945.

3. Sale, D, and MacDougall, D. Specificity in strength training: A review for the coach and athlete. *Can J Appl Sport Sci* 6:87-91, 1981.

4. Sheppard, J, and Triplett, NT. Program design for resistance training. In *Essentials of Strength Training and Conditioning.* 4th ed. Haff, GG, and Triplett, NT, eds. Champaign, IL: Human Kinetics, 439-470, 2016.

Chapter 5

1. Carlock, JM, Smith, SL, Hartman, MJ, Morris, RT, Ciroslan, DA, Pierce, KC, Newton, RU, Harman, EA, Sands, WA, and Stone, MH. The relationship between vertical jump power estimates and weightlifting ability: A field test approach. *J Strength Cond Res* 18:534-539, 2004.

2. Channell, BT, and Barfield, JP. Effect of Olympic and traditional resistance training on vertical jump improvement in high school boys. *J Strength Cond Res* 22:1522-1527, 2008.

3. Chiu, L, and Schilling, BK. A primer on weightlifting: From sport to sports training. *Strength Cond J* 27:42-48, 2005.

4. Conroy, M, Dimas, P, Dreschler, A, Feher, T, and Gattone, M. *USA Weightlifting Sports Performance Coaching Manual.* Colorado Springs, CO: USA Weightlifting, 26-29, 64, 2017.

5. Gambetta, V, and Odgers, S. *The Complete Guide to Medicine Ball Training.* Sarasota, FL: Optimum Sports Training, 1991.

6. Hori, N, Newton, RU, Nosaka, K, and Stone, MH. Weightlifting exercises enhance athletic performance that requires high-load speed strength. *Strength Cond J* 27:50-55, 2005.

Chapter 6

1. Caulfield, S, and Berninger, D. Exercise techniques for free weight and machine training. In *Essentials of Strength Training and Conditioning*. 4th ed. Haff, GG, and Triplett, NT, eds. Champaign, IL: Human Kinetics, 351-408, 2016.

2. Haff, GG, Caulfield, S, and Berninger, D. Exercise techniques for alternative modes and nontraditional implement training. In *Essentials of Strength Training and Conditioning*. 4th ed. Haff, GG, and Triplett, NT, eds. Champaign, IL: Human Kinetics, 409-438, 2016.

3. McBride, J. Biomechanics of resistance exercise. In *Essentials of Strength Training and Conditioning*. 4th ed. Haff, GG, and Triplett, NT, eds. Champaign, IL: Human Kinetics, 19-42, 2016.

4. Glassbrook, DJ, Helms, ER, Brown, SR, and Storey, AG. A review of the biomechanical differences between the high-bar and low-bar back squat. *J Strength Cond Res* 31(9):2618-2634, 2017.

Chapter 7

1. Caulfield, S., and Berninger, D. Exercise techniques for free weight and machine training. In *Essentials of Strength Training and Conditioning*. 4th ed. Haff, GG, and Triplett, NT, eds. Champaign, IL: Human Kinetics, 351-408, 2016.

2. Delavier, F. *Strength Training Anatomy*. 3rd ed. Champaign, IL: Human Kinetics, 6-119, 2010.

3. Haff, GG, Caulfield, S, and Berninger, D. Exercise techniques for alternative modes and nontraditional implement training. In *Essentials of Strength Training and Conditioning*. 4th ed. Haff, GG, and Triplett, NT, eds. Champaign, IL: Human Kinetics, 413-416, 2016.

4. Potach, DH, and Chu, DC. Program design and technique for plyometric training. In *Essentials of Strength Training and Conditioning*. 4th ed. Haff, GG, and Triplett, NT, eds. Champaign, IL: Human Kinetics, 514, 517, 2016.

Chapter 8

1. Behm, DG, Drinkwater, EJ, Willardson, JM, and Cowley, PM. Canadian Society for Exercise Physiology position stand: The use of instability to train the core in athletic and nonathletic conditioning. *Appl Physiol Nutr Metab* 35:109-112, 2010.

2. Behm, DG, Drinkwater, EJ, Willardson, JM, and Cowley, PM. The use of instability to train the core musculature. *Appl Physiol Nutr Metab* 35:91-108, 2010.

3. Haff, GG, Caulfield, S, and Berninger, D. Exercise techniques for alternative modes and nontraditional implement training. In *Essentials of Strength Training and Conditioning*. 4th ed. Haff, GG, and Triplett, NT, eds. Champaign, IL: Human Kinetics, 409-438, 2016.

4. Hamlyn, N, Behm, DG, and Young, WB. Trunk muscle activation during dynamic weight-training exercises and isometric instability activities. *J Strength Cond Res* 21:1108-1112, 2007.

5. Nuzzo, JL, McCaulley, GO, Cormie, P, Cavill, MJ, and McBride, JM. Trunk muscle activity during stability ball and free weight exercises. *J Strength Cond Res* 22:95-102, 2008.

6. Willardson, JM. Core stability training: Applications to sports conditioning programs. *J Strength Cond Res* 21:979-985, 2007.

Chapter 12

1. Comfort, P, Pearson, S, and Mather, D. An electromyographical comparison of trunk muscle activity during isometric trunk and dynamic strengthening exercises. *J Strength Cond Res* 25(1):149-154, 2011.

2. Haff, GG, Berninger, D, and Caulfield, S. Exercise technique for alternative modes and nontraditional implement training. In *Essentials of Strength Training and Conditioning*. 4th ed. Haff, GG, and Triplett, NT, eds. Champaign, IL: Human Kinetics, 409-438, 2016.

3. Yavuz, U, Erdag, D, Amca, A, and Aritan, S. Kinematic and EMG activities during front squat and back squat variations in maximum loads. *J Sport Sci* 33(10):1058-1066, 2015.

A

abdominal crunches 171-172
actin 5
acyclic sports 16
adaptation 5-6, 52
aerobic (oxidative) systems 14-15
agility
    versus change of direction 14
    defined 5
agility tests
    5-10-5 (pro agility drill or 20-yard shuttle run)
        39-41
    L-drill (3-cone) 42-44
agility training 7-8
alternating leg lower 175-176
anaerobic capacity tests
    60-50-40-yard (55-46-37 m) 46-47
    300-yard (274 m) shuttle run 45-46
anaerobic energy system 15
anatomical core, defined 9, 155
anatomical core training. *See also specific exercises*
    exercise finder 156-157
    in-season 265
    off-season 185
    overview 155-156
    postseason training 299
    preseason training 233
anti-extension exercises 156
antilateral flexion exercises 156
antirotation exercises 156
articulation 13
athletic pyramid 4-5
ATP-PC (phosphagen) system 14-15

B

back extension (stability ball) 178
back squat 91-94
band exercises
    bench press 127
    mini-band glute bridge 177
    Nordic hamstring curl 120
    pull-up 148
    terminal knee extension 111-112
    triceps push-down 150
    upright row 141
barbell farmer's walk 158
barbell rollout 170-171
base position exercises
    Pallof press 160
    stick chop 162
    stick lift 164
basic strength phase 55-56
behind-the-neck shoulder press 131
bench press
    1RM bench press test 24-25
    technique and variations 125-127
    225-pound bench press maximum repetition
        test 48-49
bent-over lateral raise 135
bent-over row 141-142
biceps curls 152-154
Big Four core exercises 58
biomechanical analysis, of football 16-17
BLOB throw 87-88
body composition 10, 296. *See also* lean body mass
bone density, and strength training 10
bridge exercises
    single-leg 120-121
    supine glute 176-177
broad (standing long) jump 33-35

C

cable curl 153
chain equipment exercises
    back squat 92-94
    bench press 127
chalk marks, for vertical jump testing 30-31
change of direction (COD) 14, 231
clean high pull 71-72
clean pull 72
close grip bench press 127
COD (change of direction) 14, 231

F

face pull (machine) 136
farmer's walk 158-159
fat-free mass 10
fat mass 10, 296
5-10-5 agility test (pro agility drill or 20-yard shuttle run) 39-41
flexibility, versus mobility 13
flexibility training
    for injury prevention 9
    off-season 181-182
    preseason 231
football
    biomechanical analysis 16-17
    force in 11
    physiological analysis 11-15
    position-specific analysis 17-21
    strength training goals 55-57
    strength training programming. *See* program design
force
    core strength and 155
    in football 11
    formula for 181
    Olympic lifts and 63
    rate of force development 12
force plate 30
40-yard (37 m) sprint test 35-38
forward step lunge 100-102
four-day-per-week routines. *See* split (four-day-per-week) routines
fourth-quarter conditioning 55
front-facing medicine ball toss 166-167
front planks 173-174
front shoulder raise 134
front squat 94-96
fullbacks
    exercises for 59
    in-season training 266, 276-278
    off-season training 186, 201-206
    physical demands on 57
    physiological characteristics 18-19
    preseason training 233, 244-246
    training goals 56
functional exercises, defined 156

G

general preparatory phase (GPP) 295, 301
glute bridges 176-177
glute-ham raise 121-122
good morning (exercise) 112-113

ground-based structural exercises. *See* core exercises

H

half-kneeling exercises
    Pallof press 160
    stick chop 162
    stick lift 164
hammer curl 154
hamstring exercises
    band-assisted Nordic hamstring curl 120
    dumbbell hamstring walk 118
    hamstring slide 116-117
    Nordic hamstring curl 119-120
hamstring injuries 9
hang clean 66
hang snatch 69
Henneman's size principle 6
high pull 70-72
high school programs
    in-season 262
    off-season 182
    postseason 296
    preseason 232
hip thrust 113-114
hypertrophy/strength endurance phase 55

I

impulse, in agility 7
incline bench press 125
individual needs, in postseason goals 295
injury prevention
    lean body mass and 12
    lower-body exercises and 89
    Olympic lifts for 63
    role of strength training in 8-10
    upper-body exercises and 123
in-season programming
    base program 270-272
    defensive backs 282-285
    exercise order 269
    exercises for 264-265
    goals and objectives 261-262
    kickers, punters 289-291
    length and structure 262-264
    offensive, defensive linemen 273-275
    position-specific adjustments 266-268
    programming tables interpretation 266
    quarterbacks 286-288
    season cycle 292-294
    tight ends, fullbacks, linebackers 276-278
    volume and intensity 268-269

The **National Strength and Conditioning Association (NSCA)** is the world's leading organization in the field of sport conditioning. Drawing on the resources and expertise of the most recognized professionals in strength training and conditioning, sport science, performance research, education, and sports medicine, the NSCA is the world's trusted source of knowledge and training guidelines for coaches and athletes. The NSCA provides the crucial link between the lab and the field.

ABOUT THE EDITORS

Jerry Palmieri, MA, CSCS, RSCC*E, was the strength and conditioning coach for the New York Giants for 12 years under Tom Coughlin. Palmieri attended Dumont High School in Dumont, New Jersey, where he played football and began competing as an amateur boxer. He attended Montclair State University and, upon earning his bachelor's degree in physical education, he returned to Dumont to begin his coaching career as an assistant football and track coach.

Courtesy William Hauser Photography.

Palmieri later earned his master's degree in exercise physiology at the University of North Carolina at Chapel Hill. He then worked as a strength and conditioning coach at Oklahoma State, Kansas State, and Boston College. In 1995, he began his NFL career with the Jacksonville Jaguars, where he coached for eight seasons. He spent 2003 with the New Orleans Saints before returning home to coach with the New York Giants in 2004. He retired from the Giants and the NFL in 2017, culminating a 34-year coaching career in strength and conditioning.

In 1999, Palmieri was honored as Coach of the Year by the Professional Football Strength and Conditioning Coaches Association, and he was named the 2007 NFL Strength and Conditioning Coach of the Year by Samson Equipment. He was a member of the New York Giants' staff during their Super Bowl Championship seasons in 2007 and 2011. He has written numerous articles on strength and conditioning and enjoys speaking not only about his profession but also on his spiritual life. Palmieri volunteers for the Fellowship of Christian Athletes.

Palmieri married his high school sweetheart, Ellen. Their daughter, Annamarie, is a vice president of Winner & Mandabach Campaigns in Santa Monica, California. Their son, Tony, is the football video coordinator at the University of Delaware. Tony and his wife, Sabrina, have blessed Jerry and Ellen with their first grandchild, Gabriel.

Darren Krein, MA, CSCS, PES, CES, currently employed by the XFL Tampa team, has 18 years of NFL coaching experience, most recently serving as the head strength and conditioning coach of the Indianapolis Colts (2016-2017) and Miami Dolphins (2011-2015). In 2013, he was recognized by his peers as the NFL Strength Coach of the Year at the league's annual strength and conditioning coaches banquet.

Darren Krein

From 1997 through 1998 and again from 2001 through 2009, Krein was an assistant strength and conditioning coach with the Seattle Seahawks, where he assisted in the coordination of the athletes' weight training and off-season conditioning program. He was also integral in the design and implementation of the rehabilitation process for injured athletes.

Prior to coaching, Krein was drafted by the San Diego Chargers in the fifth round (150th overall) of the 1994 NFL Draft, but he missed his rookie season due to a knee injury. A native of Aurora, Colorado, Krein was a four-year letterman (1989-1993) for the University of Miami Hurricanes. He was named a unanimous First Team All–Big East selection and Second Team Associated Press All-America choice as a senior. While at the University of Miami, Krein totaled 190 career tackles and 17.5 sacks as a member of the Hurricanes and earned a degree in business management. He also holds a master's degree in kinesiology from A.T. Still University.

Brett Bartholomew, MSEd, CSCS,*D, RSCC*D, is a performance coach, best-selling author, and keynote speaker. He is the founder of the coach development company Art of Coaching and his experience includes working with athletes both in the team environment and private sector along with members of the U.S. Special Forces and members of Fortune 500 companies. Together, Bartholomew has coached a diverse range of athletes across 23 sports worldwide at levels ranging from youth athletes to Olympians as well as athletes who compete in the NFL, NBA, MLB, UFC, MLS, and NCAA.

©Brett Bartholomew

Anthony Caterisano, PhD, FACSM, did his graduate studies at UNC-Chapel Hill and earned a PhD from the University of Connecticut in 1984, and has been a Fellow in the American College of Sports Medicine (FACSM) since 1999. As a professor at Furman University, he has been teaching exercise physiology in the Department of Health Sciences for over 35 years, and also served as the varsity head wrestling coach at Furman from 1984 to 1991. Dr. Caterisano co-authored two books on strength training for football with Dr. Mike Gentry, and published several papers in strength and conditioning research journals in that area.

Courtesy of Furman University.

Mike Gentry, EdD, CSCS, MSCC, RSCCE, is a former associate athletics director for Athletic Performance at Virginia Tech from 1987 through 2015. From 1982 to 1986, he was the director of strength and conditioning at East Carolina University. Dr. Gentry was the forty-second recipient of the NSCA's CSCS certification and he earned his doctorate in education at Virginia Tech in 1999. Dr. Gentry co-authored two books with Dr. Anthony Caterisano: *A Chance to Win: A Complete Guide to Physical Training for Football* in 2004 and *The Ultimate Guide to Physical Training for Football* in 2013.

Courtesy of Virginia Tech.

Jeff Hurd, MS, CSCS, RSCC*E, retired after 25 years as an NFL strength and conditioning coach. Prior to that, he was a college strength and conditioning coach for 10 years. Hurd received his BS and MS degrees from Fort Hays State University. Currently, he is the owner and CEO of Hurd Performance in Georgetown, Texas.

©Jeff Hurd

Nathaniel D.M Jenkins, PhD, CSCS,*D, NSCA-CPT,*D, is an assistant professor with joint appointments in kinesiology, applied health and recreation, and nutritional sciences at Oklahoma State University (OSU), where he mentors graduate students in the applied neuromuscular physiology and the applied nutrition and exercise science laboratories. In 2018, Dr. Jenkins was named the National Strength and Conditioning Association's Terry J. Housh Outstanding Young Investigator and the Distinguished Researcher in the College of Education, Health, and Aviation at OSU. He is a member of the NSCA, American College of Sports Medicine, American Heart Association, and American Physiological Society.

Courtesy of Oklahoma State University.

Richard C. Lansky, CSCS, ACSM-EP, USAW Senior International Coach Level 5, is the strength and conditioning coach at Braden River High School in Bradenton, Florida. During his 30-year career, he coached at nationally-ranked Manatee, Lakeland Christian, Sarasota-Booker, and also in the private sector. A 1988 Syracuse University graduate, Lansky coached weightlifting at every level, including the Pan Am Games and Worlds. His awards include the 2006 USOC Doc Counsilman Science Award for Weightlifting, 2014 Samson's Strength/American Football Monthly High School Strength Coach of the Year, and 2018 NHSSCA Southeast Regional Strength Coach of the Year.

Courtesy of Thomas Bender, Sarasota Herald Tribune.

Anthony Lomando, CSCS, CES, PES, FST Level II, is currently serving as assistant strength and conditioning coach for the Denver Broncos and is entering his eleventh year in the NFL (2019). Prior to Denver, Lomando spent three years working on the strength and conditioning staff for the Jacksonville Jaguars from 2009 to 2011. His tenure in Jacksonville came after working for Athletes' Performance (now called EXOS) as a performance specialist. He was employed overseas exclusively with the Qatar National and Olympic Soccer teams from 2007 to 2008. Lomando earned a master's degree in rehabilitation sciences from California University of Pennsylvania in 2008 and a BS degree in Kinesiology from California Polytechnic State University-San Luis Obispo in 2006.

Courtesy of Denver Broncos.

Erik Myyra, MS, CSCS, currently works at Florida State University with the men and women's track and field teams. Before arriving at FSU, Myyra was part of the staff at Butler University, Towson University, and University of Michigan at different times in his career. While getting a graduate degree at Eastern Michigan University, Myyra competed in and coached track and field. During his undergraduate years, he was a track and field athlete and football player at Albion College where he earned his Bachelor's degree in exercise science.

Courtesy of Florida State University.

Jim Peal, MS, CSCS, has 38 years of strength and conditioning experience: Four as an athlete, four as an assistant coach, and the last 30 years as a head strength coach. Peal started his career as a walk-on lineman at Miami of Ohio and he followed that up with coaching positions at Evansville, Tennessee, Kansas State, The Citadel, Buffalo, and Butler University where he recently retired. Peal's philosophy is to emphasize total body development while focusing on the demands of the sport and a strong commitment to work. Highlights of his career include being a part of two Final Four tournaments, one of the first group of individuals who became CSCS-certified by the NSCA, and, most importantly, being around some truly wonderful people.

©Jim Peal

Ted Rath is the director of strength training and performance for the Los Angeles Rams and has over a decade of coaching experience within the NFL. He began his coaching career at the high school and collegiate level, has written articles for several industry publications, and speaks regularly at conferences, clinics, and corporate events both domestically and abroad. In his first season directing his own program, Rath was named the Strength and Conditioning Coach of the year by the Professional Football Strength and Conditioning Coaches Association.

Courtesy of Lululemon.

Zac Woodfin, CSCS, USAW Level 2, is the director of football strength and conditioning at the University of Kansas. He came to KU after two years at Southern Mississippi where he served as the director of strength and conditioning. In 2014, Woodfin was named FootballScoop Strength Coach of the Year, while serving as head strength and conditioning coach at his alma mater, UAB. Previously, he spent three seasons with the Green Bay Packers as an assistant strength coach. Woodfin broke into the industry working with Athletes' Performance (now called EXOS) where he trained Olympic athletes and clients who played in the NFL, NBA, and MLB. Following a college career in which he became UAB's all-time leading tackler, Woodfin signed as a free agent with the Green Bay Packers. Later, he signed with the Baltimore Ravens and spent a season with the organization, then a season in NFL Europe, and shortly after signed with the Houston Texans.

Courtesy of The University of Kansas.